OECD Public Governance Reviews

Public Procurement Review of Mexico's PEMEX

ADAPTING TO CHANGE IN THE OIL INDUSTRY

OECD
BETTER POLICIES FOR BETTER LIVES

This document was approved by the Public Governance Committee on 16 December 2016 and prepared for publication by the OECD Secretariat.

This document and any map included herein are without prejudice to the status of or sovereignty over any territory, to the delimitation of international frontiers and boundaries and to the name of any territory, city or area.

Please cite this publication as:
OECD (2017), *Public Procurement Review of Mexico's PEMEX: Adapting to Change in the Oil Industry*, OECD Public Governance Reviews, OECD Publishing, Paris.
http://dx.doi.org/10.1787/9789264268555-en

ISBN 978-92-64-26854-8 (print)
ISBN 978-92-64-26855-5 (PDF)

Series: OECD Public Governance Reviews
ISSN 2219-0406 (print)
ISSN 2219-0414 (online)

The statistical data for Israel are supplied by and under the responsibility of the relevant Israeli authorities. The use of such data by the OECD is without prejudice to the status of the Golan Heights, East Jerusalem and Israeli settlements in the West Bank under the terms of international law.

Photo credits: Cover © PEMEX.

Corrigenda to OECD publications may be found on line at: *www.oecd.org/about/publishing/corrigenda.htm*.

Foreword

In an economic environment characterised by historically low oil prices, oil and gas companies such as *Petróleos Mexicanos* (PEMEX) face tremendous challenges in maintaining and improving their productivity. In a sector where 40 cents of every dollar earned is spent on raw materials and services, procurement systems are central to a company's competitiveness. Alongside strategies to maximise value creation, procurement frameworks are needed to safeguard the company from mismanagement and corruption. Furthermore, fierce competition among international oil companies requires flexible and agile frameworks to unlock the innovation potential of the market and develop sustainable and strategic alliances.

Following an initial evaluation of PEMEX Corporate Governance and Board arrangements in 2010, and taking into account the 2015 OECD Recommendation on Public Procurement, the report *Public Procurement Review of Mexico's PEMEX: Adapting to Change in the Oil Industry* reviews progress made by PEMEX in its procurement function since Mexico's 2013 Energy Reform, which opened up the state-controlled oil and gas sector to competition. As a result, the company's procurement function went from a decentralised to a centralised structure to maximise its purchasing power, develop a homogeneous process, facilitate planning, advance the professionalisation of the procurement workforce and implement a comprehensive supplier management framework.

The OECD was invited by PEMEX to review the governance and effectiveness of the recently adopted procurement structure (Procura) in light of good international practices. This report assesses the alignment of different, yet complementary, dimensions of procurement, such as organisations, strategies, people and tools in key areas from governance to integrity and procurement strategies, including supplier relationships.

Strategic decisions and changes made by top management in PEMEX's 2017-21 Business Plan, in response to recent market evolutions and legislative reforms, have made the company better aligned with its competitors. The positioning of the procurement function in PEMEX's organisational structure and the streamlining of procurement processes allow for synergies between business and procurement practices. Efforts to develop robust integrity strategies have led to an ambitious ethics and integrity programme. That said, the effective implementation of these changes calls for structured and co-ordinated actions throughout the company and its suppliers.

The report acknowledges the actions taken by PEMEX to implement OECD policy recommendations. In particular, the company has developed the Electronic System for PEMEX Procurement (SISCEP), which is a platform for more comprehensive e-procurement and improves simplification and transparency. In addition, PEMEX has significantly expanded the use of different procurement procedures and reduced direct awards: the contract amounts procured in April–August 2016 through direct awards represented only 23% of the total, compared to 81% in 2015.

This report puts forward recommendations for the effective implementation of transformational reforms, such as:

- continuing corporate governance reforms in line with OECD guidelines and international good practices
- standardising and upgrading procurement data and information systems
- professionalising the procurement function
- maximising competition in tender procedures, limiting further the use of direct awards
- establishing an effective and coherent integrity framework
- inviting suppliers to adhere to the values and principles of PEMEX's Code of Conduct and to develop their own integrity standards
- developing a policy on whistleblower protection and allowing anonymous reports of wrongdoing
- completing PEMEX's suppliers assessment framework to maximise competition and innovation.

The OECD remains committed to supporting PEMEX in fulfilling its mission to create value, improve competitiveness, and overcome energy market challenges so that the company can contribute to a better standard of living for Mexico's population.

Angel Gurría
OECD Secretary-General

Acknowledgements

Under the direction and oversight of Rolf Alter, OECD Director for Public Governance and Territorial Development, and János Bertók, Head of the Public Sector Integrity Division, this review was co-ordinated by Jacobo Pastor García Villarreal, Senior Policy Analyst, with the support of Paulo Magina, Head of the Procurement Unit, and Julio Bacio Terracino, Deputy Head of the Public Sector Integrity Division. The authors of the different chapters include Angelos Binis, Matthieu Cahen, Jacobo Pastor García Villarreal, Petur Matthiasson, and Giulio Nessi. The company Vazquez Nava Consultants provided the inputs to draft the chapter on review and remedy system of procurement decisions.

Valuable comments were received from Hans Christiansen and various staff members from PEMEX. Editorial assistance was provided by Thibaut Gigou and Julie Harris. Anaisa Goncalves, Pauline Alexandrov, and Alpha Zambou provided administrative assistance.

The OECD expresses its gratitude to PEMEX for its fruitful co-operation and leadership, in particular Director General, José Antonio González Anaya; Director of Corporate Administration and Services, Carlos Alberto Treviño Medina; Operative Director of Procurement and Supply, Miguel Ángel Servín Diago; former Director General Emilio Lozoya Austin; and former Director of Corporate Procurement and Supply, Arturo Henriquez Autrey, and the entire PEMEX procurement team and all the departments involved in this process. Ambassador Dionisio Pérez-Jácome Friscione, José Poblano, and Maya Alejandra Camacho Dávalos, from the Permanent Delegation of Mexico to the OECD, were instrumental in supporting the OECD in this project.

This review is part of a series of governance reviews in OECD and G20 countries. It benefited from input provided by senior officials from Mexico's Economic Competition Commission, the Superior Audit Body, the Ministry of Energy, the Ministry of Public Administration, the Office for Digital Strategy of the Presidency, as well as PEMEX's suppliers and business chambers, who participated in the domestic debates in Mexico City.

This report incorporates information shared during two OECD workshops on transparency and integrity in public procurement, which took place on 2-5 February 2016 in Mexico City and Villahermosa. Special thanks to PEMEX and its officials for the support in organising and carrying out these workshops.

The OECD is also grateful to the lead reviewers who participated in the domestic debate: Stefan Hoffmann-Kuhnt, President and Managing Director, Pohlmann & Company Canada; Dale Evans, Director of the @oneAlliance, Anglian Water Alliance; Robert Gielisse, Public Internal Control Consultant; and Jorge Díaz Padilla, Chair of the Integrity Management Committee and former President, International Federation of Consulting Engineers (FIDIC).

The OECD Mexico Centre, under the leadership of Roberto Martinez, and the staff in charge of publications, notably Alejandro Camacho, were instrumental in co-coordinating the editorial process for the Spanish publication.

Table of contents

Tables

Tables *(continued)*

Figures

Figures *(continued)*

Acronyms and abbreviations

ANAC	Italian Anti-Corruption Authority
ARI	Institutional Risk Management
ASF	Superior Audit Body
CAAOS	Committee for Acquisitions, Leasing, Works and Services
CAPAS	Attention Centres for Procurement and Supply
CAUD	Audit Committee
CEO	Director General
CFE	Federal Electricity Commission
CONOCER	National Council for Standardisation and Certification of Labour Skills
CORP	PEMEX Corporate
COSO	Committee of Sponsoring Organisations of the Treadway Commission
CPBs	Central Purchasing Bodies
CRPEMEX	Risk Committee of PEMEX
DCF	Corporate Directorate of Finance
DCPA	Corporate Directorate for Procurement and Supply
DCPCD	Corporate Directorate of Planning, Coordination and Performance
DOF	Official Gazette (*Diario Oficial de la Federación*)
EPE	*Empresa Productiva del Estado* (state productive enterprise)
EPS	State Productive Enterprise
ERP	Enterprise Resource Planning System
FTA	Free Trade Agreement
GAE	Group for Strategic Supply
GAECA	Group for the Authorisation of Exceptions to an Open Public Tender
GDP	Gross Domestic Product
GJCA	Manager for Legal Affairs and Administrative-Contentious
HIIP	Integral tool for supplier information
HR	Human Resources
ICT	Information and Communication Technology
IIA	Institute of Internal Auditors
INAI	National Institute for Transparency, Access to Information, and Personal Data Protection
INAP	National Institute for Public Administration
IT	Information Technology
JCA	Administrative-Contentious Trial
KPIs	Key Performance Indicators
LAASSP	Law of Acquisitions, Leasing, and Services of the Public Sector
LFACP	Federal Anti-Corruption Law on Public Procurement
LFRASP	Federal Law on Administrative Responsibilities of Public Servants

LGTAIP	General Law on Transparency and Freedom of Information
LOPS	Law of Public Works and Related Services
MARE	Enterprise Risk Management Framework
NAFIN	*Nacional Financiera* (Development bank)
NAFTA	North America Free Trade Agreement
NRF	Norms of Reference
OGD	Open Government Data
OIC	Internal Control Body
PAAAOS	Annual Programme for acquisitions, leasing, services, and works
PACMA	Support Program for Communities and the Environment
PEMEX	*Petróleos Mexicanos*
PEP	PEMEX Extraction and Production
PGPB	PEMEX Gas and Basic Petrochemicals
PMI	PEMEX International Trade
POBALINES	Guidelines on acquisitions, leasing and services
POT	Transparency Duties Portal
PPI	PEMEX Procurement International Inc.
PPQ	PEMEX Petrochemicals
REF	PEMEX Refining
RIA	Regulatory Impact Assessment
RPC	Relationship with Suppliers and Contractors
RR	Reconsideration request
SAAR	Automated System for Risk Management
SAI	Supreme Audit Institution
SAPRE	Strategic Procurement Solution Tool
SDRPC	Deputy Directorate for Development and Engagement of Suppliers and Contractors
SFP	Ministry of Public Administration
SHCP	Ministry of Finance and Public Credit
SIDP	Institutional System for Project Development
SIPPC	System of Public Information on Suppliers and Contractors
SIRHN	Institutional Human Resources Platform
SME	Small and Medium Enterprise
SOEs	State-Owned Enterprises
SPyA	Follow up System for Procurement and Supply
TFJA	Federal Tribunal for Administrative Justice
UCII	Institutional Internal Control Unit
UR	Responsibilities Unit

Executive summary

Since the 2013 Energy Reform, which opened up Mexico's energy sector to private investment, Petróleos Mexicanos (PEMEX) has become a state productive enterprise with the core mission of creating value. This new legislative framework granted PEMEX greater autonomy for its administration, organisation, management and budget, as well as a new corporate structure. At the same time, it changed PEMEX's organisational structure and resulted in a series of reforms in different fields, including procurement, acquisitions, leasing, services and works, in order to give PEMEX the tools required to compete in international markets. This OECD review identifies the strengths of PEMEX procurement function and the potential options for improvement to achieve its new institutional mission and compete successfully.

Key findings

PEMEX senior procurement management now reports directly to the CEO, which indicates the strategic importance given to this activity, and the function is centralised within the Corporate Directorate for Procurement and Supply (DCPA), ensuring the development of homogeneous procurement processes throughout PEMEX and its subsidiaries, as well as the consistent application of the regulatory framework. Three strategic pillars were defined to allow the new procurement structure to create value: strategic supply and category management, procurement and supply model, and suppliers' management and development.

Overall the legal environment seems to be more conducive to leveraging public procurement to achieve secondary policy objectives. Developing a vision for sustainable green growth and to achieve social objectives and support the development of small and medium-sized enterprises, innovation, and standards for responsible business conduct would contribute to an approach that seeks such objectives without sacrificing the primary objective: creating value.

PEMEX has set up a comprehensive change management strategy, identifying resistances and obstacles in order to deploy measures to minimise them. However, PEMEX still has to develop a professional procurement workforce to leverage procurement activities strategically by making systematic use of workforce planning, skills frameworks, robust and merit-based recruitment and promotion processes, and performance management.

The recent regulatory reforms led PEMEX to streamline the structure of its solicitation documents and model contracts. The development of 13 new generic model contracts represents a significant investment in the clarification of the commercial and contractual relationship PEMEX wants with its major service providers. The generic model contracts are more accessible and user-friendly and reflect precisely the specificities of a larger range of requirements and circumstances. However, improvements can be made regarding intellectual property rights, termination rights and dispute resolution.

PEMEX recognises integrity as a priority and is developing a framework to prevent, identify, and sanction corrupt and unethical behaviours. In this sense, a sound internal control system has been established to ensure integrity, fraud, and corruption risks and threats are identified and effectively mitigated. In this framework, new measures on integrity have been introduced (i.e. new Code of Ethics and Code of Conduct, as well as specific provisions on conflicts of interest) while a robust Ethics and Corporate Integrity Programme (Programa de Ética e Integridad Corporativa) was launched in February 2016.

A significant challenge for PEMEX concerns developing and implementing a single end-to-end platform for e-procurement that ensures greater efficiency of the process in a user-friendly format. The previous procurement system was fairly complex and lacked the necessary interoperability between platforms.

As PEMEX enters a more competitive market, it is taking action to identify good practices of supplier engagement, since excessive controls and a legalistic culture make it difficult to engage with suppliers for consultation and development purposes. During the review, suppliers expressed concerns about how selection criteria used in tenders are being applied. PEMEX could address such concerns by enhancing supplier relationships with new techniques, such as debriefing suppliers or applying standstill periods.

The evaluation process of the procurement function is still in its design stage. The company has also developed tools to collect information from suppliers and contractors but their usefulness for decision making is still limited. A robust system of supplier performance management would make managing risks according to the historic performance of suppliers possible and even provide incentives for good performance.

Key recommendations

Although several achievements have strengthened the PEMEX procurement function, challenges remain to allow the company to reach its new institutional mission of creating value.

Regarding the management of the procurement process, PEMEX should pay particular attention to enhancing overall competition by reducing the proportion of direct awards; aligning procurement and business strategies through the standardisation of information systems to produce more useful reports for decision makers; making procurement plans, reports and information communicated internally and externally more accessible; advancing the professionalisation of the procurement workforce; and developing an e-procurement tool to support the whole cycle of procurement operations.

PEMEX also faces a number of challenges regarding accountability and transparency, and it is thus called upon to increase efforts to establish a zero-tolerance policy against corruption. First, PEMEX could ensure a comprehensive and effective integrity framework for staff working in procurement, but also for the Board of Directors. At the same time, PEMEX would benefit from strengthening its culture of integrity, instilling it among its employees and requiring it from all subjects entering into a commercial relationship with the company and its subsidiaries. Third, improvements are needed to detect wrongdoings and channels to report them.

As for transparency, PEMEX may review the existing mechanisms to disclose information in order to make them easily accessible to the public, including through the use of open data. At the same time, PEMEX needs to seek the right balance between protecting sensitive commercial information and achieving the highest degree of transparency of its procurement activities. In addition, PEMEX could improve the existing framework on the participation of social witnesses by increasing the transparency of the selection process.

PEMEX would benefit from ensuring that all components and functions of the internal control system are present throughout the company. It is absolutely critical that line managers and personnel, (i.e. the main risk owners) are actively involved in the risk management exercise. The anti-fraud and anti-corruption policies have to be continuously monitored and adapted to prevent, detect, and respond to this type of threat. The internal audit should be the bedrock of assessing the efficiency of the system and providing assurance that proportionate controls are in place and risks are adequately mitigated.

Finally, regarding its relations with suppliers, PEMEX would greatly benefit from developing strategic relationships by reinforcing its outreach to the suppliers' communities and revising its assessment framework to increase competition and unlock innovation potential, completing the evaluation model of its procurement function, defining key performance indicators and a comprehensive evaluation framework of supplier performance.

Part I

Implementing the right procurement framework in Petróleos Mexicanos (PEMEX)

Chapter 1

Strengthening the structure and governance of Petróleos Mexicanos' procurement function

Mexico undertook a significant reform package for its energy sector in 2013. This chapter analyses the corporate governance of PEMEX, after such reforms, its organisational structure, the normative framework applicable to procurement activities, the governance and co-ordination of the procurement function, and the benefits from centralisation of its procurement activities. It will discuss the implications of the greater autonomy granted to the company for its administration, organisation, management and budget, mainly the fact that opening up Mexico's energy sector to private investment meant that PEMEX has to compete in the marketplace. Finally, this chapter assesses the core change in PEMEX's procurement structure after these reforms, which consists on the critical mission of creating value.

Corporate governance of Petróleos Mexicanos (PEMEX)

Mexico undertook a significant reform package for its energy sector in 2013. A constitutional reform published in December 2013 was the first step, which was followed by a set of secondary laws, such as the Hydrocarbons Law (Ley de Hidrocarburos), the Law for the Industrial Safety Agency and Environmental Protection of the Hydrocarbons Sector (Ley de la Agencia de Seguridad Industrial y Protección al Medio Ambiente del Sector Hidrocarburos), and the Law for Coordinated Regulatory Bodies of the Energy Sector (Ley de Órganos Reguladores Coordinados en Materia Energética), as well as amendments to other legislations, such as the Foreign Investment Law (Ley de Inversión Extranjera). The whole package is commonly known as the "Energy Reform".

As a result of the Energy Reform, Petróleos Mexicanos, or PEMEX, was granted greater autonomy for its administration, organisation, management and budget, as well as a new corporate structure. Indeed, Article 2 of the PEMEX Law (Ley de PEMEX) establishes that PEMEX is a state productive enterprise (empresa productiva del Estado, or EPE), the exclusive property of Mexico's federal government, with legal personality and its own assets, as well as technical, operative, and management autonomy.

The Energy Reform changed the organisation of PEMEX. In fact, the opening of Mexico's energy sector to private investment called for strengthening the company to allow it to compete successfully. The company is led and managed by a Management Board (or "Board") and a Director General (or chief executive officer [CEO]). The Board is the highest governing body of the enterprise and is responsible for establishing planning, guidelines and strategic visions for PEMEX, its subsidiaries and affiliated companies.

The reform to the Board focused on making it not only the highest governing body of the enterprise, but also a more specialised body with the tools required to assess and monitor the company's performance, without external interference. Concretely, the strengthening of the Board was achieved through the following measures: 1) granting it clear powers to guide the company; 2) establishing institutional guarantees to avoid external and undue interference in decision making; 3) more explicit rules regarding Board appointments; 4) reforming the Board's composition, including by reducing the number of members representing the federal government; 5) introducing "independent Board members", who can only be removed under specific circumstances established by law; and 6) the establishment of special regimes for PEMEX in matters such as responsibilities and remunerations, which are more aligned with those applicable to private companies.

Chapter II of the PEMEX Law regulates the Board, including its membership and functioning. The Board consists of ten members, as set out in Table 1.1. To provide a point of comparison, Box 1.1 presents PEMEX's corporate governance structure before the Energy Reform.

Table 1.1. **Membership of the PEMEX Board**

Member of the Board	Nomination process	Term of membership
Minister of Energy (Secretaría de Energía, or SENER), who serves as Chair of the Board and whose vote breaks a tie	Membership established by law (Article 15, Section I of PEMEX Law)	As long as the individual serves as state minister Can be discretionally removed by the president
Minister of Finance and Public Credit (Secretaría de Hacienda y Crédito Público, or SHCP)	Membership established by law (Article 15, Section I of PEMEX Law)	
Three members representing the[1] federal government and appointed by the president	Membership established by law (Article 15, Section II of PEMEX Law)	
Five independent members	Appointed by the president and ratified by the Senate (Article 15, Section III of PEMEX Law)	Five years, staggered by annual succession. Can be reappointed for one additional term (Article 22 of PEMEX Law).

1. As of January 2016, these members were the Minister of Economy, the Minister of the Environment, and the Deputy Minister for Hydrocarbons of SENER.

Source: Government of Mexico (2014), "Ley de Petróleos Mexicanos" [Pemex Law], www.diputados.gob.mx/LeyesBiblio/pdf/LPM_110814.pdf (accessed 29 September 2015).

Box 1.1. **PEMEX's corporate governance structure before the Energy Reform**

Previous to the Energy Reform, PEMEX's Board was comprised of:

- six representatives of the state appointed by the Federal Executive
- five representatives from the Petroleum Workers' Union, who had to be active members and permanent employees of PEMEX
- four members appointed by the Federal Executive and ratified by the Senate, who represented the State and, in this capacity, were considered as public officials.

Source: OECD (2010), "Corporate governance and board arrangements at Petróleos Mexicanos: Evaluations and recommendations", unclassified OECD document, www.oecd.org/officialdocuments/publicdisplaydocumentpdf/?cote=DAF/CA/SOPP(2010)5/FINAL&docLanguage=En; Government of Mexico (2014), "Ley de Petróleos Mexicanos" [Pemex Law], www.diputados.gob.mx/LeyesBiblio/pdf/LPM_110814.pdf (accessed 29 September 2015).

Members of the Board have the following responsibilities, according to Article 32 of the PEMEX Law:

- abstaining from carrying out professional or commercial transactions with PEMEX
- participating in the committees established by the Board
- contributing to the work of the Board by putting forward opinions, recommendations, and guidance derived from the analysis of the performance of PEMEX
- complying with the Board's duties of loyalty and care, as established in the PEMEX Law.

According to Article 40 of the PEMEX Law, the Board establishes, at least, the following committees:

- Audit
- Human Resources and Remunerations
- Strategy and Investments
- Procurement, Leasing, Works and Services.

The Committee for Procurement, Leasing, Works and Services is headed by an independent member of the Board, who rotates every year. The Corporate Director for Procurement and Supply of the company participates in the committee as an invitee. This committee has been granted, among others, the following attributions:

- making recommendations to the CEO on concrete reforms to the procurement policies and regulations to be presented to the Board
- issuing opinions, upon request by the Board, on specific procurement procedures
- approving cases of exceptions to open public tender so that PEMEX or the EPS may contract with PEMEX affiliates
- reviewing the annual programmes of acquisitions, leasing, works, and services and making recommendations to the Board.

Figure 1.1 presents PEMEX's current corporate governance structure.

Figure 1.1. **PEMEX's corporate governance structure**

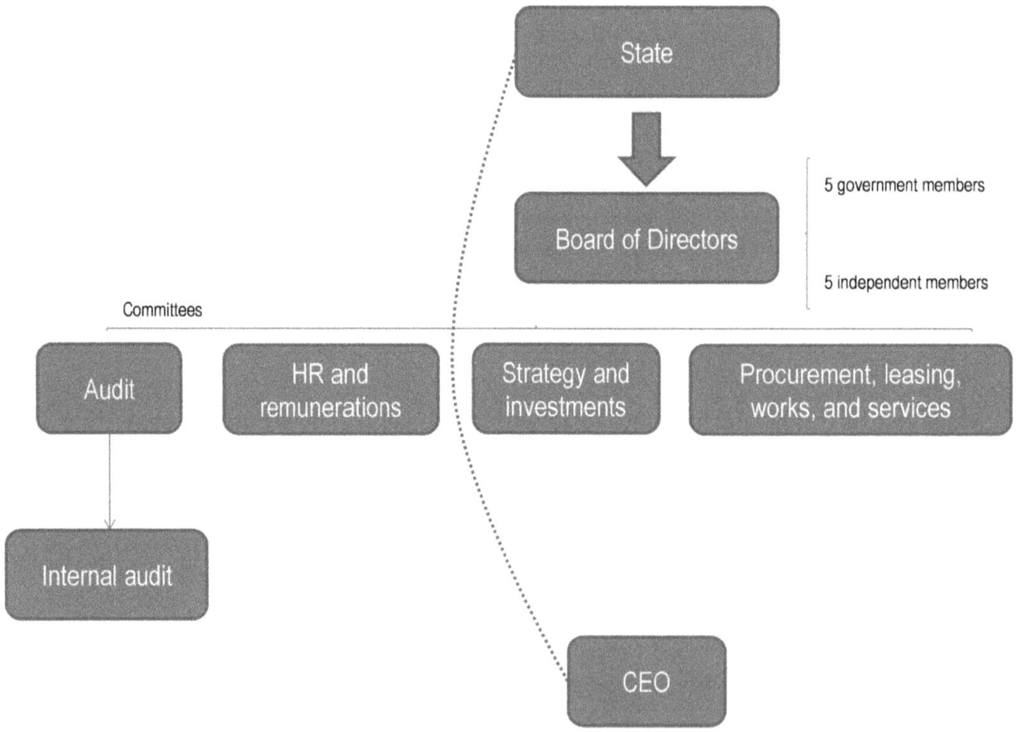

Source: Snipeliski Nischli, Ron (2014), "The new PEMEX and CFE", presentation by Ron Snipeliski Nischli, General Director for Legislation and Consultation, SHCP, to the OECD Working Party on State Ownership and Privatisation Practices, 22-23 October 2014.

Under the new structure, the federal government, acting as an owner, undertakes the following tasks (Snipeliski Nischli, 2014):

- prescribing the company's purpose and establishing financial and non-financial objectives (in some jurisdictions equivalent to a corporation's bylaws)
- appointing and removing members of the Board and assessing conflicts of interest
- appointing and removing the CEO (who may also be removed by the Board)
- determining Board members' remuneration
- determining the State dividend
- evaluating the performance of the company and the Board.

Another important change in the corporate governance of PEMEX as a result of the Energy Reform is the establishment of its own internal audit function reporting to the Board. Previously, internal audit was performed by the Internal Control Body (Órgano Interno de Control, or OIC), subordinated to the Ministry of Public Administration (Secretaría de la Función Pública, or SFP), not to PEMEX's Board (see Figure 1.2). External audit remains very much the same, carried out by external auditors and the Supreme Audit Body (Auditoría Superior de la Federación, or ASF), which is accountable to Congress.

Figure 1.2. **PEMEX's audit and control functions**

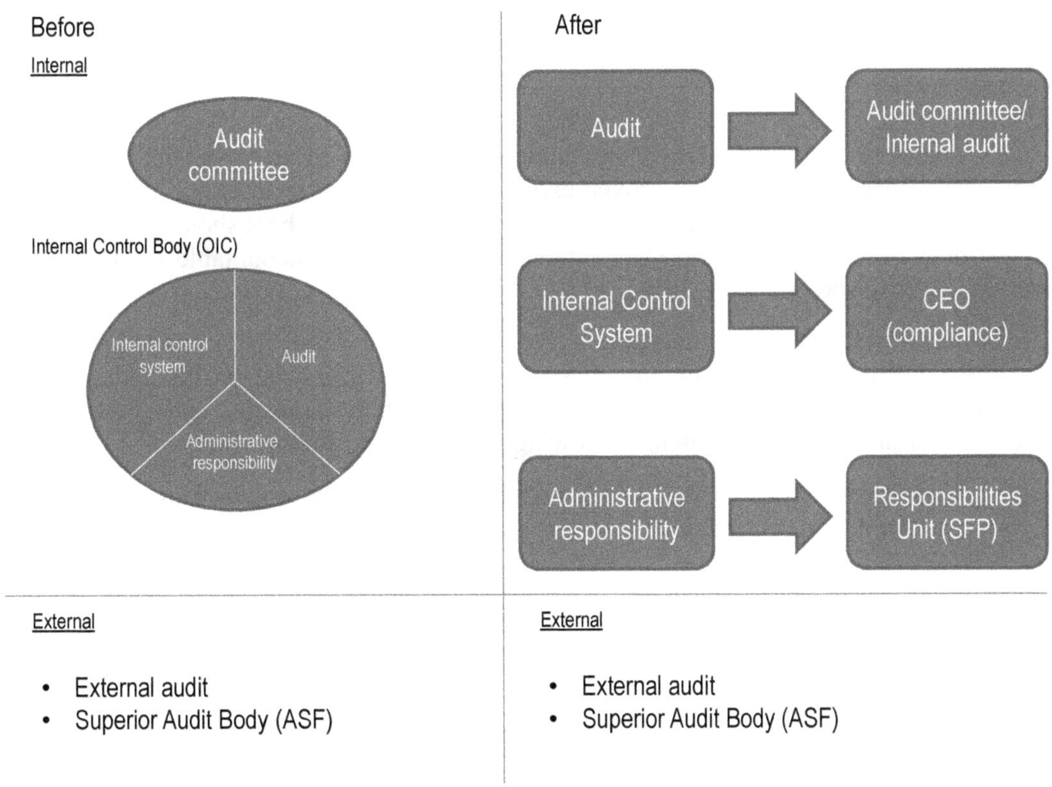

Source: Snipeliski Nischli, Ron (2014), "The new PEMEX and CFE", presentation by Ron Snipeliski Nischli, General Director for Legislation and Consultation, SHCP, to the OECD Working Party on State Ownership and Privatisation Practices, 22-23 October 2014.

The reforms to the PEMEX Board address some of the recommendations issued by the OECD in its report, "Corporate governance and board arrangements at Petroleos Mexicanos: Evaluations and recommendations" (OECD, 2010). They also follow, in some instances, the OECD Guidelines on Corporate Governance of State-Owned Enterprises (hereafter referred to as the "OECD Guidelines") (OECD, 2015a) (see Box 1.2).

Box 1.2. The OECD Guidelines on Corporate Governance of State-Owned Enterprises

The OECD Guidelines on Corporate Governance of State-Owned Enterprises are recommendations to governments on how to ensure that state-owned enterprises (SOEs) operate efficiently, transparently, and in an accountable manner. They are the internally agreed standard for how governments should exercise the state ownership function to avoid the pitfalls of both passive ownership and excessive state intervention. The guidelines were first developed in 2005 as a complement to the OECD Principles on Corporate Governance. They were updated to reflect the decade of experience with their implementation and address new issues that have arisen concerning SOEs in the domestic and international context.

The guidelines cover the following themes: 1) rationales for state ownership; 2) the state's role as an owner; 3) SOEs in the marketplace; 4) equitable treatment of shareholders and other investors; 5) stakeholder relations and responsible business; 6) disclosure and transparency; and 7) the responsibilities of the boards of SOEs.

Source: OECD (2015a), "OECD Guidelines on Corporate Governance of State-Owned Enterprises", www.oecd.org/corporate/guidelines-corporate-governance-soes.htm.

For example, in 2010 the OECD recommended that: 1) the Executive should consider appointing Board members with proven experience and expertise from the hydrocarbons sector, business, and finance; 2) the use of alternate Board members should be restricted to extreme circumstances; and 3) an internal audit function accountable to the Board should be established (OECD, 2010).

Concerning the first recommendation, Article 20 of the PEMEX Law establishes that the three members representing the federal government, as well as the independent members, shall be appointed based on their experience, capacity, and professional prestige and should comply with the following requirements, among others:

- a professional degree in law, administration, economics, engineering, accounting or a field related to the hydrocarbons sector
- at least ten years of professional experience in activities that develop the necessary expertise for PEMEX, namely professional, research and teaching.

The incorporation of independent members gives plurality to the Board and opens up the possibility of bringing in expertise from outside the government. This is a step in the right direction. Care must however be taken to ensure the actual independence of the individuals appointed.

With regard to the second recommendation, Article 17 of PEMEX Law establishes that the three members representing the federal government, as well as the independent members, shall not have alternates; only the ministers of SENER and SHCP shall have alternate members in deputy ministers.

Concerning the third recommendation, PEMEX has established its internal audit function, responding directly to the Board and substituting the audit function carried out previously by the OIC (See Figure 1.2).

In addition to these achievements, there remain areas of opportunity. For example, Board nomination is problematic when benchmarked against the OECD Guidelines. The PEMEX Law does not elaborate on alternative procedures for the president to appoint board members (i.e. nomination committees, pools of qualified candidates, headhunting firms), while OECD good practice suggests that such appointments should be based on competitive and merit-based procedures. This is not the case, and hence, there is a risk of politicising the nominations.

PEMEX's organisational structure

The Organic Statute of PEMEX, published in the Official Gazette (Diario Oficial de la Federación, or DOF) on 28 April 2015, establishes the organic structure of the company in Article 19. There are 12 second-level tiers directly dependant on the CEO, in addition to the Internal Audit function, which is accountable to the Board, and the Responsibilities Unit, accountable to SFP (see Figure 1.3). Each one of these units has deputy directorates and managers to discharge its duties.

The Organic Statute set out the most important restructuring of PEMEX in decades, as a result of the Energy Reform. The Board makes the appointments of corporate directors, based on the proposals of the CEO.

In addition, in November 2014, the Board approved the transformation of four subsidiary bodies into productive state enterprises. These include PEMEX Exploration and Production and PEMEX Industrial Transformation, as well as the creation of five EPSs that will eventually transform into affiliate companies: PEMEX Drilling and Services, PEMEX Logistics, PEMEX Coproduction and Services, PEMEX Fertilizers, and PEMEX Ethylene. The new EPSs have legal personality, their own assets, as well as technical and operative autonomy, but are subject to central direction and co-ordination by PEMEX.

Furthermore, Article 61 of PEMEX Law defines affiliate companies as those in which PEMEX participates, directly or indirectly, with more than 50% of their social capital. Affiliate companies are organised according to the private law regime of the country where they are established. An example of an affiliate company is PMI Comercio Internacional, which is a set of companies in charge of trading activities in crude oil, derivatives, and petrochemicals markets, with operations in more than 20 countries. PMI also deals with strategic projects concerning, for example, infrastructure and partnerships with other companies.

Figure 1.3. **PEMEX's organisation chart**

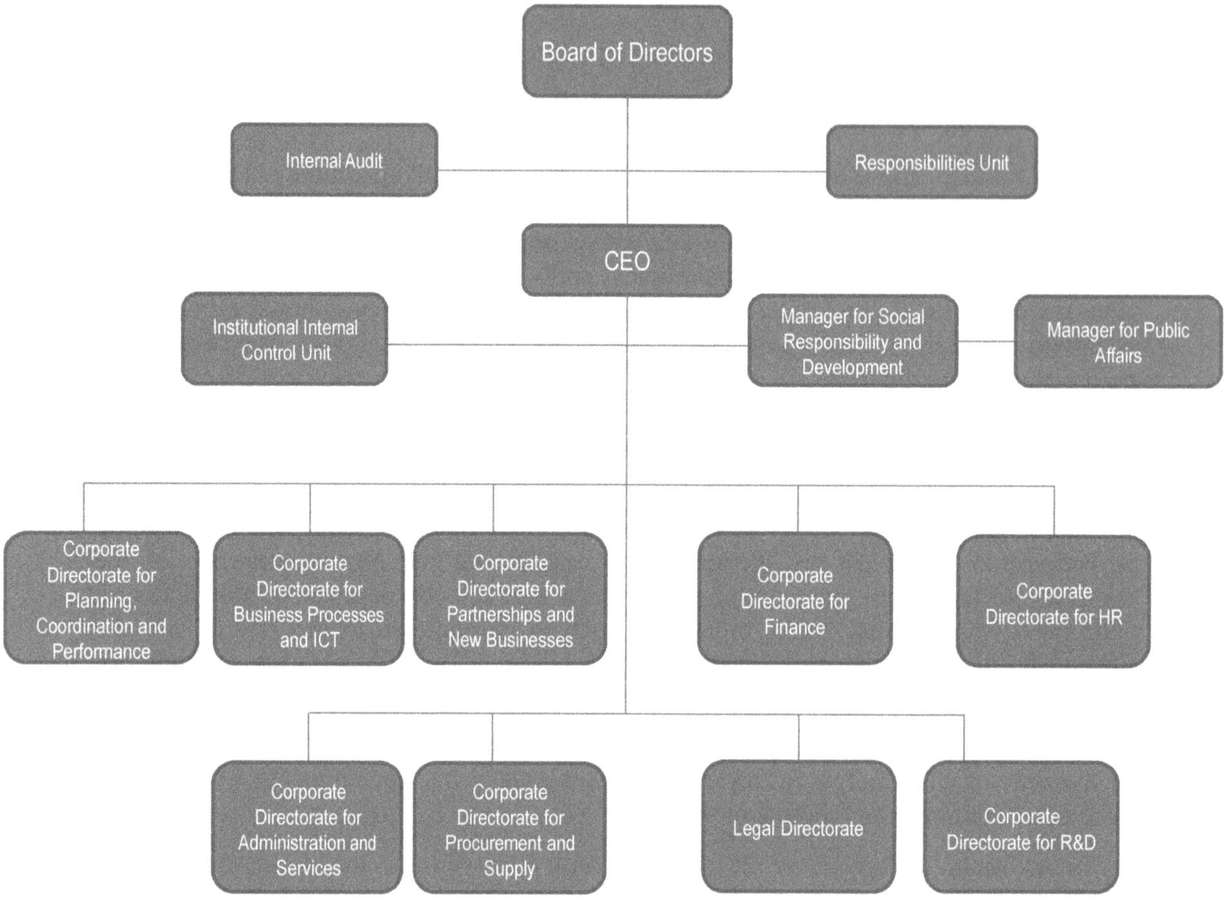

Source: PEMEX (2015), "Manual de organización de estructura básica de Petróleos Mexicanos y Organismos Subsidiarios", April.

A simple comparison with the organisation charts of other oil companies, aside from the boards of directors, reveals many common features. For example, British Petroleum (BP) organises its operations into upstream (i.e. exploration and extraction) and downstream (i.e. refining and commercialising) (BP, n. d.). Its second-tier units are in many cases similar to those of PEMEX, such as finance, legal, production, and human resources (HR). Likewise, Petrobras' second-tier units are similar to those of PEMEX, such as finance, exploration and production, and legal services (see Petrobras' organisation chart in Figure 1.4) (Petrobas, n. d.).

Figure 1.4. **Petrobras' organisation chart**

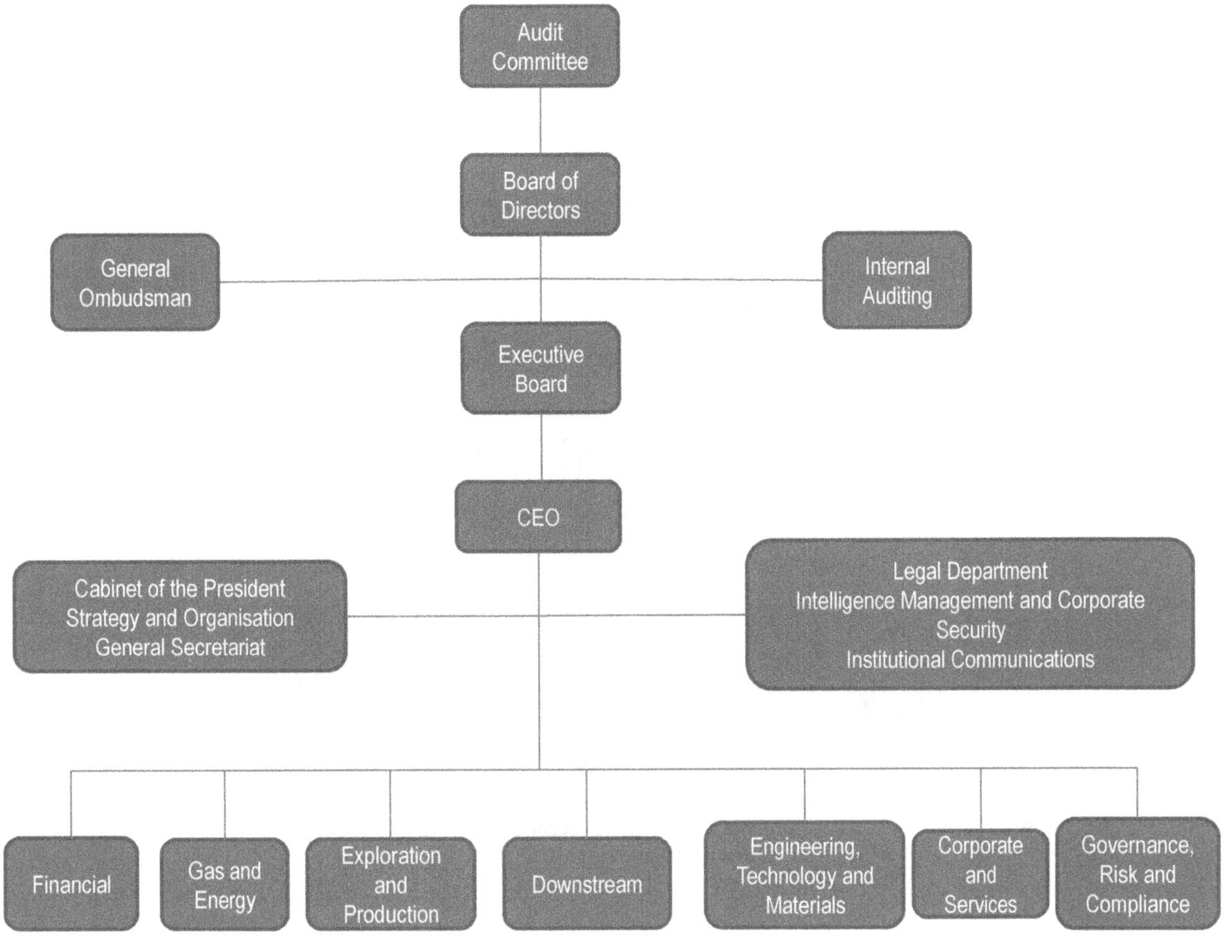

Source: Adapted from Petrobras (n. d.), "Organization chart", webpage, www.petrobras.com.br/en/about-us/organization-chart/ (accessed 14 January 2016).

The same common features are found in Statoil, where some of the second-tier areas include legal, audit, development and production, drilling, and exploration (see Figure 1.5) (Statoil, n. d.).

Figure 1.5. **Statoil's organisation chart**

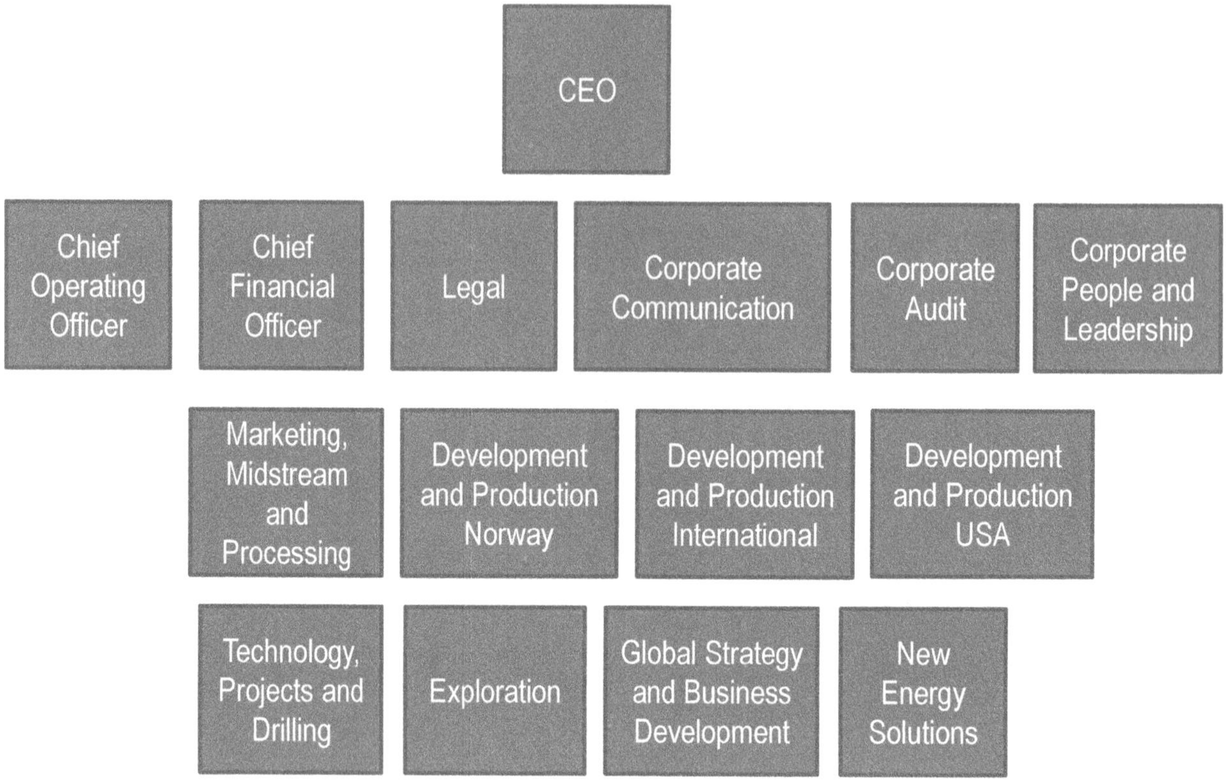

Source: Adapted from Statoil (n. d.), "Organisation chart", webpage, www.statoil.com/en/about/corporategovernance/governingbodies/orgchart/Pages/default.aspx (accessed 14 January 2016).

The normative framework for procurement in PEMEX

As a result of the Energy Reform and with the objective of giving the company flexibility to compete in international markets, PEMEX is subject to special regimes in many fields, including procurement, acquisitions, leasing, services and works, as established in Article 60 of the PEMEX Law. Hence, PEMEX is no longer subject to the Law of Acquisitions, Leasing, and Services of the Public Sector (Ley de Adquisiciones, Arrendamientos y Servicios del Sector Público, or LAASSP) or the Law of Public Works and Related Services (Ley de Obras Públicas y Servicios Relacionados con las Mismas, or LOPSR), which apply to all federal public administration.

Previous to the Energy Reform, there was a dual regime applicable to PEMEX procurement. On the one side, it was subject to the LAASP and the LOPSR. On the other side, it was regulated by the PEMEX Law. Such duality used to create confusion among PEMEX officials to determine which regime was applicable in each case. In this sense, the Energy Reform streamlined the regulatory framework for the governance of the procurement function of PEMEX.

Current PEMEX's procurement procedures are regulated first by the Constitution and the free trade agreements (FTAs) signed by Mexico, second by the PEMEX Law and its bylaws (*Reglamento*), and third by the normative instruments issued by the company itself (see Figure 1.6).

Figure 1.6. **Regulatory pyramid applicable to PEMEX's procurement**

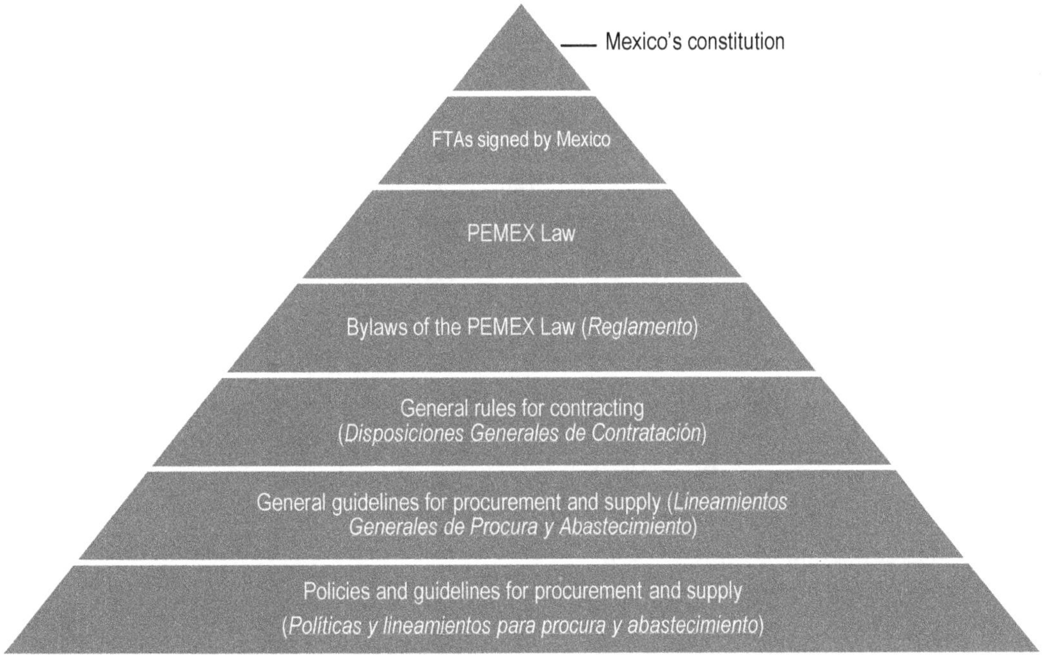

Source: Based on information provided by PEMEX.

Article 134 of the Constitution establishes that the procurement of goods and services should be carried out through public tenders in order to achieve the best terms in price, quantity, financing arrangements and convenience. As a consequence, public tender shall be the rule, unless specific and justified circumstances prevent this from happening.

The principles set out in the Constitution are then detailed in a set of normative instruments, which are applicable to PEMEX, its subsidiaries, and affiliates. In fact, Chapter III of PEMEX Law (on acquisitions, leasing, services, and works) starts by stating that PEMEX's procurement activities will abide by the principles established in Article 134 of the Constitution and the Board will issue the specific guidelines that the company and its subsidiaries should follow. It also includes a section on integrity measures for procurement activities.

The bylaws of the PEMEX Law go into detail in many of the mandates of the Law itself. Chapter III, Section I, refers to the challenge mechanism (*recurso de reconsideración*) to the award of a contract. The "General Rules for Contracting", published in the DOF on 10 June 2015, contain the following sections:

1. General rules
2. Planning, programming, and budgeting for procurement
3. Authorising procurement
4. Strategic supply and management by categories
5. Procurement procedures
6. Contracts
7. Challenge mechanism

8. Transparency in procurement
9. Specific guidelines with regard to transition Article 13 of the PEMEX Law
10. Integrity in procurement.

The "General Guidelines for Procurement and Supply" aim to establish the operative procedures for procurement and supply, as mandated in the "General Rules for Contracting", and define the operational framework for procurement and supply with regard to planning, programming, budgeting, contracting and contract management.

Finally, the "Policies and Guidelines for Procurement and Supply", in force since 11 June 2015, go into greater detail on the topics covered in each of its sections:

1. General vision
2. Planning, programming, budgeting, and strategies for procurement
3. Procurement procedures
4. Contract management
5. Master data management
6. Information and evaluation
7. Operations without contract
8. Transition
9. Definitions.

In addition to the instruments listed in the pyramid, other applicable regulations include the following:

- Federal Law on Anti-Corruption in Public Procurement (Ley Federal Anticorrupción en Contrataciones Públicas)
- Guidelines for the participation of social witnesses during procurement and supply activities and Contracting procedures by PEMEX and its subsidiary companies
- Operating rules for the Suppliers and Contractors' Public Information System of PEMEX and its subsidiary companies
- Operating rules of the Strategic Supply Group (Grupo de Abastecimiento Estratégico, or GAE) of PEMEX and its subsidiary companies
- Operating rules of the Group on Exceptions to Open Tendering (Grupo de Autorización de la Excepción al Concurso Abierto, or GAECA) in PEMEX and its subsidiary companies
- Guidelines to develop the Annual Programme for Acquisitions, Leasing, Services and Works (Programa Anual de Adquisiciones, Arrendamientos, Servicios y Obras, or PAAAOS) of PEMEX and its subsidiary companies
- Guidelines to authorise the signature of multi-year contracts and the convocation, award, and, if applicable, formalisation of contracts whose entry into force starts in the next fiscal period, for PEMEX and its subsidiary companies

- Policies and general guidelines for investments and strategic partnerships for PEMEX, its subsidiary, and affiliate companies.

As mentioned previously, the PEMEX Board issued several of the regulatory instruments applicable to its procurement activities, namely the "General Rules for Contracting", the "General Guidelines for Procurement and Supply", and the "Policies and Guidelines for Procurement and Supply". Despite the fact that PEMEX carried out internal consultations during the process to reform the procurement function, mainly with the key areas that are the clients of the Corporate Directorate for Procurement and Supply (DCPA), it would have benefited from the application of the regulatory quality standards mandatory for the federal public administration, which basically require a regulatory impact assessment (RIA) (*manifestación de impacto regulatorio*) to verify that the benefits of new regulations outweigh the costs and an open consultation period, as established in the Federal Law of Administrative Procedure (Ley Federal de Procedimiento Administrativo; see Figure 1.7).

Figure 1.7. **The regulatory impact assessment process in Mexico**

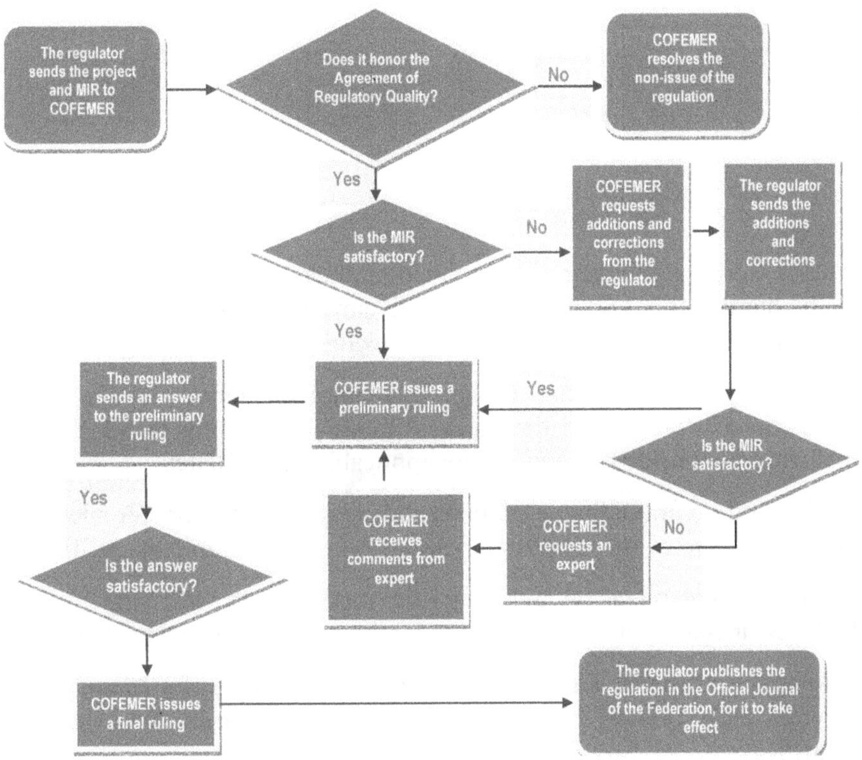

Note: COFEMER is the Federal Commission for Regulatory Improvement (Comisión Federal de Mejora Regulatoria) and is the regulatory oversight body.

Source: OECD (2015b), *OECD Regulatory Policy Outlook 2015*, OECD Publishing, Paris, http://dx.doi.org/10.1787/9789264238770-en.

Since PEMEX is not part of the federal public administration, it is not subject to such regulatory quality procedures. In fact, Mexico's regulatory consultation and RIA procedures were highly ranked in the *OECD Regulatory Policy Outlook 2015* (OECD, 2015b).

Procurement structure and governance as a result of recent reforms

According to Article 146 of the Organic Statute of PEMEX, published in the DOF on 28 April 2015, the DCPA will carry out procurement for acquisitions, leasing, services, and works through its different areas and on behalf of the EPS and, where applicable, PEMEX affiliates. The procurement structure is organised according to Article 19, Section VIII of the Organic Statute of PEMEX (see Figure 1.8).

Figure 1.8. **Corporate Directorate for Procurement and Supply (DCPA) organisation chart**

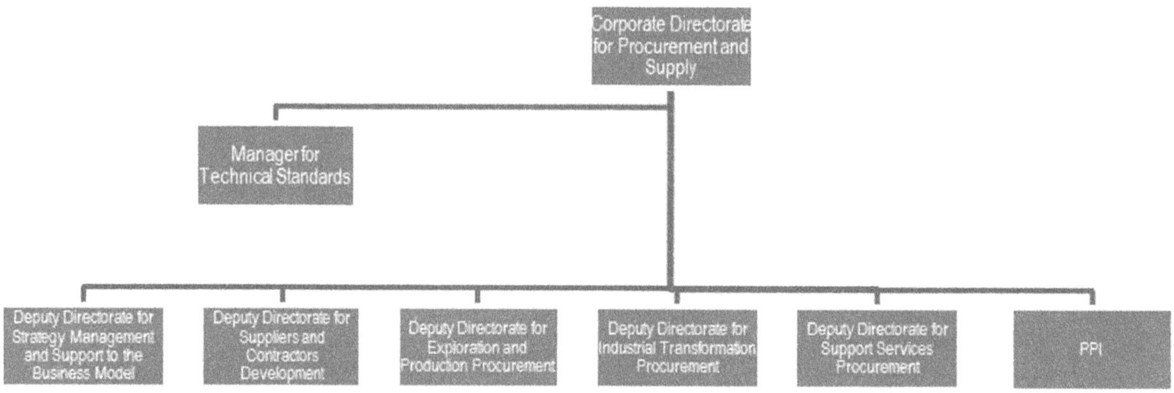

Source: Based on information provided by PEMEX.

The DCPA Corporate Director is appointed (and can be removed) by the Board upon suggestion by the PEMEX Director General. His powers are listed in the Organic Statute of PEMEX (Article 146), which include the following, among others:

- defining and steering the design and implementation of the national and international strategy and the business model concerning PEMEX procurement, including its subsidiaries and, where applicable, its affiliates
- issuing and co-ordinating guidelines and criteria for the procurement and supply of PEMEX, including its subsidiaries and, where applicable, its affiliates
- guiding procurement by applying the methodology for strategic supply for PEMEX, including its subsidiaries and, where applicable, its affiliates
- guiding the standardisation of the procurement processes for acquisitions, leasing, services, and works by PEMEX, including its subsidiaries and, where applicable, its affiliates
- guiding activities for co-operation and management with suppliers and contractors of PEMEX, including its subsidiaries and, where applicable, its affiliates.

PEMEX Procurement International Inc. (PPI) has legal status and its own assets, while its functions are aligned to the strategy and objectives of DCPA.

In addition, as part of the procurement processes, PEMEX has established several permanent committees or working groups, which are divided into two groups: those that manage procurement projects (Groups 1-3 below) and those oriented towards improving the process (Groups 4-5 below):

1. **Strategic Supply Group** (Grupo de Abastecimiento Estratégico, or GAE): It approves procurement considered as strategic supply and linked to category management. It is comprised of the Deputy Director of the EPS appointed by PEMEX Director General, responsible for procurement; three deputy directors from DCPA; a deputy director from Finance; and a deputy director from Legal. In addition, a deputy director from the Internal Institutional Control Unit (Unidad de Control Interno Institucional, or UCII); and a deputy director from Internal Audit participate as permanent invitees.
2. **Group on Exceptions to Open Tendering** (Grupo de Autorización de la Excepción al Concurso Abierto, or GAECA): It is charged with approving exceptions to public tendering to allow PEMEX to use other procedures, such as restricted invitations and direct awards. It is comprised of the Deputy Director of the EPS appointed by PEMEX Director General, responsible for procurement; two deputy directors from DCPA; a deputy director from Finance; and a deputy director from Legal. In addition, a deputy director from the UCII and a deputy director from Internal Audit participate as permanent invitees.
3. **Government Body for Procurement and Supply**: Government bodies are multidisciplinary groups created by decision of PEMEX Director General with the aim of managing the improvement, efficiency, standardisation, and systematisation of processes, while aligning the strategic objectives and value chain. The Government Body for Procurement and Supply was created in 2015 and is co-ordinated by the Corporate Directorate for Business Processes and Information and Communication Technologies
4. **Management Working Group**: This group was created in June 2015 to follow up the agreements taken by the Government Body for Procurement and Supply and facilitate the implementation of the Procurement Model 2.0 (Modelo de Procura 2.0) by standardising definitions and operations and speeding up the optimisation of the procurement function.
5. **Committee for Procurement, Leasing, Works and Services**: As mentioned before, this committee is headed by an independent member of the Board, who rotates every year. The Corporate Director for Procurement and Supply also participates as an invitee.

As a result of the reform of procurement procedures, PEMEX adopted a methodology of strategic supply. This methodology sets out analysing what is bought, who buys it, and how it is bought, assessing markets, identifying better procurement options and capturing services. It relies on several tools, such as preparatory contracts, reference agreements, auctions, price negotiation, pre-qualifications, multiannual open orders and public tenders. Figure 1.9 illustrates the steps followed to carry out strategic supply.

Figure 1.9. **PEMEX's strategic supply methodology**

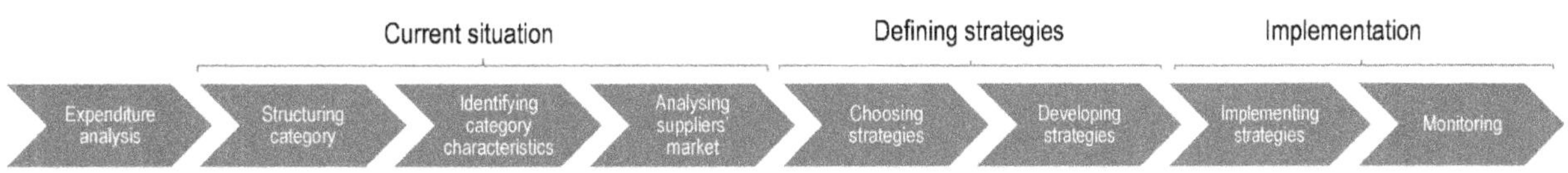

Source: Based on information provided by PEMEX.

The steps include:

- **Expenditure analysis**: Consists of classifying expenditures in groups with similar characteristics (i.e. categories) and obtaining the expenditure by supplier or business unit.
- **Structuring category**: During this step, the most important characteristics by category are identified, leading to the classification by sub-categories.
- **Identifying category characteristics**: This stage identifies users, interest groups, procurement procedures, needs that create demand and ongoing initiatives.
- **Analysing suppliers' market**: Consists of determining the market profile, including size, growth, segments, cost structure, new trends, negotiation power, and partnership or joint development opportunities.
- **Choosing and developing strategies**: During these steps, the category is assessed in a matrix comparing economic relevance in relation to implementation complexity to determine potential schemes. Likewise, supplier and purchaser powers are defined based on a market-supplier analysis and the characteristics of the category. With this information, supply strategies are selected, based on the internal situation and the market. Finally, the selected strategy is developed in specific work plans, including risks and contingency strategies.
- **Implementing strategies**: Depending on the strategy selected, procurement schemes are implemented. This phase usually entails negotiating with suppliers.
- **Monitoring**: Consists of analysing potential changes in categories and determining the applicability of the strategies selected at the beginning. It requires assessing the supply market and new trends in products, processes, materials, etc. The selected strategies are consequently refined.

Figure 1.10 presents the basic steps of homogeneous procurement and the supply process (*proceso homologado*). Step 1 (procurement planning) starts with identifying the needs for the development of strategic projects. Such procurement should be aligned with the objectives of PEMEX and its subsidiaries' business plan. An important premise is that procurement should create economic value and be evaluated according to objective key performance indicators (KPIs). The areas that participate in procurement planning include the programming departments of the EPS, the DCPA, the Corporate Directorates of Finance (DCF), and of Planning, Coordination and Performance (DCPCD).

Figure 1.10. **The basic steps of PEMEX's homogeneous procurement and supply process**

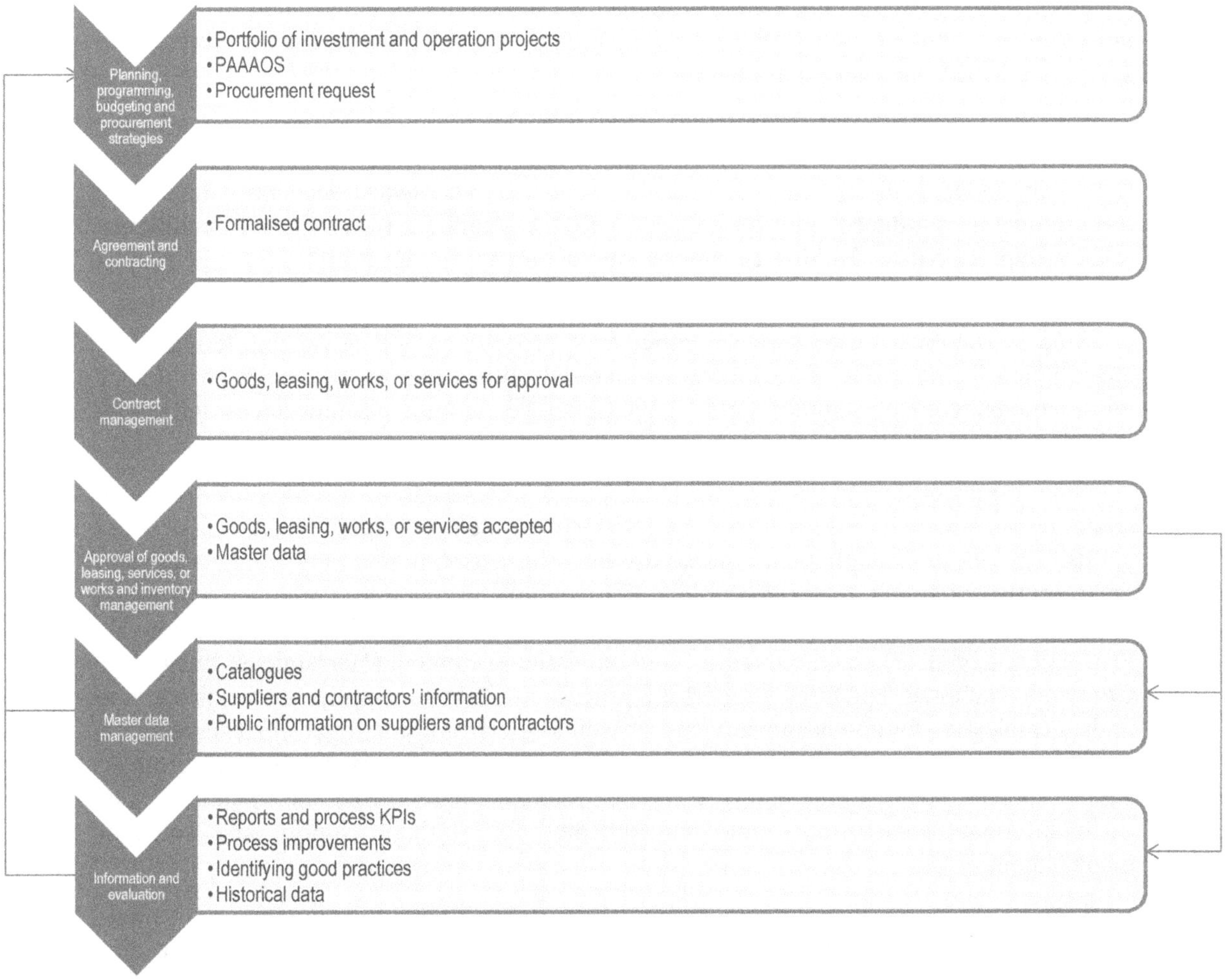

Source: Based on information provided by PEMEX.

The compilation of requirements starts on 1 April of the year previous to the one in which purchases will actually take place and the Annual Programme for Acquisitions, Leasing, Services and Works (Programa Anual de Adquisiciones, Arrendamientos, Servicios y Obras, or PAAAOS) is issued by 15 November at the latest. The PAAAOS is approved by the Director General of the corresponding EPS and the Corporate Director of DCPA. At corporate level, the PAAAOS is approved by the Corporate Directors of PEMEX.

Information concerning the procurement needs of the EPS is communicated to the DCPA via the process to identify and consolidate requirements. The procuring areas, in co-ordination with the procurement officials of the corresponding EPSs, identify their requirements according to their portfolio of projects and programmes and align them to budget availability. Then, the procurement officials (Deputy Directorate for strategy management and support to the business model of DCPA) upload the procurement initiatives in the system for procurement and supply follow-up (Sistema de Seguimiento de Procura y Abastecimiento, SPyA).

The PAAAOS assigns priorities to the procurement requirements, as defined by the DCPCD, and is linked to the available budget for procurement, determined by the DCF, indicating a tentative schedule for acquisitions, leasing, services and works, and specifying which ones have a multi-year scope.

Step 2 (agreement and contracting) starts with the reception and acceptance of the procurement request by the DCPA, which then establishes the procedure to be followed (i.e. open tender, restricted invitation or direct award). The award decision is taken and the contract is produced and formalised with the supplier. If, along the contractual relationship, PEMEX decides to amend the contract, the user area (i.e. the project manager) has to request the amendment to the DCPA.

Step 3 (contract management) anticipates procedures for advanced termination, cancellation in the event of violations to material obligations by suppliers, compliance with national content policies, and unanticipated economic circumstances impacting agreed costs and prices.[1]

Step 4 (master data management) anticipates a series of tools to collect and manage strategic procurement information. This is done through managing master risks from goods, services, and suppliers in order to use the information in planning, contracting, and the execution of supply or service orders. For example, procurement procedures feed the Integral Tool for Supplier Information (Herramienta Integral de Información de Proveedores, or HIIP) and the Integral Tool on National Content (Herramienta Integral de Contenido Nacional, HICON), support the process to evaluate supplier performance, and update catalogues for goods and services, as well as electronic catalogues that serve as the basis for price lists and commercial conditions of goods and services with determined supply sources, such as preparatory contracts, reference agreements and open contracts. Such information also feeds into the schemes for strategic supply and category management.

Finally, Step 5 (information and evaluation) comprises a model to evaluate procurement and supply processes and support management decisions. This step also includes the production of reports and KPIs on procurement management and control to support the process of continuous improvement.

Centralisation

PEMEX's Business Plan 2014-18 establishes, among its strategic objectives, creating value and increasing efficiency in procurement processes, while strengthening national supply, through a strategy to design and implement a comprehensive and single model for procurement. The core change in PEMEX's procurement structure after the Energy Reform is that it went from a decentralised to a centralised system. Previous to such reform, each of PEMEX subsidiaries had its own procurement processes. Procurement used to be carried out by each one of the subsidiaries according to their specific needs and was supervised by their own acquisitions committees. The centralised structure brings together the procurement activities of the different EPSs and the regulatory framework is the same for all of them.

The decision to modify PEMEX's organic structure to centralise the procurement function in the DCPA stemmed from an analysis of good procurement practices in 14 oil and gas companies around the world, with a focus on creating value to maximise benefits such as savings, opportunity and quality of goods, services and works purchased by PEMEX.

The benchmarking analysis found that the 14 oil and gas companies have organised their procurement functions around two basic models: partially centralised (hybrid) and fully centralised (see Table 1.2).

Table 1.2. **Benchmarking the procurement function of 14 oil and gas companies**

Model	Features	Companies
Fully centralised	All procurement units, operations and resources are accountable and assigned to a Chief Procurement Officer (CPO)	Exxon Mobil, Repsol, Shell, Chevron, ENI, Statoil, Suncor, Kuwait Petroleum
Partially centralised (hybrid)	Global procurement groups for specific categories Other categories are managed by business unit Procurement function supported by a central unit	BP, Conoco, Total, Petrobras, Petrochina
Fully decentralised	There is no procurement co-ordination group Procurement functions are assigned by business unit Supply activities carried out by each entity	PEMEX (before the Energy Reform).
Partially decentralised	Co-ordination of the procurement strategy relies on category leaders No specific business units reporting directly to a CPO	Sonangol

Source: Based on information provided by PEMEX.

The main benefits of a centralised structure are:

- taking advantage of and maximising PEMEX's purchasing power to create value and offer quality goods and services
- developing a homogeneous process with a clear governance structure
- facilitating comprehensive and long-term procurement planning
- addressing real business needs with quality and opportunity
- advancing comprehensive supplier management with complete and accurate information
- professionalising the procurement function
- managing procurement with a focus on evaluation and continuous improvement.

The centralised activities and strategies include procurement policies and guidelines, market analysis, annual procurement programmes, strategic supply and category management, contracting procedures, and formalisation of contracts, among others. Table 1.3 shows the new distribution of procurement activities.

Table 1.3. **PEMEX's new distribution of procurement activities**

Activity	Decentralised procurement scheme	DCPA centralised scheme
Planning, programming and budgeting		
Planning procurement needs	X	X
Inventory review	X	X
Draft procurement programme	X	X
Consolidation and review of procurement programmes	*	Θ
Communication of procurement programmes	*	*
Economic modelling	X	Θ
	Developing and consolidating requirements	
Procurement request	X	X
Determining the applicable regime	X	*
Market research	X	*
Technical specifications	X	Θ
Determining economic criteria	X	*
Determining technical criteria	X	Θ
	Executing procurement procedures	
Selection of the procedure: Public tender Restricted invitation Direct award	X	*
Analysis and selection of procurement strategy: Consolidation, framework agreement, preparatory contract Reference agreement	X	*
Executing the procurement procedure	*	*
	Contract management	
Contract supervision	X	X
Following up the execution of the contracts	X	*
Modification agreements		
Request	X	X
Management	X	*
Determining the anticipated termination	X	Θ

X Subsidiary body; * DCPA; Θ shared responsibility (DCPA has final responsibility)

Source: Based on information provided by PEMEX.

Three strategic pillars were defined so that the new procurement structure could create value in the transformation of PEMEX:

- **Strategic supply and category management**: This pillar develops a strategy for each defined category, builds expertise and researches the market by category. For procurement outside of the defined categories, in some cases the strategy dictates the aggregation of demand and consolidation, while in others the strategy is ad hoc or specific to the need. Category management calls for developing, evaluating and strategically monitoring supplier performance by specific categories. Each category requires its own information on market status, supply strategies, and suppliers' management making them more controllable. As illustrated in Figures 1.11 and 1.12, entities with category management programmes have shorter turnaround times from suppliers and show greater efficiency in issuing acquisitions orders.

Figure 1.11. **Difference in the number of processed acquisition orders by employee according to the use or lack of use of category management**

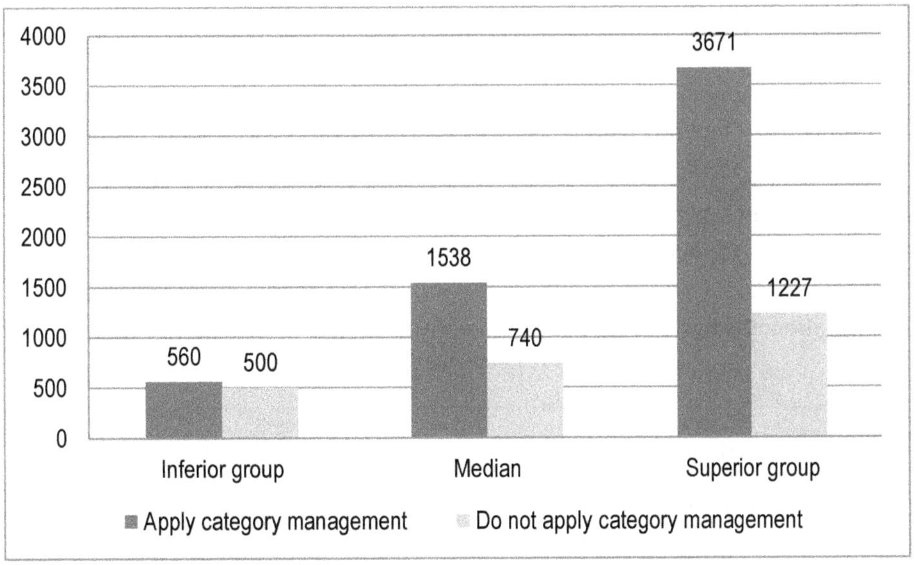

Source: APQC (2011a), "Employees significantly more efficient with category management", APQC, Houston, Texas, www.apqc.org, (accessed 22 February 2016).

Figure 1.12. **Difference in medium time for supplier delivery according to the use or lack of use of category management**

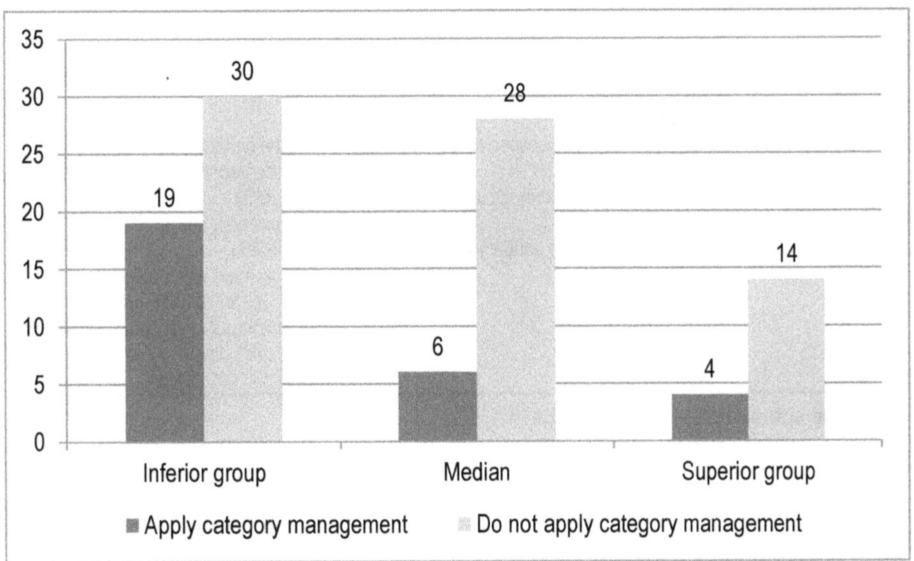

Source: APQC (2011b), "Procurement category management: Faster PO cycle time", APQC, Houston, Texas, www.apqc.org, (accessed 22 February 2016).

- **Procurement and supply model**: This pillar lies on the standardisation of the procurement function, its processes, and procedures, ensuring alignment with the companies' goals and objectives, and on the professionalisation of the procurement workforce.

- **Suppliers' management and development**: DCPA becomes the only agile and transparent point of contact between the procurement community and users. It aims to develop the supply chain and evaluate supplier performance, leveraging information technologies (i.e. PEMEX Pass, Suppliers and Contractors Information System).

Table 1.4 presents some of the benefits that the centralised procurement model and standardised business rules are already delivering to PEMEX.

Table 1.4. **Benefits to PEMEX from the centralisation of procurement activities and standardised business rules**

Issue	Problems	Benefits
Solicitation documents	Self and excessive regulation imposed by each subsidiary Different models of solicitation documents (i.e. structures, templates, contents), which weakens corporate identification Complex templates	Four models of solicitation documents, which simplify and standardise language and corporate identification Simplifying templates from approximately 60 to 30 pages, eliminating redundant and unnecessary explanations or requisites
Evaluation criteria	More than 90% of tenders are allocated using binary criteria and favouring the lowest price Insufficient use of alternative and universally recognised criteria	Definition of an evaluation methodology (binary) and six award criteria, dispensing with the lowest price criteria: 1) discount application from maximum reference prices; 2) equivalent annual cost; 3) points and percentages; 4) cost-benefit; 5) net present value; and 6) binary criteria
Market research	Research limited to requesting quotes from suppliers Staff do not have the expertise to undertake market research Collected information is not consolidated for global analysis	More comprehensive market research methodology
Procurement linked to budget	Procurement initiatives disassociated from budget availability Procurement budget January-October 2014: MXN 393 000 million Procurement programme January October 2014: MXN 919 000 million	For the first time, the PEMEX annual procurement programme is tied to budget availability Procurement budget 2015: MXN 166 000 million Procurement with payment scheduled in 2015: MXN 160 000 million Total amount of procurement programme 2015 (including multi-year procurement): MXN 590 000 million

Source: Based on information provided by PEMEX.

Co-ordination and communication

Procurement planning should ensure precision, opportunity and quality of the necessary goods, works and services to achieve PEMEX's strategic objectives, as set out in the strategies and projects established in its business plan. The background information that develops, aligns, and informs procurement flows from the projects included in the Business Direction process.

The Business Direction process is divided into six sub-processes (see Figure 1.13):

- **Strategic analysis**: Consists of analysing the environment, the opportunities, and national and international regulations applicable to the hydrocarbons business, as well as the capacities of the company to envision different business alternatives to develop a competitive advantage and strengthen its market position.
- **Strategy definition**: Defines the company strategies to achieve performance objectives dictated by senior management, ensuring they are aligned with the Programme for Executing the Strategy (Programa de Ejecución de la Estrategia) and linked to the required financial resources.
- **Strategic programming and integral management**: Once strategies are defined, this process develops the specific operating programmes to fulfil them, ensuring alignment of all the business processes with the achievement of goals.
- **Capital projects development**: Consists of detailed planning of the authorised portfolio of projects, including their related procurement, construction, testing, and launching of capital works, as established in the Institutional System for Project Development (Sistema Institucional de Desarrollo de Proyectos, or SIDP), as well as periodic assessments during the life cycle of the projects.
- **Follow up and co-ordination**: This process continuously verifies compliance with the Executive Programme of Integral Management (Programa Ejecutivo de Gestión Integral, or PEGI), including an analysis of operative and strategic results and the definition of actions for operative improvement.
- **Business evaluation and control**: Consists of an analysis of results, operative and strategic, a comprehensive business assessment, and informing the Directive Group of the necessary strategic actions to achieve objectives. It provides feedback for the strategic analysis to be considered in the updates of the plans.

Figure 1.13. **PEMEX's Business Direction process**

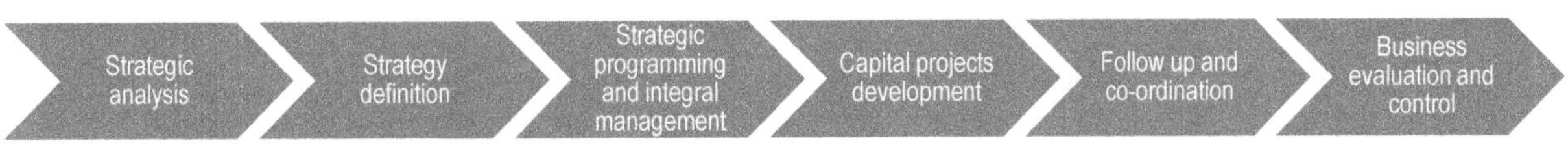

Source: Based on information provided by PEMEX.

DCPA produces several reports that do not necessarily have a fixed periodicity. Such reports are submitted to the requesting entity or to the one they are supposed to be submitted to (i.e. directorate, deputy directorate). If applicable, they are also submitted to the areas that provided input or deal with the subject matter. This may happen through institutional e-mail accounts or on paper. Likewise, news is sent to the entire procurement community through the internal email account "NotiDCPA" and DCPA's intranet portal.

A significant number of reports are prepared for senior management by the DCPA operative units. However, inputs usually come from different information systems. DCPA is currently undergoing a process of standardisation to streamline information systems and be able to produce more useful reports for decision makers. Some of the reports produced for analysis by senior management include:[2]

- Follow-up report for SPyA initiatives: This report describes the status of procurement requirements, including those from PAAAOS (not operational yet).
- Follow-up of procurement initiatives registered in the PAAAOS.
- Progress reports on the amount of the PAAAOS.
- Procurement requests.
- Tender procedures declared as void.
- Report on formalised contracts.
- Report on contracts completed before the specified time, or terminated.
- Compliance with contracts timelines.
- Report on challenges to tender decisions.
- Registration process dashboard: This tool illustrates the number of registered suppliers in the system to register and assess suppliers.

Procurement information communicated outside of PEMEX is conveyed through several channels. First, DCPA has developed a microsite within the Internet portal (www.pemex.com/procura/Paginas/default.aspx) for consultation by suppliers and the public in general. This site contains information, for example, on open public tenders, restricted invitation processes and supplier relationships.[3] Second, in compliance with the General Law on Transparency and Freedom of Information (Ley General de Transparencia y Acceso a la Información Pública, or LGTAIP) PEMEX procurement information is uploaded in the Transparency Duties Portal (Portal de Obligaciones de Transparencia, or POT), where all federal public entities actively publish information required by the LGTAIP. Third, the PEMEX Law (Article 85) and the General Rules for Contracting (Article 22) establish that PEMEX will develop a Suppliers and Contractors' Public Information System (Sistema de Información Pública de Proveedores y Contratistas, or SIPCC) which should be updated periodically and contain information on the formalised contracts during the last five years. In addition, the SIPCC contains information on the nationality and business activities of suppliers, the results of evaluations on their performances, compliance with contract terms and timelines, sanctions, compliance with environmental regulations and quality certifications.

Additionally, PPI also communicates information to suppliers through its website (pemexprocurement.com) to support international procurement activities, such as identifying and registering potential suppliers and goods not produced in Mexico (i.e. drilling and oil production equipment, motors, and chemical products). PPI's portal also contains information on international public tenders that PPI manages on behalf of PEMEX, a directory of approved suppliers, and a performance assessment of suppliers.

Finally, calls for tender on the modality of international public tender under free trade agreements are published in the DOF.

Proposals for action

While PEMEX's new corporate governance structure following the Energy Reform aligns better with the OECD Guidelines, further reforms are needed to align still more with OECD best practice.

While the incorporation of independent members is a step in the right direction, the composition of the PEMEX Board is still not fully aligned with the OECD Guidelines. A central recommendation of the OECD Guidelines is that boards should be composed to exercise "independent and objective judgment". In most OECD countries, SOE boards are composed of a mix of civil servants, other individuals tasked with pursuing the public interest and "independent" directors.[4] The trend, fuelled by a growing commercialisation of SOEs, is toward a greater reliance on independent board members – or persons with relevant commercial experience.

Given that the appointment process of independent members to the PEMEX Board starts in the Office of the President, the government could put together a committee, consisting of representatives from different ministries, to make proposals to the president. This committee would be charged with identifying a pool of qualified candidates with experience in the energy sector for the president to include in the list to be presented to the Senate. This process would provide the nomination with greater legitimacy, transparency and merit orientation.

There is also growing recognition that certain public sector representatives are not acceptable as SOE board members under any circumstance. OECD consensus holds that neither ministers, state secretaries, nor other direct representatives of, nor parties closely related to, the executive powers should be represented in SOE boards. Scandinavian countries have gone further than most jurisdictions to formally limit the weight of politicians and bureaucrats in SOE boards. For example, active politicians, including members of parliament, ministers, state secretaries, as well as civil servants who within their remit exert regulatory or controlling authority over the company or deal with matters of substantial importance for the company, cannot be elected to the board of directors in Norway.

Moreover, many countries have restrictions concerning the nomination of civil servants as board members. In Finland, for instance, only one civil servant from the ownership function (and in some cases another from a relevant administration) can serve on an SOE board, but potential conflict issues are avoided by generally not allowing the politically appointed civil servants to serve on boards. A similar approach has been adopted by Australia where appointment of departmental officers can only be considered in exceptional circumstances, having regard to their ability to represent the interests of the government, their possession of business skills, and to any potential conflicts of interest that might arise. New Zealand (which also has an express process for vetting conflict of interest) has gone farthest in instituting an absolute ban on any serving politicians or civil servants sitting on SOE boards. So, in general, good practice is to avoid officials directly linked with the executive powers from sitting on SOE boards (OECD, 2013) (see Box 1.3).

Box 1.3. Board appointment process in the United Kingdom

The General Office of the Commissioner of Public Appointments (OCPA) recruitment process is as follows (although this may vary slightly depending on the size of the SOE and the specific requirements of the post):

- The central ownership advisory unit, the Shareholder Executive (ShEx) and the SOE Chair agree on the mix of skills and experience required on the board, leading to agreement on a strategic plan of public appointments.
- A timetable for recruitment is then agreed between the SOE, the lead Director in ShEx, and an independent assessor (IA).
- A draft specification setting out the role and requirements for the board appointment is drafted and agreed with HR and the SOE. The role and person specification is then agreed with the body or minister making the final decision.
- A candidate search is undertaken with the vacant position being publicly announced (i.e. advertised) and often involving the use of recruitment agencies to ensure a more thorough search of potential candidates.
- On the basis of applications received, a long list of potential candidates is produced. An initial assessment involving ShEx, the IA, and the SOE is conducted to produce a short list of candidates to interview.
- An interview panel is established comprising the lead ShEx policy official, the IA, and the Chair of the SOE.
- The panel then reaches agreement on the preferred candidate and submits a panel report with recommendations to departmental ministers.
- Once ministers have agreed on the recommendation, the appointment can be made.
- An appointment is normally for a fixed period of three years at which point the position is subject to re-election.

Where the post is not OCPA regulated, the SOE runs the process, but follows the OCPA guidelines in most instances.

Source: OECD (2013), *Boards of Directors of State-Owned Enterprises: An Overview of National Practices*, OECD Publishing, Paris, http://dx.doi.org/10.1787/9789264200425-en, p. 41.

It is the government, not the Board, which determines the appointment – and in practice also the removal – of PEMEX's CEO. Although the Board has the legal authority to remove the CEO, it cannot fulfil its duties of oversight properly unless this authority is credible. This lack of credibility creates confusion in the vertical separation of functions. Even so, the situation is better after the approval of the Energy Reform since the government (Executive and Congress) retained more limited powers, such as setting the financial balance target, the ceiling for salary spending, and a debt ceiling. All other activities and operations are regulated by the Board, without intervention or approval requirement from the government.

Another initiative that would align PEMEX's practices still more with OECD best practice concerns self-evaluation of the Board. This applies to the Corporate Board, as well as those of the EPSs. Such evaluation would focus on the efficiency with which the Board has carried out its duties, collectively and as board members. The PEMEX CEO should deliver the Federal Executive the report concerning the Corporate Board, while the reports on the EPS Boards would be delivered to the Corporate Board. This self-evaluation would come in addition to the one mandated by Article 117 of PEMEX Law, which focuses more on PEMEX performance, its operative, programme, and financial situation, as well as its organisational and accounting structures, and not on the Board and its role as such.

Periodically review the regulatory framework for procurement to ensure that, while it gives PEMEX flexibility to compete in international markets, it also provides adequate safeguards for integrity.

One of the most pressing challenges for PEMEX is to transition to operating as a corporatised company to compete in open markets, while still having to comply with regulations applicable to the public sector. PEMEX is now subject to a special procurement regime to grant it the flexibility it needs in open markets. However, measures should be taken to ensure that this flexibility is not abused, leading to integrity breaches. On the other hand, PEMEX is subject to laws corresponding to the public sector to ensure proper accountability, such as the LGTAIP. However, this law requires PEMEX to disclose information that might be considered commercially sensitive and put the company at a disadvantage.

These balances, flexibility - in relation to safeguarding integrity -, and accountability - in relation to protecting commercially sensitive information -, are not easy to strike. The right balance will most likely be a struggle in PEMEX's near future. Hence, PEMEX should establish a system of periodic evaluation of its regulatory framework to ensure it gets closer and closer to the right balance and achieves policy objectives (i.e. strengthening PEMEX competitiveness and advancing accountability).

Evaluating regulations after a period of implementation should be primarily focused on whether the intended outcomes by the regulatory intervention have been achieved. This is the main purpose of retrospective analysis and it is its systemic application that is recommended in the 2012 Recommendation of the OECD Council on Regulatory Policy and Governance. Nowadays, there is not an internationally recognised or agreed-upon guidance for regulatory evaluation. However, the *OECD Regulatory Policy Outlook 2015* proposes a set of evaluation criteria that could form the basis for an evaluation framework (OECD, 2015b) (see Box 1.4).

Reviewing periodically its regulatory framework is a significant opportunity for PEMEX, as OECD country practices for *ex post* evaluation remain sporadic. Nonetheless, Mexico ranks well in the OECD composite indicators for regulatory management, specifically concerning *ex post* evaluation of primary laws and subordinate regulations (OECD, 2015b). PEMEX could work together with Mexico's regulatory oversight body, COFEMER, to analyse the tools it has developed for *ex post* evaluation and adapt them to the company's needs.

Most methodologies used in OECD countries for *ex post* regulatory evaluation concentrate on the unintended consequences of a regulation and on the achievement of policy goals (see Figure 1.14).

Box 1.4. Principles for setting an evaluation framework

General criteria

- Relevance: Do the policy goals cover the key issues at hand?
- Effectiveness: Was the policy appropriate and instrumental to successfully address the needs perceived and the specific problems the intervention was meant to solve?
- Efficiency: Do the results justify the resources used? Or could the results be achieved with fewer resources? How coherent and complementary have the individual parts of the intervention been? Is there scope for streamlining?
- Utility: To what degree do the achieved outcomes correspond to the intended goals?

Additional criteria

- Transparency: Was there adequate publicity? Was the information available in an appropriate format, and at an appropriate level of detail?
- Legitimacy: Has there been a buy-in effect?
- Equity and inclusiveness: Were the effects fairly distributed across the stakeholders? Was enough effort made to get appropriate access to information?
- Persistence and sustainability: What are the structural effects of the policy intervention? Is there a direct cause-effect link between them and the policy intervention? What progress has been made in reaching the policy objectives?

Source: OECD (2015b), *OECD Regulatory Policy Outlook 2015,* OECD Publishing, Paris, http://dx.doi.org/10.1787/9789264238770-en.

Figure 1.14. **Methodologies used in *ex post* evaluation (number of OECD countries)**

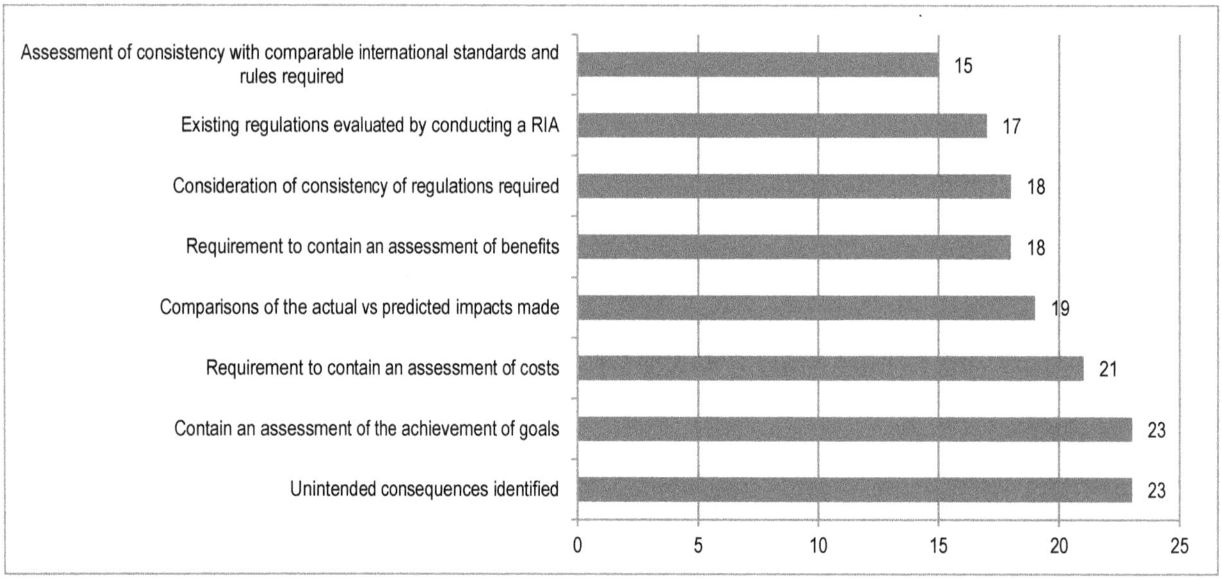

Source: OECD (2015b), *OECD Regulatory Policy Outlook 2015,* OECD Publishing, Paris, http://dx.doi.org/10.1787/9789264238770-en.

Ensure full commitment from PEMEX senior management with regard to implementing the reform and centralisation of the procurement function. Specifically, avoid long periods with acting DCPA corporate directors and deputy directors.

The position of the procurement function in the organisational structure of an institution is an indicator of the importance given to it as a strategic activity. As a general rule, the closer the procurement function is to senior management, the more strategic it becomes as an activity to create value.

In the case of PEMEX, the procurement head reports directly to the CEO, which indicates the strategic importance given to this activity. This is a notable change, as before the Energy Reform there were two or three tiers between the CEO and the procurement function.[5] This is consistent with the organisation found in many other international oil companies, where procurement is positioned one or two tiers below the CEO. For example, in 9% of the international oil companies that participated in the comparative study by CAPS Research, the procurement function reports directly to the Director General, while in 68% of the companies, procurement chiefs report one level below that of the Director General (see Box 1.5).

Box 1.5. **Position of the procurement function in 22 international oil companies**

The 2010 *Supply Management Performance Benchmarking Report - Petroleum Industry*, drafted by CAPS Research, analysed and compared the organic structure and the performance of the procurement function in 22 international oil companies: Aera Energy LLC, Alyesca Pipeline Service Company, BHP Billiton Petroleum (Americas) Inc., BP plc, Chevron Corporation, Ecopetrol, El Paso Corporation, EnCana Corporation, Eni S.p.A., Exxonmobil Global Services Company, Hess Corporation, Nabors Industries Ltd., National Cooperative Refinery Association, Nexen Inc., Plains All American Pipeline L.P., Pride International Inc., Repsol YPF, Sasol Limited, Shell International, Statoil ASA, Tesoro Companies Inc. and Transcanada Pipelines, Ltd.

Organisational tiers between the Director General and the chief procurement officer

Percentage

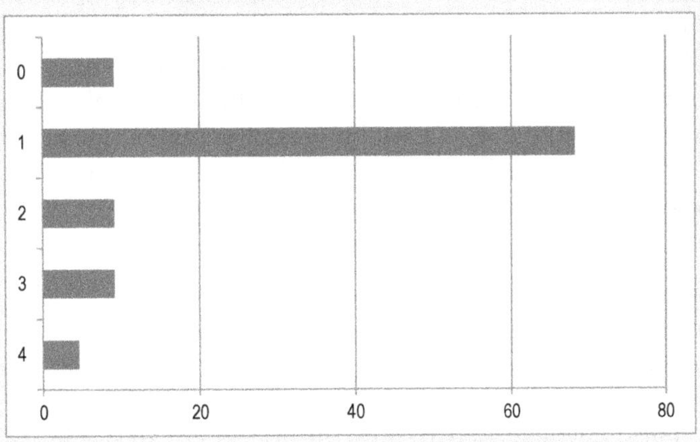

Source: Adapted from CAPS Research (2010), *2010 Supply Management Performance Benchmarking Report – Petroleum Industry*, sponsored jointly by the Institute for Supply Management and the J.P. Cary School for Business at Arizona State University.

While the position of the procurement function has been strengthened and illustrates robust back-up from senior management, in practice, there are other signals that indicate such back-up is not as strong. In particular, the lack of formal appointment of the Corporate Director for DCPA (vacant from September 2015 to April 2016) and several of its deputy directors weakened the leadership in the transformation of the procurement function. The Corporate Director of DCPA resigned in September 2015 and up to April 2016, there was an acting corporate director, without a formal appointment. The resignation cascaded down into several reallocations of staff, leading some of the deputy directors to interim positions as well. In fact, the DCPA was the only corporate directorate of PEMEX with an acting head at the time of writing this report (February 2016). The appointment of the new Corporate Director in DCPA in April 2016 created a new opportunity to send the right signals from top management as to the priority given to the transformation of the procurement function.

In the future, PEMEX should avoid long periods of time without a formal head of procurement. This situation creates lack of stability for staff, affects morale, and prevents DCPA leaders from planning beyond the short term, which is critical for the successful drive of the transformation process PEMEX is going through. Furthermore, the absence of a formal head denotes an inadequate "tone from the top" and weak change management.

PEMEX is going through a difficult financial situation, exacerbated by low oil prices. Therefore, there is no room for waste. Procurement is an activity with an important potential to realise savings and create value. However, such benefits will only be materialised if the transformation of the procurement function is completed and that requires sustained leadership and commitment from the top. Such commitment can be demonstrated by the empowerment of a strong DCPA team.

While at the central offices there seems to be awareness of the transformation process of PEMEX, advancing such transformation in the regional offices is a challenge and will require additional efforts to further employee engagement.

In line with the previous recommendation, the "tone from the top" should be illustrative for employees in PEMEX regional offices as to the commitment to the new procurement structure. The centralisation process will take away operational flexibility in the regional offices and reduce opportunities for misbehaviour, or at least, add an additional control mechanism. It is foreseeable that there will be resistance not only from the officials who might have unduly benefited from the decentralised structure, but also from others who resist change out of pure bureaucratic inertia. Hence, the centralisation of procurement should be facilitated organisation-wide, but particularly outside of headquarters, where it might be more difficult to convey senior management commitment.

Facilitation strategies could include consultation in the design and improvement of procurement procedures, training, sharing good practices, providing incentives (not necessarily economic incentives) and raising awareness concerning the advantages of the centralised structure and how it supports PEMEX in its transformation and in facing current, difficult times, characterised by low oil prices. For example, DCPA could set a number of indicators to measure compliance and progress in the transition to a centralised structure by the different regional offices. Then, it could rank them, highlighting good practices and providing recognition or awards to the top performers.

In the context of the downsizing of the company, morale might be low and there might be incentives to resist change. Highlighting the positive aspects of PEMEX's procurement transformation is therefore a must. Close interactions of senior management with regional employees would also help, even if it takes place through remote tools (i.e. videoconferencing). Such interactions must reassure regional PEMEX employees about the strategies going forward and how they will positively benefit their day-to-day activities.

Notes

1. Chapter 5 of Part III will address contract management in length.
2. Other reports are produced for different government institutions. For example, a monthly report on small and medium-sized enterprise (SME) procurement is provided to the Ministry of Economy.
3. An English version of the PEMEX webpage is also available at www.pemex.com/en/procurement/Paginas.
4. Independent directors (subject to national definitions) are individuals who do not directly represent any particular stakeholder interest in the SOE, but who are sought to bring specific skills and competencies to the Board.
5. The exact position differed between PEMEX Corporate and its subsidiaries.

References

APQC (2011a), "Employees significantly more efficient with category management", APQC, Houston, Texas, www.apqc.org (accessed 22 February 2016).

APQC (2011b), "Procurement category management: Faster PO cycle time", APQC, Houston, Texas, www.apqc.org (accessed 22 February 2016).

BP (British Petroleum) (n. d.), "Group organisation", webpage, www.bp.com/en/global/corporate/about-bp/group-organisation.html (accessed 14 January 2016).

CAPS Research (2010), *2010 Supply Management Performance Benchmarking Report – Petroleum Industry*, sponsored jointly by the Institute for Supply Management and the J.P. Cary School for Business at Arizona State University.

Government of Mexico (2014), "Ley de Petróleos Mexicanos" [Pemex Law], www.diputados.gob.mx/LeyesBiblio/pdf/LPM_110814.pdf (accessed 29 September 2015).

OECD (2015a), "OECD Guidelines on Corporate Governance of State-Owned Enterprises", www.oecd.org/corporate/guidelines-corporate-governance-soes.htm.

OECD (2015b), *OECD Regulatory Policy Outlook 2015,* OECD Publishing, Paris, http://dx.doi.org/10.1787/9789264238770-en.

OECD (2013), *Boards of Directors of State-Owned Enterprises: An Overview of National Practices*, OECD Publishing, Paris, http://dx.doi.org/10.1787/9789264200425-en.

OECD (2010), "Corporate governance and board arrangements at Petróleos Mexicanos: Evaluations and recommendations", unclassified OECD document, www.oecd.org/officialdocuments/publicdisplaydocumentpdf/?cote=DAF/CA/SOPP(2010)5/FINAL&docLanguage=En.

PEMEX (2015), "Manual de organización de estructura básica de Petróleos Mexicanos y Organismos Subsidiarios", April.

Petrobras (n. d.), "Organization chart", webpage, www.petrobras.com.br/en/about-us/organization-chart/ (accessed 14 January 2016).

Snipeliski Nischli, Ron (2014), "The new PEMEX and CFE", presentation by Ron Snipeliski Nischli, General Director for Legislation and Consultation, SHCP, to the OECD Working Party on State Ownership and Privatisation Practices, 22-23 October 2014.

Statoil (n. d.), "Organisation chart", webpage, www.statoil.com/en/about/corporate governance/governingbodies/orgchart/Pages/default.aspx (accessed 14 January 2016)

Chapter 2

Implementing strong organisational procurement strategies at Petróleos Mexicanos

This chapter assesses how the revisited procurement organisation in PEMEX is aligned with the company's business objectives and creates economic value for the Mexican state. It further suggests actions reinforcing the strategic role of the procurement function in the company, from increased oversight on procurement activities to strengthened relations with suppliers.

While Petróleos Mexicanos (or PEMEX) transforms into a state productive enterprise (empresa productiva del Estado, or EPE), its primary objectives are to compete in an open market and to maintain its status as sector leader, generating economic value in all its business lines. The company's vision, embedded into all its activities, insists upon creating economic value and profitability for the Mexican state.

The OECD Recommendation on Public Procurement (OECD, 2015a) calls upon countries to create an environment conducive to transforming procurement into a strategic function best able to meet overall government objectives. As a productive company of the state whose primary mission is to create economic value and profitability for Mexico, the principles of the OECD Recommendation apply to PEMEX (see Box 2.1).

Box 2.1. Principles of the OECD Recommendation on Public Procurement relating to organisational procurement strategies

While the 2015 OECD Recommendation on Public Procurement spells out principles aiming at driving efficiencies throughout the procurement cycle, some principles convey concepts that are closely linked to the implementation of strong organisational procurement strategies. The OECD Council notably:

1. **RECOMMENDS** that Adherents foster transparent and effective stakeholder **participation.**

To this end, Adherents should:

1. **Develop and follow a standard process when formulating changes to the public procurement system.** Such standard process should promote public consultations, invite the comments of the private sector and civil society, ensure the publication of the results of the consultation phase and explain the options chosen, all in a transparent manner.
2. **Engage in transparent and regular dialogues with suppliers and business associations to present public procurement objectives and to assure a correct understanding of markets.** Effective communication should be conducted to provide potential vendors with a better understanding of the country's needs, and government buyers with information to develop more realistic and effective tender specifications by better understanding market capabilities. Such interactions should be subject to due fairness, transparency and integrity safeguards, which vary depending on whether an active procurement process is ongoing. Such interactions should also be adapted to ensure that foreign companies participating in tenders receive transparent and effective information.
3. **Provide opportunities for direct involvement of relevant external stakeholders** in the procurement system with a view to increase transparency and integrity while assuring an adequate level of scrutiny, provided that confidentiality, equal treatment and other legal obligations in the procurement process are maintained.

2. **RECOMMENDS** that Adherents develop processes to drive **Efficiency** throughout the public procurement cycle in satisfying the needs of the government and its citizens.

To this end, Adherents should:

1. **Streamline the public procurement system and its institutional frameworks.** Adherents should evaluate existing processes and institutions to identify functional overlap, inefficient silos and other causes of waste. Where possible, a more service-oriented public procurement system should then be built around efficient and effective procurement processes and workflows to reduce administrative red tape and costs, for example through shared services.
2. **Implement sound technical processes to satisfy customer needs efficiently.** Adherents should take steps to ensure that procurement outcomes meet the needs of customers, for instance by developing appropriate technical specifications, identifying appropriate award criteria, ensuring adequate technical expertise among proposal evaluators, and ensuring adequate resources and expertise are available for contract management following the award of a contract.

Box 2.1. Principles of the OECD Recommendation on Public Procurement relating to organisational procurement strategies *(continued)*

3. **Develop and use tools to improve procurement procedures, reduce duplication and achieve greater value for money**, including centralised purchasing, framework agreements, e-catalogues, dynamic purchasing, e-auctions, joint procurements and contracts with options. Application of such tools across sub-national levels of government, where appropriate and feasible, could further drive efficiency.

3. **RECOMMENDS** that Adherents develop a procurement workforce with the **Capacity** to continually deliver value for money efficiently and effectively.

To this end, Adherents should:

1. **Ensure that procurement officials meet high professional standards for knowledge, practical implementation and integrity by providing a dedicated and regularly updated set of tools**, for example, sufficient staff in terms of numbers and skills, recognition of public procurement as a specific profession, certification and regular trainings, integrity standards for public procurement officials and the existence of a unit or team analysing public procurement information and monitoring the performance of the public procurement system.

2. **Provide attractive, competitive and merit-based career options for procurement officials**, through the provision of clear means of advancement, protection from political interference in the procurement process and the promotion of national and international good practices in career development to enhance the performance of the procurement workforce.

3. **Promote collaborative approaches with knowledge centres such as universities, think tanks or policy centres to improve skills and competences of the procurement workforce**. The expertise and pedagogical experience of knowledge centres should be enlisted as a valuable means of expanding procurement knowledge and upholding a two-way channel between theory and practice, capable of boosting application of innovation to public procurement systems.

4. **RECOMMENDS** that Adherents drive performance improvements through **Evaluation** of the effectiveness of the public procurement system from individual procurements to the system as a whole, at all levels of government where feasible and appropriate.

To this end, Adherents should:

1. **Assess periodically and consistently the results of the procurement process**. Public procurement systems should collect consistent, up-to-date and reliable information and use data on prior procurements, particularly regarding price and overall costs, in structuring new needs assessments, as they provide a valuable source of insight and could guide future procurement decisions.

2. **Develop indicators to measure performance, effectiveness and savings of the public procurement system** for benchmarking and to support strategic policy making on public procurement.

Source: OECD (2015a), "Recommendation of the Council on Public Procurement", www.oecd.org/corruption/recommendation-on-public-procurement.htm.

This vision also applies to the reform of its procurement function. Procurement activities account for a significant share of PEMEX's total budget, which amounted to approximately MXN 540 billion in 2014. Therefore efforts towards a sound and efficient management of procurement operations would directly affect the company's ability to compete in a low-oil-price environment.

Economic circumstances surrounding the current oil world force companies in this field to generate savings and create value in their operating environments more than ever, so already significantly reduced benefit margins could continue to exist, providing revenues not only for the company itself but for the state. In the case of PEMEX, 90% of its revenues are given back to the Mexican government. This illustrates that although PEMEX is transforming into a more privatised structure, it remains a strategic vehicle for public finance, exposed to recent market changes.

After five years of unprecedented stability, global oil prices have re-entered their normal commodity price cycle with a fall from over USD 100 a barrel in May 2013 to an historical low of USD 19 on 20 January 2016, with a vast majority of forecasts predicting a long-term low level of oil prices (see Box 2.2).

Box 2.2. Energy sector transformation for a low-oil-price world

Energy sector investment plans are being scaled back, with most companies significantly reducing their capital investment programmes in new projects by an average of about 30%, with far-reaching market, supply-chain, community and human implications.

Historically, the response to commodity prices falling has been short-termism, treating the emerging symptoms, not the actual cause; focus is on sustaining cash flow rather than sustaining investments. Reducing capital expenditure (CAPEX) and cancelling projects may reduce cost escalation, which preserves cash for survival. However, in the long run this will cost more and bring back all of the current pathologies once price recovers.

Analysis shows that projects are now longer, with more expensive front-end processes and stages. A US dollar buys less than half of what it did ten years ago (in project terms). Projects today are more technical and complex and have a lot of moving parts.

Recent major projects trends indicate that:

- Engineering costs have doubled since 2000.
- Pipeline costs have doubled since 2005.
- Equipment costs have doubled since 2000.
- Construction costs in the West have doubled since 2000.
- Owner's costs have increased continuously, and can be up to 25% of total installed cost (TIC).
- Team sizes are dramatically larger at all stages. In the last ten years, teams have doubled in size, with increased management and assurance – adding to the complexity of interfaces seen as the norm.

Source: Adapted from Major Projects Association (2015), "Highlights from the Major Projects Association Event held on 11 November 2015", www.majorprojects.org/highlights/389highlightslowoilprice.

PEMEX should ensure a permanent alignment of its procurement strategy with business objectives

Considering the significant share of PEMEX resources, therefore indirect public resources, allocated to this category of expenditure, an effective procurement function plays a strategic role in ensuring a sound management of those funds. In accordance with the OECD Recommendation on Public Procurement, the procurement cycle should be as streamlined as possible and integrated into the overall governance system of the organisation as a whole, recognising the procurement function as a strategically important component (OECD, 2015a).

The Energy Reform passed in 2014 led to the establishment of a new procurement framework that aimed to address the new challenges faced by PEMEX. Indeed, in this context, the PEMEX Board of Directors implemented change to its procurement function, notably by centralising procurement activities and defining unified global procurement strategies.

The Board of Directors, which is PEMEX's supreme decision body, is responsible, in accordance with Article 13 of the PEMEX Law (Ley de Petróleos Mexicanos), for defining the company' strategic orientations. It is composed of ten counsellors, five of which are independent. These counsellors are designated by the Executive branch in light of their experience and competences, and proposals are ratified by the Senate (see Chapter 1).

PEMEX developed a business plan detailing its strategic vision. This plan, covering 2016 until 2020, defines Pemex's strategic directions in value creation and operational and financial sustainability for the next five years. It includes analyses of PEMEX global performance, supported by results achieved in 2014. On this basis, the plan then details strategic orientations aiming at further developing PEMEX performance. The overarching assessment of PEMEX performance against its competitors clearly calls for the need to generate additional value, allowing for better economic performance. While its production of barrels is comparable to other international oil companies, PEMEX's corporate assets are negative (PEMEX, 2015).

Procurement strategies are not absent from these key issues. Indeed, in support of the four broad strategic objectives designed to augment PEMEX's productivity, reference is made to the necessity to increase procurement ability to create value and generate efficiency.

Adopted by the PEMEX Board on 15 December 2015, the 2016-20 business plan is the reference document that details the company's business strategic orientations. This document and the corresponding strategies integrate the new PEMEX organisational environment for the first time. This document should be completed, however, with an action plan detailing timeframes for the completion of the various objectives set out in the business plan, and allowing for a robust monitoring of progress made towards these objectives. In doing so, PEMEX would be able to implement the necessary corrective actions in case expected progress does not happen.

Aligning procurement strategies with business objectives is paramount to the implementation of strategic procurement in many different industries since the share companies spend against each dollar of revenue could be as high as 65%. Oil companies spend on average almost half (40%) of their revenues in raw materials and services (Figure 2.1). Analysing this information not only provides insights on the profit structure of oil companies, but on some of the main supply chain industries contracting with those companies.

Figure 2.1. **Total spend as a percentage of sales: Cross-industry comparison**

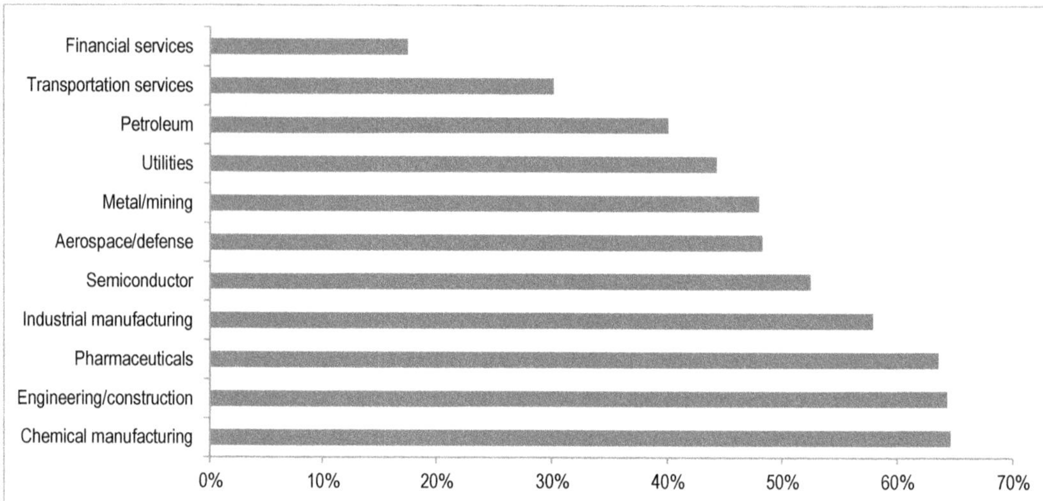

Source: Adapted from CAPS Research (2012) *Cross-Industry Report*, jointly sponsored by member companies, the W. P. Carey School of Business at Arizona State University, and the Institute for Supply Management (ISM).

Alongside the oil industry, companies in the utilities sector spend almost the same share of their revenues (44%) in raw materials and services, thus having comparable perspectives in the positioning of procurement strategies against overall business objectives. In addition, the levels of total spend managed or controlled by supply management, i.e. procurement, is equally important in both industries (see Figure 2.2) and accounts for 77%.

Figure 2.2. **Percentage of total spend managed or controlled by supply management**

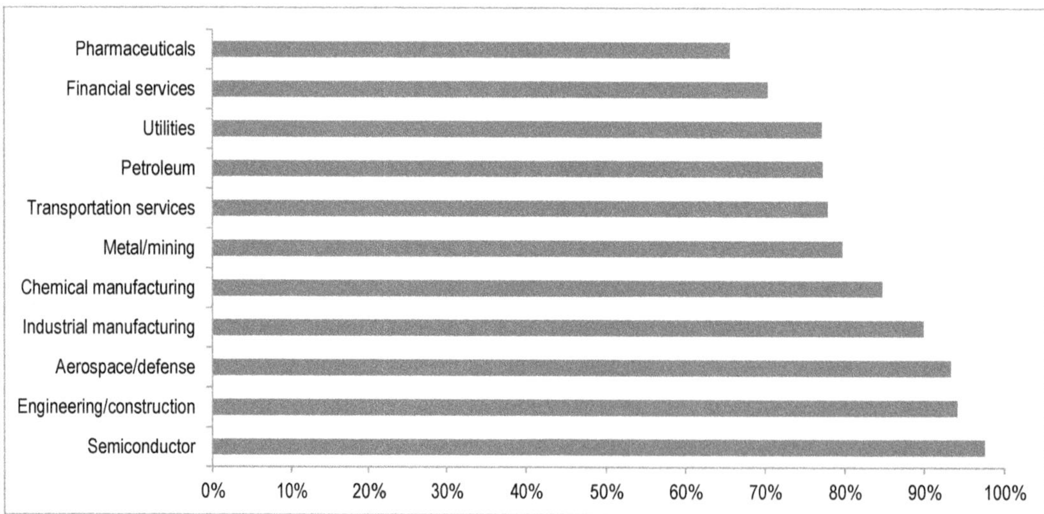

Source: Adapted from CAPS Research (2012) *Cross-Industry Report*, jointly sponsored by member companies, the W. P. Carey School of Business at Arizona State University, and the Institute for Supply Management (ISM).

In a challenging economic environment, the positioning of the procurement function in the organisation of the company could create synergies with business strategic orientations

The decision taken by the Board of Directors to revisit the procurement function was made following an analysis of existing practices in 14 different oil companies worldwide and with the view to create value that could generate savings, quality and opportunity in goods, services and works acquired by PEMEX. The Organic Statutes of PEMEX (Estatuto Organico de Petroleos Mexicanos) published in the Official Journal of the Federation (Diario Oficial de la Federacion, or DOF) on 28 April 2015 created the Corporate Directorate for Procurement and Supply (Direcion Corporativa de Procura y Abastecimiento, or DCPA).

These changes are reflected in various aspects:

- Generating value will be the prevailing criterion in PEMEX decision making, especially in procurement.
- Increasing transparency in PEMEX processes, obtaining better savings, achieving better contractual terms and conditions in opportunity, service and quality, better number of long-term procurement solutions, developing suppliers and contractors' base will be important.
- Evolving work cultures so as to increase the contribution of the procurement function in terms of team efficiency, quality of services and availability of resources will be a priority.

The benefits of the centralisation of the procurement function are expected to enhance and streamline PEMEX operating procedures, notably with the implementation of a business model whose overarching principles are to:

- meet real business needs, through an approved process and comprehensive, long-term planning
- develop an integral suppliers relationship management system, which should provide necessary, complete and reliable information
- implement an institutional strategic supply methodology for procurement operations
- conduct procurement with a focus on performance assessment and continuous process improvement along with the development and professionalisation of the procurement workforce.

In order to fulfil its missions, the PEMEX Board of Directors is directly supported by specific committees, including a committee for Acquisitions, Leases, Works and Services (Comité de Adquisiciones, Arrendamientos, Obras y Servicios, or CAAOS). The chair of this committee is one of the four independent counsellors of the Board of Directors. Such an organisation should position procurement strategies at the heart of the company's business objectives. However the fact that the chair is designated on a rotation basis each year could hinder the long-term influence of this committee on the strategic orientations decided by the PEMEX Board of Directors. Indeed in many large organisations, a frequent rotation of chairs has been found to be detrimental to strategy consistency (Ernst & Young, 2013).

In accordance with Article 45 of the PEMEX Act, the CAAOS is responsible for:

- formulating to the Director General recommendations on specific aspects that may be included in procurement policies and provisions proposed to the Board of Directors
- reviewing proposals that the Director General presents on procurement policies and provisions
- formulating opinions at the request of the Board of Directors, on contracts submitted to it, in accordance with applicable provisions
- following up on acquisitions, leasing, services and works contracts that have been authorised by the Board of Directors in accordance with Fraction V of Article 13 of the PEMEX Law
- approving, where appropriate, exceptions to public tenders for PEMEX and its subsidiary productive companies' contracts with subsidiaries of PEMEX
- reviewing the annual procurement plans for acquisitions, leases, works and services and formulating recommendations it deems appropriate to the Board of Directors
- carrying out any other task as determined by the Board of Directors.

The Mexican Federal Commission of Electricity (Comisión Federal de Electricidad, or CFE) has also been subject to the effects of the Energy Reform. As a productive company of the State, CFE, just as PEMEX, now operates in an open market for the generation and marketing of electricity and competes with other major players. To address this new competing environment, CFE's organisational structure follows the same rationale and promotes procurement as a strategic support to the corporate decision-making process.

Yet, the sharp decline of oil prices and the fall recently experienced by PEMEX on oil distribution, coupled with the share of spend for each dollar of sales, further advocates for a closer alignment between business objectives and procurement strategies.

Effective and efficient organisational structure and processes are needed to unlock the potential of procurement at PEMEX

Setting aside organisational alignment, the positioning of procurement as a strategic function also derives from its internal structure and how it operates with business units. Indeed procurement synergies are often found in procurement internal organisations that are structured in accordance with corporate needs (Rozemeijer, 2000).

The Organic Statutes of PEMEX have centralised and standardised procurement processes for the acquisition of goods, services and works for PEMEX and its subsidiary productive companies. The centralisation of the procurement process aims to better manage relations with suppliers, create standard procedures for planning long-term acquisitions and professionalise procurement officials.

In accordance with PEMEX's Organic Statutes published on 28 April 2015, a new directorate was created with the overarching responsibility of defining and managing the design and implementation of the national and international procurement strategy applicable to PEMEX, its subsidiary productive companies and other subsidiaries.

The DCPA is therefore responsible for the overall procurement strategy of the company and is tasked with the definition, implementation and monitoring of all co-ordination mechanisms relating to procurement in PEMEX's fragmented and decentralised operating universe.

Alongside the DCPA sits PEMEX Procurement International (PPI), a US-based subsidiary of PEMEX, which started its operations on 1 November 1994. Since its creation, PPI has developed over 200 long-term partnership agreements and has had contractual relationships with more than 1 700 suppliers in the oil equipment manufacturing and services industry, as well as other related industries.

Indeed PPI is specialised in the conclusion of different types of framework agreements (*contratos preparatorios, acuerdos referenciales*). These long-term contracts are agreements for the purchase of goods and contracting of services. They are negotiated between PPI and the original equipment manufacturers, producers, licensed distributors, and certified service providers that allow PEMEX and its subsidiaries to purchase equipment, parts, information technology, consumables, repairs, maintenance, and other products or services.

While PPI is an autonomous entity, it observes PEMEX's legal framework. Incorporated in Delaware and authorised to carry out business in Texas, PPI operates outside Mexican law. Nevertheless, PPI operates on behalf of PEMEX through several agency agreements with it, its subsidiaries and affiliates. While carrying out business on behalf of its principals, PPI finds itself legally obliged to fully observe and comply with PEMEX's legal framework and with its internal regulations, to some extent. Furthermore, as an affiliate company of PEMEX, PPI is committed to aligning its operations to the strategies and standard operating procedures defined by the DCPA. Yet, PPI procurement activities are not consolidated with those of PEMEX and its subsidiary productive companies, and does not therefore benefit from potential synergies.

In an effort to implement transformational changes to procurement strategies used by PEMEX purchasing entities, the DCPA developed a new procurement business model called Procurement 2.0 (Procura 2.0). This procurement process aims to better align procurement practices across business areas. It should be accompanied with an implementation plan so these improvements can be realised in a relatively short period of time. In line with the OECD Recommendation on Public Procurement (OECD, 2015a), which promotes streamlined public procurement systems and institutional frameworks, the DCPA implemented a unified strategy centred on three pillars – processes, people and systems.

The first overarching principle relates to procurement planning. In order to align centralised procurement strategies with decentralised business needs, PEMEX established internal guidelines relating to procurement forecast. Article 4 of the Procurement Guidelines (Disposiciones Generales de Contratacion par Petroleos Mexicanos y sus Empresas Productivas Subsidarias, or the "Procurement Guidelines") indicates that PEMEX and its subsidiary productive companies shall develop an annual procurement plan that shall be issued no later than 15 November of the preceding year. This procurement plan shall be designed by each entity in conjunction with the DCPA and is subject to quarterly updates.

PEMEX concentrates Mexico's biggest investment portfolio of large projects (see Figure 2.3), which necessitates thorough and detailed procurement planning to minimise the impact of the size and complexity of those projects on market participation to procurement processes.

Figure 2.3. **Mexico's 2016 investment projects and programmes, by responsible units with allocated budgets in excess of MXN 2 million**

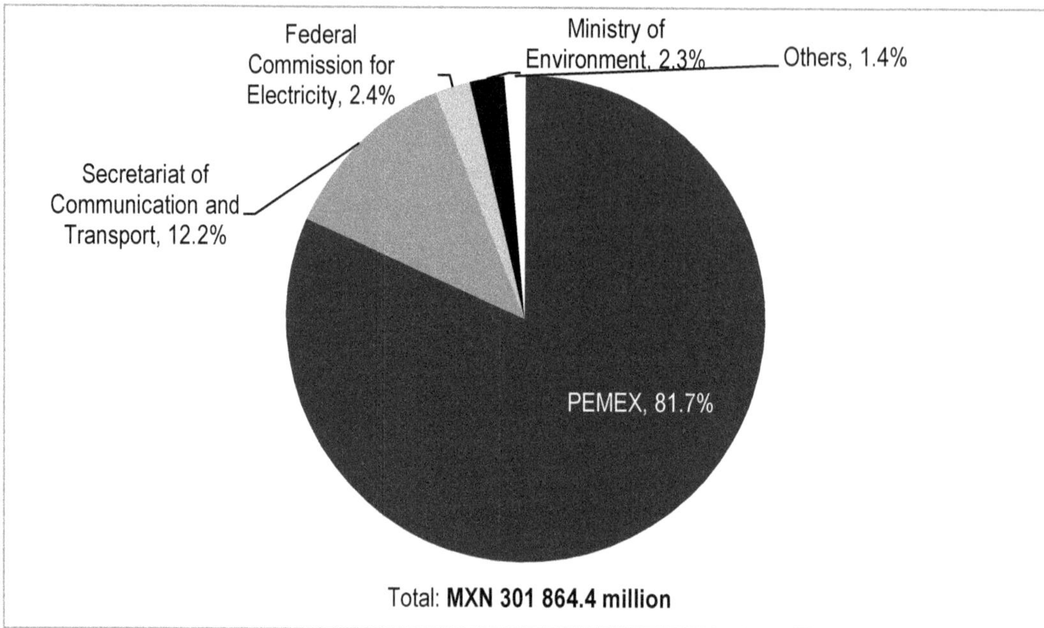

Source: Adapted from CEFP (Centro de Estudios de las Finanzas Publicas) [Centre for Studies on Public Finance] (2016), "Federal expenditure budget assigned to investments projects and programmes in 2016", Information Note of 25 January.

The indicative 2016 procurement plan lists 9 935 different processes to be carried out, mostly during the year (with few multi-annual projects), by PEMEX and its subsidiary productive companies. The planned procurement operations account for an estimated total budget of approximately MXN 340 billion. This plan does not, however, include procurement forecasted operations of PEMEX subsidiaries, for which no comprehensive information is readily available. Fragmented information about the PEMEX group global procurement operations hinders access to procurement opportunities.

The second major principle of the DCPA strategy is the development of product categories to define harmonised procurement strategies for certain product families. As of September 2015, PEMEX identified 17 product families and 42 product categories. Dividing the procurement portfolio into product categories should help PEMEX implement tailored procurement strategies that respond best to end users' needs and market capabilities.

PEMEX has adopted a new methodology for defining its strategies for the procurement of most common goods and services. This methodology, called "Strategic Supply and Management by Categories" (Abastecimiento estratégico y gestión por categorías), first analyses the company's expenditure. On this basis, PEMEX defines categories of products that can be subject to the same procurement strategy. The outcomes of this strategic assessment and the deriving contracts are validated afterwards by an ad hoc group called the Group for Strategic Supply (Grupo de Abastecimiento Estratégico, or GAE), in accordance with Article 10 of the Procurement Guidelines.

This strategic sourcing method (see Figure 2.4) should help PEMEX structure its procurement portfolio, adapting strategies to business objectives and risks management. By streamlining procurement processes for a given category, PEMEX devotes efforts to drive efficiencies throughout its procurement organisations, notably in its attempts to reduce duplication and red tape costs.

Figure 2.4. **PEMEX's strategic sourcing methodology**

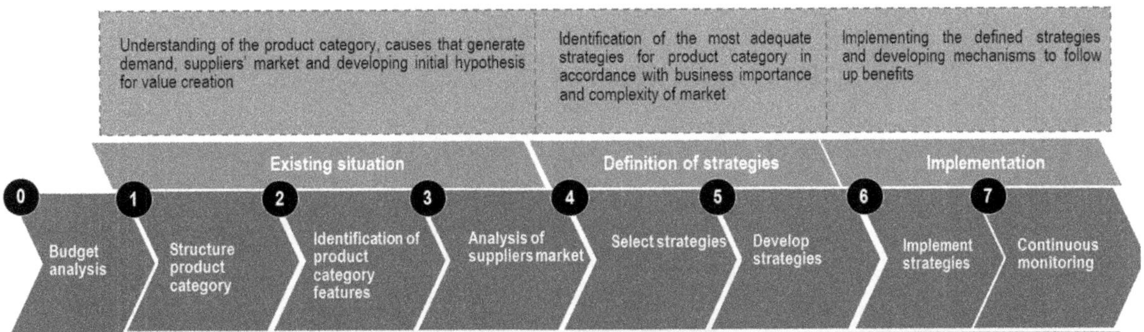

Step	Main activities
Structure of product category	▪ Identification of the most important variables such as technical specifications, spending volume and build the category tree
Identification of the product category features	▪ Analysis of existing contracts ▪ Analysis of budget spending by activity and business units ▪ Analysis of procurement processes, existing strategies and key stakeholders in the process ▪ Interviews with users to understand demand
Analysis of suppliers market	▪ Identification of new national or international suppliers ▪ Understand value creation for suppliers ▪ Design and issuance of request for information to understand market capabilities and gain market intelligence
Select and develop strategies	▪ On the basis of previous analyses, identification of the most appropriate strategies
Implementation of strategies	▪ Carrying out the contracting process
Monitoring	▪ Mechanism to monitor benefits and indicators for the assessment of savings and other benefits

Source: Adapted from information provided by PEMEX.

To roll out procurement processes defined in accordance with the strategic sourcing methodology and to ensure alignment with business needs, the DCPA runs each specific procurement project together with a project manager. The project manager is a director of PEMEX or one of its subsidiary productive companies appointed by PEMEX's Director General.

In a decentralised business environment and with highly specialised goods or services, tailored procurement strategies should help address the complexity of procurement operations. Yet, oftentimes, product categories management also includes an assessment of the criticality of the goods or services, considering business objectives or taking the company's competitive environment into account. The literature offers a wide range of policy options allowing organisations to structure their procurement portfolio.

A long-standing theoretical model was developed by Kraljic for the first time in 1983. This model proposes to categorise goods and services in accordance with their relative financial impact and risk of supply (Kraljic, 1983). The supply market complexity assesses, among other things, the number and size of the supplier market, the level of competitive pressure or the substitution possibilities. The importance of profit is evaluated through the prisms of corresponding procurement expenditure, the percentage of the organisation's total procurement expenditure or the impact on quality, availability or reliability of the end products. By allocating companies' procurement portfolios in one of the quadrants found in Figure 2.5, a specific procurement strategy can then be applied.

Figure 2.5. **Krajlic model**

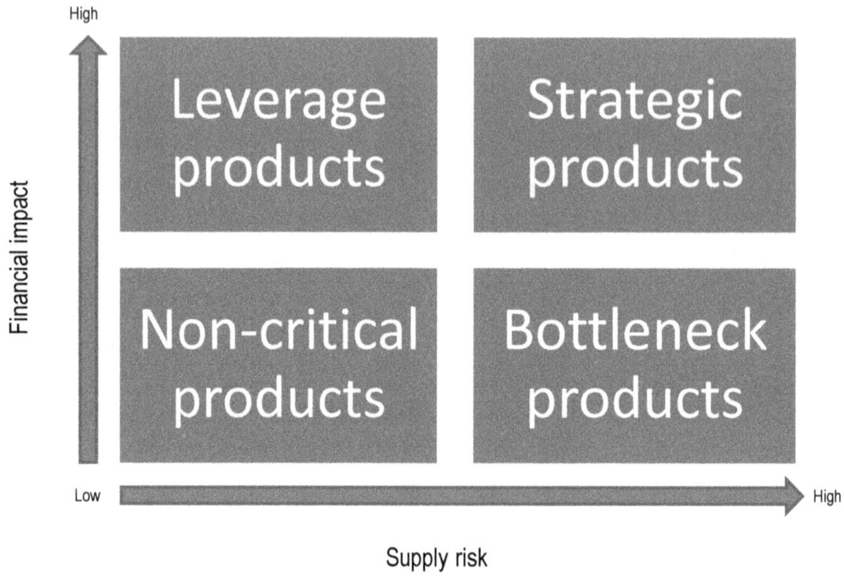

Source: Adapted from Kraljic, P. (1983), "Purchasing Must Become Management", *Harvard Business Review*, https://hbr.org/1983/09/purchasing-must-become-supply-management.

Aligning PEMEX and suppliers' strategies could create an environment conducive to increased productivity on both ends

Beyond the initial negotiation strategies of oil companies affected by the sharp fall in prices that led to harsh renegotiations of contracts with suppliers, companies need to define more sustainable procurement strategies in the long term.

In addition to the product-category-driven approach, other procurement portfolio management theories have been developed. Indeed, one of the main criticisms of the Kraljic matrix is that it oversimplifies the procurement context and does not sufficiently take into account suppliers' perspectives. Therefore alternative theories have developed that focus procurement portfolio management on the relationship between the buyer and the supplier. The framework by Cox et al. (2003) defines strategies on the basis of the relationship between the two actors (buyer dominance, supplier dominance, interdependence and independence).

Other theories have focused on supply chain in procurement portfolios where strategies are defined according to the contextual factors influencing the supply chain (Fisher, 1997). The core argument of these theories is that the procurement relationship between a buyer and a supplier is influenced by the degree of innovation attached to the goods or services procured. For products categorised as functional, demand will be relatively stable and predictable. Because of the absence or little significance of customisation, suppliers will compete on financial aspects. In the case of innovative products, demand is relatively unpredictable and a large number of variants will be proposed. Suppliers might also be able to limit competition.

These theories illustrate the different perspectives from which the procurement portfolio of an organisation can be assessed and structured. These models are not exclusive of the other and each can complement the assessment of PEMEX's procurement portfolio.

Besides categorisation of procurement spending and strategic analyses, efficient global procurement strategies also define processes that are able to create synergies with suppliers. In addition to the "what we buy", specific attention is devoted to the "how we buy". This is particularly true in the oil industry where complex and large-scale infrastructure projects are necessary to maintain companies' productivity. PEMEX infrastructures, and most notably refineries, are in need of major repairs and upgrades, and often operate at below their stated capacity (CRS, 2015). Coupled with low oil prices affecting capital expenditure, innovative procurement strategies should be identified to meet PEMEX's financial constraints and investment needs (see Box 2.3 to see other oil company examples).

Box 2.3. Strategic alignment in procurement strategies

For the last ten years, large-scale projects carried out by oil companies have seen procurement strategies developed to favour synergies between buyers and suppliers and ensure strategic alignment. Two examples illustrate how combining technical expertise from both sides with procurement skills can help to enhance the value for money of large infrastructure projects.

ExxonMobil "Design One, Build Many" strategy

ExxonMobil Development implemented a procurement strategy called "Design One, Build Multiple" for the delivery of large-scale deepwater projects offshore Angola on Block 15. The projects in Block 15, approximately 90 miles off the coast of Angola, established industry benchmarks for completion time and unit development costs for deepwater projects of their size and complexity.

"The success of our Design One, Build Multiple strategy in Angola would not have been possible without the collaboration in a shared vision among ExxonMobil, Sonangol and Block 15 contractor group," said Jeff Woodbury, Executive Vice President of ExxonMobil Development Company.

Between 2003 and 2008, ExxonMobil Development applied the "Design One, Build Multiple" strategy to deliver two tension leg platforms and five of the world's largest floating production, storage and offloading vessels to Block 15. The use of many of the same suppliers, service providers and workers, including Angolans, to build and install the facilities enhanced safety, quality, efficiency and reliability.

The company received the award at the annual dinner for the world's largest conference for offshore development at the George R. Brown Convention Center in Houston. Susan Cunningham, Chair of the OTC Board of Directors, said, "Each year, OTC recognises individuals and companies that have made outstanding contributions to the offshore industry. ExxonMobil Development earned this honor for its industry-leading approach to Angola deepwater project development."

BP Suppliers Led Solutions

In developing Suppliers Led Solutions, BP (British Petroleum) used the concept of smart standardisation to ensure effective competition among suppliers and competitive prices. The first effort carried out by BP hardware product teams composed of procurement staff, engineers and quality assurance specialists had focused on categorisation of products classified against three tiers of relative importance to the risk-management strategy of the company.

Box 2.3. **Strategic alignment in procurement strategies** *(continued)*

By developing lean engineering, BP procurement teams have been able to integrate standard technical specifications and quality requirements, reducing the number of bespoke documentation required for each project. This strategy helped significantly reduce the time needed for suppliers to respond to BP's needs, hence augmenting the overall attractiveness of procurement operations.

Suppliers Led Solutions not only proved useful in decreasing the level of engineering efforts required on the suppliers' end, it also provided benefits in terms of overall project completion. BP experienced an unprecedented 70% decrease of time to completion, which also helped reduced its internal engineering and project costs.

Source: Adapted from Reuters (2011), "ExxonMobil recognized for industry-leading approach to develop Angola deepwater projects", press release, 2 May; Smith, R. (2015), "Energy sector transformation for a low-oil-price world", presentation given at Major Projects Association, 11 November.

One factor that is often overlooked in implementing strong organisational procurement strategies is the analytical capacity that allows the procurement unit to understand trends and patterns and participate in the attainment of business objectives. Unsurprisingly a large share of powerful information is to be found in corporate information technology (IT) systems that somehow relate to procurement.

PEMEX should ensure that information systems support its strategic internal procurement organisation

In a decentralised operating environment with multiple autonomous subsidiary productive companies and subsidiaries, the collection of procurement information that informs the DCPA's decision-making process with strong and reliable evidence is paramount to the effectiveness of the centralised procurement function.

The DCPA relies on information provided by IT systems that collect and process procurement-related information. Data that can be collected and generated by a comprehensive e-procurement system supports a host of important procurement functions, including ongoing performance evaluation of the system and its outcomes; the development and deployment of risk-management strategies; and internal and external accountability (OECD, 2016). In so doing, e-procurement systems create an environment conducive to efficient procurement organisations.

PEMEX, and notably the DCPA, have a number of IT systems that cover the procurement cycle. Procurement-related information is inputted into at least 18 different systems (see Table 2.1). Beyond potential duplication, hence efficiency and productivity losses, PEMEX is clearly exposed to risks with regard to the quality and reliability of the information processed. The fragmented structure of the PEMEX group and decentralised business areas might further prevent a comprehensive analysis of procurement performance, thus hindering the transformation of the DCPA into a strategic partner. However in an effort to streamline the collection and analysis of procurement-related information, PEMEX recently introduced a transitional platform supporting procurement operations, homologating processes, integrating documents and producing data used to inform future procurement decisions.

Although PEMEX has been developing a specific taxonomy to ensure data consistency, the multiplicity of IT systems shown in Table 2.1 clearly suggests risk for human error and discrepancies in the understanding of e-procurement vocabulary in the different business areas. The DCPA runs the risk of not being provided with the reasonable assurance that strategic procurement decisions are supported by reliable data analyses. Mitigation measures such as robust, yet manual and repetitive, quality assurance processes could address this risk, but may not be sustainable in the long term. In addition, the multiplicity of platforms covering the tendering phase suggests multiple interactions with potential bidders being required to provide administrative documentation on various occasions. This calls for the swift implementation of an integral information system covering the entire procurement cycle and promoting the once-only principle (European Commission, 2016).

While procurement experts participate in ad hoc IT projects, the DCPA does not have a dedicated technical team that combines IT experience and procurement understanding in its structure. The absence of procurement knowledge in teams designing e-procurement systems has often been identified as an e-procurement risk, resulting in sub-optimal benefits for the procurement function (UN, 2006).

Table 2.1. **Information technology systems where PEMEX and DCPA procurement-related information is stored**

Procurement phases	IT systems
Procurement planning	SPyA (Sistema de Seguimiento de Procura y Abastecimiento) ERP SAP (Enterprise Resource Planning; Systems, Applications and Products) PICS (Proceso Integral de Contratacion de Suministros) in SAP for PEP (Exploracion y Produccion) PDBS (Pronostico de Demanda de Bienes y Servicios de Petroleos Mexicanos)
Development of procurement strategies	SAPRE Ariba HIIP (Herramentia de Integral de Informacion de Proveedores y Contratistas)
Tendering and contracting	SAPRE Ariba Online system for collective groups PICS in SAP for PEP HITEC for PEMEX Procurement International SRM for PGPB (Gas y Petroquímica Básica) Boveda Electronica de Documentos Module MM of SAP for PREF (Producción y Refinación) Oracle for PPQ (Petroquímica)
Contract administration	Oracle SAP PICS HITEC for PEMEX Procurement International SRM for PGPB
Management of master data	Achilles for suppliers registration, performance assessments and audit findings ARIBA Supplier Information and Performance Management Suppliers portal SAP HITEC
Management of goods, services, works, leases and stocks	SAP Boveda Electronica de Documentos
Information and evaluation	SAP Oracle SPyA Intranet portals
Integration with financial management systems	PLURIPEP (Pluri-annual Pemex Exploración y Producción) SAP
Knowledge management tool on processes	ARIS
Management of internal exchange of information	SAC (Sistema de Administración de Correspondencia)

Source: Information provided by PEMEX.

Meaningful performance assessments of the procurement function could support the strategic positioning of the DCPA

A performing procurement organisation, aligned with business objectives, implementing tailored procurement strategies and supported by specialised electronic tools will, however, be of little relevance to the company's business strategy if its performance is not measured over time. In particularly challenging macroeconomic environments, establishing indicators and measurement mechanisms that track progress against selected objectives and identify opportunities to further improve the procurement function is of paramount importance.

The DCPA and the revisited procurement business model have recently established that assessing the results of procurement operations in past years in various areas. This should provide meaningful insights to measure the impact of the revisited organisational structure of the procurement function.

Figure 2.6 demonstrates that contracts are awarded for an overwhelming majority via direct award. While direct awards include some sort of collaborative procurement tools established on the basis of proprietary rights, this number de facto reduces procurement opportunities for suppliers of all sizes. Article 77 of the PEMEX Law stipulates that open public tenders should be the general rule unless this procurement procedure is deemed not to be the most favourable to ensure the best economic conditions. However, the practice clearly differs from this provision as evidenced by Figures 2.6 and 2.7. Additionally, the DCPA might not be in a position to demonstrate the value for money of the awarded proposal due to the absence of comparative analyses. The share of direct awards in terms of overall value as shown by Figure 2.7 also signals that the recourse to discretionary awarding of contract does not only affect small purchases for which the cost of bidding could be an impediment to suppliers' participation. It could also suggest that additional consolidation efforts could be carried to avoid repetitive small purchases under direct award.

Figure 2.6. **PEMEX's use of different types of contracting procedures (by volume), 2010-15**

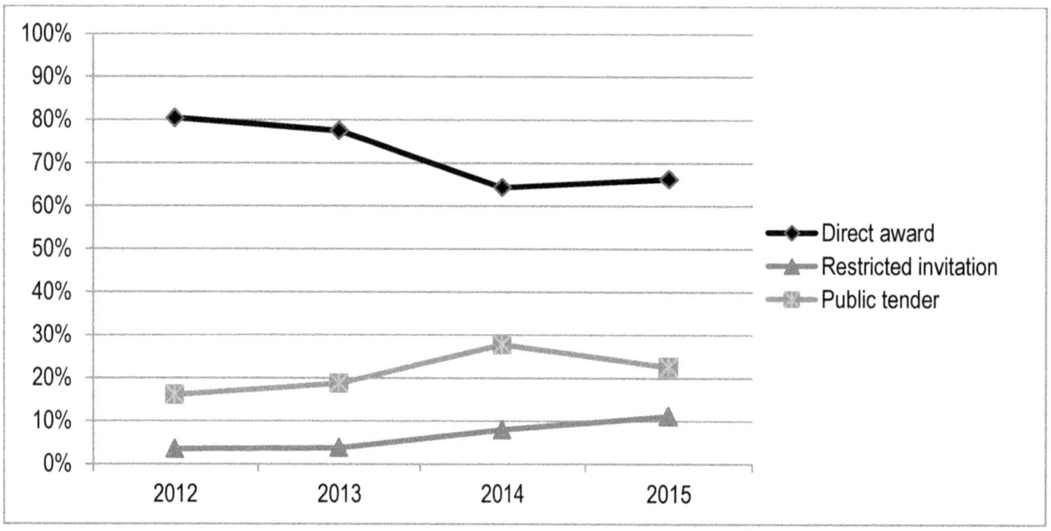

Source: Based on information provided by PEMEX.

Figure 2.7. **PEMEX's use of different types of contracting procedures (by value), 2010-15**

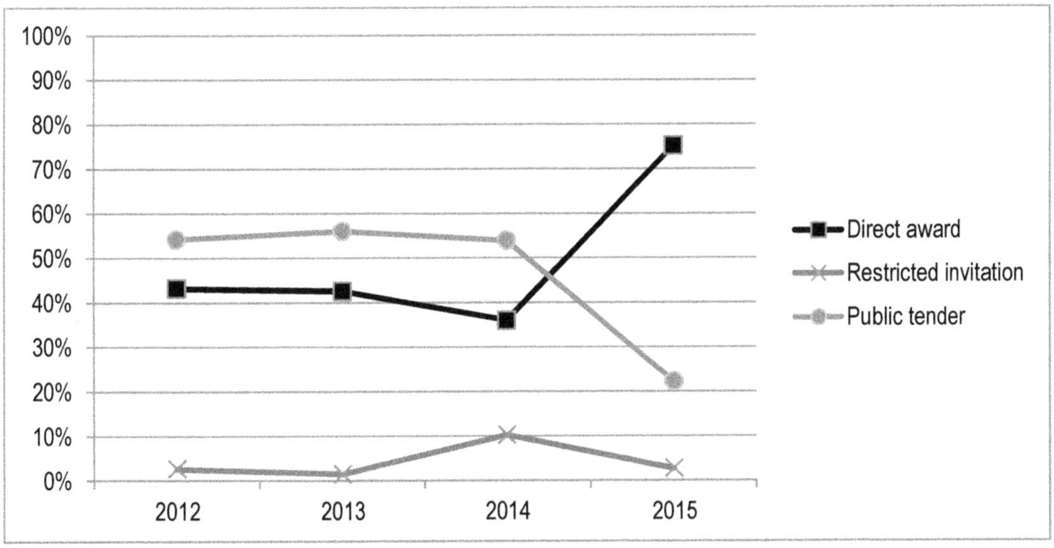

Source: Based on information provided by PEMEX.

The Group for the Authorisation of Exceptions to an Open Public Tender (Grupo de Autorización de la Excepción al Concurso Abierto, or GAECA) approves the exceptions to an open tender, authorising the productive company to use other procedures, such as restricted invitations and direct award. Chaired by the subdirector of the productive company that the Director General has appointed as responsible for concluding the contract, the group also comprises two subdirectors from the DCPA, a subdirector of Finance and a subdirector of the Legal Directorate. This group also includes two permanent invited representatives: a subdirector of the Internal Control Unit and a subdirector of Internal Audit.

Responsible for authorising exceptions to open public tender in accordance with Article 78 of the PEMEX Law, save for Fractions II, III, XVI, XVIII and XXI, the GAECA analyses documentation submitted to it that should justify the recourse to exception to open public tender. Yet, the Procurement Guidelines do not indicate which information should, at a minimum, be provided to the GAECA. Absence of guidance could pose consistency issues in the nature and format of the supporting documentation, which should allow the GAECA to decide if the exception is the adequate driver for value creation.

The OECD Recommendation on Public Procurement suggests driving performance improvements through evaluation of the effectiveness of the public procurement system from individual procurements to the system as a whole. It notably calls upon the development of indicators to measure performance, effectiveness and saving of the public procurement system (OECD, 2015a).

Considering the budget allocated to procurement, the DCPA contributes significantly to achieving the overall objectives of PEMEX, which are to create economic value and profitability for the Mexican state. Therefore, the outcomes of the public procurement processes shall be measured and assessed against these objectives.

The DCPA already developed a series of indicators to assess progress in the different procurement phases. They, however, mostly provide indications on activities and not on performance. For example, the DCPA monitors the time needed for completion of procurement processes, which provides indications on the activity. Yet without factoring in the assessment the number and level of efforts of employees participating in procurement processes, this indicator does not provide evidence of the efficiency of the procurement workforce.

Tools for measuring the performance of public procurement has generated a lot of attention in OECD countries and discussions have highlighted the main challenges involved in evaluating the performance of a procurement system as a whole, and notably the scarcity of standardised data to showcase meaningful information and analyses (OECD, 2013). Because of its decentralised business organisation, PEMEX could be exposed to similar challenges. Yet, they might be overcome more easily with the support of interoperable IT systems and commonly agreed methodologies.

Key performance indicators (KPIs) not only measure aggregated procurement performance, but also prove extremely helpful in assessing specific procurement process performance and providing grounds for procurement officials to guide future procurement decisions (OECD, 2015a). In so doing, the DCPA would transform itself into an agile organisation able to adapt to changing environments and pursue business strategic objectives. Experience in the oil industry suggests that setting clear objectives in terms of procurement savings helps to reinforce the position of the procurement function in the company (Rozemeijer, 2000).

According to the *Harvard Business School Review*, procurement costs in the oil industry account for approximately 50% of the total company's costs and 5% savings on procurement costs could increase the organisation's profit margin by 30% to 50%. Savings in PEMEX procurement would therefore directly impact the overall company's profitability, thus aligning procurement objectives with business objectives (see Box 2.4).

Box 2.4. **Challenges in evaluating savings**

Several challenges exist with regard to conducting a comparative evaluation of savings achieved with procurement:

Calculation methodology: A broad range of calculation methods are applied across OECD countries depending either on the nature of contracting mechanisms to which it applies or on the perspective identified, notably:

- comparison between historical prices or reference price based on market analysis and final price proposed by the awarded supplier
- assessment of the total cost of ownership of products or services procured and comparison with reference prices
- in the case of framework agreements, comparison between the price list proposed by the awarded suppliers in the first competition stage or the average historical price and the discounted price obtained after second stage competition
- comparison between historical processing or labour costs and new processing or labour costs.

Source: OECD (2014a), "OECD Survey on Public Procurement", OECD, Paris; OECD (2015b), "OECD Survey on Centralised Framework Agreements", OECD, Paris.

Beyond strict financial savings, fostering competition also generates, albeit more indirectly, savings (Estache and Iimi, 2008). Indeed, according to a study based on a sample of 200 infrastructure projects, the mere fact of promoting competition generates approximately 8.2% of savings. Therefore, assessing the level of competition in PEMEX procurement operations could provide useful insights regarding the effectiveness of its organisation. While assessing the number of bids received in open public tenders will only provide PEMEX with activity indicators, factoring in the number of bids having passed the technical threshold required could signal efficiencies or deficiencies in preparatory market analysis or choice of procurement strategies (see Box 2.5).

Box 2.5. Key performance indicators: Efficiency of competition

$$\text{Ratio of qualified bids received} = \frac{Qualified\ bids}{Bids\ received\ per\ open\ public\ tender}$$

Bids received per open public tender: This indicates the number of proposals received by the deadline of the public tender.

Qualified bidders: This indicates bidders that have been assessed and judged of sufficient technical quality to warrant the assessment of their financial proposal.

Source: Adapted from OECD (2014b), "Towards procurement performance indicators: First set of indicators", www.oecd.org/officialdocuments/publicdisplaydocumentpdf/?cote=GOV/PGC/ETH(2014)5&docLanguage=En.

Finally, since PEMEX developed a new strategic sourcing methodology from which procurement strategies are identified and implemented in each product category with the aim to maximise value generation, performance indicators could assess the level of global spend managed or controlled under these strategies in order to both assess the level of implementation of procurement strategies across the PEMEX group (including subsidiaries) and the relative effect of strategic sourcing on processes, time and cost.

Proposals for action

While the new law, the creation of the DCPA and the development of a unified strategic sourcing methodology already provide an organisational framework conducive to procurement performance, PEMEX operates within an economic context that requires additional efforts. Scarce resources coupled with increased competition from big oil companies will force PEMEX's procurement function to become an agile organisation able to adapt to rapidly changing business priorities.

In order to improve the management of its procurement function and align it with the OECD Recommendation on Public Procurement, PEMEX may wish to consider the following proposals:

- The DCPA could benefit from developing a comprehensive procurement strategy detailing procurement objectives in addition to processes to facilitate a common understanding across the PEMEX group of its strategic importance.

- In order to maximise volume leverage in procurement operations and provide all suppliers with a streamlined framework, PEMEX could consider expanding the consolidation strategies included in its new procurement model to all entities of the PEMEX group and notably to its subsidiary.
- To strengthen the role of the CAAOS in defining and implementing corporate strategies at the Board of Directors' level, PEMEX could consider supporting a change in the law to expand the duration of the term of office of its Chair.
- PEMEX may seek to expand procurement opportunities information and make it freely accessible on its website by: 1) including procurement forecasts of all entities of the PEMEX group, not only for its productive subsidiary companies; and 2) providing such information in a usable rather than static format. In doing so, PEMEX would increase transparency of procurement information, facilitating access of suppliers of all sizes and regions to procurement opportunities.
- PEMEX may seek to promote strategic alliance between the PEMEX group and its suppliers' objectives in further development of its sourcing methodology, so as to develop sustainable relationships with suppliers in a tense economic environment and to increase productivity on both sides.
- As a priority, PEMEX could implement an IT system to support the whole cycle of procurement operations, including the once-only principle, not only to ensure consistency across entities and integration with other financial management systems, but also to reduce procurement risks linked to data quality, and reduce red tape costs for bidders.
- The DCPA could develop, implement and monitor performance indicators beyond information on transactional activity. These indicators would allow the DCPA to show the PEMEX Board of Directors that it is reaping the benefits of centralisation by focusing on performance assessment and continuous process improvements.
- PEMEX could enhance overall competition in its procurement processes by reducing the share, both in numbers and value, of direct awards.
- In cases where exceptions to public tender are considered to be the most appropriate strategic approach to the market, clear, evidence-based supporting documentation could be submitted to the GAECA in order to make informed decisions. This would allow the procurement function to align with the PEMEX vision statement, which is that generating value is the prevailing criterion in PEMEX decision making.

References

CAPS Research (2012), *Cross-Industry Report,* jointly sponsored by member companies, the W. P. Carey School of Business at Arizona State University, and the Institute for Supply Management (ISM).

CEFP (Centro de Estudios de las Finanzas Publicas) [Centre for Studies on Public Finance] (2016), "Federal expenditure budget assigned to investments projects and programmes in 2016", Information Note of 25 January.

Cox, A. et al. (2003), *Supply Chain Management: A Guide to Best Practice*, Financial Times/Prentice Hall, London.

CRS (Congressional Research Service) (2015), "Mexico's oil and gas sector: Background, reform efforts and implications for the United States", CRS.

Ernst & Young (2013), "Effective Board and Committee Leadership, Audit Committee Leadership Network in North America", Ernst & Young.

Estache, A. and A. Iimi (2008), "Procurement efficiency for infrastructure development and financial needs reassessed", *Policy Research Working Paper* 4662, World Bank.

European Commission (2016), "Electronic public procurement will reduce administrative burden and stop unfair bidding", European Commission.

Fisher, M. (1997), "What Is the Right Supply Chain for Your Product?", *Harvard Business Review.*

Kraljic, P. (1983), "Purchasing Must Become Management", *Harvard Business Review,* https://hbr.org/1983/09/purchasing-must-become-supply-management.

OECD (2016), *The Korean Public Procurement Service: Innovating for Effectiveness*, OECD Public Governance Reviews, OECD Publishing, Paris, http://dx.doi.org/10.1787/9789264249431-en.

OECD (2015a), "Recommendation of the Council on Public Procurement", www.oecd.org/corruption/recommendation-on-public-procurement.htm.

OECD (2015b), "OECD Survey on Centralised Framework Agreements", OECD, Paris.

OECD (2014a), "OECD Survey on Public Procurement", OECD, Paris.

OECD (2014b), "Towards procurement performance indicators: First set of indicators", www.oecd.org/officialdocuments/publicdisplaydocumentpdf/?cote=GOV/PGC/ETH(2014)5&docLanguage=En.

OECD (2013), "Towards procurement performance indicators: Stocktaking report on procurement information collected in countries", declassified OECD document, www.oecd.org/officialdocuments/publicdisplaydocumentpdf/?cote=GOV/PGC/ETH(2013)9&docLanguage=En.

PEMEX (2015), "Main elements of the Business Plan of Petróleos Mexicanos and its productive subsidiary companies 2016-2020" [Principales elementos del Plan de Negocios de Petróleos Mexicanos y sus empresas productivas subsidiarias 2016-2020], Petróleos Mexicanos.

Reuters (2011), "ExxonMobil recognized for industry-leading approach to develop Angola deepwater projects", press release, 2 May.

Rozemeijer, F.A. (2000), "Creating corporate advantage in purchasing", Technische Universiteit Eindhoven, https://pure.tue.nl/ws/files/1542318/200012802.pdf.

Smith, R. (2015), "Energy sector transformation for a low-oil-price world", presentation given at Major Projects Association, 11 November.

UN (United Nations) (2006), *UN Procurement Practitioners Handbook*, Interagency Procurement Working Group (IAPWG), UN, updated September 2012, www.ungm.org/Areas/Public/pph/channels/PPH.pdf.

Chapter 3

Promoting complementary policy objectives through Petróleos Mexicanos' procurement

This chapter assesses how PEMEX is promoting complementary policy objectives such as supporting the participation of small and medium sized enterprises, promoting environmental considerations and social responsibility. It further suggests what PEMEX can do to foster improvements in the field of green policy and social objectives.

The relevance of diminishing SMEs in the Mexican economy

This chapter looks at how Petróleos Mexicanos (or PEMEX) has been using its substantial buying power in the marketplace and how it can leverage the procurement process to actively promote complementary policy objectives. While efficiency and cost effectiveness are among the primary objectives of public procurement, governments increasingly use this purchasing power as a policy lever to support various secondary objectives such as green growth, promotion of locally sourced or innovative goods and services, or giving preference to small and medium-sized enterprises (SMEs).

The OECD Recommendation on Public Procurement (hereafter, the "OECD Recommendation") encourages a balanced approach towards achieving governmental objectives through the use of public procurement (OECD, 2015a). The OECD recognises that the delivery of goods and services in an economical and efficient manner as the primary procurement objective, while promoting other methods in pursuit of secondary policy objectives such as sustainable green growth, the development of SMEs, innovation, standards for responsible business conduct or broader industrial policy objectives. The decision to pursue secondary policy objectives in public procurement will vary by government and the needs of citizens, but the OECD Recommendation identifies steps that should be taken whenever such objectives are pursued (see Box 3.1).

Box 3.1. The OECD Recommendation on Public Procurement on secondary policy objectives

5. **RECOMMENDS** that Adherents recognise that any use of the public procurement system to pursue secondary policy objectives should be **balanced** against the primary procurement objective.

   To this end, Adherents should:

   1. **Evaluate the use of public procurement as one method of pursuing secondary policy objectives in accordance with clear national priorities**, balancing the potential benefits against the need to achieve value for money. Both the capacity of the procurement workforce to support secondary policy objectives and the burden associated with monitoring progress in promoting such objectives should be considered.

   2. **Develop an appropriate strategy for the integration of secondary policy objectives in public procurement systems**. For secondary policy objectives that will be supported by public procurement, appropriate planning, baseline analysis, risk assessment and target outcomes should be established as the basis for the development of action plans or guidelines for implementation.

   3. **Employ appropriate impact assessment methodology to measure the effectiveness of procurement in achieving secondary policy objectives**. The results of any use of the public procurement system to support secondary policy objectives should be measured according to appropriate milestones to provide policy makers with necessary information regarding the benefits and costs of such use. Effectiveness should be measured both at the level of individual procurements, and against policy objective target outcomes. Additionally, the aggregate effect of pursuing secondary policy objectives on the public procurement system should be periodically assessed to address potential objective overload.

Source: OECD (2015a), "Recommendation of the Council on Public Procurement", www.oecd.org/corruption/recommendation-on-public-procurement.htm

SMEs constitute more than 90% of all established businesses worldwide and are a key driver for economic growth and development. In Mexico, SMEs represent over 99% of formal enterprises and contribute to providing 34.7% of gross domestic product (GDP) and seven out ten formal jobs in the country.[1] SMEs in Mexico are still very significant to the labour market but their contribution to the overall GDP has diminished in the last five years by one-third. As in many other countries, the importance of SMEs to the Mexican economy and the labour market cannot be underestimated. However, most SMEs in Mexico are restricted because of limited access to capital or financing. When faced with excessive administrative burdens, SMEs are more likely to make illegal payments in order to circumvent the burden. UNIDO and UNODC (2007) states that SMEs are more susceptible to bureaucratic corruption than larger companies. In addition, SMEs are also more susceptible to administrative corruption due to the fact that they often lack the time and resources necessary to be informed about complex regulations and requirements, making illegal payments to cover up mistakes or avoid overly bureaucratic procedures more likely. Therefore, a large corporation such as PEMEX should make use of variety of measures at their disposal to encourage SME participation in public procurement and enable SME participation through capacity development, limit corruption risks affecting SMEs and reduce bureaucracy (OECD, 2015a).

It has been more than five years since the Mexican government began to pursue complementary policies through public procurement. From the start, PEMEX had a major role to play in following the federal complementary policies established by the Ministry of Economy (Secretaría de Economía). With the changes made to the legal framework in 2014 and again in 2015 the consequent transformation of PEMEX into a state productive enterprise (empresa productiva del Estado) has resulted in it no longer falling under the definition of a public agency for the development of national industry. Hence, PEMEX is no longer required to abide by the Law of Acquisitions, Leasing and Services of the Public Sector (LAASSP) or the Law of Public Works and Related Services (LOPSRM). On 10 June 2015 PEMEX published their general procurement provisions for PEMEX and its subsidiary productive companies (EPS), after having been approved by the PEMEX Board of Directors. The reform envisages that PEMEX will now be able to contract goods and services in a more commercially oriented environment, its contracts fully governed by commercial law. These new general contracting provisions, which are now in effect, have replaced the former administrative contracting provisions issued by the PEMEX Board of Directors in 2008.

It is too early to tell how the new legal framework will impact the procurement processes of PEMEX and its subsidiaries companies. The reform envisages that PEMEX will now be able to contract goods and services in a more commercially oriented environment. The new legal framework does not make a distinction between suppliers regarding the size of companies and, even better, it allows for the participation of consortia, which means that SMEs can now participate jointly. Despite the new legal framework, the principles and best practices recommended need to be adhered to and PEMEX should stand firm on not lessening its effort towards supporting complementary objectives.

The need for a holistic strategy to enhance SME participation

In 2009, the Mexican Ministry of Economy established a plan to promote the development of local SMEs, partly through participation in public procurement. As such, the Ministry of Economy set specific annual goals for each federal entity to award contracts to SMEs. According to the Law for Development of the Competitiveness of SMEs, the planning and implementation of policies and actions to promote the competitiveness of SMEs should encourage agencies and entities of the federal government to gradually acquire the minimum of 35% for all goods, services and public works procured. Even though PEMEX has a new legal framework, the company continues to participate in governmental programmes regarding acquisitions from SMEs such as Programa de Compras de Gobierno from the Ministry of Economy. The programme is automatically renewed each year by the ministry and is relevant in order to quantify the purchases from SMEs. Through this programme PEMEX commits to a certain annual goal of acquisitions from SMEs and presents the results on a monthly basis. Due to the legislative reforms PEMEX is promoting a reassessment of the plan in order to reflect the changes of the oil and gas industry in Mexico.

The federal government, through the Ministry of Economy has been responsible for establishing the appropriate policy for the energy industry. In 2010, the Mexican public administration entities generally achieved or exceeded the proposed goal for domestic content. For several years PEMEX has surpassed the target set by the ministry, sometime by nearly 80%. Among all subsidiaries, REF (Refinación) purchases the most from SMEs, followed by PEP (Exploracion y Produccion) and CORP (Corporativo). The target set by the Ministry of Economy for PEMEX in 2015 was MXN 17 680 million; at the end of November PEMEX had spent MXN 12 847 million (see Figure 3.1). For the first time the company did not achieve the federal goal for SMEs purchases.

Figure 3.1. **Objective for purchases from SMEs set by the Ministry of Economy for PEMEX, and the actual purchases made for 2010-14 in MXN millions**

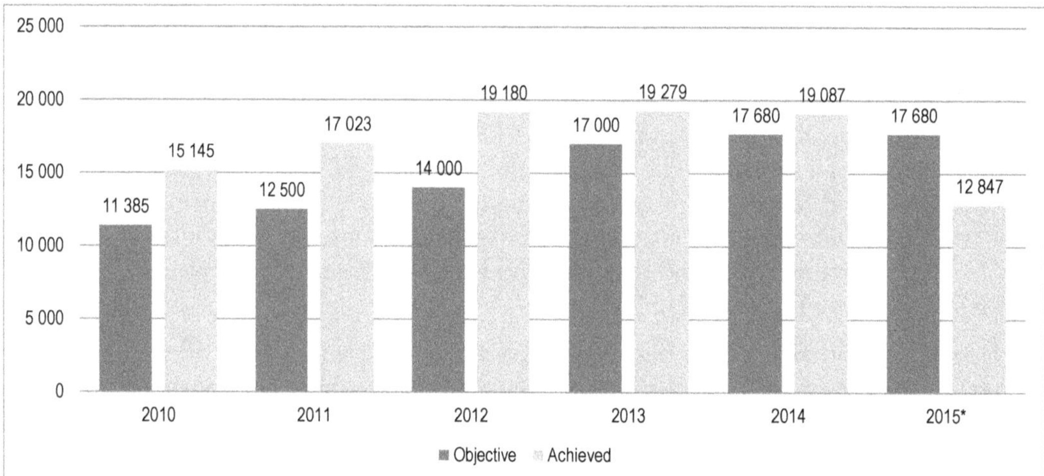

Note: *As of November 2015.

Source: Based on information provided by PEMEX.

Of the total government procurement expenditures for SMEs in Mexico, PEMEX accounts for approximately 20%, which has been the trend in recent years (see Figure 3.2). Furthermore, public procurement and supply operations through different procurement methods (open competition, direct awards or restricted invitations) granted to SMEs by PEMEX amounted to about 5% of the total purchases made by the company in 2014 and 3.5-4% in 2015. Declining crude oil prices, energy reforms, focus on productivity and concerns about the capability of SMEs to deliver were possible explanations offered by PEMEX officials for declining SMEs purchases during the OECD fact-finding mission. The purchases are focused on specialised products and SMEs in Mexico in general lack the necessary skills and the capital to deliver.

Figure 3.2. **The total amount of government operations assigned to SMEs and the amount procured by PEMEX in 2010-14 in MXN millions**

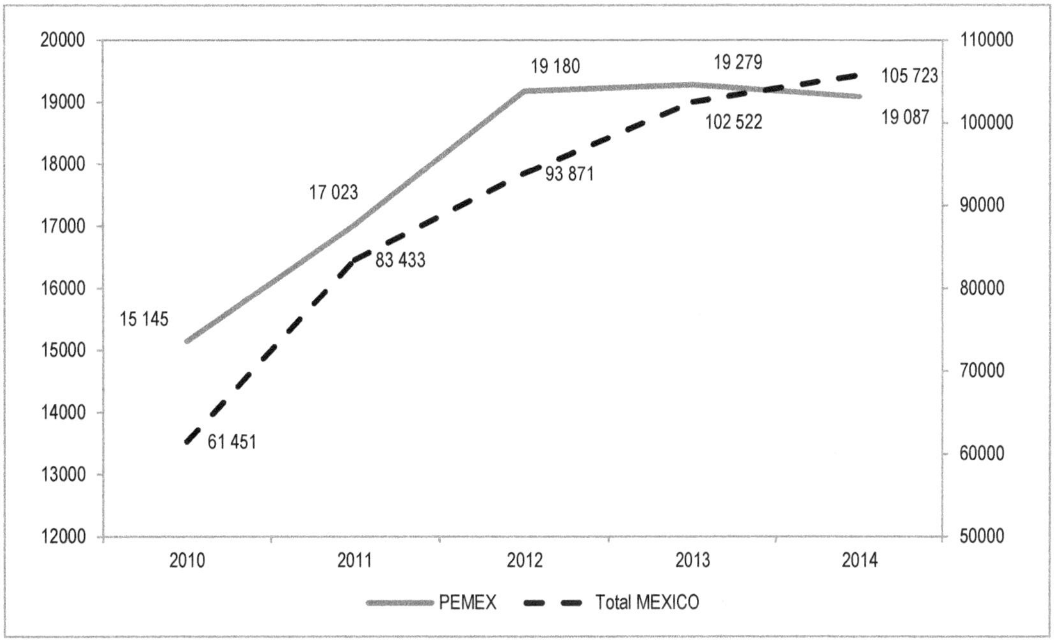

Source: Based on answers provided by PEMEX.

PEMEX developed a supplier development strategy in 2009 based on the 2008 PEMEX Law. The strategy was comprised of two main themes: 1) policies for national content and support to SMEs in the procurement process; and 2) sustainable development of suppliers and supply chains in order to strengthen the capacity of the domestic industry. The strategy is no longer in place, but it was developed due to the fact that PEMEX was the only oil company operating in Mexico. With the new Hydrocarbons Law the general principles of the government's suppliers development strategy that PEMEX now follows, is based on the fact that it is a productive state enterprise. Furthermore the new legislation led to new programmes like the National Productivity Council, the Hydrocarbons Consultative Board and the new Fideicomiso.

In the PEMEX strategy, a target was set that by the last quarter of 2009, PEMEX would be requesting a minimum of 10% local content purchasing for projects with major integrated contracts, pursuant to the provisions of free trade agreements. The Ministry of Economy defines such projects as public works. The average local content requested in international public tenders held under the coverage of Free Trade Agreements, for contracting public works in PEMEX rose steadfastly from 10% in 2011 to 18% in 2013, but then dropped to 13% in 2014.

The policies for national content defined by the federal government encourage the participation of SMEs in PEMEX's operations as contractors or suppliers of PEMEX.

This is so PEMEX can meet the minimum established limit for local content that should be incorporated into their supply chains by national companies, of which many are SMEs. There are no specific procedures in place dedicated to SMEs but there is a point system in place that encourages suppliers to commit to subcontract part of their work to SMEs. The point system works in favour of participants who are said to belong to an SME or are committed to subcontract part of their work to SMEs. In Korea, certain measures have been put in place to increase public purchases from SMEs (see Box 3.2).

Box 3.2. Support for SMEs in Korea

Support for SMEs in Korea is a strong priority, given the make-up of the economy. There are approximately 3.3 million SMEs in Korea, while there are only 2 900 large businesses: SMEs make up 99.9% of Korean businesses. Public Procurement Service (PPS) implements the government's policies for increasing public purchases from a variety of types of entities, including small and medium-sized businesses, local businesses, women-owned businesses and other social enterprises.

- The legal basis of support of SMEs requires the heads of public institutions to provide small and medium-sized businesses with increased opportunities to receive orders when they intend to make procurement contracts for goods, services and construction works.
- A recent change, which took effect on 1 January 2015, now defines SMEs solely in terms of sales volume (either annual or average). In addition to the criteria for being included as an SME, there are specific factors that can exclude an enterprise from SME status, including total assets exceeding USD 423.8 million.
- A business must be deemed independent in ownership and business operation (not a subsidiary of a large enterprise) with respect to the relevant laws and regulations.
- Article 4 of the Enforcement Decree of the Act on Facilitation of Purchase of Small and Medium Enterprise-Manufactured Products and Support for Development of their Markets sets an annual purchasing goal for SME-manufactured products of 50% or more of total purchasing value.
- An SME set-aside programme is run in co-operation with the Small and Medium Business Administration (SMBA). Under this programme, SMBA designates specific products for SMEs, and currently there are 207 products with this designation. For these products to be designated as competitive products, only SMEs that directly manufacture such products are invited to participate in competitive tenders.

Source: OECD (2016), *The Korean Public Procurement Service: Innovating for Effectiveness*, OECD Public Governance Reviews, OECD Publishing, Paris, http://dx.doi.org/10.1787/9789264249431-en.

The Hydrocarbons Law establishes that the minimum average percentage of local content in exploration and extraction of hydrocarbons will gradually increase, from 25% in 2015 to at least 35% in 2025; these objectives will be reviewed every five years. This percentage will be different for deep and ultra-deep water activities, which will be set by the Ministry of Economy. PEMEX and all operators within the hydrocarbons industry that conduct this type of activity in Mexico must contribute to achieving these goals. PEMEX has achieved results in increasing SME participation and national content. With a calculated national content level of 42.4% for 2012 to 2014, it has gradually increased since 2009-11, when it was 40.5% (see Figure 3.3).

Figure 3.3. **Level of local content in PEMEX procurement in 2012-14**

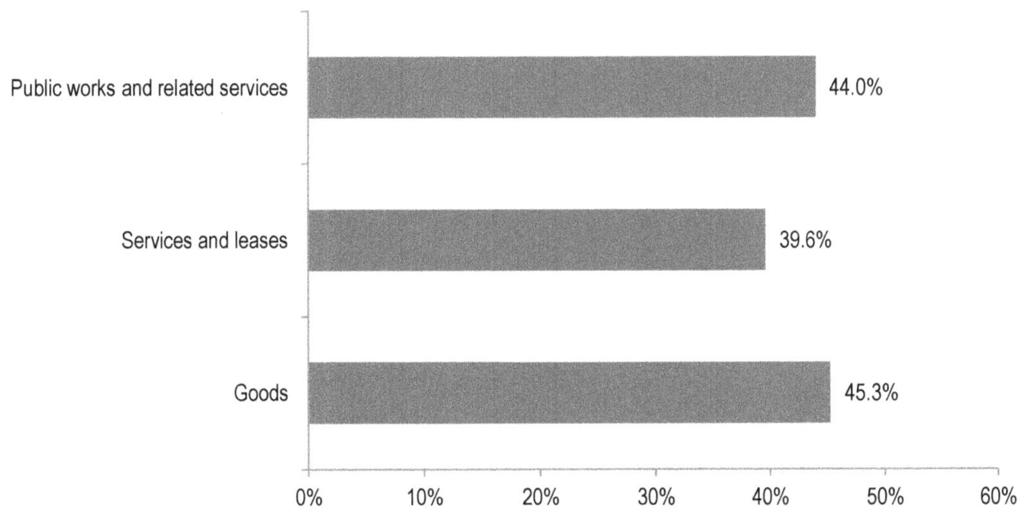

Source: Information provided by PEMEX.

Even though PEMEX has been one of the largest public entities in Mexico to procure from SMEs, the total amount was only about 5% of PEMEXs total procurement in 2014. It is not clear whether SMEs are to a large extent used as subcontractors to larger corporations that are working for PEMEX. Better data on subcontractors could provide a better overall picture of the amount of financial resources spent by PEMEX on SMEs and national content. It is important for PEMEX to acquire more detailed information from their contractors on the use of SMEs as subcontractors, but as it stands the company is not able to do so. During the OECD fact-finding mission, a PEMEX official referred to a proposal allowing PEMEX to include or count SMEs that are being subcontracted by primary contractors. The changes made to the regulatory framework in 2014-15 exclude direct statues committed to SMEs. The strategy that was developed in 2009 and the good intentions to improve on this front seem to have slowed down since 2011. The strategy and legal statues concerning the matter of national content and SMEs needs to be evaluated and clear goals should be set for the participation of SMEs.

In 2009 PEMEX and NAFIN created the Public Trust to Promote Development of National Suppliers and Contractors for the State Oil Industry to help SMEs access funding. Since 2014 the Public Trust has not been operating. A new trust has been established following the induction of the new legal framework. PEMEX and other companies competing with PEMEX can now seek funding on equal terms from this new fund. During the five-year period of the Public Trust some 11 projects were funded involving 235 companies. The support in technical assistance amounted to MXN 24 640 403.

Data available from PEMEX indicates that the company is displaying increased competition in its procurement activities for goods, services and leases. The subsidiaries presented in Figure 3.4 indicate that both the number of contracts made by public bidding and the total value awarded is growing. There is still a significant level of PEMEX contracts recorded as being awarded directly to selected suppliers, but a relatively high proportion of them are derived from low amounts (Article 42).

Figure 3.4. **Type of competition procedure used by PEMEX subsidiary bodies**

% total number and value of goods, service and lease contracts, 2014-15

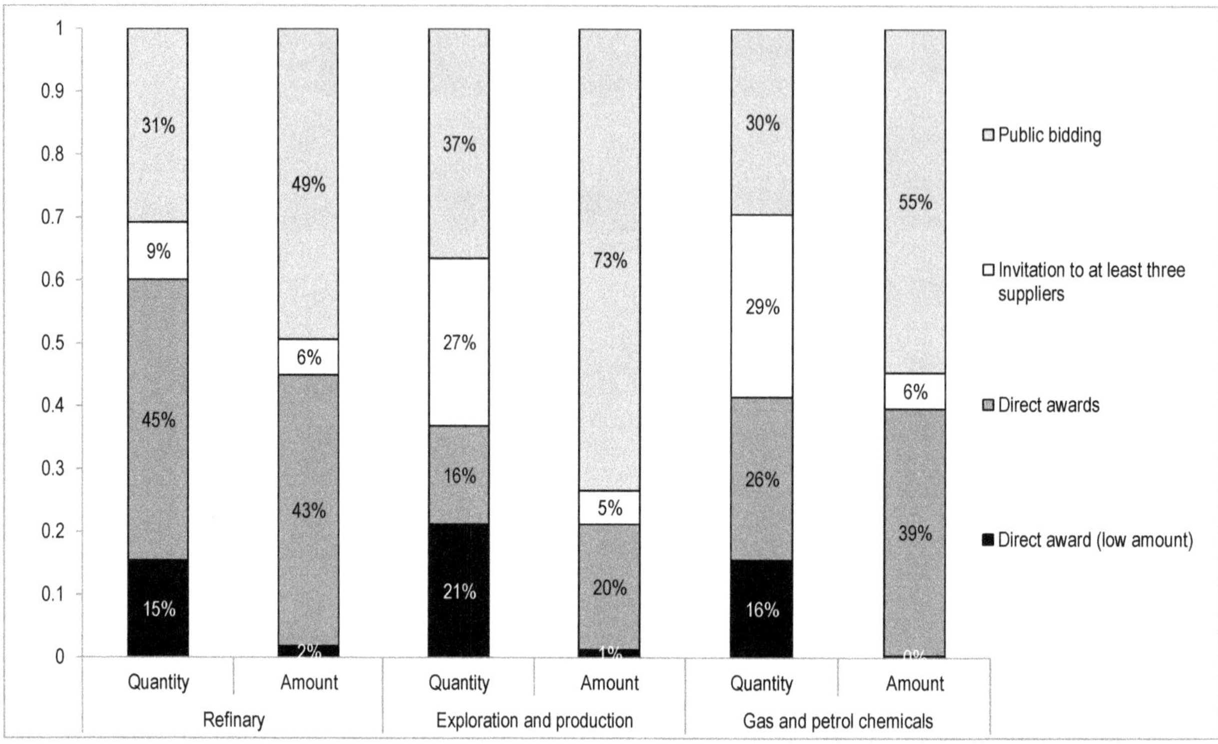

Source: Information provided by PEMEX.

Moreover, payments from PEMEX are sometimes late, which further serves to undermine smaller companies with lower cash flows. A mechanism should thus be put in place that prioritises payments to SMEs since late payments can seriously affect the cash flow of a company and its survival in the market. There is no specific protocol that prioritises payments to SMEs; the same overall guidelines and payments can take up to 180 days according to conditions 4.18 of the Treasury General guidelines. It is important to look at the promotion of small local businesses as something that has a positive impact on the supply chain through diversification of supply. These are some of the immediate issues that PEMEX needs to address, but there are others that should be addressed that relate to the further advancement of tools and processes.

The need for a robust green procurement policy

Green procurement is defined as the process through which a contracting authority procures goods, services or works that have reduced environmental impact throughout their life cycle when compared to other alternatives in the market (European Commission, 2008). It is traditionally associated with the procurement of energy-efficient vehicles or equipment, recycled materials or waste reduction (Box 3.3). However, for environmental considerations to comply with the best-value principle, it must take into account all the associated costs to the life-cycle costs – including operation, ownership, maintenance, and disposal – and not only upfront costs. Efforts should be made to account for environmental externalities into the overall cost of the good or service to the community, and not just the financial cost to the procuring agency. OECD countries are increasingly adopting green policies in their procurement function.

Box 3.3. Products most commonly acquired through green public procurement

There are certain similarities in countries promoting green procurement:

- **Construction, renovation and maintenance of public buildings**: Low resource consumption (energy, water, raw materials, landscape) throughout their whole life cycle, use of recycled materials, waste management, etc.
- **Transport**: Type of vehicles (hybrids, electrics), reduction of fossil fuels and increase of biofuels, CO_2 emission limits for new vehicles, training courses for drivers, use of bicycles for short administrative tasks, etc.
- **Office equipment and office supplies**: Energy efficiency, using computers, copiers, printers, monitors and other equipment meeting the standard ENERGY STAR; two-sided printing in order to reduce paper consumption; use of recycled paper or of virgin fibre paper coming from sustainably managed forests (FSC or equivalent label).
- **Cleaning**: Cleaning products "highly biodegradable", "free from hazardous substances", or not impairing water quality, etc.
- **Services**: Messenger enterprises with reduced fossil fuel use in vehicles, printer enterprises with ISO 14001 certification, etc.

Source: Based on US Environmental Protection Agency web site, www.epa.gov/ in OECD (2013a), *Public Procurement Review of the Mexican Institute of Social Security: Enhancing Efficiency and Integrity for Better Health Care*, OECD Publishing, Paris, http://dx.doi.org/10.1787/9789264197480-en.

For a period there was a common belief among countries that green policies were expensive, especially in times of fiscal consolidation. However, greener products and services are less costly to public agencies, in terms of life-cycle costs, than less green products. The vast majority of OECD member countries use public procurement now as a tool to implement policies or strategies to foster secondary policy objectives. In fact, 26 OECD member countries have developed strategies or policies to support green public procurement, SMEs and innovative goods and services (see Table 3.1). Many countries are realising that when they consider the social externalities, green products and services generally have less long-term total social costs. It was not until recently that Mexican authorities developed a federal green procurement policy.

Table 3.1. **Development of strategic public procurement by objective in selected OECD member countries and partner economies**

	Green public procurement	Support to SMEs	Support to innovative goods and services
Australia	•	•	•
Austria	•	○	•
Canada	♦•	•	•
Chile	♦•	♦•	•
Denmark	•	•	•
Estonia	○	○	○
Finland	•	♦	♦
France	♦•	♦•	♦•
Germany	•	•	•
Greece	♦•	•	○
Hungary	♦	•	•
Ireland	•	•	•
Italy	♦	♦	♦
Japan	•	•	•
Korea	•	•	•
Luxembourg	♦•	♦•	♦
Mexico	•	•	•
New Zealand	♦•	♦•	♦•
Norway	◘	♦•	♦•
Poland	•	•	•
Portugal	•	♦	♦
Slovak Republic	○	○	○
Slovenia	♦•	•	•
Spain	♦•	♦•	♦•
Sweden	♦•	•	•
Switzerland	♦•	♦•	♦
United Kingdom	•	•	•
United States	•	•	♦•
Brazil	♦•	♦•	•
Colombia	♦	•	•
OECD29			
♦ A strategy / policy has been developed by some procuring entities	13	10	10
• A strategy/policy has been developed at a central level	24	23	20
◘ A strategy / policy has been rescinded	1	0	0
○ A strategy/policy has never been developed	2	3	3

Source: OECD (2015b), *Government at a Glance 2015*, OECD Publishing, Paris, http://dx.doi.org/10.1787/gov_glance-2015-en.

PEMEX green procurement was limited to the requirements stipulated in the LAASSP as well as the PEMEX Act in order to ensure environmental sustainability. There appears to be no link between PEMEX policies for the preservation of the environment and achievement of sustainable development and the use of green procurement. PEMEX has not developed and implemented its own green procurement policy to support its sustainable development efforts. Despite the positive steps taken by the Mexican government in recent years, progress has been negligible. There is still no green procurement policy in place. Nevertheless, PEMEX has considered jointly designing a policy of that nature with the sustainable development unit. This will be based on the Energy Reforms, which require PEMEX to reflect, in contractual terms, participants to focus on green issues while promoting the generation of value and the advantage of being socially responsible within a competitive environment.

The PEMEX Act created the Environmental and Sustainability Committee for the purpose of assisting PEMEX in the implementation of, and compliance with, policies for the preservation of the environment and achievement of sustainable development. However, PEMEX does not have a policy on green procurement, nor has it developed a directory or a catalogue of green products. The new legislation doesn't prevent PEMEX from being more proactive, but there is a lack of direct encouragement in the new legislation. The 2012 Guidelines on Acquisitions, Leasing and Services (Políticas, Bases y Lineamentos en Materia de Adquisiciones, Arrendamientos e Servicios, or POBALINES) gave PEMEX a clear mandate for the use of natural resources and to respect national and international green standards. However, no information or data is available to assess whether PEMEX complied with those requirements. The POBALINES are no longer in place but PEMEX is currently working on developing indicators as part of a total assessment model.

In order to achieve successful implementation of a green procurement policy, it is necessary to consider measurement and capacity building. Indicators and information on contracts establishing environmental performance as the basis for bid evaluation and contract are necessary to measure the level of take-up of the policy. Furthermore, procurement officers need to be provided with specific guidance on how to incorporate environmental considerations into their procurement activities. PEMEX could do more to institutionalise and conduct proactive capacity-building efforts. PEMEX's progress in green procurement will be dependent on the market's capacity to deliver green products, which is a further challenge for PEMEX if there is not a satisfactory supply, although PEMEX could aim to promote the creation of this kind of supply. There are good examples from South American countries that PEMEX can benefit from on how to incorporate social and environmental criteria for awarding contracts into its procurement process. It is now, for example, compulsory to have award criteria that takes into consideration national industries and disabled people in Colombia,[2] (see Box 3.4).

Box 3.4. Incorporating social and environmental criteria in Colombia

The government of Colombia has had a strong social focus in the past in creating incentives in regulations for the support of SMEs, national industry and disabled people. More recently the government decided to promote green procurement by setting environmental objectives.

The National Development Plan (Plan Nacional de Desarrollo para Todos) 2010-14 prioritises sustainable production and processes and optimal use of natural resources. To promote these objectives, in 2012 the Colombian Ministry of Environment collected information on environmentally sustainable public procurement and selected five products (coffee; printed materials including books, maps and publications; lightbulbs; paper; and mining materials) on which it is conducting market research in order to arrive at environmental procurement targets (e.g. product specifications, selection criteria).

Alongside such market research, the Ministry of Environment has issued 15 guidelines on how to include green criteria in procurement, 5 of which include life-cycle analysis of products. The likelihood of success of such green procurement projects will to an extent depend on the adoption of adequate monitoring mechanisms to assess their progress and results.

Source: OECD (2013b), *Colombia: Implementing Good Governance*, OECD Publishing, Paris, http://dx.doi.org/10.1787/9789264202177-en.

There are policies or guidelines on procurement activities that promote innovation. They are to a certain extent encouraged by Article 78 of the PEMEX Act, which allows for, in cases where the procedure of open competition is not the ideal method to ensure the best conditions available, the company being able to choose to use other procedures that may be, among others, restricted invitation or direct award. Every time the company decides to use other procedures, they refer to a specific article. Also, in Article 13, Section IV of the PEMEX Act, strategic alliances and partnerships with individuals or companies is encouraged. The promotion of innovation of the procurement and supply of PEMEX is permitted according to the new legislation, but more guidance for procurement officials is needed, as there is little information available on whether this approach is ever used. There is a need to make the innovation programme much more visible to PEMEX staff and the public.

Towards social objectives through social responsibility

It is important to distinguish between different complementary policy objectives in procurement, like environmental or social objectives. Complementary environmental policy goals might include the promotion of recycled materials, environmental disposal plans, or low-polluting goods and services. Complementary social policy objectives might include, on the other hand, the procurement of goods and services that favour a specific minority or gender (see Box 3.5). PEMEX's approach to environmental or social objectives seems to be based on the social responsibility approach. However, it should be clear what is meant by achieving social and environmental objectives through public procurement and social responsibility through public procurement, as these two approaches are distinct. Targeting social responsibility through procurement is not uncommon; in Norway there is an Action Plan for Environmental and Social Responsibility in Public Procurement.[3]

In Mexico, the procurement legal framework only makes reference to providing preference in bidding proceedings to disabled persons or companies that employ disabled persons (at least 5% of total employees for at least six months of employment).[4] There is no data available on the number of contracts awarded to businesses employing people with disabilities. Given that the pursuit of social objectives was inherent in PEMEX's legal framework (LAASSP), the company could still aim to apply the preference for disabled persons provided by the LAASSP. Despite these legal changes, it is important for PEMEX to set high goals and develop its own social objectives (health-related) that could be pursued through its procurement process.

Information gathered during the OECD fact-finding mission to Mexico indicates that PEMEX is encouraging social responsibility where the aim is to enhance the contribution that PEMEX can make to improving social and environmental conditions, including labour and other human rights within communities. This is implemented through projects like the foundation of PACMA (Support Program for Communities and the Environment), whose objective is *"Creating an investment program for the welfare and quality of life of those living in oil-producing areas."* The provisions of PACMA are of a general and mandatory nature for suppliers or contractors of PEMEX, and under certain conditions the amount and term, which might be 1-2% of the total contract amount, will go to support the community and environment (see Box 3.6).

Box 3.5. The promotion of women's businesses in the United States

The US government instituted a women-owned small business (WOSB) contracting programme, as part of the administration's broader commitment to increasing competition in the award of federal contracts to women, socially and economically disadvantaged persons and veterans. The new regulations set forth procedures authorised by the Small Business Act to help ensure a level playing field on which WOSBs can compete for federal contracting opportunities, while helping achieve the existing statutory 5% goal. The regulations entered into force on 4 February 2011 with the SBA charged with implementing and administering the programme. Some 83 industries are identified in which WOSBs are under-represented or substantially under-represented in terms of the award of federal contracts. The rule removes the requirement, set forth in a prior proposed version that each federal agency must certify that it had engaged in discrimination against women-owned small businesses in order for the programme to apply to contracting by that agency. The rule allows women-owned small businesses to self-certify as "WOSBs" or to be certified by third-party certifiers, including government entities and private certification groups. At this stage, it is too early to assess the impact of the new programme. However, it has been praised by stakeholders and women's organisations and represents a proactive trend in the US federal procurement strategy.

Source: Based on US Small Business Administration web site, www.sba.gov/offices/headquarters/oed/resources/3690 in OECD (2013a), *Public Procurement Review of the Mexican Institute of Social Security: Enhancing Efficiency and Integrity for Better Health Care*, http://dx.doi.org/10.1787/9789264197480-en.

Box 3.6. The objectives of the Support Program for Communities and the Environment (PACMA)

PACMA offers support in seven basic areas (health, safety, infrastructure, equity, environmental protection, education and productive projects) and contributes to mitigating risks in the non-technical operations of PEMEX in communities.

The implementation of programmes, projects and actions have the following benefits:

1. helps build a climate of collaboration or mutual understanding with residents, authorities, institutions and organisations located in the vicinity of oil installations
2. facilitates compliance with the operational goals of PEMEX and its subsidiary companies production
3. prevents impacts that could conflict with environmental stakeholders
4. assists the government in social development
5. links to other sustainable development programmes
6. allows for harnessing the potential of the oil industry to promote social development to their areas of influence
7. gives greater room for manoeuvre and negotiation with key environment entities.

PACMA establishes the participation of all stakeholders, promoting programmes, projects and specific actions, with financial support from suppliers and contractors of PEMEX, which is mandatory for them.

Source: Based on information provided by PEMEX.

PEMEX considers secondary objectives when designing and drafting the documentation and the contract, including requirements, evaluation criteria and weighting, which are reflected in the annex called "Support Program for Communities and the Environment" (PACMA), "S 4 2 a", which states the need to promote environmental protection as an explicit recognition of the social and environmental responsibility of PEMEX. The corporate social responsibility reflects well in the considerations relating to the environment that are integrated into PEMEX's open competition documentation. Depending on the nature and complexity of the procurement, certain aspects of industrial safety, occupational health and environmental protection are listed and used as part of the evaluation criteria. In accordance with the internal regulations there are minimum environmental requirements that need to be met by suppliers or contractors, its staff and its subcontractors, in order to prevent incidents and accidents at PEMEX facilities. Such obligations are clearly defined at the early stages of the publication of tenders, but they are not subject to assessment; however, failure to comply with those requirements can have consequences ranging from making deductions to payments or to termination of contracts.

The PACMA reflects the strategy of top management, which is to make "PEMEX a more competitive business, transparent to remain the pillar for national development ... consolidating efforts of corporate social responsibility that includes a social policy focus to reconcile the industry growth aspirations with that of increasing well-being in communities, through public and private social responsibility." In addition to this, PACMA conforms to the mandate of Article 25 of the Constitution in which it is stated that, "When national economic development with social responsibility, the public sector, the social sector and the private sector ..." just as (the state) "may participate by themselves or with the social and private sectors, according to the law, to promote and organise the priority areas of development," further it may "provide conditions for the development of the private sector to contribute to the development national economic...".

The objective of PACMA is to create a set of programmes, works and/or actions, which contribute to, obtain, expand and consolidate the social license to operate (LSO), allowing human development, generating productive capacities, addressing social gaps and forging a long-term sustainable development projects in the communities located within the areas of influence of PEMEX. The PACMA projects have to last for more than a year and have a budget of over MXN 100 million, for the offshore projects budget needs to exceed MXN 300 million. A technical committee comprised of PEMEX personnel and outside stakeholders collegially decides which project to support.

For this, PEMEX provides the basis for the implementation of the PACMA strategy and commitment to sustainable development, basing its strategy on:

- a generation of projects having favourable and sustainable social impact in nearby communities where there is extraction and production
- a consolidation of a sustainable model that integrates economic, environmental and social operation
- development of specific and measurable actions for the population, emphasising the benefit of vulnerable groups and support to women.

With the new PEMEX regulation the company is working towards becoming a "socially responsible company". The new Hydrocarbon Law requires assignees like PEMEX to develop impact assessments and management plans for all contracts relative to oil extraction. These requirements were not part of the previous legal framework.

Furthermore, the new legal framework seems to encourage PEMEX to do more to achieve social objectives as it requires the company to carry out social impact analysis in every contract relating to the distraction of oil. These requirements were not a part of the previous PEMEX legal framework.

A new landscape for complementary objectives

When designing and promoting complementary policies for public procurement, PEMEX needs to balance the benefits and potential costs of such policies as they can carry the risk of trading off integrity and value for money. By putting more emphasis on complementary criteria in tender evaluation the significance of value for money will be diminished. This can increase complexity, costs and risks in the procurement cycle by increasing demands placed on suppliers, procurement officers and systems of monitoring and evaluation. More countries and companies are now including economic, environmental or social considerations in the procurement process while ensuring that procurement decisions remain fair and transparent. Apart from programming such complementary policies into the evaluation mechanism, one of the ongoing difficulties lies in monitoring the implementation of the contract by contractors and subcontractors, who often operate across borders. There is also the issue of value for money and transparency that need not be traded off directly with complementary policy objectives. For example, by considering whole of life-cycle costs, more environmentally conscious decisions are ensured whilst also promoting more sound long-term financial management practices. Furthermore, one of the main challenges faced by all countries that promote complementary goals through public procurement is the development of performance indicators that are appropriate for assessing the success of applying complementary criteria in a public procurement regime.

On the three key topics - SMEs, green procurement and social objectives - steps have been taken by PEMEX in recent years to initiate more projects on sustainable development, and PACMA is a good example of what the company is doing. The changes in the legal framework do not prohibit PEMEX from doing business with SMEs; however, the competitive environment can lead PEMEX to move away from contracting SMEs if they are not competitive. The size of small contracts that PEMEX is making would by most standards be considered quite high, i.e. the "small" contracts do require companies with a certain level of capacity to be able to fulfil requirements.

During the OECD fact-finding mission, PEMEX officials understood that the total value of SMEs was decreasing, but there were also concerns that SMEs with the necessary knowledge and expertise might not exist. PEMEX has worked closely with industrial chambers and associations in order to inform their supply chain about the most relevant changes in the legislation. PEMEX has organised workshops for the new registry and conferences about the new procurement model. An effort has been made in the electronic media to update and make more transparent the information available for the public in general, mainly for suppliers. However, despite this commitment from the company, the economic environment does not seem favourable for SMEs. How the combined effects of the new legal framework and the current situation of tumbling oil prices and widespread deflationary forces affect the SMEs in Mexico in the long term is uncertain. It seems likely though that the falling price of oil will require PEMEX to be even more competitive, which may mean fewer SMEs will be contracted.

Proposals for action

The transformation of PEMEX into a state enterprise production has had an impact on how the company now approaches complementary objectives. Overall the legal environment seems to be more conducive to secondary objectives while the current economic situation is not. There is room for improvement: there is a need for a green policy, more direct actions to achieve social objectives, and steps needed to refocus PEMEX's SMEs strategy. The promotion of SMEs has not progressed since 2012, which could have a serious impact on small businesses in Mexico.

In order to further promote complementary policy objectives through its procurement, PEMEX could consider the following:

- PEMEX could develop a strategy that addresses the challenges that the company is now confronted with in the new environment with a view to enhancing SME competitiveness.
- PEMEX could set out incentives in regulations for the support of SMEs, national industry and disabled people, for example by benefiting primary contractors that are subcontracting to these industries.
- PEMEX could be more proactive in gathering data on SMEs being subcontracted by primary contractors.
- PEMEX could set up a framework for measuring results of the strategies/policies to use procurement to support socio-economic or environmental objectives. Part of that framework should include assessments of the extent to which public procurement is used in practice to support socio-economic or environmental objectives compared to other methods.
- PEMEX could support SMEs through a broad range of programmes. For example by designating specific products as competitive products; then only invite SMEs that directly manufacture such products to take part in competitive tenders.
- PEMEX could define a number of categories that allow for preferential purchasing of products with new technology. Products manufactured by newly developed technology would be evaluated and awarded certification, which allowed preferential purchasing.
- PEMEX could more forcefully apply various procurement mechanisms to promote complementary policy objectives, such as:
    - proactively publishing yearly forecasts of contracts of interest for targeted companies (based on complementary policy objectives)
    - setting aside lots specifically for target organisations (based on complementary objectives)
    - developing systems that ensure prompt payment to small and medium-sized suppliers
    - reducing the value of performance bonds required to obtain a contract
    - providing quality feedback to participants.

- PEMEX could support sustainable growth and promote innovation by developing a policy on green procurement to reduce the negative environmental impacts and environmental cost of public procurement.
- PEMEX could develop guidelines on how to better understand social impact procurement; to identify potential suppliers in Mexico and to develop a procurement process that assesses both financial and social value. This could help PEMEX achieve social objectives.

Notes

1. Information gathered during the OECD fact-finding mission.
2. Benefits for enterprises that hire handicapped persons (Law 361 of 1997 – Article 4.2.5.5); see www.secretariasenado.gov.co/senado/basedoc/ley/1997/ley_0361_1997.html.
3. For more information, see www.regjeringen.no/en/dokumenter/Environmental-and-Social-Responsibility-/id476600/.
4. LAASSP, Article 14.

References

European Commission (2008), "Public procurement for a better environment", Communication to the European Parliament, the Council, the European Economic and Social Committee and the Committee of Regions, European Commission", Brussels, http://eur-lex.europa.eu/LexUriServ/LexUriServ.do?uri=COM:2008:0400:FIN:EN:PDF (accessed 23 February 2012).

OECD (2016), *The Korean Public Procurement Service: Innovating for Effectiveness*, OECD Public Governance Reviews, OECD Publishing, Paris, http://dx.doi.org/10.1787/9789264249431-en.

OECD (2015a), "Recommendation of the Council on Public Procurement", www.oecd.org/corruption/recommendation-on-public-procurement.htm.

OECD (2015b), *Government at a Glance 2015*, OECD Publishing, Paris, http://dx.doi.org/10.1787/gov_glance-2015-en.

OECD (2013a), *Public Procurement Review of the Mexican Institute of Social Security: Enhancing Efficiency and Integrity for Better Health Care*, OECD Publishing, Paris, http://dx.doi.org/10.1787/9789264197480-en

OECD (2013b), *Colombia: Implementing Good Governance*, OECD Publishing, Paris, http://dx.doi.org/10.1787/9789264202177-en.

UNIDO (United Nations Industrial Development Organization) and UNODC (United Nations Office on Drugs and Crime) (2007), "Corruption prevention to foster small and medium-sized enterprises development", Vienna, www.unodc.org/documents/corruption/Publications/2012/UNIDO-UNODC_Publication_on_Small_Business_Development_and_Corruption_Vol1.pdf.

Chapter 4

Enhancing procurement capabilities in Petróleos Mexicanos

This chapter analyses how Petroleos Mexicanos, or PEMEX, could transform the procurement function into a strategic activity for value creation, including by making use of strategic workforce planning, change management, a skills framework, recruitment and promotion processes, training and performance management. It assesses the institutional model for human resources management in PEMEX, including processes such as recruitment, development and retention. Since it is critical for the company to be endowed with the right number of procurement officials with a fit-for-purpose set of competencies and skills, this chapter provides recommendations to improve the management of the procurement workforce in order to fulfil the company objectives and quickly evolve bearing in mind the company's new institutional mission focused on creating value.

Overview of Petróleos Mexicanos' workforce organisation

The procurement workforce is responsible for taking stock of the company's assets and determining the external resources it needs, or might need in the future, facilitating access and management of such resources, so that the company can fulfil its strategic objectives. In consequence, procurement professionals ought to leverage their knowledge and experience to manage resources and supply, and explore market opportunities to achieve the best outcome for Petróleos Mexicanos (or PEMEX). This section will discuss the extent to which procurement officials have the capacities to fulfil such responsibilities and contribute to the transformation of the procurement function, in the context of the wider reform to PEMEX.

PEMEX recognises that personnel is currently facing a significant challenge considering the need of the company to quickly evolve bearing in mind its institutional mission (i.e. becoming a state productive enterprise that operates to create value, following principles of efficiency and transparency). The staff structure is therefore not stable at the moment; its stabilisation will be necessary to systematically develop professionalisation plans. This situation is aggravated by the current financial situation of the company, which calls for downsizing.

According to PEMEX's Yearly Statistical Report, the company had 153 085 employees at the end of 2014 (PEMEX, 2014). Table 4.1 presents the trends and distribution by subsidiary.

Table 4.1. **PEMEX's employee numbers by subsidiary**

Subsidiary	2010	2011	2012	2013	2014	% change 2010-14
PEMEX corporate	14 254	14 192	14 404	14 425	14 960	4.9
Exploration and production	49 802	51 713	51 998	53 404	52 403	5.2
Refining	45 306	46 909	46 236	47 980	47 576	5.0
Gas and basic petrochemicals	12 327	11 918	12 191	12 905	12 669	2.8
Petrochemicals	13 542	13 541	13 487	13 758	13 476	-0.5
Medical services	12 137	12 288	12 381	12 302	12 001	-1.1
Total	147 368	150 561	150 697	154 774	153 085	3.9

Source: PEMEX (2014a), *Anuario Estadístico 2014*, PEMEX, www.pemex.com/ri/Publicaciones/Anuario%20Estadistico%20Archivos/2014_ae_00_vc_e.pdf (accessed 14 March 2016).

A small increase in employees of 3.9% took place during the period 2010-14, with increases of about 5% in PEMEX Corporate, Exploration and production, and Refining, and slight decreases in Petrochemicals and Medical services. The growing overall trend reverted in 2014.[1] Despite the adjustment plan announced on 29 February 2016, by May 2016 total staff amounted to 169 638 employees, which represents an increase of 10.8% relative to 2014 (see Table 4.2).

Table 4.2. **PEMEX's employee numbers by subsidiary and type (as of May 2016)**

Subsidiary	*Confianza* (freely appointed)	%	Unionised	%	Total
Exploration and production	10 482	19	44 603	81	55 085
Refining	5 197	9.5	49 501	90.5	54 698
PEMEX corporate	8 414	25.9	24 101	74.1	32 515
Gas and basic petrochemicals	1 883	13.5	12 105	86.5	13 988
Petrochemicals	1 300	9.8	11 936	90.2	13 236
Industrial transformation	46	100	0	0	46
Logistics	25	100	0	0	25
Co-generation and services	22	100	0	0	22
Drilling	15	100	0	0	15
Ethylene	4	100	0	0	4
Fertilisers	4	100	0	0	4
Total	27 392	16.1	142 246	83.9	169 638

Source: Based on information provided by PEMEX.

PEMEX employees are divided into two types: unionised workers (*de base o sindicalizados*), which represent 83.9%, and freely appointed (*de confianza*), which represent the other 16.1%. Union membership is restricted to technical and administrative personnel who have a relatively stable status, while *confianza* employees have permanent contracts and include superior and intermediate management, and professional staff. However, *confianza* employees can be removed or transferred according to company needs and when new superiors come in. In general, unionised staff have more limited capacities relative to *confianza* employees. In addition to these two types of personnel, PEMEX can hire short-term staff or consultants (*honorarios*).

Human resources management is regulated by the Federal Labour Law (Ley Federal del Trabajo), the PEMEX Law and other PEMEX-specific regulations, such as PEMEX's Organic Statute (Estatuto Orgánico de Petróleos Mexicanos) and the Organisation Manual of the Basic Structure of PEMEX and its Subsidiaries (Manual de Organización de Estructura Básica de Petróleos Mexicanos y Organismos Subsidiarios), as well as the Collective Work Contract, which is the collective contract between PEMEX and the Union of Oil Workers of Mexico (Sindicato de Trabajadores Petroleros de la República Mexicana, or STPRM) and the Working Bylaws for *Confianza* Employees (Reglamento de Trabajo del Personal de Confianza).[2] Since PEMEX is not part of the central public administration, the Professional Civil Service Law does not apply.[3]

Human resources management follows an institutional model, which includes the following processes:

- **Recruitment**: Key positions, starting in the middle management ranks, are subject to competitive recruitment processes, in which at least three candidates with the right profiles are interviewed and, according to the complexity of the job to be performed, may have to take an exam to assess their skills. The main recruitment sources are the jobseeker section (*bolsa de trabajo*; see Box 4.1) hosted on PEMEX's website, and internal candidates from the recruiting area or who have been part of professional development plans (*planes de carrera*).
- **Development**: Employee development is planned between the corresponding functional area and the individual employee, on the basis of the skill needs to fulfil business objectives.

- **Retention**: In co-operation with the human resources management department, the different corporate directorates establish the key positions to run their main activities efficiently. Based on analyses and measurements of the skills of the employees performing different functions, replacements are prepared for key positions. In addition, there are variable remuneration schemes to recognise superior performance.

Box 4.1. The jobseeker section on PEMEX's website

The jobseeker section on PEMEX's website provides information for jobseekers and students looking for internship and service opportunities. For the case of jobseekers, the website provides an application form in pdf format, which is downloaded and filled out before it is sent by e-mail to PEMEX. The application form requires personal and contact information from the applicant, as well as academic and work history. Additionally, it includes a section for PEMEX staff.

For the case of applicants for internships and social service, the website provides information about requirements and the address to which the documents should be sent.

Source: PEMEX (2015), "Trabaja en Pemex", webpage, www.pemex.com/acerca/recursos-humanos/Paginas/Trabaja-en-Pemex.aspx (accessed 14 March 2016).

Regarding the Corporate Directorate for Procurement and Supply (Dirección Corporativa de Procura y Abastecimiento, or DCPA), 1 034 *confianza* employees work in this area, including senior and middle management (i.e. the director, deputy directors and middle managers). The duties of these employees are strictly limited to procurement functions. They include two areas focused on category management: the manager for categories for exploration and production and the manager for categories for industrial transformation and support and health services.

Regarding the operation of regional offices, PEMEX has developed a model called Attention Centres for Procurement and Supply (Centros de Atención de Procura y Abastecimiento, or CAPAs). This model aims to carry out procurement efficiently and transparently, following from the centralised management of the process and under the leadership of DCPA. Figure 4.1 illustrates the way CAPAs will rationalise procurement at the regional level:

Figure 4.1. **PEMEX's CAPAS structure**

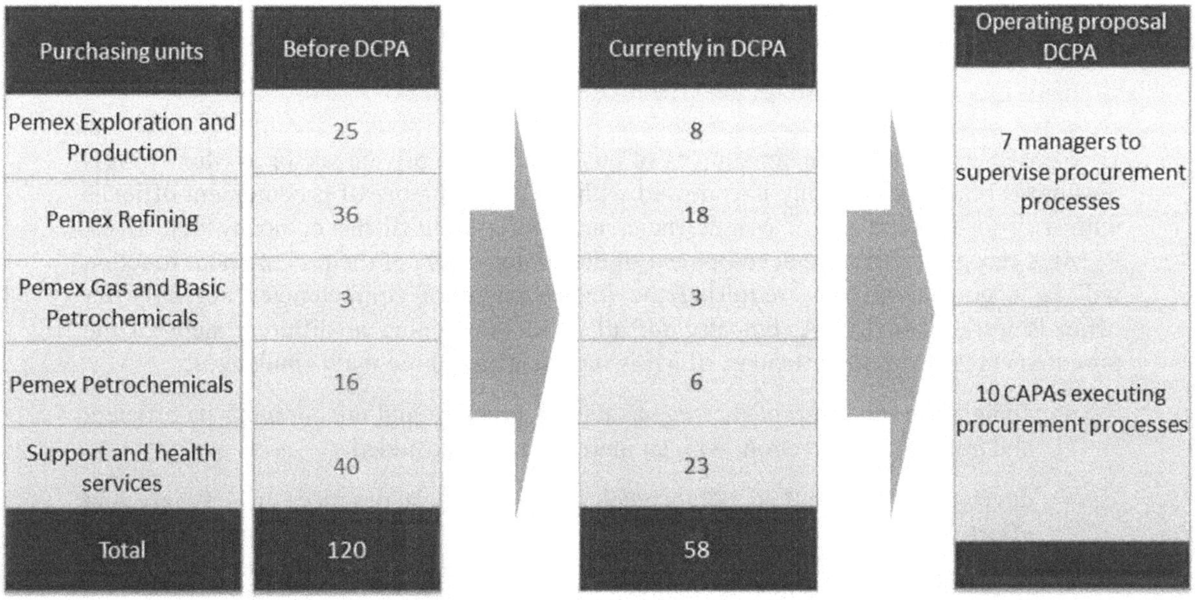

Source: PEMEX (2015), "Centros de Atención de Procura y Abastecimiento", presentation provided by PEMEX.

Procurement managers will carry out their functions at the central level, while CAPAs will take care of the procurement requirements of the geographic area under their responsibility. The number of CAPAs was determined on the basis of geographic location and requirements of the users who will be provided with procurement and supply services. Concerning strategic supply and category management, the strategy is set at the central level, while the procurement tools are implemented through the web or the PEMEX network.

The CAPAs are staffed as indicated in Table 4.3.

Table 4.3. **CAPAs' employee numbers by region and type**

CAPA	*Confianza* (freely appointed)	Temporary	Unionised	Total
Reynosa	17	0	42	59
Monterrey	35	13	20	68
Altamira	21	12	16	49
Guadalajara	6	0	0	6
Queretaro	58	19	19	96
Poza Rica	47	0	67	114
Veracruz	6	0	15	21
Coatzacoalcos	126	33	186	345
Villahermosa	264	0	257	521
Ciudad del Carmen	139	0	137	276
Total	719	77	759	1555

Source: PEMEX (2015), "Centros de Atención de Procura y Abastecimiento", presentation provided by PEMEX.

Confianza employees in CAPAs represent 70% of the *confianza* staff of DCPA (1 034 employees). Change management will therefore be as important at PEMEX headquarters as it will be in the regions.

Strengthening the strategic role of the procurement workforce

PEMEX is one of the main sources of business for the private sector in Mexico; it is thus critical that the company is endowed with the right number of procurement officials with a fit-for-purpose set of competencies and skills to fulfil the company objectives. PEMEX recognises that the development of the strategic role of the procurement function will be a gradual process, requiring the improvement of competencies not only for officials working in DCPA, but also for all those intervening at different steps of the procurement process. In particular, PEMEX has identified three main challenges:

- completing the setup of the organisational structure and encouraging its efficient and transparent operation, with an incremental value added
- developing the required competencies to adopt best practices in a timely and effective manner
- developing the personnel to facilitate the continuity of operations in key posts.

The strategy "Professionalising to Transform" (Profesionalizar para Transformar) is the first intensive effort by the DCPA to establish a basic platform of standardised knowledge relative to the business practices that will advance the feasibility of the procurement business model, where the guiding criterion is value creation. Nonetheless, the main challenge is to facilitate cultural change, not only in the practices to manage human resources, but also in the behaviour of officials, who have been used to a highly bureaucratic culture proper of a state monopoly. In consequence, there is an opportunity to develop a human resource management (HRM) system that allows for flexibility and advances impartiality and transparency.

An important factor to keep in mind is that PEMEX is under pressure to transform and, therefore, to reform its HRM policies. PEMEX's HRM system is quite rigid, as is the case in Mexico's public administration, and requires reform to align with the needs and demands for specialised skills. An inflexible regulatory framework, topped with the role of the union, make it difficult for managers to plan and select the right applicants to fill vacancies.

Strategic workforce planning

A key element of reform of the public sector, including state-owned enterprises (SOEs), in OECD countries has been the introduction of strategic workforce planning. There is no evidence that DCPA has carried out the planning to estimate the size of the procurement workforce needed in upcoming years, let alone the medium and long-term. This implies a risk that PEMEX, at some point, may not have enough human resources to face the procurement workload, and that officials will not receive specific training to address skills weaknesses. This is aggravated by the fact that DCPA does not have a register or an estimate of the degree of turnover of procurement officials.

There are few incentives to retain personnel and it is hard to replace staff given the specialised knowledge and experience required. An additional constraint is that vacancies which, by nature, are reserved for unionised workers, are filled by PEMEX with employees suggested by the STPRM within 72 hours upon request, according to Article 4 of the Collective Contract. One of the issues is that unionised workers cannot be dismissed easily. A removal should be requested by the employee himself. In consequence, managers cannot plan based on competencies and skills, as basically the union proposes the staff to fill vacancies reserved for it.

Bearing in mind such structural constraints, PEMEX could invest in the development of its capacity for strategic workforce planning by:

- allocating responsibilities among senior officials for strategic workforce management
- ensuring the right profile of the workforce to fulfil the company's strategic objectives
- defining general objectives regarding workforce planning, particularly in terms of numbers and costs
- defining general objectives concerning diversity, competencies, skills, and education requirements.

Strategic management of the workforce anticipates future developments and maintains a structured and representative workforce of the appropriate size – one that is able to meet the changing needs of organisations in a cost-efficient manner. In consequence, effective workforce planning requires quality information that is linked to organisational strategies, efficiency concerns, and organisational arrangements that support workforce decisions. PEMEX should engage in strategic workforce planning based on a strategic vision and quality information, strengthening DCPA capacities and holding procurement managers accountable for the strategic management of their teams. Such workforce planning would contribute to:

- spreading a common understanding of PEMEX's vision and procurement business model
- raising awareness of current and future skill and competency needs, and identifying gaps within the company
- anticipating future developments and maintaining a structured and representative workforce of an appropriate size, able to meet the changing needs of the company in a cost-efficient manner
- allowing for a more efficient and effective use of the workforce, preparing for restructuring, reducing or expanding the procurement workforce.

Workforce planning requires following up the number of staff, costs, and competencies; flexibility in workforce management, as well as commitment from, and accountability of, senior officials. PEMEX could establish processes to link workforce planning with the company's overall strategic plans, including accountability mechanisms for senior management to report on its workforce planning. PEMEX could benefit from the experience of OECD countries, such as the United States, which have advanced initiatives to align workforce planning with strategic objectives (see Box 4.2). The US experience offers two important lessons: 1) human resources needs should stem from organisational objectives, mission, functions, workload, and desired performance standards; and 2) institutions should determine the skill set and the number of staff required to carry them out effectively and efficiently.

Box 4.2. The system for strategic alignment of workforce planning in the United States

Workforce planning is part of the strategy of the US Federal Government to align human capital with the mission, goals, and objectives of federal institutions. It is supervised by senior managers and, particularly, human resources chiefs, through analysis, planning, investment, and management of human resources programmes.

HRM strategies are incorporated in strategic programmes, execution plans, and budgets, and are guided by the following criteria: planning of human capital, good practices relative to human capital, knowledge-sharing, and human resources as a strategic partner. Each criterion is linked to indicators that illustrate how well each institution is running HRM. Activities and outcomes are evaluated in light of a Human Capital Strategic Plan, which includes goals, objectives, and strategies, as well as performance indicators. Institutions are required by the US Office of Personnel Management (OPM) to annually submit their Human Capital Strategic Plans.

Human resources plans are directly linked to strategic performance annual plans in each institution and are used to make decisions regarding the structure and distribution of the workforce. Key tasks and competencies to fulfil the institution's mission are identified and documented, which then provide inputs for the strategies to hire, develop, and retain talent. The human resources planning of each institution identifies current and future competencies and the corresponding gaps that need to be closed.

In addition, a review process forecasts the possible adjustments of the workforce, allowing senior management to anticipate and act accordingly to ensure fulfilment of programme objectives. A functional analysis facilitates structuring the institution so as to achieve the right mix and distribution of employees to support mission accomplishment.

Source: Office of Personnel Management (n. d.), www.opm.gov (accessed 16 March 2016); and presentation by Jonathan Foley, US Delegate to the OECD Public Employment and Management Working Party, 9-10 December 2010.

Co-ordination of DCPA with CAPAs

Co-ordination mechanisms are key to allow CAPAs to carry out procurement processes in compliance with DCPA policies. These mechanisms should aim to facilitate the exchange of knowledge and good practices, improve learning, and above all, commit the different units to a set of common goals and programmes. In other words, DCPA should strive to maintain procurement policy coherence, while allowing CAPAs managerial flexibility. In doing so, DCPA would support the process by setting guidelines and disseminating knowledge and good procurement practices to advance understanding and skills.

In line with previous discussion, it should be understood that centre-led procurement does not necessarily mean "centralised procurement". CAPAs will provide procurement services to the users in the geographic areas under their responsibility, but technical advice and training provided by the central office (DCPA) should be at the disposition of those units at all times. Expanding and improving interaction between DCPA and CAPAs for conducting procurement should then be a priority.

PEMEX could leverage the use of information and communication technologies (ICTs), especially for long-distance assistance and supervision in conducting recruitment for procurement. The use of such technologies for recruitment would not only increase efficiency, but also allow DCPA and the human resources unit to see who is being hired in CAPAs. The use of ICT in human resources functions should be aligned to PEMEX's business needs and therefore be backed by a vision of HRM and how ICT can contribute to realising such vision. The vision should plan for five years ahead, according to the experience of Belgium, and ideally for the longer term.

Creating a specific procurement profession in PEMEX

The 2015 Recommendation of the Council on Public Procurement suggests developing a procurement workforce with the capacity to continually deliver value for money efficiently and effectively. To this end, the Recommendation (OECD, 2015) suggests the following:

- ensuring that procurement officials meet high professional standards for knowledge, practical implementation, and integrity by providing a dedicated and regularly updated set of tools, among others, the recognition of public procurement as a specific profession, certification, and regular training
- providing attractive, competitive, and merit-based career options for procurement officials
- promoting collaborative approaches with knowledge centres such as universities, think-tanks and policy centres to improve skills and competences of the procurement workforce.

PEMEX needs to address several opportunities in order to develop a specific procurement profession and get closer to best OECD practices.

Change management

HRM strategies should facilitate cultural change in support of the Energy Reform and the new centralised procurement model. The Energy Reform by itself requires a cultural change, as the company will be transitioning to a competitive market. As PEMEX itself recognises, human resources and organisational reforms take time and results will not materialise immediately. PEMEX officials could consider the different normative tools used by other OECD countries to plan, implement, and sustain reform (see Table 4.4).

The DCPA Deputy Directorate for Strategy Management and Support to the Business Model (Subdirección de Gestión de Estrategia y Soporte al Modelo de Negocio) is in charge of co-ordinating the change management strategy for the implementation of the business model for procurement in PEMEX, its EPS and affiliates. The change management methodology developed by PEMEX aims at advancing change initiatives by identifying the reasons that justify them and turn them into the leading forces of the company. This methodology also identifies stakeholders and audiences, different resistances, and obstacles in order to deploy measures to minimise them and achieve change and improvement as soon as possible. The methodology consists of six building blocks (see Figure 4.2) and is accompanied by a communications and awareness plan, which aims to communicate structured information about the objectives and the scope of DCPA and create awareness of the benefits of DCPA by explaining its functioning and innovations to internal and external audiences.

Table 4.4. **Challenges to public administration reforms and alternative normative tools**

Key challenges	Normative tools
Reform planning phase	
• Addressing information gaps and agreeing on a timeline with measurable milestones and final results • Developing support for reform: users and employees	• Independent systems of specialised knowledge and preliminary assessments • Public debate and consultation • Taking advantage of crises
Reform implementation phase	
• Leadership and political commitment with reform • Overcoming resistance and developing reform ownership • Building capacities and knowledge	• Clear electoral mandates • Compensating losers from reform • Implementing complementary reforms • Training plans and public administration schools • Communicating reform
Reform sustainability phase	
• Evaluating reform and estimating success	• Evaluation tools • Independent reform-tracking institutions • High-level committees

Source: OECD (2010), "Making Reform Happen: Lessons from OECD Countries", OECD Publishing, Paris, p. 214. http://dx.doi.org/10.1787/9789264086296-en

Figure 4.2. **PEMEX's change management methodology**

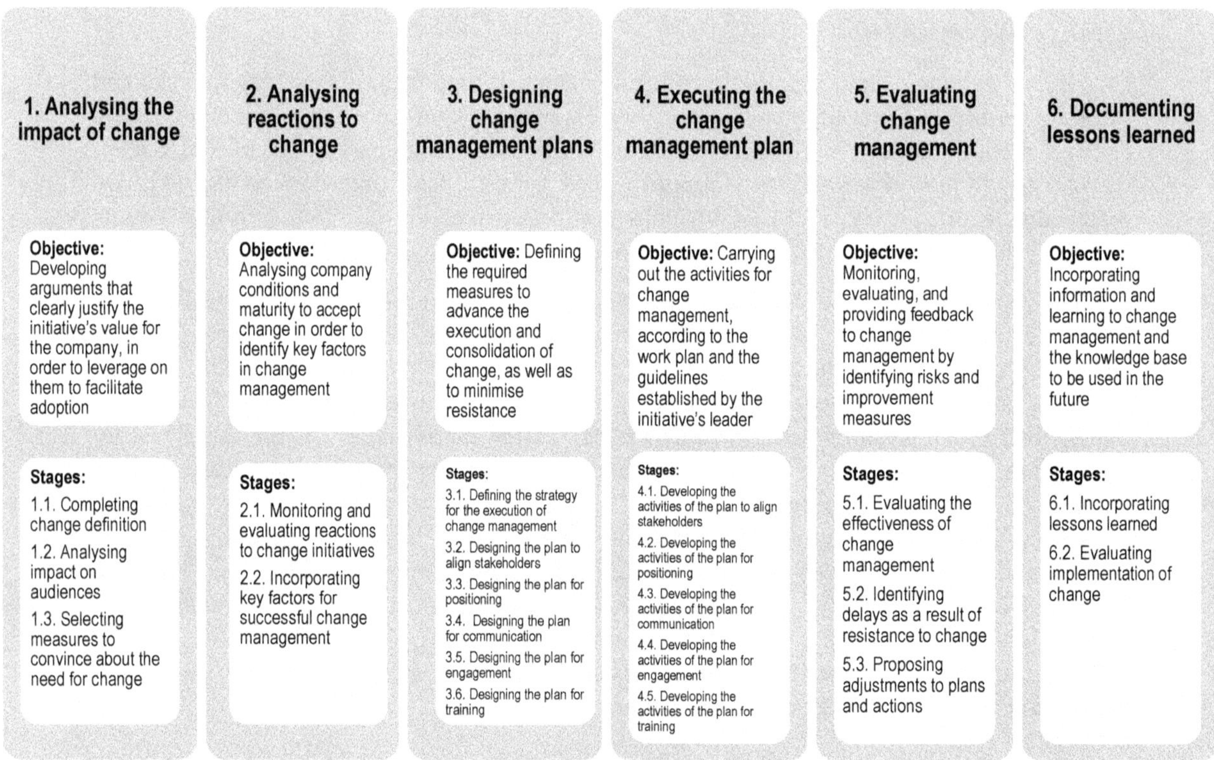

Source: PEMEX (2014b), "Estrategia Integral de Gestión del Cambio para fortalecer la adopción y operación de la DCPA", DCPA January.

Some of the tools being used to facilitate change include a survey on willingness to change and plans for widespread training. The survey, conducted in October 2014 to 1 420 officials, found a favourable perception towards the establishment of DCPA and the need for PEMEX's organisational structure to evolve. However, officials also expressed high expectations regarding the professionalisation of the procurement function and doubts concerning the degree to which professional experience will be considered for career development. In addition, staff expressed concerns regarding job stability. These findings speak to the awareness of staff regarding the importance of human resources for a successful change management strategy. PEMEX's efforts should address these expectations and concerns to avoid "reform fatigue" and keep employees' attitudes positive about change.

Regarding training, it was launched in June 2014, with different e-courses divided into four modules: 1) procurement context in PEMEX: structure and procedures under the PEMEX Law; 2) strategic supply; 3) framework agreements and preparatory contracts; and 4) bidding evaluation methods (see Tables 4.6 and 4.7 later in this chapter for a complete description of the courses and the number of officials taking them).

PEMEX could learn from Finland's programme, "Finwin: Towards a New Leadership" and develop a similar initiative for senior management aiming at the design of a change-management strategy, identification of challenges and opportunities, and sharing of good practices (see Box 4.3).

Box 4.3. Finland's change management programme: Finwin – Towards a New Leadership

In December 2006, the Ministerial Committee for Economic Policy of Finland established the change management programme called, "Finwin – Towards a New Leadership". The aim of the programme was to bring about a shared understanding and vision concerning future challenges and ways to manage them. Finwin facilitated horizontal dialogue among senior managers from different ministries and agencies through seminars for discussion. Its intention was to facilitate change by disseminating information and exchanging positive and negative lessons on reform programmes in different areas and levels of government.

The programme was organised around seminars which served as fora for discussion on topics like well-being at work, social innovations, functions of the state sector and regional administration reform. There were also other working methods such as learning cafés and workshops that complemented the discussions held at the seminars. Managers had the opportunity to discuss a common vision of where they were going, what they wanted from the future, where they would be in ten years, and the desired level of quality to operate. One of the concrete results of Finwin was the elaboration of a five-point programme for better management.

Source: Huerta Melchor, O. (2008), "Managing change in OECD governments: An introductory framework", *OECD Working Papers on Public Governance*, No. 12, OECD Publishing, Paris, http://dx.doi.org/10.1787/227141782188.

Competencies and skills

Although PEMEX's procurement team demonstrates high levels of commitment and professionalism, there appear to be opportunities to strengthen competencies and skills, including handling supplier and contract management, and performing complex procurement. For example, key profiles could be better defined. Upgrading competencies and skills would strengthen the procurement function. Procurement professionals need a set of flexible skills due to changing contexts and priorities. The strategic role of PEMEX requires procurement professionals with high-level strategic, tactical, as well as operational skills, particularly now that the company has the mandate of creating value.

Focusing on developing competencies is critical. Across OECD countries, competency management has proved to be an effective way to define the abilities and behaviours needed for people to do their jobs properly. Moreover, it links up a number of key human resources activities to ensure that an organisation is staffed by competent people who perform effectively. In OECD countries like Belgium, Canada, Korea and the United States, competencies are being integrated into various activities to ensure these are well-aligned with organisational needs. Such activities include recruitment and selection of staff, training and development, as well as succession and career planning.

The DCPA should perform the dual role of developing skills and capabilities for the procurement function in PEMEX. It should work together with members of staff to set challenging standards for skills and competencies within procurement and provide procurement professionals with access to learning and development opportunities to reach those standards. Drawing on the experience of the United Kingdom, DCPA and the Corporate Directorate for Administration and Services, which has incorporated the HR functions since March 2016, could collaborate to build the procurement profession and develop a "Skills Frameworks for Procurement Practitioners and Procurement Leaders". These frameworks can be used by individuals to assess their skills and identify development needs when planning and progressing their career in the procurement profession in PEMEX. These frameworks can be adapted when needed. The objective would be to lay the foundations for the development of a procurement profession in PEMEX. Procurement professionals should add value to the quality and cost-effectiveness of the acquisition of goods, services, leasing, and works, and draw up contracts that secure value for money and comply with legal and policy requirements.

As a way to define and measure the skills, abilities, and behaviours considered necessary for the job, many organisations use competencies as part of job profiles. If used properly and supported by appropriate assessment methods, a competency framework provides a rigorous and reasonably objective way to assess whether a candidate is likely to be effective in the job. The competencies required are defined by the job profile: for example, social competencies could include the ability to work in teams or build networks; for staff with managerial responsibilities competencies could include interpersonal skills and leadership abilities; other examples of competencies might entail strategic thinking, client focus, or analytical skills. Depending on the type of job, both generic competencies and job-specific competencies may be included in the job profile (see Table 4.5).

Table 4.5. **Skills framework for PEMEX's procurement professionals: An example**

Skills	Procurement management roles			
	Procurement officer	Senior procurement officer	Deputy directors	Head of DCPA
Strategic awareness: • Awareness of the marketplace, commodities, and products: Spend category and sector awareness, knowledge of commodities and services usually purchased, awareness of new technologies • Awareness of procurement strategy	• Limited strategic awareness • Awareness of markets as a source of supply, but not detailed market/product knowledge, limited commercial focus • Administrative capacity only, requires close supervision	• Awareness of strategic issues • Capable of identifying circumstances where value and risk require a particular approach to be taken • Knowledge of markets and products, with ability to apply basic procurement processes in search of best value for money • Some commercial focus, with enough experience of strategic procurement to know when to seek advice	• Knowledge and some experience in developing corporate procurement strategy • Able to identify appropriate procurement strategies and approaches and recommend preferred option • Experience with supplier management and principles of supplier development • Commercially aware and credible internally and externally • Experience and knowledge of specific markets, with the ability to exploit them through application of well-developed procurement skills • Experience of working on strategic projects as part of cross-functional teams	• Expert in procurement strategy and leads development • Skilled and experienced in market exploitation • Able to identify appropriate tactics dependent on supplier position in the market • Capable of playing a leading role in cross-functional teams managing strategic procurement • Capable of managing all aspects of projects, from business case to delivery • Capable of identifying and implementing appropriate procurement strategies and approaches • Actively manages and develops relationships with key suppliers
Managing the procurement process: • Procurement cycle • Roles and responsibilities for supplier databases • Low value procurement: Requests for quotations, framework agreements, procurement cards. • Projects: Risk-based approach, roles and responsibilities, critical success factors, identifying needs, business case/option appraisal, scoping, market sounding, procurement approach and rules.	• Limited awareness of procurement processes • Involvement in supporting/administrative capacity, in line with pre-determined rules and under close supervision	• Understands and is able to apply basic procurement processes to routine situations. Some experience with negotiation, but requires support • Experienced enough to know when to seek help or advice • Some commercial focus, with enough experience to know when to seek advice	• Knowledgeable about and comfortable with all aspects of procurement processes • Capable of providing advice on all types of specifications and to take the lead on procurement aspects as part of a cross-functional team • Experience in negotiating high value contracts, commending credibility and respect internally and externally • Commercially aware and credible internally and externally	• Expert in all aspects of procurement processes, through experience and applied knowledge • Able to apply judgement to determine how best to apply processes to secure best value in any particular set of circumstances • Able to direct and coach others, capable of commending credibility internally and externally

Source: OECD (2013), *Public Procurement Review of the Mexican Institute of Social Security: Enhancing Efficiency and Integrity for Better Health Care*, OECD Public Governance Reviews, OECD Publishing, http://dx.doi.org/10.1787/9789264197480-en.

Recruitment and promotion processes

OECD good practices suggest that recruitment and promotion processes should be transparent and based on merit and clearly defined competencies. Impartiality in recruitment processes can be advanced by open competitions to fill vacancies. Regarding promotion, impartiality is advanced by a positive assessment of individual performance.

Key positions, starting in middle management, are subject to competitive recruitment processes, in which at least three candidates with the right profiles are interviewed and, according to the complexity of the job to be performed, may have to take an exam to assess their skills. However, such competitive processes are not standardised and do not apply to all types of employees. There is still a high degree of discretion from the office where the vacancy is, jeopardising the merit principle. The margin for external applicants to fill vacancies is limited to instances where highly specialised skills are not found in the company's workforce, as internal candidates are given preference. In other words, there are no systematic robust practices to ensure transparency and merit-based selection, such as competitive processes and selection panels. In addition, performance assessment of the individual employees can be improved since PEMEX lacks an accountability framework, like the one found in Canada (see Box 4.4). Increased transparency could be pursued in the appointment for different positions, supported by the systematic assessment of employees' performance, to avoid undue influence in promotions.

Box 4.4. **Canada's Management Accountability Framework**

The Management Accountability Framework (MAF) is a framework for management excellence, accompanied by an annual assessment of management practices and performance in most departments and agencies of the Government of Canada. The MAF is a key tool of oversight that is used by the Treasury Board of Canada Secretariat (TBS) to help ensure that federal departments and agencies are well managed, accountable and that resources are allocated to achieve results.

The MAF establishes the expectations for sound public sector management practices and performance. It supports the management accountability of organisational deputy heads and improves management practices across government departments and agencies. The framework establishes indicators and measurements to assess performance through time and help senior management strengthen accountability for management results. The objectives of the MAF are to:

- obtain an organisational and government-wide view of the state of management practices and performance
- inform Deputy Ministers and Heads of Agencies about their organisations' management capacity
- inform the Treasury Board of Canada Secretariat about the state of policy implementation and practices
- identify areas of management strength and any areas that require attention
- communicate and track progress on government-wide management priorities
- continuously improve management capabilities, effectiveness, and efficiency government-wide.

Source: Treasury Board Secretariat (2009), "Management Accountability Framework", www.tbs-sct.gc.ca/hgw-cgf/oversight-surveillance/maf-crg/index-eng.asp (accessed 22 March 2016).

PEMEX could take the following actions to upgrade recruitment and selection processes, render them more transparent, and ensure that they are based on merit and the assessment of competencies:

- Engaging the HR bureau of the Corporate Directorate for Administration and Services and delegating to it some of the activities involved in recruitment, such as drafting/developing exams, organising interviews, objectively assessing the skills and competencies of candidates, and producing a short list from which DCPA could make the final selection. Engagement by HR experts would enhance the credibility and sophistication of the recruitment processes.
- Opening the recruitment process to real competition for internal and external applicants. This practice has improved the performance culture in OECD countries. While it is a good practice to offer personnel career advancement opportunities, this should not come at the expense of open competition, as careers should be developed by upgrading the skills, competencies, and professional experience of the staff, not by preparing an employee to substitute for a retiring one. Opening recruitment processes more widely to competition would also contribute to changing a dominant bureaucratic culture based on complying with procedures to one that rewards merit, results and performance. The main lesson here is that a promotion should be earned rather than assumed a given. Opening up vacant managerial positions for competition will promote fairness and merit.
- Adjusting jobs profiles and descriptions. PEMEX should take advantage of its transformation process to introduce modern tools for skills and competencies management, starting with jobs profiles. This tool, by defining the main responsibilities and expected results, sets the framework to assess performance objectives and measure such results, as well as to analyse which skills, behaviours, and attributes are required to carry out the corresponding functions effectively. Jobs profiles are tools to build flexible, performance-oriented, and forward-looking recruitment processes. In this regard, the jobs profiles used by PEMEX are quite complete and, for example, by describing the outputs or results expected from the job and including statements about the required skills and personal attributes. Still, they show some opportunities for improvement regarding the definition of indicators to assess performance and their linkage to job competencies. This is critical to facilitate an effective performance management process to assess what is achieved and giving employees feedback to address shortcomings. Furthermore, in the context of DCPA, only senior managerial positions (i.e. the Head of DCPA and deputy directors) have comprehensive job profiles, while those for lower level positions still need to be developed.
- Introducing a system for competency management. Such a system would be useful to define the attitudes and behaviours employees need to carry out their jobs effectively and link different HR activities to recruit personnel who work efficiently. The experience of OECD countries suggests different steps to introduce competency management systems with a long-term perspective in mind (see Box 4.5).

Box 4.5. Route map to introduce, develop and implement competency management

The experience of OECD countries suggests some basic steps (i.e. a checklist) to introduce, develop, and implement competency management.

- **Step 1. Create a long-term planning structure***:* The introduction of competency management is a strategic decision and a long-term commitment. However, competency management is not an end in itself, but the means to an end. First, competency management should be linked to the mission and vision of the institution (vertical integration). Some of the questions to be answered at this stage are the following: Why the institution wants to introduce competency management? and How does competency management link with the institution's mission and vision? One of the main reasons behind the introduction of competency management in OECD countries has been generalised organisational and cultural reforms in the public administration. In other words, it has aimed to transform traditional and rigid bureaucracies into modern and flexible organisations.
- **Step 2. Organise, plan and communicate change towards competency-based management***:* This stage includes three elements:
  - Define how to organise competency management (governance of HR): Some of the questions to answer are: Who is going to develop competency management? and Who will co-ordinate its implementation? The main choice to make at this step is whether competency management will be led in a centralised or decentralised manner. OECD countries usually recur to a mix in which there is a decentralised approach to implementation while following guidelines established by a central HR service.
  - Plan the development of a competency management system: Defining concepts is key to avoid misunderstandings in the short term during the development of the competency management scheme and in the long term during its implementation. Some of the concepts to be defined include "competency" and "competency management". Likewise, decisions should be taken on which areas of the institution will apply competency management (i.e. the whole organisation, a specific department, particular kinds of staff).
  - Develop and roll out communication plans: The introduction of competency management requires staff support. Hence, it is critical to inform staff and different stakeholders (i.e. HR professionals, supervisors, employees, union) about the reform process. This requires a proactive communication campaign.
- **Step 3. Identify competencies and develop models for the selected groups***:* There are several options, such as a set of competencies for all public employees, or one set for senior management and another for operative staff, or one for every hierarchical level. OECD countries usually prioritise senior management. In any case, a good system should always be aligned to the institution's strategy, mission and vision.
- **Step 4. Incorporate competencies into different HR processes***:* The next step consists of applying the model to HR management, such as in recruitment, career development, and HR planning. This incorporation can take place gradually or horizontally. If the gradual approach is selected, the process can start with a pilot in a department, with a group of employees, or a specific HR process. Early engagement of top management sends a strong message to the rest of the institution. Likewise, the HR processes in which the competency model will be applied have to be chosen.
- **Step 5. Update the competency management system periodically***:* The effectiveness of the whole system (i.e. the models and incorporating competencies into HR processes) should be evaluated. Some questions to be answered at this stage are: How can the competency management system be improved? and How well are the different components of the model working? The list of competencies should be updated when the business strategy is modified.

Source: OECD (2013), *Public Procurement Review of the Mexican Institute of Social Security: Enhancing Efficiency and Integrity for Better Health Care*, OECD Public Governance Reviews, OECD Publishing, http://dx.doi.org/10.1787/9789264197480-en.

Performance management

The recurrent practice of favouring internal candidates to fill vacancies is not an effective way to create opportunities for career advancement and value added for the company. According to PEMEX's HR Model, variable remunerations, such as a productivity bonus, are provided to reward good performance and fulfilment of the objectives and goals of the company. However, it is not clear how "good performance" is measured, which is in part due to the fact that job profiles have not incorporated indicators to measure staff performance. In many of Mexico's public institutions, bonuses are given by default, without proper and individualised performance measurement, unless the public official does something terribly wrong. In other words, PEMEX should avoid this widespread practice that does not really motivate good performance. In addition, performance assessment is restricted to *confianza* employees and does not apply to unionised workers, as established in the Collective Work Contract.

PEMEX's transition opens up the opportunity to introduce a performance assessment model based on indicators aligned with the company's mission to create value. In order to achieve the best result, employees should understand what is expected from them, as well as receive feedback and support from their superiors to improve performance.

Adopting staff performance management frameworks focused on key results aligned with the organisational priorities and performance targets would allow the procurement function to be oriented towards long-term objectives rather than daily needs. It would also assist in identifying the competencies required to perform well. To reach full benefit, it is essential that this system is not only used to assess performance results, but also that regular feedback is provided to employees and actions are taken to address shortcomings. The aim should be to enable operational managers to work with their staff to align their individual needs, interests, and career aspirations with PEMEX's business needs. The focus should be on the future, on what the employee needs to be able to do, and how he/she can do things better. The experience of OECD member countries suggests that effective performance management recognises good work performance and addresses poor performance. It identifies staff training or development needs, and addresses other barriers to good performance.

Performance management should be an explicit strategy for the procurement workforce. In this sense, three obstacles tend to be commonplace:

- Assessing performance implies a cultural change for which neither the company nor its employees are prepared. As mentioned before, there is no evidence that a change management strategy has been put in place. Hence, there might be resistance to performance assessment. Middle and senior management also need to be trained to carry out the evaluations of their teams.
- There is a need to create a system and a structure for performance management. As a prerequisite, PEMEX should develop its capacity to describe expected results and translate them into actionable operations. This would support PEMEX's senior management to carry out performance evaluation at the organisation, team, and individual levels. Furthermore, developing indicators is a precondition, but a complex and difficult task that requires time and resources (see Box 4.6).

Box 4.6. Criteria to develop key performance indicators

The work by the Learning Team Human Resources and Administration of the European Public Administration Network has led to the definition of basic criteria for good key performance indicators, such as the following:

- **Pertinent**: Representative indicator for Critical Success Factors (CSF). It is necessary for follow up.
- **Correctly defined**: Detailed description of the indicator, understandable and comprehensive, so that its meaning is clear for everyone.
- **Measurable**: Data are available to measure progress.
- **Cost-effective**: The cost of measuring is justified by the results and benefits.
- **Timely**: The frequency of measurement is realistic and acceptable for the different stakeholders.
- **Reliable**: Measurement is precise and objective.

Source: Hamande, Jack (2015), "EUPAN", presentation from FPS P&O Belgium before the Learning Team Human Resources and Administration of the European Public Administration Network (EUPAN LTHRA).

- Middle and senior management should be held accountable for performance assessment. This requires striking a difficult balance between accountability and flexibility. Too many restrictions create conditions that hinder the freedom of management to improve performance. Management should have the necessary means and flexibility to facilitate the fulfilment of objectives. Canada's MAF is a good example of how to make management accountable for performance (see Box 4.4).

Finally, the experience of OECD countries suggests that a performance management system should encourage the systematic engagement of employees, as individuals and as part of the team, to improve organisational effectiveness in the achievement of the institution's mission and goals.

Training and certification

Formal and on-the-job training programmes should be available for entry-level as well as more experienced procurement officials, to ensure that officials involved in public procurement have the necessary skills and knowledge to carry out their responsibilities and keep abreast of changes. Despite the fact that PEMEX is in the middle of its transition process, training has been provided to DCPA staff and all those employees taking part in the procurement process as part of the strategy "Professionalising to Transform". Seven e-learning courses concentrated on the basic procurement concepts, methodologies, and strategies (see Table 4.6). These courses provide harmonised knowledge to incorporate good practices and standardise the procurement function. They are available in the institutional human resources platform (SIRHN) and are thus available to all PEMEX staff, but they are particularly promoted among procurement officials.

Table 4.6. **PEMEX's seven e-learning courses**

Title and length	Objective
Module 1. Framework for PEMEX procurement	
Structure and procurement procedures under the PEMEX Law (9 hours)	Identify the regulatory framework applicable to PEMEX procurement in substantive activities.
Procurement under the PEMEX Law (4 hours)	Identify PEMEX's areas involved in procurement under its special procurement regime. Likewise, provide general and practical information to support the elaboration of the documents needed to carry out procurement procedures.
Module 2. Strategic supply	
Introduction to strategic supply (2 hours) Expenditure analysis in strategic supply (1.5 hours) Implementing the Strategic Supply Methodology (2 hours)	Identify the concepts and stages of the Strategic Supply Methodology to understand its importance to create value in the company, as well as to indicate the relevance of expenditure analysis.
Module 3. Preparatory contracts (*Contratos preparatorios*)	
Preparatory contracts (5 hours)	Define preparatory contracts; identify the different types, and their advantages. Likewise, discuss the agreement, management and implementation of preparatory contracts.
Module 4. Methodologies to assess proposals	
Methodologies to assess proposals (9 hours)	Discuss different methodologies to assess proposals to facilitate a comprehensive analysis, identify optimal criteria, and allow the selection of the proposal with the best conditions.

Source: Based on information provided by PEMEX.

Table 4.7 illustrates the progress made with regard to the implementation of the strategy "Professionalising to Transform" in DCPA concerning the e-learning courses.

Table 4.7. **PEMEX e-learning courses participation (as of August 2015)**

Area	Registered	Module 1: Approved	Module 2: Approved	Module 3: Approved	Module 4: Approved
Total DCPA	1 619	2 436	3 243	1 988	659
SGESMN	67	79	109	53	13
SRPC	21	26	26	0	0
SPA	1 427	2 159	2 911	1 914	642
PPI	104	172	197	21	4

Notes: Module 1 includes two courses; Module 2 includes three; Module 3 includes two; and Module 4 includes one.

SGESMN: Deputy Directorate for Strategy Management and Support to the Business Model

SRPC: Deputy Directorate for Suppliers and Contractors Development

SPA: Deputy directorates for procurement (Exploration and production, Industrial transformation, and Support services)

PPI: PEMEX Procurement International

Source: Based on information provided by PEMEX.

DCPA staff is also offered three additional courses on substance concerning strategic supply: Expenditure analysis (14 hours); Prioritising and selecting categories, stages of the methodology (15.5 hours); and Negotiation.

Training initiatives launched by DCPA have been directed towards both kinds of employees, *confianza* and unionised. However, there is no standard frequency for training to take place; it usually responds to requests by staff and their corresponding areas. Furthermore, the kinds of training that each type of employees needs will differ according to their activities. An additional weakness is the lack of training on integrity issues, particularly those related to procurement.

More incentives could be offered to employees who take training, for example, by linking such training with performance evaluation and certification of skills. Procurement officials are not certified, which hinders their opportunities for professional development. Certification could take place with the support of external entities, such as the National Institute for Public Administration (Instituto Nacional de Administración Pública, or INAP) or the National Council for Standardisation and Certification of Labour Skills (Consejo Nacional de Normalización y Certificación de Competencias Laborales, or CONOCER). Certification could include not only procurement management skills, but also commitment to ethics and integrity. Some OECD countries, such as Canada, Chile, and the United States have developed certification programmes for procurement staff (see Box 4.7). The main lesson for PEMEX is that certification helps define the key competencies of procurement professionals along with education and experience requirements.

While continuing to leverage the use of ICTs for training purposes, PEMEX should make courses available through different means and open up other topics, such as financial analysis of suppliers, analysis of supply and value chains, market research, managing suppliers, risk management, contract management, and so on. The use of ICTs is key to increasing the supply and coverage of training activities while making it cost-efficient, particularly to reach out to staff located outside of PEMEX headquarters, such as those in CAPAs.

Above all, it is important to avoid having isolated training courses, but to pursue comprehensive training programmes for procurement officials. Training should be seen as an important element to improve and develop capabilities and skills in procurement, prepare public servants for positions at higher levels of responsibility and certify their capabilities. In order to make better use of training facilities, PEMEX could develop a broad framework for providing training in procurement – but it is important that training is established by line managers together with employees. This would foster accountability for managers to ensure career development for their employees. The objectives of all learning activities (workshops, courses, seminars) should be based on the development of specific competencies required for the procurement function.

Box 4.7. Certification of procurement officials in Canada, Chile and the United States

Canada: The Procurement, Materiel Management and Real Property Communities Management Office (PMMRP CMO) promotes professionalism in over 16 000 public service employees who work in procurement, material management, and real property. The Communities Management Office provides programmes and services for the development of individual members, as well as for the communities as a whole. These programmes and services are provided in collaboration with departments and agencies, and through agreements with the Canada School of Public Service for the training component and with the Canadian General Standards Board for the Certification Programme.

Community members have access to the Certification Program for the Federal Government Procurement and Materiel Management Communities; competency suites for each community that describe proficiency in a particular job function in terms of knowledge, skills and abilities, including procurement competencies; competency-based guides designed to help build and strengthen individuals' proficiency levels for each of the core competencies; and workshops, learning events, and a curriculum of classroom and online training available from the Canada School of Public Service.

Chile: The Chilean acquisition workforce is composed of 13 000 officials scattered throughout the territory. They need ongoing training, which is delivered as follows:

- The first level corresponds to a basic mandatory training designed for new procurement officials. It includes an induction into public procurement regulation and to the use of ICT procurement systems. This training is provided via e-learning.
- The second level includes workshops covering primary topics such as calls for tenders, non-competitive procurement, framework agreements, and contract management. There is a high demand to participate in this workshop as it helps participants prepare for the certification test.
- The certification test is mandatory for every civil servant with a login and password in the procurement system. This certification evaluates basic knowledge and skills. Contracting officials must re-certificate every two years. Contracting officials cannot procure without having proper clearance through this certification process.
- The third level corresponds to advanced training courses, which involve more complex topics and target specific audiences. This level has a smaller scope than the previous ones.

United States: The American Purchasing Society (APS) is a professional association of buyers and purchasing managers. It was the first organisation to establish a nationally recognised certification for buyers and purchasing professionals. APS offers four different certification programmes: 1) the Certified Purchasing Professional programme directed at professionals who have demonstrated the skills to successfully implement improved purchasing and supply chain practices as part of a business solution in an organisation; 2) the Certified Professional Purchasing Manager programme, aimed at those in managerial positions and who have managerial experience; 3) the Certified Green Purchasing Professional; and 4) the Certified Professional Purchasing Consultant programme, aimed at Certified Purchasing Professionals who either consult or teach purchasing to people outside their own employer.

Source: Treasury Board Secretariat (n. d.), www.tbs-sct.gc.ca/pd-pp/index-eng.asp (accessed on 27 March 2016); OECD (2013), *Public Procurement Review of the Mexican Institute of Social Security: Enhancing Efficiency and Integrity for Better Health Care*, OECD Public Governance Reviews, OECD Publishing, http://dx.doi.org/10.1787/9789264197480-en; American Purchasing Society (2016), "Certification programs", webpage, www.american-purchasing.com/page.php?PageID=6 (accessed 27 March 2016).

Proposals for action

- PEMEX could engage in strategic workforce planning to facilitate monitoring of the numbers, costs, and competencies of staff, as well as align the future needs of human capital with the strategies of the company. Strategic workforce planning should also help address identified gaps and strengthen the strategic role of the procurement function in the transformation of PEMEX.
- PEMEX could enhance the co-operation and communication between DCPA and CAPAs in order to build procurement capacities through the sharing of good practices and the management and training of staff.
- PEMEX could execute, in a participative manner, the change management strategy for the implementation of its centralised procurement model and the alignment of the HR function.
- PEMEX could develop a competency management framework to identify the skills and behaviours required for procurement staff to carry out its job effectively. Job profiling is also an element to set the foundations of a new procurement profession in PEMEX.
- PEMEX could strengthen the HR Unit of the Corporate Directorate for Administration and Services and engage it in the processes related to procurement staff (i.e. recruitment, selection, career planning). Bringing HR expertise into DCPA would make its processes more transparent, sophisticated and reliable.
- PEMEX could provide recruitment processes with more transparency and flexibility on the basis of merit and competencies. This entails opening vacant managerial positions up for competition, allowing internal and external applicants. Fair processes should be the mechanism to open opportunities for employees with procurement experience to move up in the hierarchy of the company.
- PEMEX could introduce a performance management system and hold senior management accountable for performance. This entails setting performance objectives and implementing staff performance management frameworks in all HR tools and processes, including job profiling, recruitment, selection and continuous evaluation.
- PEMEX could step up systematic and comprehensive training to procurement staff, initially concentrating on the most critical weaknesses. Different training means, including the use of ICTs, should be facilitated, particularly for CAPAs. The professionalisation of the procurement function could also be supported through the certification of skills and competencies of officials.
- PEMEX could advance a system of secondments for procurement officials to public and private institutions in order to develop their skills and facilitate career advancement, as well as to bring in external expertise. Currently, secondments are not promoted.

Notes

1. For more information, see www.pemex.com/saladeprensa/boletines_nacionales/Paginas/2016-015-nacional.aspx.
2. The two latter instruments can be found at www.pemex.com/acerca/informes_publicaciones/Paginas/default.aspx (accessed 14 March 2016).
3. The Professional Civil Service Law, issued in April 2003, regulates the organisation, operation, and development of the civil service scheme for the central public administration.

References

American Purchasing Society (2016), "Certification programs", webpage, www.american-purchasing.com/page.php?PageID=6 (accessed 27 March 2016).

Hamande, Jack (2015), "EUPAN" , presentation from FPS P&O Belgium before the Learning Team Human Resources and Administration of the European Public Administration Network (EUPAN LTHRA).

Huerta Melchor, O. (2008), "Managing change in OECD governments: An introductory framework", *OECD Working Papers on Public Governance*, No. 12, OECD Publishing, Paris, http://dx.doi.org/10.1787/227141782188.

OECD (2015), "Recommendation of the Council on Public Procurement", www.oecd.org/corruption/recommendation-on-public-procurement.htm.

OECD (2013), *Public Procurement Review of the Mexican Institute of Social Security: Enhancing Efficiency and Integrity for Better Health Care*, OECD Public Governance Reviews, OECD Publishing, http://dx.doi.org/10.1787/9789264197480-en.

OECD (2010), "Making Reform Happen: Lessons from OECD Countries", OECD Publishing, Paris. http://dx.doi.org/10.1787/9789264086296-en

Office of Personnel Management (n. d.), www.opm.gov (accessed 16 March 2016).

PEMEX (Petróleos Mexicanos) (2015), "Trabaja en Pemex", webpage, www.pemex.com/acerca/recursos-humanos/Paginas/Trabaja-en-Pemex.aspx (accessed 14 March 2016).

PEMEX (2015), "Centros de Atención de Procura y Abastecimiento", presentation provided by PEMEX.

PEMEX (2014a), *Anuario Estadístico 2014*, PEMEX, www.pemex.com/ri/Publicaciones/Anuario%20Estadistico%20Archivos/2014_ae_00_vc_e.pdf (accessed 14 March 2016).

PEMEX (2014b), "Estrategia Integral de Gestión del Cambio para fortalecer la adopción y operación de la DCPA", DCPA January.

Treasury Board Secretariat (2009), "Management Accountability Framework", www.tbs-sct.gc.ca/hgw-cgf/oversight-surveillance/maf-crg/index-eng.asp (accessed 22 March 2016).

Treasury Board Secretariat (n. d.), www.tbs-sct.gc.ca/pd-pp/index-eng.asp (accessed on 27 March 2016).

Chapter 5

Ensuring clarity and minimising procurement risks in Petróleos Mexicanos through strong tender documents and model contracts

This chapter assesses the strengths and weaknesses of the template tendering documents and contracts used by PEMEX. It further explores the novelties of the new generic model contracts and whether PEMEX has been able to streamline the development process for solicitation documents and model contracts according the legislative reforms. Potential improvements to the template contracts are proposed to increase certainty and reduce risks in PEMEX procurement activities.

Reform of solicitation documents and model contracts

As alluded to in previous chapters the regulatory reforms implemented in 2014-15 allow Petróleos Mexicanos (or PEMEX) to contract goods and services in a more commercially oriented environment; excluding exceptions, its contracts will be fully governed by commercial law in accordance with Article 80 of the PEMEX Law. These new general contracting provisions, which are now in effect, have replaced the former administrative contracting provisions. The new general contracting provisions govern the procurement and contracting of PEMEX and its subsidiary productive enterprises. They include, among others, rules and regulations on bidding processes, exemptions from the bidding process, the publication of projects and contracts to be awarded in a given calendar year, required features of all contracts and different types of dispute resolution mechanisms. One of the fundamental changes resulting from the new general provisions for tendering is the elimination of the unilateral administrative rescission that characterised the general scheme of the Act on Public Works and Related Services. In the model contracts, there is a provision permitting both parties the right to terminate prior to judicial declaration being made.

The new legal framework must be applicable to any public procurement procedure under which PEMEX is to contract with private and public bodies. Tendering documents comprising comprehensive rules on the three most relevant phases of the tendering process (invitation to tender; evaluation; and award) tend to privilege competition between bidders and are likely to ensure a level playing field as well as transparency and integrity in contracting procedures (OECD, 2009). It seems to be that contractual terms in the PEMEX documents are structured in compliance with the regulatory framework applicable to the process of procurement and supply. For the purpose of clarifying doubts so that potential tenderers have the necessary information to make a decision on whether to participate in the tender or not.

The OECD Recommendation on Public Procurement (2015) encourages a coherent and stable institutional, legal and regulatory framework to increase business as it is the key starting point to assure sustainable and efficient public procurement systems (see Box 5.1). Creating clear and integrated tender documents, standardised where possible and proportionate to the size and complexity of the procurement, should encourage broad participation from potential competitors, including new entrants and small and medium-sized enterprises.

Consistent and systematic use of strong templates of contractual documents provides clarity, security and consistency to both the buying organisation and the marketplace, and reduces risks in the contractual process. Hence, it is important to analyse whether the template contract and tendering documents developed by the relevant entities comply with the applicable legislation, have a sound structure and provide the required clarity. The purpose of this chapter is to undertake the assessment of the template contractual documents currently used by PEMEX for the acquisition of goods and services, through the different perspectives referred to above, and to provide some proposals for action to increase the results of PEMEX's contracting procedures.

Box 5.1. The OECD Recommendation on Public Procurement on access to procurement

1. **RECOMMENDS** that Adherents facilitate access to procurement opportunities for potential competitors of all sizes.

To this end, Adherents should:

1. **Have in place coherent and stable institutional, legal and regulatory frameworks,** which are essential to increase participation in doing business with the public sector and are key starting points to assure sustainable and efficient public procurement systems. These frameworks should:
    1. be as clear and simple as possible
    2. avoid including requirements which duplicate or conflict with other legislation or regulation
    3. treat bidders, including foreign suppliers, in a fair, transparent and equitable manner, taking into account Adherents' international commitments (e.g. the Agreement on Government Procurement within the framework of the World Trade Organization, the European Union Procurement Directives, and bilateral or multilateral trade agreements).
2. **Deliver clear and integrated tender documentation, standardised where possible and proportionate to the need,** to ensure that:
    1. Specific tender opportunities are designed so as to encourage broad participation from potential competitors, including new entrants and small and medium-sized enterprises. This requires providing clear guidance to inform buyers' expectations (including specifications and contract as well as payment terms) and binding information about evaluation and award criteria and their weights (whether they are focused specifically on price, include elements of price/quality ratio or support secondary policy objectives).
    2. The extent and complexity of information required in tender documentation and the time allotted for suppliers to respond is proportionate to the size and complexity of the procurement, taking into account any exigent circumstances such as emergency procurement.

Source: OECD (2015), "Recommendation of the Council on Public Procurement", www.oecd.org/corruption/recommendation-on-public-procurement.htm.

The legislative framework for solicitation document and contract models

One of the main goals of the constitutional reform in the energy sector promoted by the Federal Executive, was to provide PEMEX with operational flexibility and administrative simplicity, through the new regulatory framework on procurement contracts, leases, works and services; so that the new contractual terms could incorporate premises based on simplicity, flexibility and value creation. The PEMEX Act 2014 is a fundamental change to the previous regulatory framework that was put in place with the 2008 PEMEX Law. All the new contracts will be created in a mercantile environment; before they were all of an administrative nature. PEMEX now works on equal terms with the suppliers and they now have similar legal recourses to PEMEX. The new framework has led to changes being made to solicitation documents and model contracts. The model contracts that were founded on the previous framework, sometimes called institutional model contracts will cease to exist and new model contracts, generic model contracts will be incorporated into the procurement process. The generic models will be introduced in 2016. The contracts are being presented almost 18 months after the introduction of the PEMEX Act, due to the fact that the subsidiary companies of PEMEX were not created until November 2015.

In December 2013 the Mexican Constitution was modified[1] with the purpose of reforming the energy sector. Article 134 of the Mexican Constitution, which sets the legal basis for public procurement in Mexico,[2] the PEMEX Act and its implementing regulation define the general principles for the new public procurement regime in PEMEX. Public procurement activities were reorganised and on the basis of this reform, a new set of rules on procurement were adopted for PEMEX (Ley de Petróleos Mexicanos) on 11 August 2014 and its implementing regulation (Reglamento de la Ley de Petróleos Mexicanos) on 31 October 2014. As a state productive company, PEMEX will no longer apply the general public procurement laws.[3]

The main legal requirements of PEMEX covering both the solicitation process of documents and the development of model contracts include:

- The Mexican Constitution (Constitución Política de los Estados Unidos Mexicanos)
- Free Trade Agreements that are subject to purchasing provisions (Tratados de Libre Comercio en los que México sea parte en lo correspondiente al Capítulo de Compras)
- PEMEX Act (Ley de Petróleos Mexicanos)
- Regulations (Su Reglamento)
- General Contracting Provisions for PEMEX and its subsidiary companies (Disposiciones Generales de Contratación para Petróleos Mexicanos y sus Empresas Productivas Subsidiarias)
- General Guidelines for Procurement and Supply (Lineamientos Generales de Procura y Abastecimiento)
- Policies and Guidelines for Procurement and Supply (Políticas y Lineamientos para Procura y Abastecimiento).

Article 134 of the Mexican Constitution is mainly referred to in the solicitations documents and model contracts. Articles 75 and 77 of the PEMEX Act illustrate the general framework for procurement, i.e. reference to Article 134 in the Mexican Constitution and some other key principles like effectiveness, efficiency and results that PEMEX has to adhere to. Article 77 also refers to some key principles in addition to providing the authorisation to choose specific procurement methods under certain circumstances. Article 11 of the General Contracting Provisions (the "Provisions") categorises procurement methods available to PEMEX, i.e. open tendering, restricted invitation and direct awards. Article 25 is quite detailed in the sense it stipulates the information needed to enable interested parties to decide on their participation in the contest. These are issues that need to be, among other things, included in solicitation documents and model contracts; they describe the complexity and magnitude of the procurement process. Article 38 of the Provisions refers specifically to model contracts and how the terms are supposed to be based on the nature and purpose of a contract. The article allows for adaptability content wise but requires a specific framework for the contract to be maintained.

The General Guidelines for Procurement and Supply specify that the requirements and contents of the contractual terms must be appropriate to the requirements and nature of the procurement and the implemented strategy, aiming to simplify these documents. These contractual documents are subject to the PEMEX Act, PEMEX Regulation and the Provisions. The reform of the legislative framework has provided the company with more freedom in the field of procurement than it used to have under the previous legislative regime. The model contract is prepared considering the provisions needed for model contracts, which are developed as outlined in Article 6 of the Provisions by a project manager. The contracting model will include at least according to the type of contract, the identification of risks linked to the project, procurement process and execution of contracts, prevention and mitigation of risks, as well as the concentration of contracts in a single supplier or contractor based on the nature, scale and complexity of the object of the contract. Furthermore, contracts need to be in accordance with Free Trade Agreements, containing a chapter on government procurement that have been adopted by the Mexican government.

Towards a new framework: Assessment of the solicitation documents and model contracts used in PEMEX

The lawfulness of solicitation documents and their compliance with the applicable legislation constitutes the first step towards a transparent awarding procedure. Considering the volume and diversity of public contracts to be awarded and the known vulnerability of procurement systems to corruption and fraud, the rule of law in the context of public procurement is of the utmost importance to assure sustainable and efficient public procurement systems.[4] Tender documents and model contracts that do not contravene the applicable legislation provide for a higher degree of transparency while granting a sound level of legal certainty to tenderers.

For the purpose of this review, the following contractual documents were assessed:

- five template contracts (hereafter referred to as the "model contracts") provided by PEMEX, applicable with the PEMEX Act, PEMEX Regulation, Provisions and General Guidelines for Procurement and Supply
- three actual solicitation documents associated with public tendering under the applicable PEMEX Act, PEMEX Regulation and the Provisions
- one signed version of an open contract for the acquisition of goods entered into by PEMEX Exploration under the applicable PEMEX legislation.

All tender documents assessed have more or less the same general contents. While there are between 20 and 30 clauses in the solicitation document, some of the terms are further developed in annexes. These annexes provide, for example, details on how to present a joint bid, the form and terms of performance bonds, and the clear description of the quality and characteristics of the goods, rentals and services being acquired. This use of annexes completing and complementing the solicitation documents has the virtue of offering a more comprehensive tender framework, which strongly details the most relevant features of the awarding procedure, and therefore of increasing its transparency. Also, it is a standard to have an annex on PACMA, the "Support Program for Communities and the Environment".

The terms of the solicitation documents provide the prospective bidders with a reasonable and sufficient set of tender rules ordering the relevant aspects of the tender procedure. The fact that all analysed solicitation documents contain similar provisions and follow the same format, as opposed to the use of several different and diffuse solicitation documents for the awarding of objectively similar contracts, strengthens PEMEX's procurement procedures. By pursuing uniform tender procedures PEMEX is building the foundations that could lead to a specialisation of its employees. It allows prospective bidders to better prepare themselves to participate in PEMEX tenders by referring to their previous experiences and participation in different tenders launched by PEMEX. A thorough review of PEMEX solicitation documents shows that they are generally in line with the relevant terms of the applicable legislation, with no particular flaws identified. Most importantly, they contain all the elements required by the Provisions (Article 25) to be included in tender invitations. Before 2014, solicitation documents under the applicable PEMEX legislation could be quite different from solicitation document under the Law of Acquisitions, Leasing and Services of the Public Sector (LAASSP).

The regulatory framework requires PEMEX to use the binary approach in the awarding process. The approach is operationalised in two phases, the first using solely mandatory requirements to narrow the field of bidders. The second stage can include several different award criteria:

1. lowest price
2. equivalent annual cost
3. points or percentages
4. cost-benefit
5. net present value
6. cost total equivalent
7. life-cycle cost
8. auction
9. price negotiation.

In the past PEMEX has mainly used the lowest price criteria for public works and points and percentages for service contracts. The most commonly used method during the second stage is still the lowest price, however with the change in regulation there is an intention to use other methods in the future.

All reviewed solicitation documents include the template version of the contract, which is fundamental for a transparent procurement system. It guarantees that the contract is in line with both the relevant legislation and the terms of the tender invitation (if not, the bidders may immediately challenge its terms), and that all bidders will be executing the agreement under the same general terms.

The OECD Secretariat reviewed the five model contracts against the relevant terms of the applicable legislation, considering, among others, the following:

- obligations and liability of the parties
- basis and method of payment

- inspection, acceptance and warranty
- dispute resolution mechanisms
- pre-established damages and penalties
- adequate provision for a clear description of the goods or services to be provided by the contractor
- intellectual property
- subcontracting
- replacement of contractor personnel
- transfer of ownership
- termination clauses
- performance guarantee.

The review showed that the model contracts are more or less in line with the relevant terms of the applicable legislation. However, gaps were identified, that if closed could improve the contracts per se if more effort were put into clarifying such issues as dispute resolution mechanism, termination clauses and transfer of ownership. With a new legislative framework associated with model contracts, the requirements have changed and they are not as detailed as the applicable LAASSP legislation. The new PEMEX Act does not require that associated contracts include a clause on the negotiation of the transfer and awarding of the relevant intellectual property rights arising out of the contract to PEMEX, as the previous legislation did. PEMEX has however decided to continue to include a clause on this issue in all generic contracts.

Signed contract aligned with model contracts

A rigorous framework for model contracts will benefit organisation to the extent to which they are adhered to in actual procurement activities, so a comparison with actual contracts awarded is appropriate to identify eventual deviations, flaws and improvements. PEMEX has provided one signed contract to be reviewed by the OECD. The comparison with model contracts should provide an indication of the extent to which the latter are adhered to at time of contract award. The review has identified a significant level of coherence between the two sets of documents. No substantial or material deviations have been found that could affect the transparency or legality of the awarded contract. Furthermore, a common structure between the model contracts and the contract is clearly traceable; not only are the most relevant clauses being replicated, but also in the contract annexes. The main difference lies in the number annexes, which are fewer in the model contracts. The main explanation lies in the number of specification annexes related to the subject in the signed contract. The description of the goods set forth in the annexes of the contract evaluated is fairly exhaustive and technically clear.

Identification of potential improvements to the model contracts: The transitional phase 2014-16

The assessment of the capability of the model contracts used in PEMEX resides in the evaluation of their strengths, weaknesses and risks by comparing them with relevant benchmarking legislations and good practices. It was found as a result of said review that the current provisions of the model contracts present some interesting strengths. However, opportunities remain for PEMEX to improve its contracts. With the new generic model contracts, some of those issues will be addressed but they have yet to be implemented. The development of model contracts is not solely for the purpose of ensuring clarity and equity throughout the procurement process but can also clarify internal procedures and communication between the supplier and the contracting authority (see Box 5.2).

Box 5.2. Government model contracts in New Zealand

The New Zealand Ministry of Business, Innovation and Employment (MBIE) has developed a set of standard conditions of contract for routine government purchases. These conditions are called government model contracts (GMCs).

The Second Edition GMCs were launched by MBIE in October 2011, replacing the First Edition GMCs, launched in July 2010.

The development and implementation of GMCs is part of the Government Procurement Reform Programme and was mandated by a Cabinet Directive requiring MBIE to:

"... create a standard, simple, plain English set of conditions of contract for common goods and services to be used by all Public Service Departments and State Services."

The GMCs are aimed at low-value, low-risk common goods and services. They have been designed as the default government contract. It is up to each agency using the GMCs to determine what constitutes low-value, low-risk common goods and services. This definition is subjective and will depend on the size of the agency and the scale and complexity of its procurement function. Through the use of GMCs across the Public Service and State Services, the New Zealand government aims to:

- provide simple, plain English contracts that are easy to use for both agencies and suppliers
- provide a fairer balance of risk between buyer and supplier
- standardise the treatment of legal risk in low-value, low-risk contracts
- reduce the need for negotiations and legal advice in routine purchases
- promote consistent practice across government
- promote process efficiencies in high-volume, low-value transactional contracting
- simplify doing business with government
- support improved procurement practice and align with international best practice.

Source: Information provided by Grant Lyons, Manager Collaborative Procurement, New Zealand Government Procurement, Ministry of Business, Innovation and Employment. Also see New Zealand Government Procurement (2016), "Government Model Contracts", webpage, www.business.govt.nz/procurement/for-agencies/government-model-contracts#Background.

Intellectual property

The main legal framework for PEMEX does not include detailed clauses on the subject of intellectual property rights. Article 38 of the Provisions necessitates that there be a term on intellectual property rights in the model contracts. All the model contracts reviewed included per se clauses and most of them the same reference prohibiting suppliers under any circumstances from using for commercial, advertising or any other purposes, the name PEP, PEMEX and/or any of its subsidiaries productive enterprises and/or its subsidiaries, logos or any other sign or symbol distinctive property. The rights of suppliers to retain copyright and other intellectual property rights of the deliverables are clearly stated in the model contracts, as well as the rights specifying that the ownership lies with PEMEX. The issue of "locked-in" with a single supplier has not been an issue for PEMEX as it has been allowed to use a much larger level of information created under the resulting contracts (including technical drawing and specifications) in future activities without the risk of litigation. This potentially allows PEMEX to obtain better value later through competition.

Obligations and liabilities

The breakdown of obligations and liabilities between PEMEX and private contractors overall appears to be well balanced under the model contracts. Notably, the transfer of risks is in line with the experience of OECD countries. Liabilities are determined on a case-by-case basis and it is common that they are capped to the contract price, but this limit is not applied in case of negligence or misconduct. The contractor is fully liable for third-party damages and lost profits (*daños y perjuicios*), including environmental damages. Under Mexican law, damages have to be direct. There are no indirect or consequential damages. The PEMEX Act requires that associated contracts have clear dispositions on the parties' contractual liabilities, further stipulating that the project manager must foresee in all contracts a statute determining the liabilities (and the respective limits) of each party in accordance to the risk profile of the contract.

Basis and method of payment

The model contracts may contain an advance payment regime, which is reasonable and in line with the PEMEX Guidelines. Such payments are only allowed when specified in the contract. In the model contracts there is either a clause permitting advance payment or not. It depends on the objective, purpose, length of solicitation period, duration of the contract, etc. It also depends on the market environment, whether there is scarcity in the market, new suppliers, few suppliers, etc. The evidence gathered will contribute to the analysis and final decision on whether to allow advance payment. Before the new PEMEX Act, the use of advance payment was more frequent. It is now more controlled as it is carried out in a more centralised manner.

It is clear in every solicitation document which costs are included or excluded. The model contracts could be more conclusive regarding whether value-added tax (VAT) is to be added to the contracted price or not. Furthermore, the majority of the model contracts have a specific clause on insurance, whereby it is merely stated that the contracting of insurance policies is the contractor's responsibility, leaving doubts about the specific time until which it has that obligation (this issue being further complicated by the unclear timing of transfer of ownership, as discussed later). PEMEX could consider reviewing the applicable model contracts to ensure full clarity on the timing of the responsibilities of each party and on whether and when the associated elements of costs are included and excluded from the contract price, reducing the confusion and risk of dispute between the parties.

Under the previous legislation, mandatory price reviews were limited to public works contracts. The new regime foresees mandatory price reviews for multi-year contracts for public works, services and goods. The price reviews may be motivated by the adoption of technological developments or by market price variations of the equipment being used in the contract's execution.

Subcontracting rules

While the PEMEX Act has no provisions on subcontracting, the Provisions encompass clauses relating to subcontracting, the most relevant being Article 25, which requires solicitation documents to include terms of subcontracting, and Article 38, which requires all model contracts to include a chapter on subcontracting. The only other reference can be identified in Article 44 in the contracts of services for exploration and extraction, there it states that it is forbidden to subcontract the management of activities under the contract for exploration. All PEMEX model contracts specify, in accordance with the applicable PEMEX legislation, that the contractor cannot transfer, in part or in totality, these rights and obligations without prior and written approval from PEMEX.

The five model contracts include clauses on subcontracting in accordance with the legislative framework. The content is developed on a case-by-case basis; under certain circumstances subcontracting has been considered specifically as part of the work in the solicitation process and in others it is more unforeseen subcontracting and requested by the contractor after the contract has been awarded. The majority of the model contracts include a provision allowing subcontracting. It is important to have clear guidelines for subcontracting as loose subcontracting rules may jeopardise the integrity of a contract if the winning bidder subcontracts a significant portion of the contract in order to reduce its costs or as part of a collusion agreement (OECD, 2005). The opportunity, however, to subcontract a share of a public contract is an important prerogative of a procurement system aimed at encouraging the involvement of small and medium-sized enterprises in the public contracts procurement market (see the US example in Box 5.3). Allowing subcontracting does not only promote the development of that important sector of the economy but also increases the level of competition in public procurement.

PEMEX could consider aligning the subcontracting provisions in all relevant model contracts in order to clarify the subcontracting rules, especially as it relates to the possibilities and conditions of subcontracts not considered in the initial contract. Doing so would increase clarity for suppliers, while setting forth sufficient checks and balances and increasing transparency and integrity in the procurement process. There are conducive examples in PEMEX model contracts that should be included in most contracts; the clauses refer to the need for suppliers that wish to replace subcontractors to request permission from a project area administration. Also in relating to responsibility, a clause referring to the supplier being solely responsible for the obligations of the contract and that subcontractor have no recourse or any right to assert claims against PEMEX.

Box 5.3. Small business subcontracting in the United States

As an additional method of encouraging participation by small businesses in federal contracting opportunities, the United States has implemented a mandatory Small Business Subcontracting Program. For contracts or contract modifications that contain subcontracting opportunities, the supplier selected for award is required to submit a detailed subcontracting plan. Failure to submit a subcontracting plan renders the supplier ineligible for award, and any contractor or subcontractor that fails to comply in good faith with the requirements of the subcontracting plan is considered in material breach of its contract. The requirement for a subcontracting plan does not apply when the selected supplier is itself a small business, to personal services contracts, or to contracts performed entirely outside of the United States (FAR 19.702).

Each subcontracting plan must include:

1. separate percentage goals for small business, veteran-owned small business, disabled-veteran-owned small business, HUBZone small business, small disadvantaged business and women-owned small business concerns as subcontractors
2. a statement of the total dollars planned to be subcontracted and the total dollars planned to be subcontracted to the categories of concerns identified in (1)
3. a description of the principal types of supplies and services to be subcontracted, including identification of the types to be subcontracted to the relevant concerns
4. a description of the method used to develop the subcontracting goals
5. a description of the method used to identify potential sources for solicitation purposes
6. a statement as to whether indirect cost considerations were included in the establishment of goals and estimated share of subcontracts
7. the name of an individual who will administer the subcontracting program, and a description of the duties of the individual;
8. a description of the efforts the offeror will make to ensure that relevant suppliers have an equitable opportunity to compete for the subcontracts
9. assurances that the offeror will include the clause that mandates the Small Business Subcontracting Program in all subcontracts that offer further subcontracting opportunities and require any such subcontracts that exceed USD 650 000 to include their own small business subcontracting plan
10. assurances that the offeror will co-operate in any surveys, studies and reporting requirements necessary
11. a description of the types of records that will be maintained concerning procedures adopted to comply with the requirements and goals in the plan.

Source: US Government (n. d.), "Subpart 19.7—The Small Business Subcontracting Program", United States Federal Acquisition Regulation 48 CFR 19.7, www.acquisition.gov/sites/default/files/current/far/html/Subpart%2019_7.html#wp1088741.

Transfer of ownership

The transfer of ownership of the acquired goods is not being clearly dealt with in the legislation. Model contracts contain several rules that are generally in one way or another connected with the transfer of ownership of the acquired goods (such as acceptance of goods, liability and responsibility for all costs until delivery, documents to be presented upon payment, coverage of relevant insurance policy, substitution of defective goods, etc.). There is not a direct, clear and undisputed clause stating that as from a given date or event, the goods become PEMEX's property. The transfer of ownership of acquired goods is specified in the clause "Time and Place of Delivery", which under the terms established by PEMEX in the respective contract, states how the goods to be delivered by the supplier to PEMEX will become part of the assets and/or assets of Mexican oil. The transfer of ownership of property acquired by PEMEX is given at the time of delivery or on the terms of their respective contracts. In addition, its scope is contained in the technical annexes that form part of it.

Inspection, acceptance and warranty

The statutes on inspection, acceptance and warranty could be made more comprehensive in the PEMEX Act. However, the model contracts analysed determined that the goods are subject to an inspection and sufficiently cover the right to return/replace products that do not meet the contractual requirements. However, for contracts requiring testing of the acquired goods after installation, additional clarity could be introduced as to the nature of the specific verifications and tests to be done and the associated respective responsibilities and liability of each party (especially as it relates to the contractor's obligations should any test be failed). The new generic models will include a clause that states that goods that do not meet requirements can be replaced and returned.

Furthermore, the model contracts could be amended to clearly state that the first inspection is to occur upon delivery of the goods and that formal reception is only to take place if the goods are approved under subsequent technical inspections and testing. PEMEX could consider including in the clause on reception of goods a paragraph referring to a written "confirmation of delivery, reception, installation, start up and operation" being provided when formal reception is concluded. There is no written notice in the model contracts, but in the annexes to model contracts there are clauses specifying date for testing, completion of work, etc. The model contract could incorporate clear provisions governing the timeframe within which the private contractors are liable for the integrity and quality of the goods or services rendered. A specific timeframe should be reflected in the contracts for the benefit of legal certainty.

Dispute resolution mechanisms

None of the model contracts mentioned the possibility of arbitration in some situations or the provisions to be used if such an approach is selected. Dispute resolution mechanisms may enhance some suppliers' confidence. PEMEX has decided to make it optional to include arbitration provisions in the new generic model contracts. Contrary to an established practice in some OECD countries, none of the model contracts includes provisions indicating that, in case of dispute, the contractor is not allowed to stop performance under the contract before a decision has been passed. While such an approach prevents delays in the procuring agency fulfilling its requirements, it is important that such provisions include a right for the contractor to be compensated for associated damages should the decision be in its favour. The generic model contracts will include provisions indicating that, in case of dispute, the contractor is not allowed to stop performance under the contract before a decision has been passed. The contractor will also continue to receive payment throughout this period as long as he continues with his work. This signifies a change in policy but is not founded in the regulatory framework. It is encouraging that the model contracts encompass wide-ranging clauses on the prevention of disputes and on the resolution of disagreements, including conciliation mechanism. This results in a reduction in the occurrence of judicial litigations and saves time and money for both parties.

Termination

The model contracts include the various provisions for contract termination required by the regulatory framework, such as for contractor's default of the contractual provisions, public interest or a force majeure. PEMEX used to have the right to rescind the contract without the need to obtain a court decision. That is not the case with the new legal framework. In the new generic models all contracts will include a termination clause allowing the suppliers to terminate the contract as a consequence of a grave default by PEMEX.

PEMEX could consider extending the use of that clause to other model contracts, adapting it as needed. The existence of stipulations allowing the private party to terminate the contract as a consequence of a grave default by PEMEX and entitling the private entity to compensation could induce greater confidence in the public procurement system. This would result in the emergence of more bidders and broader competition, ultimately improving the transparency of the procedures and better value for money in the contracts. This is traditionally particularly important in international contracts based on foreign investment.

In accordance with the regulatory framework, PEMEX is allowed to choose to grant a remedy period to the private contractor in the event of default. While this is praised as being in line with a common practice in many countries, it may be appropriate for PEMEX to reduce the current level of case-by-case discretion under some non-standard or complex contracts. This could be achieved by automatically providing such a remedy period in situations pre-established under each specific contract (when deemed appropriate). It order to ensure visibility and understanding of that possibility, PEMEX could consider including optional clauses in its model contracts under the PEMEX Act identifying pre-established situations that may be appropriate.

Replacement of contractor personnel

Depending on the nature and complexity of the requirement to be met, the experience and qualification of the individual providing part of the work may be of utmost importance. This is particularly true for some complex service requirements required by PEMEX, such as the exploration and production contracts (integrated EP contracts). In such instances, these elements can form part of the proposal evaluation and the associated individual may be identified by name in the resulting contract(s). In accordance to what was agreed in the respective contract, associated provisions can be found in model contracts annexes that state that in the event of replacement of personnel the contractor needs prior authorisation and approval from PEMEX. It is the role of the project manager to assess and determine that the employees have the proper qualification in accordance with the contract in case of changes to personnel.

Pre-established damages

The model contracts analysed include a provision addressing the terms and conditions applicable to the enforcement of contractual fines on account of delay in the delivery of the goods or execution of the services. Pursuant to Article 38 of the new PEMEX Act, the associated contracts shall encompass a provision setting forth the terms, conditions and proceedings applicable to the enforcement of contractual fines on account of non-compliance with specified performance indicators and on account of negative environmental impact of the execution of the contract by the contractor.

If relevant contractual conditions are employed, under the premise of who generates the damage it is obliged to repair in accordance with the provisions of Article 1910 of the Federal Civil Code. Coupled with environmental legislation, it obliges that the one who causes the damage in an area is to clean it up and leave it in the state it was in before the damage occurred. Similarly, even though these model contracts foresee the implementation of penalties due to environmental damages, there is no densification of this matter. PEMEX could consider clarifying under which terms and to what extent penalties could be implemented due to environmental issues.

PEMEX planning to introduce new generic model contracts reflecting various requirements and circumstances, and reducing the risks of inadequate use of optional clauses

In the past PEMEX has been confronted with various risks relating to optional clauses being inappropriately used in contracts (such as arbitration provisions for short-term services contracts). The new legal framework for PEMEX has provided it with an opportunity to tackle these issues. The legal department has developed 13 generic model contracts that will replace the current institutional contracts. Each of them has their own optional clauses and will be subject to the negotiation process that will now take place between PEMEX and the supplier under the new legal regime. The centralisation of the procurement function should also help mitigate the risk of optional clauses being introduced. In addition, most models of contract are made by the Legal Department and are a function of the nature, complexity and scope of the contract.

During the OECD fact-finding mission, PEMEX representatives discussed some of the most significant changes to the model contracts. Among them are steps taken to include arbitration provisions that were foreseen as an optional clause in previous model contracts. Within the new model contracts, PEMEX will have the ability to define alternative dispute resolution mechanisms based on international best practices. There will be an optional clause regarding dispute settlement prior to a specific and contractual procedure agreed between the parties, such as direct consultation, conciliation, negotiation, mediation and dispute resolution panel. The choice of method can depend on the nature, scope and magnitude of recruitment as well as the characteristics of the supplier and contractor.

In older model contracts, clauses covering the possibility of termination as a consequence of grave default by PEMEX and entitling the private entity to compensation were considered as optional clauses. The generic model contracts will provide a clause related to the "Early Termination for breach of the parties" in accordance with corporate law. Furthermore, PEMEX didn't in the older model contract have optional clauses in its model contracts identifying pre-established situations that may grant a remedy period to the private contractor in the event of default. In the new model contracts there will be a clause related to waiting periods, grace or courtesy to the fulfilment of contractual obligations of the supplier/contractor. Once the application of penalties is exhausted, PEMEX can proceed with the application of the termination clause of the contract.

Proposals for action

The PEMEX tender documents and template contracts that the OECD Secretariat analysed are fairly advanced. The documents, if correctly enforced, generally provide a reasonable level of impartiality, competition and integrity. The new public procurement regime has taken steps to centralise and standardise for PEMEX and its state subsidiary companies the process of acquiring goods, services and leasing arrangements. The legislative reforms have encouraged PEMEX to streamline the development process for solicitation documents and model contracts. The development of new generic model contracts represents significant investment by PEMEX in the clarification of the commercial and contractual relationship it wants with its major service providers. The new model contract has been drafted to be more accessible and user-friendly than the contract it will replace and it is set out in a new and more accessible structure. The improvements that can be expected in the new generic contracts are the following:

- There will be 13 models contract documents to more precisely reflect the specificities of a larger range of requirements and circumstances, and reduce the risk of optional clauses being inappropriately used.
- There will be provisions clearly describing the timing and operating terms of the transfer of ownership of any product produced under the contract.
- There will be a clear warranty provision providing specific dates or timeframe within which the private contractors are liable for the integrity and quality of the goods or services rendered.
- There will be optional arbitration provisions.
- There will be an optional mechanism for advance payments.
- Contractors will be prohibited in situation of dispute from stopping performance under the contracts before a decision has been passed, with associated rights to be compensated for damages should that decision be in his/her favour.
- There will be provisions describing the conditions and approval process to replace contractor personnel.
- There will be a statement confirming both parties' right to request conciliation at any time under the resulting contracts.
- There will be a clause covering the possibility of termination as a consequence of grave default by PEMEX and entitling the private entity to compensation.

These amendments to the model contracts are positive and align with the new regulatory framework for PEMEX and the Mexican Common Law. It is therefore important that these model contracts become fully functional as soon as possible. Despite these improvements PEMEX could consider adding the following proposals to the new generic contracts:

- Improve access of both parties to pertinent intellectual property rights by allowing for the possibility to provide to the contractor a licence to use such intellectual property developed at certain stages of the project, when it is determined that the associated benefits offset the costs of getting these rights.
- Have clear provisions associated with enforcement of contractual fines on account of non-compliance with identified performance indicators.
- Include incentive payment provisions, when considered appropriate, allowing additional compensation to the contractor in specific situations.
- Include termination rights for the supplier for non-payment of overdue undisputed charges a certain number of working days after receipt of notice of non-payment.
- Gradually build up the dispute resolution procedures beginning with an attempt at "good faith" resolution by the parties' representatives, failing which the parties must use "reasonable endeavours" to resolve through "commercial negotiation". Failing this, either party may opt for mediation conducted in accordance with a mediation agreement.
- Introduce a "remedial adviser" as a way to resolve issues and bring on board third-party expertise in the hope of saving the contract and improving the operating environment in the event of certain performance failures.
- Give PEMEX the option to invoke a new "remedial adviser" process, which in essence involves the appointment of an independent body by the authority to monitor the suppliers' performance.
- Include an acknowledgement that the supplier's profit margin over the term will not exceed the "maximum permitted profit margin". That is, the profit margin identified in the supplier's financial model plus 5%. This mechanism gives the contracting authority the ability to renegotiate the charges should this point be reached, or, if suitable adjustments to the charges cannot be agreed, terminate for convenience.
- Incorporate a clause that PEMEX does not, in general, need to own specially-written or project-specific intellectual property rights but that a perpetual, royalty-free licence, and the right to sub-licence, will suffice in most cases.

Notes

1. A Decree of 20 December 2013 introduces modifications to Articles 25, 27 and 28 of the Constitution and 21 transitory articles.

2. Article 134 states that "The economic resources available to the federal government, the states, the municipalities, the government of the Federal District and the political-administrative organs thereof, and to the respective decentralised agencies or government controlled companies, shall be managed with efficiency, effectiveness, economy, openness and honesty in order to comply with the purposes for which they are intended. (…) Any acquisitions, leases and transfers of any kind of goods, the rendering of services (…) shall be awarded or carried out through public biddings, through the issuance of public summons so that solvent propositions may be submitted in a closed envelope, which shall be opened in public with the aim of assuring the best conditions available in benefit of the state in regards to price, quality, financing, opportunity and all other pertinent circumstances (…)."

3. The Public Procurement Act (Ley de Adquisiciones, Arrendamientos y Servicios del Sector Público, or LAASSP), the Public Procurement Regulation (Reglamento de la Ley de Adquisiciones, Arrendamientos y Servicios del Sector Público), the General Procurement Manual (Manual Administrativo de Aplicación General en Materia de Adquisiciones, Arrendamientos y Servicios del Sector Público), the Public Works Act (Ley de Obras Públicas y Servicios Relacionados con las Mismas), the Public Works Regulation (Reglamento de la Ley de Obras Públicas y Servicios Relacionados con las Mismas).

4. According to the 2005 World Bank indicators, bribery in OECD countries government procurement is estimated to be adding 10% to 20% to total contract costs. Furthermore, the *World Economic Forum Global Competiveness Report for 2010-2011* refers to corruption as the second most problematic factor for doing business in Mexico (right after inefficient government bureaucracy).

References

New Zealand Government Procurement (2016), "Government Model Contracts", webpage, www.business.govt.nz/procurement/for-agencies/government-model-contracts#Background.

OECD (2015), "Recommendation of the Council on Public Procurement", www.oecd.org/corruption/recommendation-on-public-procurement.htm.

OECD (2009), *OECD Principles for Integrity in Public Procurement*, OECD Publishing, Paris, http://dx.doi.org/10.1787/9789264056527-en.

OECD (2005), *Fighting Corruption and Promoting Integrity in Public Procurement*, OECD Publishing, Paris, http://dx.doi.org/10.1787/9789264014008-en.

US Government (n. d.), "Subpart 19.7—The Small Business Subcontracting Program", United States Federal Acquisition Regulation 48 CFR 19.7, www.acquisition.gov/sites/default/files/current/far/html/Subpart%2019_7.html#wp1088741.

Part II

Ensuring integrity, transparency and accountability in Petróleos Mexicanos' procurement function

Chapter 6

Ensuring integrity throughout Petróleos Mexicanos' procurement cycle

Public procurement operations in the extractive sector present a high risk of corruption throughout OECD countries because of the significant level of expenditure involved and the complexity of the whole procurement cycle. Petróleos Mexicanos (PEMEX) is not immune to such risks and although it is developing initiatives and mechanisms to promote integrity in its activities and within the organisation, it still faces a number of challenges in building a coherent and comprehensive integrity system and in creating a culture of integrity. This chapter analyses PEMEX's integrity policy and legal framework, highlighting recent developments and emphasising areas where further efforts are needed, which include: corruption risk-mapping, disclosure and management of conflict of interest, integrity training and awareness programmes and whistleblowing protection. The chapter also addresses the key role of the private sector and the importance of setting high standards of integrity for all stakeholders in the procurement cycle.

The legal framework applicable to Petróleos Mexicanos (or PEMEX) has changed in recent years after Mexico launched a major reform of the oil and gas sectors (the "Energy Reform" or Reforma Energética), following years of declining oil production by the state-owned company PEMEX, high energy costs for the business sector, and a lack of funding and technology to exploit new energy resources (OECD, 2015a). In 2014 the constitutional reform was complemented by secondary legislation (the PEMEX Law or Ley de Petróleos Mexicanos), which sets out PEMEX's new governance and outlines a Board of Directors. PEMEX also has a new legal status and although it is still fully exclusively owned by the Mexican federal government, it is now a state productive enterprise (empresa productiva del Estado, or EPE), having its own legal personality and assets, as well as technical, operational and managerial autonomy. Through these changes PEMEX is expected to improve its efficiency and concurrently become an international player in the competitive energy market.

In this new context, PEMEX identifies integrity as a priority and is developing a framework to prevent, identify, and sanction corrupt and unethical behaviours in the context of its activities. In this sense, one may recall the new Code of Ethics and Code of Conduct, specific provisions on conflicts of interest as well as the Ethics and Corporate Integrity Programme (Programa de Ética e Integridad Corporativa), which was presented in February 2016 and intends to build PEMEX's integrity framework upon the following pillars: creating an ethical and integrity environment; carrying out anti-corruption actions; improving due diligence of third parties; and developing co-ordination and communication mechanisms.

In spite of the latter developments, PEMEX faces a number of challenges in establishing appropriate accountability and transparency mechanisms, and it is thus called upon to increase efforts to establish a zero-tolerance policy against corruption. Firstly, PEMEX could ensure a comprehensive and effective integrity framework for staff working in procurement, but also for the Board of Directors, which plays a strategic role in relation to the procurement activity of the company and its subsidiaries. At the same time, PEMEX would benefit from strengthening its culture of integrity, instilling it among its employees and expecting it from all subjects entering into relationship with the company and its subsidiaries. Thirdly, improvements are needed to detect wrongdoings and channels to report them: in this sense, the Ethical Helpline (Linea Ética de Ayuda) presented in 2015 should be implemented as an essential tool to build a culture of integrity where officials feel confident coming forward to report breaches of integrity and wrongdoings.

In advancing its integrity and anti-corruption strategy and tools, PEMEX needs to pay specific attention to its procurement activity, where the risk of corruption is usually enhanced by the high levels of expenditure at stake as well as by the complex and technical issues involved in such procedures. This is confirmed by an OECD report that found that out of 427 foreign bribery cases concluded between February 1999 and June 2014, 57% were related to public procurement (Figure 6.1).

Figure 6.1. **Foreign bribery cases between 1999 and 2014 by area**

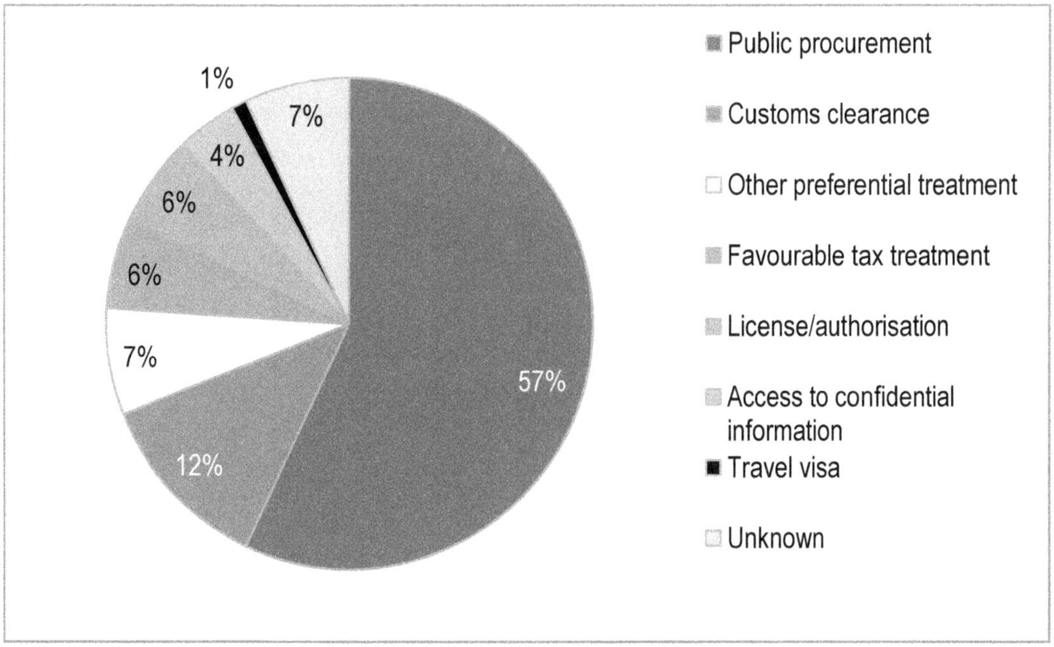

Source: Based on OECD (2014), *OECD Foreign Bribery Report: An Analysis of the Crime of Bribery of Foreign Public Officials*, OECD Publishing, Paris, http://dx.doi.org/10.1787/9789264226616-en.

The vulnerability of public investment goes beyond the risk of foreign bribery and may be represented by other corrupt conduct, such as undue influence, capture of the investment project by specific interests, and conflicts of interest. The latter risks affect all the different stages of the procurement cycle, posing different kinds of threats to the different steps of the project, from the needs assessment phase to the execution and evaluation phases (Table 6.1).

The risks of corruption faced by PEMEX during the procurement cycle are even higher considering the extractive sector where it operates and which includes mining, quarrying, petroleum and gas extraction. Mining support services activities is one of the most vulnerable to corruption, due to multiple actors at different levels involved in the process to release relevant licenses, permits and concessions. This vulnerability was also detected by the above-mentioned OECD study on foreign bribery (OECD, 2014), where the extractive sector did not only emerge as the one where most cases occurred between February 1999 and June 2014 (Figure 6.2), but it was also the one with the highest relative "cost" of bribes, i.e. the highest percentage of the total amount paid in bribes relative to the transaction value (Figure 6.3).

Table 6.1. **Corruption risks associated with the different stages of the procurement cycle**

Phase	Stage	Risks
Risks of the pre-tendering phase	Needs assessment	• Lack of adequate needs assessment • Influence of external actors on official decisions • Informal agreement on contract
	Planning and budgeting	• Poor procurement planning • Procurement not aligned with overall investment decision-making process • Failure to budget realistically or deficiency in the budget
	Development of specifications/ requirements	• Technical specifications tailored for a specific company • Selection criteria not objectively defined and not established in advance • Requesting samples of goods and services that can influence • Buying information on the project specifications
Risks of the tendering phase	Choice of procurement procedure	• Lack of procurement integrity for the use of non-competitive procedures • Abuse of non-competitive procedures on the basis of legal exceptions: contract splitting, abuse of extreme urgency, non-supported modifications
	Request for proposal/bid	• Absence of public notice for the invitation to bid • Evaluation and award criteria not announced • Procurement information disclosed and made public
	Bid submission	• Lack of competition or cases of collusive bidding: – cover bidding – bid suppression – bid rotation – market allocation
	Bid evaluation	• Conflict of interest and corruption in the evaluation process through: – familiarity with bidders over time – personal interests such as gifts or future/additional employment – no effective implementation of the "four-eyes principle"
	Contract award	• Vendors fail to disclose accurate cost or pricing data in their price proposals, resulting in an increased contract price (i.e. invoice mark-ups, channel stuffing) • Conflict of interest and corruption in the approval process (i.e. no effective separation of financial, contractual and project authorities) • Lack of access to records on the procedure
Risks of the post-award phase	Contract management/ performance	• Abuses of the supplier in performing the contract, in particular in relation to its quality, price and timing: – substantial change in contract conditions to allow more time and/ or higher prices for the bidder – product substitution or sub-standard work or service not meeting contract specifications – theft of new assets before delivery to end user or before being recorded • Insufficient supervision from public officials and/or collusion between contractors and supervising officials • Subcontractors and partners chosen in a non-transparent way or not held accountable
	Order and payment	• Insufficient separation of financial duties and/or lack of supervision of public officials leading to: – false accounting and cost misallocation or cost migration between contracts – late payments of invoices – false or duplicate invoicing for goods and services not supplied and for interim payment in advance entitlement

Source: Based on OECD (2009), *OECD Principles for Integrity in Public Procurement*, OECD Publishing, Paris, http://dx.doi.org/10.1787/9789264056527-en.

Figure 6.2. **Foreign bribery cases between 1999 and 2014 by sector**

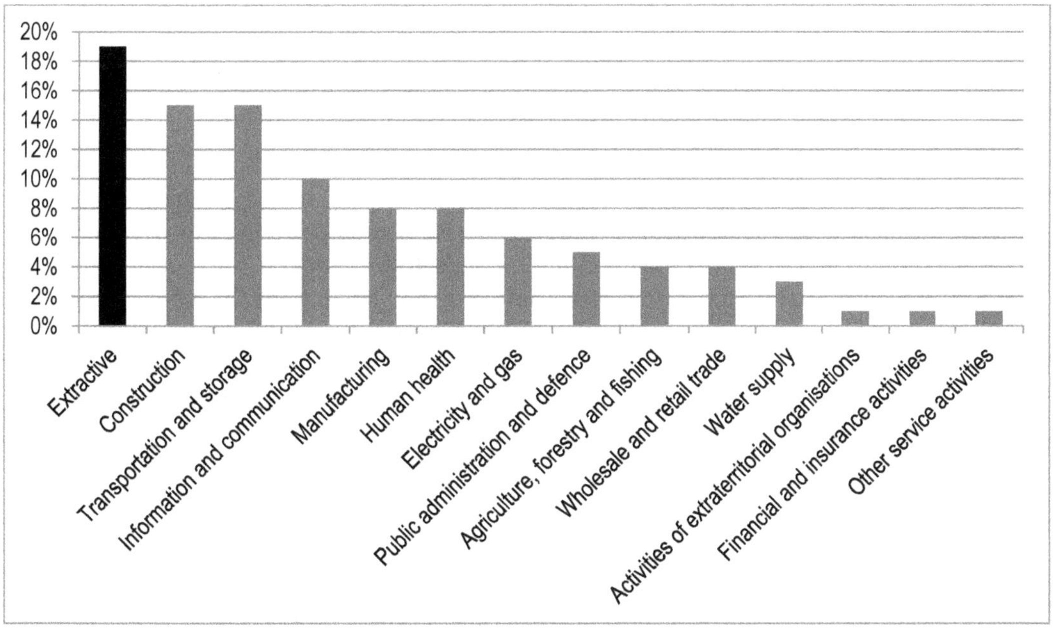

Source: Based on OECD (2014), *OECD Foreign Bribery Report: An Analysis of the Crime of Bribery of Foreign Public Officials*, OECD Publishing, Paris, http://dx.doi.org/10.1787/9789264226616-en.

Figure 6.3. **Bribes as a percentage of the transaction value by sector**

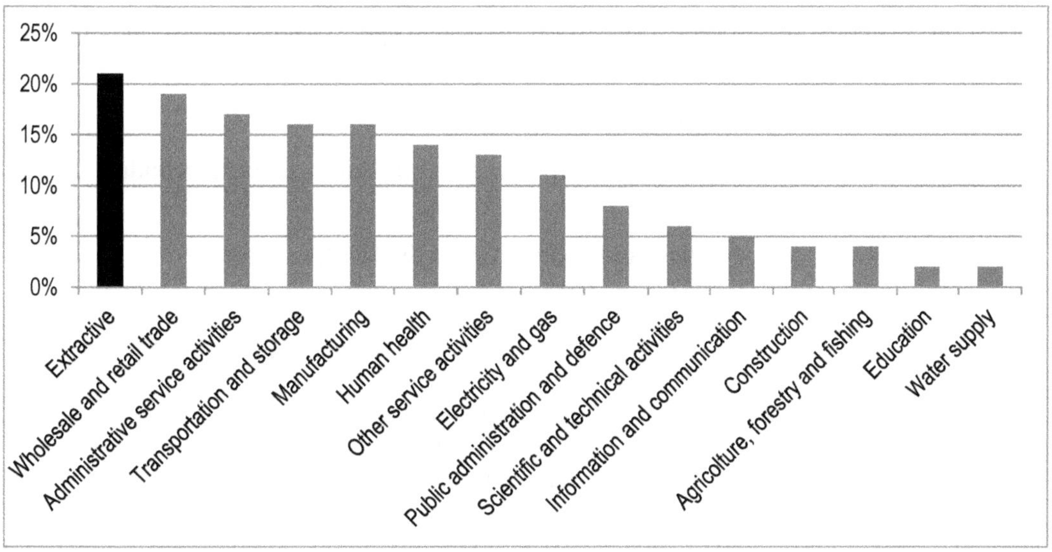

Source: OECD (2014), *OECD Foreign Bribery Report: An Analysis of the Crime of Bribery of Foreign Public Officials*, OECD Publishing, Paris, http://dx.doi.org/10.1787/9789264226616-en.

Addressing weaknesses in PEMEX's legal and policy framework for integrity

Mexico's recent Energy Reform should be accompanied by urgent steps to strengthen PEMEX's legal framework for corruption prevention.

The Energy Reform established an independent legal framework for PEMEX and its subsidiaries. Accordingly, PEMEX and its subsidiaries are now primarily subject to PEMEX Law and its implementing regulation (Reglamento de la Ley de Petróleos Mexicanos, or PEMEX Regulation) and they should follow federal rules only insofar as they are explicitly mentioned or do not contradict the latter body of rules (Article 3, PEMEX Law). This change, aiming to give PEMEX more flexibility and independence in the new energy market, also has an impact on the applicable legal framework to PEMEX procurement activity insofar as the application of the relevant legal framework (Ley de Adquisiciones, Arrendamientos y Servicios del Sector Público, or LAASSP; and Ley de Obras Públicas y Servicios relacionados con las Mismas, or LOPSRM) is explicitly excluded by PEMEX Law.

The applicability of the federal legal framework is also limited in relation to two other sets of norms that are relevant for integrity and corruption in PEMEX's procurement activity. The Federal Anti-Corruption Law on Public Procurement (Ley Federal Anticorrupción en Contrataciones Públicas, or LFACP) (Box 6.1) applies during the contracting phase together with the other provisions set in PEMEX Law to ensure integrity in procurement (Articles 82-86 of the PEMEX Law). The latter provisions set out the main policies and initiatives that should be implemented to prevent, identify, correct and sanction illicit behaviours in the context of PEMEX contracting activity, namely:

- mechanisms to identify, systemise and manage corruption-risk factors and elements as well as action to follow before their detection
- general eligibility criteria to contract with PEMEX
- a system to receive anonymous reports and complaints about misconduct during the contracting procedures
- the publication of suppliers and contractors of the last five years.

Box 6.1. The Federal Anti-Corruption Law on Public Procurement (LFACP)

The Federal Anti-Corruption Law on Public Procurement (Ley Federal Anticorrupción en Contrataciones Públicas, or LFACP) was adopted in June 2012 and provides the following provisions to address issues of corruption and fraud in public procurement:

- Penalties and liabilities on both Mexican and foreign individuals and entities for infringing the law during their participation in any federal procurement process, applying to other related professions that may have an influence on the integrity of the public procurement process (including, but not limited to, public servants).
- Mexican individuals and entities involved in corruption in international business transactions are equally liable.

Box 6.1. **The Federal Anti-Corruption Law on Public Procurement (LFACP)** *(continued)*

- Acts such as influence, bribery, collusion, shams, omission, evasion, filing false information, and forgery are considered infringements (Article 8).
- Penalties for violation of the law include fines and legal disqualification (*inhabilitación*) from the pertinent working sector for periods ranging from three months to eight years for individuals and three months to ten years for entities (Article 27).
- Pleading guilty and co-operating in the investigation reduces the sanctions up to 50%, if the plead takes place within 15 working days following the notification of the administrative disciplinary proceedings (Articles 20 and 31).
- Whistleblowers' identities must remain confidential (Article 10).

Source: OECD (2013), *Public Procurement Review of the State's Employees' Social Security and Social Services Institute in Mexico*, OECD Public Governance Reviews, OECD Publishing. http://dx.doi.org/10.1787/9789264197305-en.

As for the administrative responsibility arising from the corrupt practice of personnel, two legal frameworks currently apply to PEMEX (Table 6.2). On one hand, public servants working in PEMEX and its subsidiaries are subject to the Federal Law on Administrative Responsibilities of Public Servants (Ley Federal de Responsabilidades Administrativas de los Servidores Públicos, or LFRASP),[1] which aims to enhance the legality and integrity of public servants' performance of their administrative duties by establishing the administrative faults, the procedure for taking legal action, and the modality and degree of sanctioning to be applied to public servants. Specifically, the LFRASP prohibits procurement officials from:

- contracting with any person who performs a public function, or with any company in which such a person participates
- contracting with any person that has been prohibited from holding a job, position or commission in the public administration
- intervening in any situation that may create any personal or business-related conflict of interest
- participating in any act or procedure where integrity might be compromised
- exercising any form of influence peddling to former public servants, up to one year after they conclude their public function
- inhibiting whistleblowing or the filing of a complaint. (OECD, 2013)

On the other hand, PEMEX Law establishes a special regime for members of the Board of Directors in relation to the activity performed in such function, setting out some obligations as well as a number of situations that exclude responsibilities in the following situations:

- when they comply with the requirements for the approval of the matters that are the competence of the Board

- when they make decisions during sessions of the Board based on information provided by PEMEX Directors, the external auditor or independent experts
- when they chose the most appropriate alternative or the negative asset effects were not foreseeable.

Table 6.2. **Integrity obligations as regulated by legal frameworks applicable to PEMEX's Board of Directors and personnel**

	Board of Directors	Personnel
Disciplinary regime	Special regime established in PEMEX Law	Federal regime (LFRASP)
Conflict of interest	Special regime established in PEMEX Law and PEMEX Code of Conduct	Federal regime (LFRASP) and PEMEX Code of Conduct

Source: PEMEX Law, LFRASP, PEMEX Code of Conduct.

Considering the specificity of PEMEX's new legal status and the mixed integrity and anti-corruption legal frameworks applicable to each category of PEMEX personnel, defining the exact scope and application of rules could contribute to increasing the understanding and awareness of suppliers and external stakeholders. For this purpose, relevant authorities may consider providing guidance on this matter following the example of the resolution released in 2015 by the Italian Anti-Corruption Authority (Autoritá Nazionale Anticorruzione, or ANAC) to clarify relevant anti-corruption and transparency obligations for state-owned enterprises (Box 6.2).

Box 6.2. **Guiding the implementation of anti-corruption standards by state-owned enterprises**

In June 2015, ANAC adopted a resolution to guide state-owned enterprises in the application of the anti-corruption and transparency legal framework introduced by Law No. 190/2012. Furthermore, they identified the relevant consequence – also in organisational terms – for those enterprises as well as for the corresponding public administrations.

More specifically, they consist of the following parts:

- a general introduction of the legal framework together with general interpretive guidance
- ad hoc sections with specific indications for different kinds of state-owned enterprises
- the oversight role of the ANAC
- transitory regulation.

Source: ANAC (2015), "Linee guida per l'attuazione della normativa in materia di prevenzione della corruzione e trasparenza da parte delle società e degli enti di diritto privato controllati e partecipati dalle pubbliche amministrazioni e degli enti pubblici economici", Resolution no. 8/2015, www.anticorruzione.it/portal/public/classic/AttivitaAutorita/AttiDellAutorita/_Atto?ca=6170.

The scope of PEMEX's existing integrity policy and standards could be extended to all those working for PEMEX and its suppliers.

After the adoption of the reform, PEMEX's Board of Directors reviewed its internal integrity policy and standards by adopting a new Code of Ethics and a new Code of Conduct. While the former summarises the corporate philosophy and ethics to orient PEMEX's activities in a transparent, honest, efficient and responsible way, the latter illustrates the expected standards of conduct stemming from the Code of Ethics.

Both the Code of Ethics and Code of Conduct are quite comprehensive insofar as they provide for rules to tackle issues such as corruption, conflict of interest, influence peddling and bribes and gifts/invitations. However, so far they only apply to the personnel and the members of the Board of Directors, thereby leaving aside key partners such as consultants and suppliers, whose behaviour may also influence the reputation and image of the company. Ensuring that integrity, transparency and accountability standards are applied to any subject entering into contact with the company can contribute to preventing the risk of corruption and creates a uniform, higher level of integrity expectations throughout PEMEX's activities.

On the one hand, external suppliers may be used to different business cultures and practice, so they may not be aware of expected behaviour when interacting with PEMEX. As a consequence they may well benefit from receiving guidance from PEMEX's codes on ethical and integrity matters, which may prevent dilemmas and misunderstanding.

With specific regard to consultants, extending them the application of PEMEX's integrity rule would also contribute to levelling the playing field among people working in the company as well as setting clear standards for dealing with the confidential and privileged information they might have at their disposal. Guidance to deal with conflict-of-interest situations may also be particularly relevant in this context since the dependency that often develops between consultants and clients may lead to a bias in the selection of future consultants (Transparency International, 2011).

PEMEX would benefit from extending the scope of its Code of Ethics and Code of Conduct to all the partners interacting with the company and expect from them the same level of integrity required for its personnel. A way to apply PEMEX's integrity standards and rules to consultants is to broaden the application of the codes to anybody working in PEMEX capacity, in line with the practice of the Government of Queensland, Australia, for its public service activity (Box 6.3). Alternatively, PEMEX may directly address ethical commitments and integrity issues in its consultancy agreements, as in Hong Kong (Box 6.4).

Box 6.3. Code of Conduct for the Queensland Public Service

In the Queensland Public Service, the Code of Conduct applies to employees of its public service agencies, which according to the Public Sector Ethics Act 1994 encompass:

- a department
- a technical and further education (TAFE) institute or statutory TAFE institute
- the administrative office of a court or tribunal
- an entity prescribed by regulation.

Box 6.3. **Code of Conduct for the Queensland Public Service** *(continued)*

At the same time, for the purpose of the Code of Conduct, employees (other than judicial officials) are defined as:

- any Queensland public service employee whether permanent, temporary, full-time, part-time or casual
- any volunteer, student, contractor, consultant or anyone who works in any other capacity for Queensland public service agency.

The Code of Conduct always applies at all times when the latter subjects perform official duties, including when they represent the Queensland Government at conferences, training events, on business trips and attending work-related social events.

Source: Queensland Government (2011), "Code of Conduct for the Queensland Public Service", www.psc.qld.gov.au/includes/assets/qps-code-conduct.pdf (accessed 10 February 2016).

Box 6.4. **Ethical commitment clauses for inclusion in consultancy agreements: Hong Kong's Independent Commission Against Corruption (ICAC) Best Practice Checklist**

Hong Kong's ICAC Best Practice Checklist aims to provide organisations with a user-friendly and step-by-step procedural guide, with recommendations on safeguards to minimise corruption risks, for the employment of consultants and monitoring of their services. Organisations are expected to adapt the recommended safeguards to suit their organisational structure, resources, risk exposures, and any statutory requirements applicable to the works projects.

Ethical commitment clauses for inclusion in the consultancy agreements have four major areas of focus, including: 1) confidentiality; 2) prevention of bribery; 3) declaration of interest; and 4) a declaration of ethical commitment.

- The confidentiality clause commits the consultant to not disclose information such as the terms of the agreement or any report, document, specification, software, data, etc., to outsiders, whether they are furnished by the employer or generated by the consultant.
- The prevention of bribery clauses require consultants to prohibit their directors, agents, subcontractors or staff involved in the agreement from offering, soliciting or accepting any advantage as defined in the Hong Kong's Prevention of Bribery ordinance. Consultants should also caution their staff from soliciting or accepting excessive hospitality, entertainment or inducement that may compromise their impartiality in relation to the assignment.
- The declaration of interest clause commits the consultant to declare in writing any conflict of interest or potential conflict between their personal/financial interest and their duties in connection with the agreement.
- The declaration of ethical commitment clauses consist of a declaration of compliance with the confidentiality and prevention of bribery clauses in a form provided by the contracting authority when requesting payment of services. Payment can be withheld until the consultant submits the signed declaration.

Box 6.4. **Ethical commitment clauses for inclusion in consultancy agreements: Hong Kong's Independent Commission Against Corruption (ICAC) Best Practice Checklist** *(continued)*

The checklist provides sample forms that can be adopted or adapted where applicable. It includes sample codes of conduct with report forms on gifts received, declaration of conflict of interest, sample probity, anti-collusion and debarment clauses as well as declaration forms on compliance.

The checklist can be found at www.icac.org.hk/filemanager/en/Content_1031/manworkconsult.pdf.

Source: U4 (2011), "Examples of integrity agreements for consultants and advisors", U4 Anti-Corruption Resource Centre, Chr. Michelsen Institute, Bergen, Norway, www.u4.no/publications/examples-of-integrity-agreements-for-consultants-and-advisors/ (accessed 10 February 2016).

Mapping corruption risks is key to strengthening PEMEX's broader integrity framework, and particularly to informing preventive measures.

PEMEX has developed a risk-management strategy in relation to its procurement processes as well as a matrix that identifies 183 critical activities, 205 risks and 175 controls. According to the information provided by PEMEX, such a risk map does not include corruption or other integrity breaches. Furthermore, PEMEX declared in its response to the OECD questionnaire circulated in preparation for the OECD fact-finding mission that corruption is not a common problem. Although PEMEX is expected to review the design of a monitoring, evaluation, and risk-mitigation system, currently there is no alert mechanism or red flag that could help to detect corruption and unethical behaviour in a systematic and timely manner.

In order to effectively prevent corruption in the procurement process, PEMEX needs to put in place formal mechanisms for monitoring associated risks. As an initial step, PEMEX could develop a corruption risk map of the organisation and its processes in order to identify issues such as vulnerable positions, as well as risky activities and projects. To do this, PEMEX could consider the checklist developed by the Government of Tasmania that identifies potential risks in the public works, goods and services procurement process (Box 6.5).

Box 6.5. Tasmania's checklist of potential risks in the goods and services procurement process

The Tasmanian government developed a checklist of potential risks in the procurement cycle that is composed of 11 parts:

1. identifying the need and planning the purchase
2. developing the specification
3. selecting the purchasing method
4. purchasing documentation
5. inviting, clarifying and closing offers
6. evaluating offers
7. selecting the successful tenderer
8. negotiations
9. contract management
10. evaluating the procurement process
11. disposals.

Box 6.5. Tasmania's checklist of potential risks in the goods and services procurement process *(continued)*

For instance, these are the risks identified for the first phase:

Risk	Likely consequences	Action
Understatement of the need	Purchase of unsuitable product or service Money wasted Need not satisfied	Analyse need accurately
Overstatement of the need	Greater expense Poor competition	Analyse need accurately Use functional performance requirements
Misinterpretation of user needs	Totally unacceptable purchase or not most suitable product or service Time lost Increased costs Possible downtime	Improve consultation with users Obtain clear statement of work and definition of need
Insufficient funding	Delay in making the purchase Additional costs for re-tender	Obtain appropriate approvals before undertaking process Improve planning
Impractical timeframe	Inadequate responses from tenderers Reduced competition Delivery schedule not met	Improve forecasting, planning and consultation with users Improve communication with potential tenderers
Probity issues	Increased procurement costs Misuse of resources Most suitable product not obtained Unethical conduct	Implement best practice policies, guidelines and practices Maintain ethical environment Improve training of personnel Put suitable controls and reviews in place Consider using a probity adviser Improve communication with potential tenderers

Source: OECD (2015b), *Effective Delivery of Large Infrastructure Projects: The Case of the New International Airport of Mexico City*, OECD Public Governance Reviews, OECD Publishing, Paris, http://dx.doi.org/10.1787/9789264248335-en, p. 150-151.

Once the risks of the organisation are analysed and mapped, PEMEX may also develop a system of warning signals – such as red-flags – in relation to critical processes, vulnerable positions, as well as risky activities and projects. In this exercise, PEMEX may consider the red flags that are identified at the international level, such as the ones of the Chartered Institute of Public Finance and Accountancy (Box 6.6).

Box 6.6. Chartered Institute of Public Finance and Accountancy red flags

Recognising the risk of procurement corruption through "red flags" helps to prevent and detect it. Examples of "red flags" are:

- physical losses
- unusual relationship with suppliers
- manipulation of data
- photocopied documents
- incomplete management/audit trail
- IT-controls of audit logs disabled
- budget overspends`
- IT-login outside working hours
- unusual invoices (e.g. format, numbers, address, phone, VAT number)
- vague description of goods/services to be supplied
- duplicate/photocopy invoice
- high number of failed IT logins
- round sum amounts invoiced
- favoured customer treatment
- sequential invoice numbers over an extended period of time
- interest/ownership in external organisation
- non-declaration of interest/gifts/ hospitality
- lack of supporting records
- no process identifying risks (e.g. risk register)
- unusual increases/decreases

Source: World Bank (n. d.), "Most common red flags of fraud and corruption in procurement", http://siteresources.worldbank.org/INTDOII/Resources/Red_flags_reader_friendly.pdf (accessed 8 October 2016).

On top of that, PEMEX might also set up a system to map risks in each project, which would also ensure the integrity and responsibility for all stakeholders involved in each procurement process. In this context, PEMEX may consider the introduction of an "integrity document" in line with the probity plan developed by Australia's Procurement Transformation Division. The probity plan is part of the planning documentation and identifies the probity risks and related management strategies for each procurement process (Box 6.7).

Box 6.7. Australia's procurement probity plans

Australia's Procurement Transformation Division has developed a procurement guidance document that provides that a probity plan should be prepared before the commencement of each procurement process and forms part of procurement planning documentation. It should identify the probity risks and related management strategies for the procurement, including the role and responsibilities of each stakeholder in responding to those risks. Where the procurement is part of a broader project, the probity plan should be agreed with the project's governing body and management.

As part of the probity plan, a description should be provided of the probity services that are to be sourced, including whether a probity auditor and/or probity advisor is to be engaged, and the scope and nature of the probity services that will be delivered. All members involved in the procurement, or project, including the steering committee, advisors and other project stakeholders should be aware of arrangements put in place to preserve the probity of the process and should be provided with a copy of the probity plan.

Box 6.7. **Australia's procurement probity plans** *(continued)*

In those procurement situations where more than one agency is involved in different elements of the procurement process, it is essential that the roles and responsibilities in relation to probity be addressed within the probity plan to ensure that accountabilities are clear and that governance practices are in place. The responsibility for probity remains with the agency to which funds have been appropriated. Where this agency engages service providers (government or private) to engage in procurement activities on its behalf, it should require those providers to meet its (the agency's) responsibility and particular requirements regarding probity. However, this does not transfer the responsibility for probity to the service provider, which remains with the agency.

Source: Procurement Transformation Division (2014), "Procurement guidance - Use of probity auditors and advisors in procurement", www.hpw.qld.gov.au/SiteCollectionDocuments/ProcurementGuideProbityAuditorsAdvisors.pdf (accessed 23 February 2016).

Risks of corruption are not static but evolve together with the changes taking place within the organisation and in the outside world, so a further element to enhance PEMEX's corruption risk assessment strategy could be to introduce a system to monitor and periodically evaluate it in order to ensure it is coherent with reality and thus effective. In elaborating such a mechanism, PEMEX could consider the leading practices identified by the US Government Accountability Office (Table 6.3).

Table 6.3. **The US Government Accountability Office's leading practices for monitoring, evaluating, and adapting fraud risk-management activities**

1.	Conduct risk-based monitoring and evaluate all components of the Fraud Risk-Management Framework
•	Monitor and evaluate the effectiveness of preventive activities, including fraud risk assessments and the anti-fraud strategy, as well as controls to detect fraud and response efforts.
•	Collect and analyse data, including data from reporting mechanisms and instances of detected fraud, for real-time monitoring of fraud trends and identification of potential control deficiencies.
•	Employ a risk-based approach to monitoring by taking into account internal and external factors that can influence the control environment, such as organisational changes and emerging risks.
•	Engage stakeholders responsible for specific fraud risk-management activities in the monitoring and evaluation process.
2.	Monitor and evaluate fraud risk-management activities with a focus on measuring outcomes
•	Measure outcomes, in addition to outputs, of fraud risk-management activities.
•	In the absence of sufficient data, assess how well managers follow recommended "leading practices" for designing fraud risk-management activities.
3.	Adapt fraud risk-management activities and communicate the results of monitoring and evaluations
•	Use the results of monitoring and evaluations to improve the design and implementation of fraud risk-management activities.
•	Use analysis of identified instances of fraud and fraud trends to improve fraud risk-management activities, including prioritising and taking corrective actions, as well as enhancing fraud-awareness trainings.
•	Use results of investigations and prosecutions to enhance fraud prevention and detection.
•	Communicate results of monitoring and evaluations, including corrective actions taken, if any, to relevant stakeholders.

Source: GAO (2015), "A Framework for Managing Fraud Risks in Federal Programs", GAO-15-593SP, www.gao.gov/products/GAO-15-593SP.

PEMEX needs a comprehensive policy framework on conflict of interest.

In spite of the changes brought by the Energy Reform, PEMEX remains a company completely owned by the Mexican government that should serve the public interest and carry out its functions in an impartial and efficient way in order to avoid eroding citizen and public trust. Accordingly, the PEMEX Law states the obligation to act in a transparent, honest and efficient way. This means that the private interests of its personnel should not influence any of their decisions, including their procurement activities. However, since all public officials have legitimate interests that arise from their capacity as private citizens, conflicts of interest cannot simply be avoided or prohibited; they must be defined, identified and managed in order to prevent them from resulting in corruption.

Generally speaking, conflict-of-interest obligations for Mexican public officials are established in LFRASP, which defines a conflict-of-interest situation as when "the personal, familiar or commercial interests of the public official may influence the impartial performance of her/his work, duty or task." LFRASP also sets out a few obligations related to conflict of interest in public service as well as in the pre/post-public employment phase. In particular it prohibits public officials from:

- dealing with duties where they have personal interests
- accepting/requesting gifts or money from people and companies connected to their duties (up to one year after retirement)
- obtaining/asking for any additional benefits as part of their official duties
- improperly influencing a human resources decision where they have a personal, familiar or commercial interest
- taking advantage of their position to influence the decision of another public official to gain a personal interest
- purchasing any property which will be affected by a decision taken within her/his duty
- taking advantage of the post a public official held in the public administration
- taking advantage of the information or documents that a public official had access to and were not public.

Agreement CA-125/2015 of PEMEX's Board of Directors on General Provisions for Contracting ("PEMEX Agreement CA-125/2015") contains a section on integrity that specifically targets the staff of the procurement area (Área de Procura y Abastecimiento) and project managers. In relation to conflict of interest, it reiterates the need to respect the Codes of Ethics and Conduct and to obliges them to present the asset declaration in line with the obligation provided for by the LFRASP for certain categories of public servants.

However, as previously noted (Table 6.2), the federal regime on administrative responsibilities of public officials does not apply to the members of the Board of Directors, who are subject to the PEMEX Law and PEMEX Regulation. The latter body of norms provides for a special conflict-of-interest regime for Board of Directors' members, which includes a list of prohibited and non-prohibited conducts, a yearly obligation to disclose extra-professional activities, as a well a mechanism to assess situations where there could be a conflict of interest in the latter activities.

Conflict of interest is also addressed in the Code of Conduct, which applies to both personnel and members of the Board of Directors. The latter Code sets out desirable conducts as well as recommendations to be followed by PEMEX's staff.

Considering the existing fragmented regime characterising conflict-of-interest regulation, there seems to be a lack of a consistent and comprehensive framework to manage conflict-of-interest situations within PEMEX. Clarity seems to be missing in distinguishing between an asset declaration and a conflict-of-interest disclosure, which should be dealt with separately in order to distinguish the appropriate use to make of the corresponding information.

A related issue that emerges from the analysis is the lack of adequate standards and procedures for managing and resolving the conflict-of-interest situations that may concern PEMEX's staff. In this context guidance may be sought in the OECD Guidelines for Managing Conflict of Interest in the Public Service (OECD, 2004), which stress how disclosure of a private interest does not in itself resolve a conflict, but it enables the necessary steps to be taken to determine what measures are needed to resolve or manage the conflict positively. In particular, the OECD Guidelines propose a few alternatives that could be considered by PEMEX in developing its conflict-of-interest policy:

- divestment or liquidation of the interest by the public official
- recusal of the public official from involvement in an affected decision-making process
- restriction of access by the affected public official to particular information
- transfer of the public official to duty in a non-conflicting function
- re-arrangement of the public official's duties and responsibilities
- assignment of the conflicting interest in a genuinely "blind trust" arrangement
- resignation of the public official from the conflicting private-capacity function
- resignation of the public official from their public office
- recusal and restriction (e.g. not participating in decision making).

Furthermore, PEMEX may consider enhancing transparency over the qualification and selection process of the independent members of the Board of Directors, which the OECD considers a useful way to identify potential conflict of interest as well as to increase the professionalism of the Board itself. According to the OECD, this is particularly true in state-owned enterprises, where board member nomination is often the direct responsibility of the government and as such, carries a risk that board members will be perceived as acting on behalf of the state or specific political constituencies, rather than in the long-term interest of the enterprise and its shareholders (OECD, 2015c).

Given the sensitivity of the procurement activity, PEMEX might also consider introducing mechanisms that could extend conflict-of-interest reporting obligations to private actors at an early stage of the procurement process. In this sense, bidders could be asked to disclose prohibited or potential conflicts of interest that they may have with the contracting organisation or with the other bidders in line with the "Financial Disclosures and Conflicts of Interest" form designed by the State of Illinois in the United States (Box 6.8).

Box 6.8. Financial disclosures and conflicts of interest: State of Illinois, United States

The Financial Disclosures and Conflicts of Interest form ("form") must be accurately completed and submitted by the vendor, parent entity(ies), and subcontractors. There are eight steps on this form and each must be completed as instructed in the step heading and within the step. A bid, offer, or proposal that does not include this form shall be considered non-responsive.

The agency/university will consider this form when evaluating the bid, offer, or proposal or awarding the contract. The form is divided into eight steps as follows:

- Step 1. Supporting documentation submittal
- Step 2. Disclosure of financial interest or Board of Directors
- Step 3. Disclosure of lobbyist or agent
- Step 4. Prohibited conflicts of interest
- Step 5. Potential conflicts of interest relating to personal relationships
- Step 6. Explanation of affirmative responses
- Step 7. Potential conflicts of interest relating to debarment and legal proceedings
- Step 8. Disclosure of current and pending contracts.

The requirement of disclosure of financial interests and conflicts of interest is a continuing obligation. If circumstances change and the disclosure is no longer accurate, then disclosing entities must provide an updated form. Separate forms are required for the vendor, any parent entity(ies) and any subcontractors.

Source: State of Illinois (n. d.), "Financial Disclosures and Conflicts of Interest", www.siue.edu/text/purchasing/staff/pdf/Financial%20Disclosures%20and%20Conflicts%20of%20Interest%20V%2014%202-2.pdf (accessed 12 February 2016).

While preventative measures should be a priority for PEMEX, ensuring these are effectively enforced is essential to a comprehensive integrity framework. One existing gap for instance is disciplinary liability for independent members of the Board of Directors.

As a consequence of the new PEMEX legal framework, while public officials and ministers sitting as members of the Board of Directors are subject to the LFRASP, the responsibility regime for the independent members of the Board is established in the PEMEX Law. Although the latter instrument provides for a disciplinary regime that encompasses diligence and loyalty obligations, it does not include integrity and anti-corruption-related conduct, which could also be explicitly addressed. Furthermore, administrative procedures are only envisaged for public servants, who can be sanctioned by PEMEX's Responsibility Unit (Unidad de Responsabilidades de Petróleos Mexicanos), whereas actions for Board members' responsibility can only be brought through civil proceedings for compensation purposes (Article 31 of PEMEX Law). Considering that the Board of Directors is assigned several crucial responsibilities with respect to procurement, PEMEX may consider introducing administrative rules and procedures with respect to the investigation and sanctions for cases of disciplinary breaches committed by its members. Such a mechanism should ensure that the independence of the Board is not impaired.

More generally, PEMEX may develop statistical data on the disciplinary procedures of both its personnel and its Board, and publish a yearly report on its website with information about the outcomes of cases and the effectiveness of the enforcement mechanisms. Such an initiative would improve the confidence of PEMEX officials in its integrity system and may convey the message that the fight against corruption is a priority of the company and that integrity breaches will not go unpunished.

PEMEX could incentivise stronger integrity on the part of its suppliers through various means, including greater transparency, introducing integrity standards for eligibility, and ensuring effective sanctions.

Extending the scope of PEMEX ethical standards to suppliers may not be sufficient to discourage wrongdoing and breaches of integrity from suppliers, who are as capable of participating in a corrupt deal as public officials. In this sense, the obligation for PEMEX's suppliers to declare that they have an integrity and ethics scheme (Article 53 of PEMEX Law) doesn't seem to be an effective tool to ensure an adequate degree of integrity of private counterparts, and this is particularly true considering that such declarations are not made public and controls are carried out randomly.

Considering the key role of the private sector in ensuring the integrity of the procurement process, PEMEX may consider publishing the standard content of such declarations and to introduce systemic controls to check whether they correspond to reality. At the same time, Mexico could induce the private sector to develop its own integrity standards and programmes similarly to the one developed by the US Construction Industry Ethics and Compliance Initiative (CIECI) (Box 6.9).

Box 6.9. The Construction Industry Ethics and Compliance Initiative in the United States

The Construction Industry Ethics and Compliance Initiative (CIECI) is a non-profit private association that brings together more than 50 companies in the US construction industry to establish a process for the industry to promote integrity and ethical conduct.

The construction industry is the United States' largest industry, ranging from building contractors who construct homes, schools, hospitals, skyscrapers and shopping centres to the heavy construction industry that builds power plants, highways, bridges, airports, dams, water treatment facilities and the like. Vast and diverse, the construction industry consists of architect/engineers, contractors and subcontractors who tend to specialise. The essential goals of the initiative are the advancement of organisational cultures that encourage and support ethical behaviour and compliance with the law, and the sharing of best ethical and compliance practices within the industry.

The initiative requires each signatory company to pledge to follow six core ethical principles, to adhere to these principles, and to participate in an Annual Best Practices Forum to discuss best ethical and business conduct practices among its members and with representatives from government and other organisations. The core principles are:

Box 6.9. **The Construction Industry Ethics and Compliance Initiative in the United States**

- Each member shall have and adhere to a written Code of Business Conduct. The Code shall establish high ethical values and compliance with the law applicable to the US construction industry.
- Each member shall train its personnel as to their personal responsibilities under the Code.
- Each member commits itself to work together toward maintaining open competition in the industry, free of conflicts of interest and undue influences.
- Each member shall be responsible for sharing best ethical and compliance practices in implementing the principles with others.
- Each member shall participate in the Annual Best Practices Forum.
- Each member, through participation in this initiative, shall be accountable to the public.

Source: CIECI (2014), "Frequently Asked Questions", webpage, www.ciecinitiative.org/Faqs (accessed 23 March 2016).

Moving beyond compliance towards the implementation of a values-based strategy

PEMEX needs to strengthen its culture of integrity through more ambitious efforts for awareness raising and capacity building

The legal framework governing PEMEX provides for a number of specific provisions to ensure integrity of its procurement cycle. In particular, PEMEX Agreement CA-125/2014 sets out some specific provisions on PEMEX contracting activity, which include obligations for procurement personnel and mechanisms to prevent corruption, such as the rotation of personnel, the elaboration of indicators to improve its activity and a system to monitor the controls established in the contracting proceedings.

While in principle such regulation addresses many important issues to ensure integrity in the procurement cycle, it is hard to understand how PEMEX is trying to build a culture of integrity, especially in its procurement activities. In this sense, Agreement CA-125/2014 recalls the need to respect the Codes of Ethics and Conduct, obliges procurement personnel to present an asset declaration, and commits the Responsibility Unit to share the mechanism to report complaints and misconducts to suppliers.

A comprehensive strategy to fight corruption within an organisation should not be based on a legal framework setting out obligations and procedures, but should also aim at building institutional integrity through the promotion of moral values and ethical principles. For this reason, PEMEX should enhance its values-based strategy and stimulate the active involvement and commitment of public officials in establishing a culture of integrity within its organisation.

Raising awareness and understanding of the risks of corruption and counter measures to breaches of integrity are an important element to instil a culture of prevention to develop an effective strategy against corruption. Codes of ethics and conduct play a significant role in this context since they define the values and standards within the organisation. As discussed earlier, the Code of Ethics and Code of Conduct of PEMEX are quite comprehensive insofar as they provide for rules to tackle issues such as corruption, conflict of interest, influence peddling and on bribes and gifts/invitations. However, they do not have specific provisions regarding integrity standards for PEMEX personnel in relation to its procurement activity. At the same time, PEMEX should also purse the intended project to assess its employees' knowledge of the Codes of Ethics and Conduct and publish results on its website, in order to further commit to improving the expected ethical knowledge and behaviours from its personnel.

Although codes of ethics and conduct are necessary to instil values within an organisation, their effectiveness is limited if not coupled with support and training, which further contributes to raising awareness and building a culture of integrity. According to the information provided by PEMEX, the company organises an induction e-learning course; however, it is not clear how and to what extent it addresses issues related to ethics, integrity and corruption. Furthermore, such a programme is only made available to one category of employees (so-called "trust personnel" or *personal de confianza*), so PEMEX could consider extending to all other personnel.

At the same time, training should be tailored according to the needs of its target audience and should have a strong link with day-to-day practical issues. Since PEMEX did not provide any evidence of specific training for its procurement officials and officials in high-risk positions, PEMEX may consider providing ad hoc training on integrity and ethics-related issues, in line with the practice followed by other OECD countries, such as France (Box 6.10).

Box 6.10. Specialised training for public procurement in France

The Central Service of Corruption Prevention, an inter-ministerial body attached to the Ministry of Justice in France has developed training materials for public procurement to help officials identify irregularities and corruption in procurement. Below is a case study taken from the training materials, which illustrates the challenges faced by various actors at different steps of the procedure. It also highlights the difficulty of gathering evidence on irregularities and corruption.

Issue at stake

Following an open invitation to bid, an unsuccessful bidder complains to the mayor of a commune accusing the bidding panel of irregularities because his bid was lower than that submitted by the winning bidder. How should the mayor deal with the problem?

Stage 1: Checking compliance with public procurement procedures

The firm making the complaint is well known and is not considered "litigious". The mayor therefore gives its claim his attention and requests the internal audit service to check the conditions of the award of contract, particularly whether the procedure was in compliance with regulations (the lowest bidder is not necessarily the best bidder) and with the notices published in the official journal. The mayor learns from the report prepared by the bidding committee that although the procedure was in accordance with the regulations, the bid by the firm in question had been revised upwards by the technical service responsible for comparing the offers. Apparently, the firm had omitted certain cost headings, which were added onto its initial bid.

Box 6.10. **Specialised training for public procurement in France** *(continued)*

Stage 2: Replying to the losing bidder

The mayor lets the losing bidder know exactly why its bid was unsuccessful. However, by return post, he receives a letter pointing out that no one had informed the company of the change made to its bid, which was in fact unjustified since the expenditure that had purportedly been omitted had in fact been included in the bid under another heading.

Stage 3: Suspicions

The internal audit service confirms the unsuccessful bidder's claim and points out that nothing in the report helps to establish any grounds for the change made by the technical service. It also points out that it would be difficult for an official with any experience, however little, not to see that the expenses had been accounted for under another heading. The mayor now requests the audit service to find out whether the technical service is in the habit of making such changes, whether it has already processed bids from the winning bidder and if contracts were frequently awarded to the latter. He also requests that it check out the background of the officials concerned by the audit. Do they have experience? Have they been trained? Do they have links with the successful contractor? Could they have had links with them in their previous posts? What do their wives and children do? Examination of the personnel files of the officials and the shares of the company that won the contract fail to find anything conclusive: the only links between the officials or their families and the successful bidder are indirect.

Stage 4: Handing the case over to authorities of the Ministry of Justice

Having suspicions, but no proof, the mayor hands over information so that investigations can begin. The investigators now have to find proof that a criminal offence (favouritism, corruption, undue advantage, etc.) has been committed and will exercise their powers to examine bank accounts, conduct hearings, surveillance, etc. The case has now moved out of the domain of public procurement regulations and into the domain of criminal proceedings.

Conclusion

Unable to gather any evidence and with no authority to conduct an in-depth investigation or question the parties concerned, the mayor makes the only decision that is within his power, which is to reorganise internally and change the duties of the two members of staff concerned. However, he must proceed cautiously when giving the reasons for his decision so as to avoid exposing innocent people to public condemnation or himself to accusations of defamation while the criminal investigation is in progress.

The mayor also decides that from then on the report by the technical services to the bidding committee should give a fuller explanation of its calculations and any changes it makes to the bids, as well as systematically inform bidders of any changes.

Source: OECD (2007), *Integrity in Public Procurement: Good Practice from A to Z*, OECD Publishing, Paris, http://dx.doi.org/10.1787/9789264027510-en.

In strengthening its values-based strategy, PEMEX could also consider investing in creating an open organisation culture that could guide and support its staff in applying ethical values and integrity standards in their daily activity. In particular, the OECD has recognised the importance of developing the necessary judgement and skills enabling public servants to apply ethical principles in concrete circumstances and, for this purpose, it has recommended not only to set up specific training on these issues but also to provide impartial advice to expose, discuss and resolve ethical dilemmas and questions.

Currently, within PEMEX there is an Ethics Committee (*Comité de Etica*) that is composed of representatives from each corporate unit and supports PEMEX in improving ethical standards within the organisation. Furthermore, it analyses reports over potential breaches to the Code of Ethics, provides strategies to increasing compliance with the corresponding standards as well as their knowledge and practice among employees. Most relevantly, the Ethics Committee is assigned the function to act as a consulting and advising entity specialised in issues related to the application of, and compliance with, the Codes of Ethics and Conduct (Reglas de Operación Del Comité de Ética de Petróleos Mexicanos, sus empresas productivas subsidiarias y empresas filiales).

In spite of the latter mandate, there is no evidence that the Ethics Committee, and PEMEX in general, offers its employees the opportunity to discuss ethical issues arising in the workplace or provides guidance on how to behave in dubious situations, so formal mechanisms may be introduced to offer guidance and internal consultation to PEMEX employees, which could take the form of advice from supervisors but also from an impartial subject where open dialogue and confidentiality is ensured. In this context, PEMEX may consider the example of the Norwegian state-owned company Statoil's online portal where ethical advice is provided to both internal and external subjects and anonymity can be requested. Moreover, the ethical advice function is provided on the same webpage where misconduct can be reported (Box 6.11).

Box 6.11. Statoil's EthicsPoint

StatOil, Norway's state-owned oil company, operates on a values-based business strategy, which gives its employees the possibility to raise questions about its Code of Conduct through the Statoil's Ethics Helpline, the same platform used to report misconduct (see Box 6.12).

For this purpose, StatOil provides a 24-hour phone service and a web submission portal, where any internal or external person may ask any question about the Code of Conduct, in an anonymous way.

Once the question is submitted, a report key is generated in order to review any follow-up questions or submit more information about the question.

The question is then processed by the Ethics and Anti-corruption compliance function (CFO LEG COL), headed by the Corporate Compliance Officer, who has advice responsibilities in relation to:

- the Ethics Code of Conduct
- corruption prevention
- interpretation and adherence to applicable anti-corruption legislation, governing documents or other relevant internal policies.

With specific regard to managers, all compliance officers – who are designated by each Business Area and central staff function manager – also provide advice to line management on ethics and corruption issues in the corresponding business unit.

Source: Statoil (2016), "Statoil's Ethics Helpline", website, https://secure.ethicspoint.eu/domain/media/en/gui/102166/index.html; and Statoil (2009), "Anti-corruption compliance program", www.statoil.com/no/About/EthicsValues/Downloads/Anti-corruption%20compliance%20program.pdf.

Moreover, PEMEX could also follow the G20/OECD Corporate Governance Principles that suggest offering a contact point for employees who wish to report concerns about unethical or illegal behaviour that might also compromise the integrity of financial statements. All these mechanisms would not only help employees discuss ethical dilemmas and moral reasoning, but would also allow the Code of Ethics and Conduct to be practically applicable and eventually improved in case they do not reflect the reality and challenges of the organisation.

Protecting whistleblowers is essential to building a culture of integrity where officials feel confident coming forward to report wrongdoing.

Promoting a system to disclose wrongdoing within both private and public organisations contributes significantly to creating a culture of integrity insofar as it leads to a working environment where unethical behaviour is rejected and sanctioned, even when traditional forms of control do not detect it. However, in order for these kinds of mechanisms to function effectively, organisations have to encourage reporting misconduct, make sure that reporting channels are clear and well known throughout the organisation and, at the same time, ensure that the confidentiality of whistleblowers is protected and retaliation prevented.

In PEMEX there are currently two separate channels to report misconduct related to ethical behaviours: one for breaches of the Code of Conduct (Mecanismo para la Atención del Incumplimiento al Código de Conducta) and the other for any kind of complaints (www.quejasoic.pemex.com). While the former reports are assessed by the Internal Institutional Control Unit (Unidad de Control Interno Institucional, or UCII), the latter are handled by the Responsibilities Unit (Unidad de Responsabilidades), which is under the umbrella of the Ministry of Public Administration (Secretaría de la Función Pública, or SFP). The two channels are available on different websites, the first one on PEMEX's Code of Conduct webpage (www.pemex.com/acerca/codigo-de-conducta/Paginas/default.aspx), the second on a website managed by the SFP (www.quejasoic.pemex.com/Index.html). Neither of the two webpages informs the user of the existence of the other mechanism, nor provides a link to it. More generally, the accessibility from the homepage is not straightforward and requires navigating PEMEX's website through different levels.

Considering that channels of disclosure should be clearly demarcated and favour disclosure of wrongdoing in order to build confidence in the overall system (OECD, 2016), PEMEX could improve accessibility to the two channels and make the differences and purposes clear in order to ensure the coherence of the overall reporting system. In this sense, PEMEX may also consider creating a single reporting procedure or, at least, presenting the existing ones in a single webpage together with tools to support users in deciding which channel to use.

In 2015, PEMEX launched an Ethical Help Line (Línea Ética de Ayuda) with the aim to improve clarity and ensure co-ordination in the receipt and elaboration of the reports received. According to the information provided by PEMEX, there should be a single channel to report misconduct, which will then be filtered and forwarded to either the UCII or the Responsibilities Unit (Figure 6.4).

Figure 6.4. **Outline of the PEMEX Ethical Help Line (Línea Ética de Ayuda)**

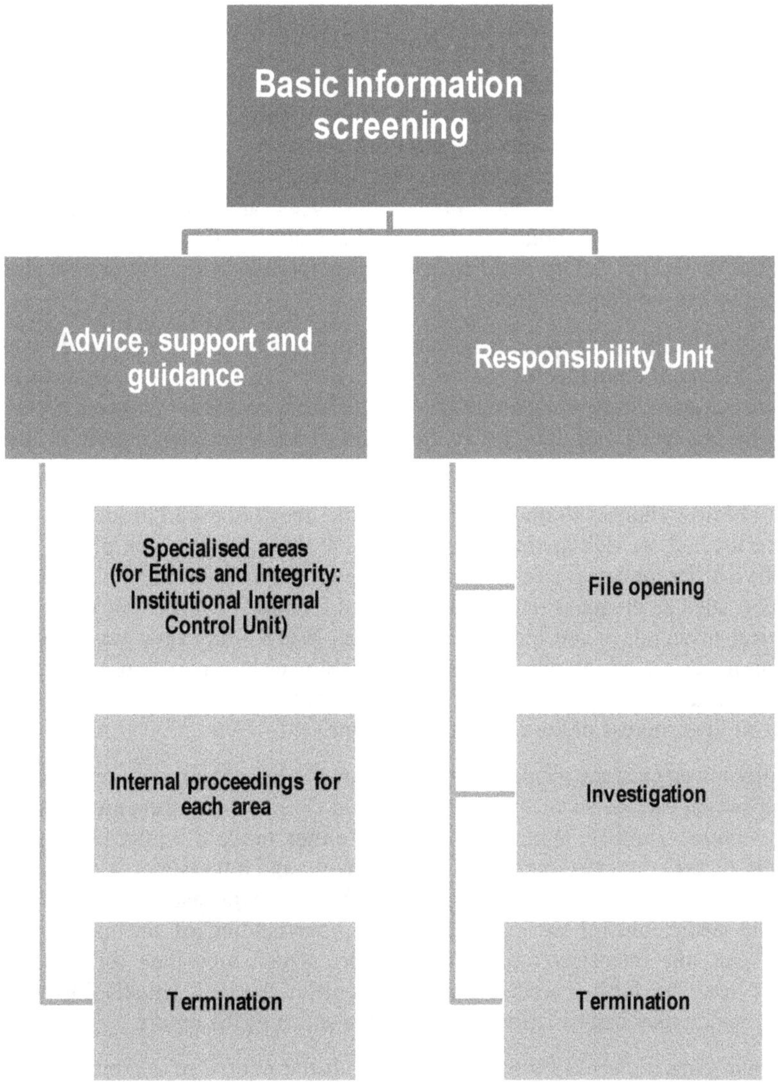

Source: Based on PEMEX (2016), "Línea ética de ayuda y mecanismos de coordinación para la atención de denuncias", presentation by PEMEX.

Unifying the receipt of wrongdoings may increase users' confidence in reporting misconduct without fearing that the wrong institution has been addressed. However, there is no evidence on how the new mechanism works in practice so it is difficult to assess whether it addresses some of the above-mentioned challenges related to co-ordination and accessibility. In the current implementation phase, PEMEX may nevertheless consider the Ethics Helpline set up by the Norwegian state-owned company Statoil, which presents all the possible channels to interact with the company in a single webpage, easily accessible from Statoil's homepage (Box 6.12).

Box 6.12. Ethics Helpline at Statoil

Recognising that clear access to whistleblowing channels is a crucial part of values and ethics, Statoil provides several avenues through which employees and third parties interacting with Statoil can raise concerns. Employees and third parties have the option to either bring their concerns forward to a superior or other relevant internal entity, or report their concerns to Statoil's Ethics Helpline. Statoil encourages employees and third-party entities to make disclosures related to possible breaches to Statoil's Code of Conduct; applicable laws and regulations; Statoils Health, Safety and Environment responsibilities; and/or concerns related to internationally recognised human rights.

Statoil's Ethics Helpline webpage is hosted by a third-party helpline provider, which ensures the anonymity and confidentiality of the whistleblower. The webpage is easy to access from Statoil's homepage, and offers whistleblowers four different options: 1) make a report on line; 2) make a report by phone; 3) follow up on a report; and 4) ask a question regarding Statoil's Code of Conduct.

If a whistleblower chooses to make a report on line, they are asked to identify the country in which they are located, as well as the country in which the violation took place. They can then choose from five different categories that best represents the incident they wish report. Integrity-related offences, such as breaches to Statoil's Code of Conduct, conflicts of interest, corruption, fraud and ethical misconduct, are included in this list. When filing their report, whistleblowers have the option to remain anonymous. After a whistleblower has made a report on line, they are assigned a "report key", which is a unique code and a password. Using their report key, callers can follow up on the progress of their report at any time.

If a whistleblower chooses to make a report over the telephone, they are asked to indicate the country in which they wish to make the report in. From there, they are provided with the appropriate telephone number. Whistleblowers can either make a report in English or in the language of any of the countries Statoil has operations in, and a translator is on hand to translate for them. Whistleblowers are connected to an interviewer, who asks questions related to the concerns of the whistleblower to ensure a better understanding of the nature of the report. Following the call, the interviewer prepares a report, which they then forward to the Ethics Helpline for review and further processing. At the end of the call, whistleblowers are given a report number, which they can use to follow up on the status of the report.

Any personal data collected by Statoil throughout the course of a report is processed and retained in accordance with the Norwegian Personal Data Act and other applicable laws and legislation. Statoil holds a license from the Norwegian Data Protection Authorities for the operation of the Ethics Helpline.

Source: Statoil (2016), "Statoil's Ethics Helpline", website, https://secure.ethicspoint.eu/domain/media/en/gui/102166/index.html

A further point to take into consideration in setting up the new Ethical Help Line is to ensure the possibility to make anonymous disclosures: although the desirability of the latter option is still very much debated, anonymous disclosure may encourage reporting, especially in countries where whistleblowing is not a common practice. One of the two reporting mechanisms that are currently in place (Mecanismo para la Atención del Incumplimiento al Código de Conducta) does not ensure complete anonymity insofar as the reporting person can decide not to provide information on identity (with the exception of sexual harassment cases); however, the form has to be sent via email, which often discloses the identity of the sender.

In reviewing the existing system, PEMEX may want to provide whistleblowers the opportunity to remain anonymous, as in the example of Statoil, whose Ethics Helpline webpage is hosted by a third-party helpline provider and which assigns a unique code and a password ("report key") after a whistleblower has made a report on line in order to provide confidentiality and anonymity of the reporting process (Box 6.12).

Another crucial element to address in implementing the new Ethical Help Line will be to raise awareness about it among employees, since there is no evidence that PEMEX has set up any programme with such a purpose in relation to the current mechanism. This aspect represents one of the key recommendations highlighted by an OECD report on whistleblowing, which lists a series of ways to raise awareness, such as training, newsletters, and information sessions about reporting channels and procedures to facilitate disclosures (OECD, 2016). In this sense, PEMEX could consider assigning such responsibility to the management, in line with practice followed in the United States where the head of each agency has to ensure that agency employees are informed of the rights and remedies available to them, including how to make lawful disclosure of information that is specifically required by law or executive order to be kept classified (Box 6.13).

Box 6.13. The United States' approach to increasing awareness through the Whistleblower Protection Enhancement Act

In the United States, the Whistleblower Protection Enhancement Act (WPEA) places the responsibility with the head of agency to increase the awareness of the rights and responsibilities of whistleblowers. Under 5 U.S.C. § 2302(c) of the WPEA, it is stipulated that "the head of each agency shall be responsible for the prevention of prohibited personnel practices, for the compliance with and enforcement of applicable civil service laws, rules, and regulations, and other aspects of personnel management, and for ensuring (...) that agency employees are informed of the rights and remedies available to them under (...), including how to make a lawful disclosure of information that is specifically required by law or Executive order to be kept classified in the interest of national defence or the conduct of foreign affairs to the Special Counsel, the Inspector General of an agency, Congress, or other agency employee designated to receive such disclosures."

Furthermore, Section 117 of the Act "designates a Whistleblower Protection Ombudsman who shall educate agency employees:

1. about prohibitions on retaliation for protected disclosures
2. who have made or are contemplating making a protected disclosure about the rights and remedies against retaliation for protected disclosures."

Source: American Bar Association (2012), "Congress strengthens whistleblower protections for federal employees", *Newsletter*, Issue: November-December 2012, www.americanbar.org/content/newsletter/groups/labor_law/ll_flash/1212_abalel_flash/lel_flash12_2012spec.html.

Another useful tool to improve public awareness, transparency and confidence in PEMEX's whistleblowing mechanism would be to publish reports to illustrate the yearly activity of the company on this issue. This could also help assess the effectiveness of the whistleblowing system.

In this context, PEMEX could consider the practice of the Italian state-owned company, Ente Nazionale Idrocarburi (Eni) which, on its website, publishes a written report on the "Whistleblowing reports received (including anonymously) by Eni and by its subsidiaries in Italy and abroad". It includes graphs to illustrate and report the number of reports received by sector and the consequences of the investigations. Both the report and the webpage with graphs are available in Italian and English (see Eni, n. d.).

Proposals for action

PEMEX could seize the opportunities provided by the Energy Reform to strengthen its legal framework for corruption prevention.

- Define the exact scope and application of integrity rules to increase understanding and awareness from suppliers and external stakeholders.
- Provide comprehensive guidance on integrity matters and publicly clarify applicable anti-corruption and transparency obligations.

PEMEX could extend the existing integrity policy and standards to all those working for PEMEX and its suppliers.

- Extend the application of PEMEX's integrity rule to consultants in order to level the playing field among people working in the company, while setting clear standards to deal with the confidential and privileged information they might have at their disposal.
- Provide guidance to deal with conflict-of-interest situations that may arise between consultants and clients.
- Extend the scope of PEMEX's Code of Ethics and Code of Conduct to all the partners interacting with the company and expect from them the same level of integrity required of its personnel.
- Address ethical commitments and integrity issues within consultancy agreements.

PEMEX could strengthen anti-corruption by mapping its corruption risks.

- Put in place formal mechanisms for monitoring risks to corruption.
- Develop a corruption risk map of the organisation and its processes in order to identify issues such as vulnerable positions, as well as risky activities and projects.
- Develop a system of warning signals – such as red flags – in relation to critical processes, vulnerable positions, risky activities and projects.
- Set up a system to map risks of corruption in relation to each project in order to ensure the integrity and responsibility for all stakeholders involved in each procurement process.
- Introduce a system to monitor and periodically evaluate the map in order to ensure that its corruption risk-assessment strategy remains up-to-date and effective.

PEMEX needs a comprehensive policy framework on conflict of interest.

- Develop a consistent and comprehensive framework to manage conflict of interest, defining the disclosure of a private interest as a first necessary step to be taken to determine what measures are needed to resolve or manage the conflict positively.
- Improve transparency over the qualification and selection process of the independent members of the Board of Directors.
- Introduce mechanisms to extend conflict-of-interest reporting obligations to private actors at an early stage of the procurement process.

PEMEX could further ensure that integrity measures are effectively enforced, especially in relation to the disciplinary liability for independent members of the Board of Directors.

- Introduce administrative rules and procedures with respect to the investigation and sanctions for cases of disciplinary breaches committed by members of the Board of Directors without impairing their independence.
- Develop statistical data on the disciplinary procedures of both its personnel and the Board, and publish a yearly report on its website with information about the outcomes of cases and the effectiveness of the enforcement mechanisms.

PEMEX could incentivise stronger integrity on the part of its suppliers through various means, including greater transparency, introducing integrity standards for eligibility, and ensuring effective sanctions.

- Publish the content of the declaration that PEMEX's suppliers have to submit in relation to their integrity and ethics schemes.
- Introduce systemic controls to check whether such declarations correspond to reality.
- Stimulate suppliers to develop their own integrity standards and programmes.

PEMEX needs to strengthen its culture of integrity through more ambitious efforts for awareness raising and capacity building.

- Pursue the intended project to assess employee knowledge of the Codes of Ethics and Conduct and publish results on its website, in order to further engage them and improve their expected ethical knowledge and behaviours.
- Provide ad hoc training on integrity and ethics-related issues for procurement officials and officials in high-risk positions.
- Stimulate the creation of an open organisation culture to guide and support the staff in applying ethical values and integrity standards in their daily activity. In this sense, develop mechanisms to provide impartial advice to expose, discuss and resolve ethical dilemmas and questions.
- Consider setting up an online portal to provide ethical advice to both internal and external subjects, including anonymously.

Protecting whistleblowers is essential to building a culture of integrity where officials feel confident coming forward to report wrongdoing.

- Improve the accessibility of existing channels to disclose wrongdoing in order to build confidence in the overall integrity system.
- Consider creating a single reporting procedure or, at least, presenting the existing ones in a single webpage together with tools to support users in deciding which channel to use.
- In implementing the Ethical Help Line (Línea Ética de Ayuda), ensure the possibility to make anonymous disclosures, and raise awareness about it among employees.
- Publish reports about whistleblowing activity in order to publicly illustrate the yearly activity of the company on this issue as well as to assess and monitor its effectiveness.

Notes

1. In July 2016 a new law on administrative responsibility of public servants was enacted (Ley General de Responsabilidades Administrativas) and will replace the existing LFRASP once it will enter into force on 19 July 2017. The new law lays out the duties and responsibilities of public officials (including for the disclosure of private interest) and sets out administrative disciplinary procedures for misconduct, differentiating between less serious and serious offences, the latter of which may now fall under the jurisdiction of the Federal Tribunal of Administrative Justice.

References

American Bar Association (2012), "Congress strengthens whistleblower protections for federal employees", *Newsletter*, Issue: November-December 2012, www.americanbar.org/content/newsletter/groups/labor_law/ll_flash/1212_abalel_flash/lel_flash12_2012spec.html.

ANAC (Autoritá Nazionale Anticorruzione) (2015), "Linee guida per l'attuazione della normativa in materia di prevenzione della corruzione e trasparenza da parte delle società e degli enti di diritto privato controllati e partecipati dalle pubbliche amministrazioni e degli enti pubblici economici", Resolution no. 8/2015, www.anticorruzione.it/portal/public/classic/AttivitaAutorita/AttiDellAutorita/_Atto?ca=6170.

CIECI (Construction Industry Ethics and Compliance Initiative) (2014), "Frequently Asked Questions", webpage, www.ciecinitiative.org/Faqs (accessed 23 March 2016).

Eni (n. d.), "Whistleblowing Reports Received by ENI", Anticorruption and whistleblowing, www.eni.com/en_DE/deutschland/corporate-governance/whistleblowing-reports/whistleblowing-reports.shtml.

GAO (Government Accountability Office) (2015), "A Framework for Managing Fraud Risks in Federal Programs", GAO-15-593SP, www.gao.gov/products/GAO-15-593SP.

OECD (2016), *Committing to Effective Whistleblower Protection*, OECD Publishing, Paris, http://dx.doi.org/10.1787/9789264252639-en.

OECD (2015a), *OECD Economic Surveys: Mexico 2015*, OECD Publishing, Paris, http://dx.doi.org/10.1787/eco_surveys-mex-2015-en.

OECD (2015b), *Effective Delivery of Large Infrastructure Projects: The Case of the New International Airport of Mexico City*, OECD Public Governance Reviews, OECD Publishing, Paris. http://dx.doi.org/10.1787/9789264248335-en.

OECD (2015c), *OECD Guidelines on Corporate Governance of State-Owned Enterprises, 2015 Edition*, OECD Publishing, Paris, http://dx.doi.org/10.1787/9789264244160-en.

OECD (2014), *OECD Foreign Bribery Report: An Analysis of the Crime of Bribery of Foreign Public Officials*, OECD Publishing, Paris, http://dx.doi.org/10.1787/9789264226616-en.

OECD (2013), *Public Procurement Review of the State's Employees' Social Security and Social Services Institute in Mexico*, OECD Public Governance Reviews, OECD Publishing, http://dx.doi.org/10.1787/9789264197305-en.

OECD (2009), *OECD Principles for Integrity in Public Procurement*, OECD Publishing, Paris, http://dx.doi.org/10.1787/9789264056527-en.

OECD (2007), *Integrity in Public Procurement: Good Practice from A to Z*, OECD Publishing, Paris, http://dx.doi.org/10.1787/9789264027510-en.

OECD (2004), *Managing Conflict of Interest in the Public Service: OECD Guidelines and Country Experiences*, OECD Publishing, Paris, http://dx.doi.org/10.1787/9789264104938-en.

PEMEX (2016), "Línea ética de ayuda y mecanismos de coordinación para la atención de denuncias", presentation by PEMEX.

Procurement Transformation Division (2014), "Procurement guidance - Use of probity auditors and advisors in procurement", www.hpw.qld.gov.au/SiteCollectionDocuments/ProcurementGuideProbityAuditorsAdvisors.pdf (accessed 23 February 2016).

Queensland Government (2011), "Code of Conduct for the Queensland Public Service", www.psc.qld.gov.au/includes/assets/qps-code-conduct.pdf (accessed 10 February 2016).

State of Illinois (n. d.), "Financial Disclosures and Conflicts of Interest", www.siue.edu/text/purchasing/staff/pdf/Financial%20Disclosures%20and%20Conflicts%20of%20Interest%20V%2014%202-2.pdf (accessed 12 February 2016).

Statoil (2016), "Statoil's Ethics Helpline", website, https://secure.ethicspoint.eu/domain/media/en/gui/102166/index.html.

Statoil (2009), "Anti-corruption compliance program", www.statoil.com/no/About/EthicsValues/Downloads/Anti-corruption%20compliance%20program.pdf.

Tasmanian Government (2015), "Checklist of potential risks in the goods and services procurement process", www.purchasing.tas.gov.au/buyingforgovernment/getpage.jsp?uid=07CC4222E4F10F00CA256C8D007F9FC6.

Transparency International, (2011), Corruption Risk Assessment Topic Guide, http://gateway.transparency.org/files/uploads/Corruption_Risk_Assessment_Topic_Guide.pdf.

U4 (2011), "Examples of integrity agreements for consultants and advisors", U4 Anti-Corruption Resource Centre, Chr. Michelsen Institute, Bergen, Norway, www.u4.no/publications/examples-of-integrity-agreements-for-consultants-and-advisors/ (accessed 10 February 2016).

World Bank (n. d.), "Most common red flags of fraud and corruption in procurement", http://siteresources.worldbank.org/INTDOII/Resources/Red_flags_reader_friendly.pdf (accessed 8 October 2016).

Chapter 7

Ensuring Petróleos Mexicanos' accountability through transparency and stronger engagement with civil society

Ensuring an open and transparent procurement system in all stages of the procurement cycle is a fundamental element to guarantee fair and equitable treatment for PEMEX's potential suppliers and to promote accountability of its activities toward all stakeholders. The Mexican legal framework on transparency and access to information has improved in recent years due a federal reform which introduced several changes at the institutional and substantial level. Further obligations apply to all public entities working in the energy sector and provide for enhanced transparency for PEMEX procurement information. This Chapter assesses the impact of the latter changes and elaborates recommendations on how to further ensure that transparency measures and mechanisms for stakeholder participation lead to effective accountability of PEMEX's activity. Such assessment does not only consider the accessibility and the format of public procurement information, but it also addresses the balance between transparency and confidentiality, as well as the participation of social witnesses and the engagement with the private sector.

Increasing access and availability of procurement information

Transparency is a crucial tool to ensure integrity in all stages of the procurement cycle. Disclosing information to the public and making it available to external stakeholders not only promotes a level playing field for potential suppliers, but also enables civil society to monitor activities and prevent corruption and misconduct. More generally, it allows the general public to become aware of public money spending and, eventually, to gain trust in public institutions.

Mexico has been working to improve its framework on transparency and access to information through a major reform that addressed both institutional and substantial issues (Ley General de Transparencia y Acceso a la Información Pública, or the Transparency Law). In particular, the reform has created the National Transparency System, which is led and co-ordinated by the National Institute for Transparency and Access to Information (Instituto Nacional de Transparencia, Acceso a la Información y Protección de Datos Personales, or INAI). It envisages the creation of a National Transparency Platform (Plataforma Nacional de Transparencia) that was launched in May 2016, aims at allowing citizens to request information in a standardised way, and provides for a number of transparency obligations.

Petróleos Mexicanos (or PEMEX), as any other entity receiving public funding or exercising public authority, is subject to the new regulation. It also has to comply with specific provisions for entities working in the energy sector, which requires maximum transparency of some acts (contracts, permits, joint ventures, companies) and sets a minimum set of information to be disclosed through mechanisms that guarantee circulation and public consultation (Article 83 of the PEMEX Law). Further obligations are set for federal and constitutionally autonomous entities by the Federal Law on Transparency and Access to Public Government Information (Ley Federal de Transparencia y Acceso a la Información Pública Gubernamental).

With specific regard to PEMEX's contracting activity, the PEMEX Law has introduced an online system of public information about suppliers that should be regularly updated and contain information on the contracts signed in the last five years (Sistema de información pública de proveedores y contratistas). At the institutional level, in May 2015 PEMEX and INAI signed a co-operation agreement (*convenio general de colaboración*) and agreed to work together on a number of initiatives that aim to strengthen the culture of transparency, openness, and personal data protection. In particular, the two institutions agreed to:

- organise courses, workshops and seminars for PEMEX personnel to raise awareness about transparency and personal data protection
- elaborate a strategy that favours the automatic publication of information
- set up an adequate mechanism to make public any relevant information for society
- carry out media campaigns to instil a culture of transparency
- improve the capacity and development of PEMEX personnel on access to information
- create dialogue and exchange of experiences among the two institutions.

Although the framework provided for by federal and PEMEX-specific laws represent a solid starting point to establish an open and transparent contracting activity, PEMEX may address the existing mechanisms to disclose information in order to make them easily accessible to the public, including through the use of open data. In this context PEMEX needs to ensure that protecting sensitive commercial information and competition would not undermine the highest degree of transparency of its procurement activity. Further challenges concern the participation of social witnesses to observe the steps of the contracting process whereas PEMEX could improve the existing framework by enhancing the transparency of the criteria for their participation, as well their impact on PEMEX procurement activity. More generally, PEMEX could benefit from establishing further mechanisms to engage with private sector representatives.

It is not sufficient to merely publish information; true transparency and accountability can only be achieved when such information is easily accessible to the public for analysis. PEMEX may wish to improve the accessibility of its public procurement information, particularly through a single database.

Considering the existing legal framework, data and information on PEMEX procurement activity can currently be found in a number of venues:

- on the National Transparency Obligations Portal (Portal de Obligaciones de Transparencia), which contains the information to be published pursuant to the Transparency Law (http://portaltransparencia.gob.mx/buscador/search/search.do?method=begin)
- on PEMEX's website, providing information about suppliers and contractors' profiles related to open competitions, restricted procedures and relationship with suppliers over the last five years (www.pemex.com/procura/relacion-con-proveedores/Paginas/info-proveedores-contratistas.aspx) (cf. Article 85, PEMEX Law and Articles 22-25, PEMEX Agreement CA-125/2014)
- on PEMEX Procurement International's website - a company 100% owned by PEMEX and incorporated in Delaware – containing international public tenders
- in Mexico's Official Gazette (Diario Oficial de la Federación, or DOF), where all international open competitions under the scope of Free Trade Agreements signed by Mexico are published.

The answers and the evidence provided show that PEMEX is making efforts to align to the relevant legal framework and to ensure proactive disclosure of information concerning its procurement activity. However, concerns remain on the fragmentation and accessibility of the information, which affects its overall quality and creates difficulties for citizens and suppliers who wish to consult it. In this sense, three sets of shortcomings have emerged from the analysis of the existing channels of information:

- The National Transparency Obligations Portal provides detailed information on PEMEX's contracting activity; however, it is hard to filter and consult contracts according to certain important criteria, such as the type of contracting procedure (*procedimiento de contratación*).
- PEMEX's Public Information System of Suppliers (Sistema de información pública de proveedores y contratistas) is a useful tool containing a significant amount of relevant information, yet it is presented in an Excel file through the use

of several acronyms, making it difficult to process its information for those who do not have the technical knowledge to do so or previous experience with PEMEX's procedures. Furthermore, it is not straightforward to find such a document in the website, as it is found after entering the "Suppliers" section and then the "Relation to Suppliers" sub-section.

- PEMEX Procurement International's website contains a page giving access to international public tenders divided in three sections (in registration; in process; concluded); however, as of October 2016, it only contains five contracts. This raises doubts over the exhaustiveness of its information (http://pemexprocurement.com/es/proveedores/licitaciones-publicas/).

In spite of recent efforts to increase the transparency of its contracting activity, PEMEX needs to simplify the existing means to publish its information. To this end, it may consider providing a single database containing all the information that is currently spread across various channels. Such an instrument should be user-friendly and easily accessible on the PEMEX website. It should also make it easy for users to visualise procurement information by the type of procedure used in terms of numbers and value. At the same time, it should be compatible with national transparency obligations and contain information on what will be procured in the future, including procurement plans and future procurements, which are currently available in a separate page (www.pemex.com/bienes-y-servicios/ley-pemex/Paginas/default.aspx). In designing a single and comprehensive database containing these features, PEMEX may consider the example provided by New York City, which set up an interactive and user-friendly portal to publish all its financial information (Box 7.1).

Box 7.1. Checkbook NYC: An online transparency tool

In July 2010, the New York City Comptroller's Office launched Checkbook NYC, an online transparency tool that for the first time placed the City's day-to-day spending in the public domain. Using an intuitive dashboard approach that combines a series of graphs and user-friendly tables, Checkbook NYC provides up-to-date information about the City's financial condition.

The website provides information about:

- budget
- revenue
- spending
- contracts
- payroll
- sub-vendors
- Minority and Women-owned Business Enterprises (M/WBE).

Box 7.1. **Checkbook NYC: An online transparency tool** ***(continued)***

The contracts section, in turn, is divided into six sub-sections classifying the information according to their status, namely:

- active expense contracts
- registered expense contracts
- active revenue contracts
- pending expense contracts
- pending revenue contracts.

Contracts include information on the contracting agency, prime supplier, current amount of the contract, original amount and how much has been spent to date.

Information on contract modification includes, among other things, the percentage between the original contract amount and the current amount, as well as how much the contract has been modified.

In order to guide citizens and firms in using the website and all the information provided therein, a Help section contains a number of useful tools which contribute to the website's effectiveness and accessibility. In particular, one can receive guidance and interact with the website through the following sections:

- site navigation and glossary
- instructional videos
- FAQs
- ask a question
- report a problem
- share an idea.

Source: New York City Comptroller (2014), "Checkbook NYC", official New York City website, www.checkbooknyc.com/contracts_landing/status/A/yeartype/B/year/116 (accessed 22 February 2016).

Publishing procurement information in open data format could contribute to enhancing PEMEX transparency and accountability

A relatively recent trend undertaken by many countries to increase the transparency and accountability of public institutions is to make their data available to the public and allow the use, reuse and free distribution of datasets through the so-called open data format. The OECD has been analysing such an increasingly relevant phenomenon and has identified the potentials of the extraordinary quantity and centrality of data collected by governments, not only in terms openness, transparency and accountability, but also as a means to enhance sharing, collaborating and higher public engagement. As for the difference with the concept of access to information, while the focus of the latter is whether the government ensures the right to access information, open government tends to assess how governments release large volumes of information in terms of formats and reusability (Ubaldi, 2013). In 2013, G8 countries adopted an Open Data Charter, which represents the first international instrument to guide the implementation of open government data (OGD) strategies; it defines five principles:

1. open data by default
2. quality and quantity data
3. usable by all
4. releasing data for improved governance
5. releasing data for innovation, as well as three collective actions to guide the implementation of those principles. (UK Government, 2013)

In this context, Mexico scores above the OECD average according the OECD pilot Index on Open Government Data (OECD OURdata Index). which assesses governments' efforts to implement open data in three dimensions based on its methodology and structured around the following principles of the G7 Open Data Charter: 1) data availability on the national portal (based on Principle 1 and Collective action 2); 2) data accessibility on the national portal (based on Principle 3); and 3) governments' support to innovative re-use and stakeholder engagement (Principle 5) (see Figure 7.1).

Figure 7.1. **OECD OURdata Index: Open, useful, reusable government data, 2014**[1]

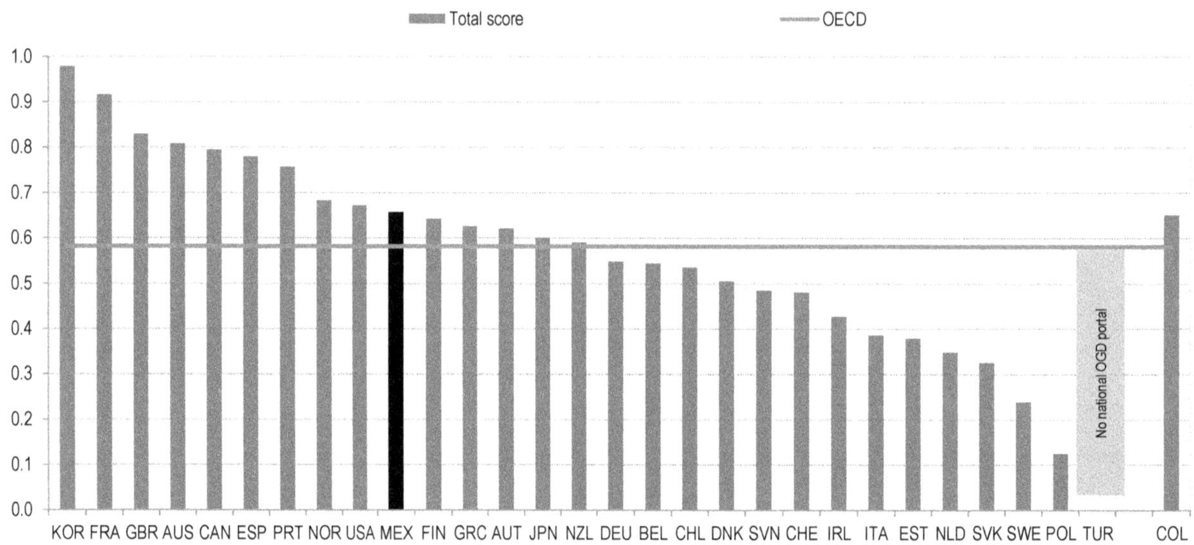

Notes: The OECD OURdata Index assesses governments' efforts to implement open data in the three critical areas - openness, usefulness and re-usability of government data. Data for the index is taken from member countries and focuses on government efforts to ensure public sector data availability and accessibility and to spur a greater re-use. The Index is based on OECD methodology and the guidelines of the G7 OGD Charter. The graph shows a composite index where 0 is lowest and 1 highest.

1. Data for the Czech Republic, Hungary, Iceland, Israel and Luxembourg are not available.

Source: OECD (2015a), *Government at a Glance 2015*, OECD Publishing, Paris, http://dx.doi.org/10.1787/gov_glance-2015-en.

In spite of Mexico's score, PEMEX is still lagging behind in the use of open data for its procurement activity, as no evidence was provided or found on this topic. As consequence, PEMEX could develop its own open data framework and instruments, taking into consideration the Open Contracting Global Principles (Box 7.2). Such principles aim to make contracting more competitive and fair, improving contract performance, and securing development outcomes through the disclosure of documents and information "in a manner that enables meaningful understanding, effective monitoring, efficient performance and accountability for outcomes." (Preamble of Open Contracting Global Principles in Open Contracting Partnership, 2016).

Box 7.2. Open Contracting Global Principles

Affirmative disclosure

1. Governments shall recognise the right of the public to access information related to the formation, award, execution, performance, and completion of public contracts.
2. Public contracting shall be conducted in a transparent and equitable manner, in accordance with publicly disclosed rules that explain the functioning of the process, including policies regarding disclosure.
3. Governments shall require the timely, current, and routine publication of enough information about the formation, award, execution, performance, and completion of public contracts to enable the public, including media and civil society, to understand and monitor as a safeguard against inefficient, ineffective, or corrupt use of public resources. This would require affirmative disclosure of:
    1. contracts, including licenses, concessions, permits, grants or any other document exchanging public goods, assets, or resources (including all annexes, schedules and documents incorporated by reference) and any amendments thereto
    2. related pre-studies, bid documents, performance evaluations, guarantees, and auditing reports
    3. information concerning contract formation, including:
        1. the planning process of the procurement
        2. the method of procurement or award and the justification thereof
        3. the scope and specifications for each contract
        4. the criteria for evaluation and selection
        5. the bidders or participants in the process, their validation documents, and any procedural exemptions for which they qualify
        6. any conflicts of interest uncovered or debarments issued
        7. the results of the evaluation, including the justification for the award
        8. the identity of the contract recipient and any statements of beneficial ownership provided
    4. information related to performance and completion of public contracts, including information regarding subcontracting arrangements, such as
        1. general schedules, including major milestones in execution, and any changes thereto
        2. status of implementation against milestones
        3. dates and amounts of stage payments made or received (against total amount) and the source of those payments

Box 7.2. **Open Contracting Global Principles** ***(continued)***

4. service delivery and pricing
5. arrangements for ending contracts
6. final settlements and responsibilities
7. risk assessments, including environmental and social impact assessments
8. assessments of assets and liabilities of government related to the contract
9. provisions in place to ensure appropriate management of ongoing risks and liabilities
10. appropriate financial information regarding revenues and expenditures, such as time and cost overruns, if any.

4. Governments shall develop systems to collect, manage, simplify and publish contracting data regarding the formation, award, execution, performance and completion of public contracts in an open and structured format, in accordance with the Open Contracting Data Standards as they are developed, in a user-friendly and searchable manner.
5. Contracting information made available to the public shall be as complete as possible, with any exceptions or limitations narrowly defined by law, ensuring that citizens have effective access to recourse in instances where access to this information is in dispute.
6. Contracting parties, including international financial institutions, shall support disclosure in future contracting by precluding confidentiality clauses, drafting confidentiality narrowly to cover only permissible limited exemptions, or including provisions within the contractual terms and conditions to allow for the contract and related information to be published.

Participation, monitoring, and oversight

1. Governments shall recognise the right of the public to participate in the oversight of the formation, award, execution, performance, and completion of public contracts.
2. Governments shall foster an enabling environment, which may include legislation that recognises, promotes, protects, and creates opportunities for public consultation and monitoring of public contracting, from the planning stage to the completion of contractual obligations.
3. Governments shall work together with the private sector, donors, and civil society to build the capacities of all relevant stakeholders to understand, monitor and improve public contracting and to create sustainable funding mechanisms to support participatory public contracting.
4. Governments have a duty to ensure oversight authorities, including parliaments, audit institutions, and implementing agencies, to access and utilise disclosed information, acknowledge and act upon citizen feedback, and encourage dialogue and consultations between contracting parties and civil society organisations in order to improve the quality of contracting outcomes.
5. With regard to individual contracts of significant impact, contracting parties should craft strategies for citizen consultation and engagement in the management of the contract.

Source: Open Contracting Partnership (2016), "Open Contracting Global Principles", www.open-contracting.org/get-started/global-principles/.

As for more practical examples, PEMEX may consider the portals set up by the Italian government to monitor ongoing public infrastructures (Opencantieri) as well as the work done for the Universal Exhibition Expo Milan 2015 (OpenExpo) (Box 7.3).

Box 7.3. **Open data portals in Italy**

Opencantieri

Opencantieri is a project managed by the Ministry of Infrastructure and Transportation (Ministero delle infrastrutture e dei trasporti) to provide open, complete and up-to-date information on Italy's ongoing public infrastructure projects. The website (http://opencantieri.mit.gov.it/) that hosts the platform contains the available data and provides a synthesis as well as specific insights on issues such as financing, costs, timing and delays. All the information is publicly accessible and can be downloaded through the Ministry of Infrastructure and Transportation's open data website (http://dati.mit.gov.it/catalog/dataset).

OpenExpo

OpenExpo was the portal set up for the 2015 Universal Exposition of Milan (http://dati.openexpo2015.it/en); it dealt with several data and transparency issues, including the following sections:

- Why Open Expo
- Expo Barometro
- Open data
- Expo2015 works
- Reporting
- Transparent administration
- Visit Expo
- Use cases

The Open data section, in particular, contains all data related to the exhibition, which is displayed in open format similarly to the corresponding datasets (http://dati.openexpo2015.it/catalog/en/dataset). Datasets can be sought via a search engine by filtering data in the map, or by surfing datasets per description tag. For the data the licence used is Creative Commons - Attribution 4.0 International (CC BY 4.0), which allows users to copy and redistribute the material in any medium or format as well as to remix, transform, and build upon the material for any purpose, even commercially, giving appropriate credit, providing a link to the license, and indicating if changes were made (https://creativecommons.org/licenses/by/4.0/legalcode). Interestingly, the website provides exhaustive information on the format of the data as well as a section with examples of the re-use of the OpenExpo dataset (http://dati.openexpo2015.it/catalog/related, available in Italian only).

Establishing and publicising a disclosure policy identifying what information should be publicly disclosed by law, the appropriate channels for disclosure, and mechanisms for ensuring access to information.

The legal framework applicable to PEMEX provides for some notable exceptions to transparency insofar as it considers a number of situations where the information may be classified as reserved or confidential (Articles 113-119 of the Transparency Law and Articles 13-19 of the Federal Law on Transparency, respectively). In particular, the PEMEX Law (Article 111) refers to the latter cases and envisages the adoption of measures to protect information related to business, economic and industrial activity, as well as to maintain a competitive or economic advantage over third parties in the realisation of its activity. Such rules have been specified in PEMEX Agreement CA-117/2014, establishing that all information is public unless it is considered an industrial or commercial secret according to the Intellectual Property Law (Ley de la Propriedad Industrial) and that the heads of administrative units should restrict the disclosure of such information.

Given the new competitive context and the sensitivity of some information activity, PEMEX is faced with the challenge of protecting sensitive commercial information and competition, but at the same time ensuring full transparency of its procurement activity. On the one hand, the OECD acknowledges that transparency has to be balanced with legitimate needs for protection of trade secrets and proprietary information and other privacy concerns (OECD, 2015b). Similarly, the OECD recognises that governments may restrict the availability of some information in order to protect commercially sensitive information for bidders (e.g. content of competitive bids such as commercial secrets, individual prices, etc.) or security-sensitive information for the state (e.g. defence, national security) that could harm interests of the bidders or of the state. With regard to the former issue, the risk of publishing the names of the bidders before the actual submission of the bids may lead to uncompetitive practices (e.g. collusion or price fixing) as well as to the elimination of competition in case firms decide to submit common bids or to plan which will be the winner (OECD, 2007, pp. 29-30). On the other hand, PEMEX should ensure clarity and consistency about the transparency framework in order to promote fair and equitable treatment for potential suppliers. For this purpose, PEMEX may consider establishing a set of guidelines illustrating its policy on transparency and confidentiality, as well as clarifying which kind of information is disclosed and publish them on line. In the same context, PEMEX may also illustrate the procedure to access information and provide an accessible link to the relevant mechanism. In defining its policy on this matter, PEMEX may consider the guidance provided by the Australian government on its website, which consists of a set of principles (Box 7.4) completed by a set of practical indications.

Box 7.4. Principles on confidentiality throughout the procurement cycle in Australia

1. Entities undertaking procurement should be familiar with Australian Government legislation and policies relevant to confidentiality in procurement, including the Privacy Act (1988), the Freedom of Information Act 1982 (FOI Act) and the Australian Government Protective Security Policy Framework.
2. Throughout the procurement process, the Australian Government's confidentiality interests must be appropriately protected.
3. When planning a procurement, entities should consider the nature of the procurement and whether it is likely to raise confidentiality issues for the Australian Government. Such issues can arise in a number of ways including where:
    1. Potential suppliers need to have access to confidential information in order to understand the procurement and lodge a submission.

Box 7.4. **Principles on confidentiality throughout the procurement cycle in Australia** *(continued)*

2. The successful tenderer needs access to confidential information in order to fulfil the requirements of the contract.
3. The information generated as a result of performing the contract is confidential.

4. Request documentation, including any draft contract, should reflect the entity's requirements for confidentiality and position on commercially sensitive information as assessed by the entity during the procurement planning process.
5. Entities must ensure all submissions are treated as confidential for the duration of the procurement process. Similarly, all submissions must be kept confidential after the award of the contract. However, this does not preclude the reporting on AusTender of data that may have been included in the successful submission that is in turn transferred to the ultimate contract.
6. Following the evaluation process, entities need to assess any supplier claims to confidentiality to determine whether the information should be treated as confidential. Entities should not agree to confidentiality clauses in contracts unless an assessment has determined, in accordance with this guidance, that the information to be covered by the clauses is confidential.
7. There are two broad types of confidentiality clauses used in contracts:
    1. **general confidentiality clauses**, which either restate legislative obligations for confidentiality (such as under the Privacy Act (1988) or a secrecy provision) or set out a general understanding between the parties in relation to how they will deal with information when performing the contract
    2. **specific confidentiality clauses**, which protect the confidentiality of:
        1. all or part of the contract itself - such clauses would only be necessary where the contract needs to specify the information that the entity has determined is confidential
        2. information obtained or generated in performing the contract – such clauses can be used to protect commercial information that an entity has determined is confidential or for the protection of Australian Government material. Examples of such clauses include:
            - The entity has access to the supplier's confidential intellectual property during the performance of the contract.
            - A supplier needs to have access to sensitive security information in order to perform the requirements of the contract.
            - New software is created under the contract giving rise to new confidential intellectual property.
            - The contract is for a consultant to prepare a confidential report that is expected to deal with sensitive public interest issues.
8. Confidential information should be managed in accordance with any relevant legislation and confidentiality provisions in the contract. Irrespective of the terms of the contract, disclosure of a supplier's confidential information may be necessary in some cases, for example to a parliamentary committee.

Source: Australian Government's Department of Finance (2014), "Confidentiality throughout the procurement cycle", www.finance.gov.au/procurement/procurement-policy-and-guidance/buying/contract-issues/confidentiality-procurement-cycle/principles.html.

Enhancing social scrutiny and citizen participation

Existing mechanisms to involve social actors in PEMEX's procurement process

Creating a culture of openness in the public sector does not only derive from proactive disclosure of information; it is also achieved through the involvement of citizens, experts and civil society in the policy-making process through forms of "direct social control". Mexico has been at the forefront in this context, whereas it introduced an innovative way for society to perform such controls, namely through the so-called "social witnesses" (*testigos sociales*), first experimented with in 2001 and then established in the Public Procurement Law (Ley de Adquisiciones, Arrendamientos y Servicios del Sector Público). The Public Procurement Law envisages the mandatory participation of social witnesses in all stages of public tendering procedures above certain thresholds, which in 2015 were MXN 350 million (approximately USD 23 million) for goods and services and MXN 710 million (approximately USD 47 million) for public works. Social witnesses are elected by the Ministry of Public Administration (SFP) through public tendering and once they participate in the procurement process, they release a final report providing comments and recommendations on the process. These reports must subsequently be published on the Mexican federal e-procurement platform (CompraNet) (Box 7.5).

Box 7.5. Social witnesses in Mexico

Social witnesses are non-government organisations and individuals selected by the Ministry of Public Administration (SFP) through public tendering. SFP keeps a registry of the approved social witnesses and evaluates their performance; unsatisfactory performance potentially results in their removal from the registry.

When a federal entity requires the involvement of a social witness, it informs SFP who designates one from the registry.

As of January 2014, SFP had registered 39 social witnesses for public procurement projects, 5 civil society organisations and 34 individuals. This number grew from 5 social witnesses in 2005 to 40 in 2014.

SFP notes that "the monitoring of the most relevant procurement processes of the federal government through social witnesses has had an impact in improving procurement procedures by virtue of their contributions and experience, to the point that they have become a strategic element for ensuring the transparency and credibility of the procurement system." An OECD-World Bank Institute study (2006) indicates that the participation of social witnesses in procurement processes of the Federal Electricity Commission (Comisión Federal de Electricidad) created savings of approximately USD 26 million in 2006 and increased the number of bidders by over 50%.

Source: OECD (2014), *Compendium of Good Practices for Integrity in Public Procurement: Meeting of the Leading Practitioners in Procurement*, OECD, Paris.

Although the Public Procurement Law does not apply to PEMEX, PEMEX Law (Article 75[III]) and the Social Witness Guidelines (Lineamientos para la participación de testigos sociales durante actividades de procura y abastecimiento y procedimientos de contratación de Petróleos Mexicanos y sus Empresas Productivas Subsidiarias) also foresee the participation of social witnesses to observe the steps of the contracting process, release a final report with comments, and eventually report irregularities to the Internal Audit Office. At the same time, social witnesses in PEMEX are not nominated by SFP but rather by an internal Appointment Committee (Grupo de Designación). Another crucial difference with the federal model concerns the typologies of contracting procedures where they may participate, namely:

- when the procedures are authorised by the Board of Directors
- when required by the Procurement Committee
- when solicited by the Procurement Area.

The Social Witness Guidelines also establish that the reports of social witnesses are published and that the relevant comments are analysed and taken into consideration insofar as they are considered appropriate and contribute to the efficient performance of the procurement activities.

In addition to social witnesses, PEMEX also declared other ways for civil society to exercise scrutiny over its procurement process. Firstly, there is a programme called "Electronic witness" (*testigo electrónico*) whereby procurement events are transmitted via the Internet. Secondly, experts participate in the elaboration of the Norms of Reference (Normas de Referencia, or NRF) for particularly sensitive procurement. However, t the latter method of participation is not relevant anymore after the entry into force of the PEMEX Law.

Increasing the transparency around how PEMEX selects social witnesses would increase the legitimacy of the initiative and ensure trust around the contracting processes in which they are involved.

The presence of social witnesses during the contracting proceedings is an important element testifying to PEMEX's commitment to ensure social scrutiny over its procurement activity in line with the model successfully implemented at the federal level. At the same time, it is important that PEMEX currently publishes the sessions of the Appointment Committee as well as its minutes (www.pemex.com/procura/procedimientos-de-contratacion/testigo-social/Paginas/sesiones.aspx), thereby ensuring an adequate level of transparency of its activity. However, the Committee is internal to PEMEX, so additional measures could be taken to ensure its objectivity. In this sense, PEMEX may consider increasing the transparency of the Appointment Committee's functioning process, for instance, by making the relevant section of the website clearly accessible from the main procurement page or by introducing additional integrity requirements for PEMEX officials who select social witnesses, together with the obligation to make public their asset and conflict-of-interest declarations.

Introducing clear and non-discretionary criteria for participation of social witnesses.

The criteria provided for by PEMEX's legal framework are dependent on decisions taken by other bodies (Board of Directors, Procurement Committee, Procurement Area), thus they may be conducive to more discretionary decisions and eventually to a lower level of predictability of social witnesses' role in PEMEX's procurement activity. In order to prevent this, PEMEX may consider aligning with the federal legislation and introduce a set of thresholds above which PEMEX is legally required to include participation by social witnesses in all stages of public tendering procedures. Participation in procedures below the legal threshold could be also considered as optional, even though any criteria to introduce such possibility should be put in writing (e.g. in procurement manuals) and prevent any discretionary decision.

Improving the impact of social witness' activity through greater transparency around their observations and steps taken by PEMEX to respond to or consider their inputs.

A further crucial issue PEMEX is called to address is the impact of social witnesses' observations, which are contained in a final report and may be taken into consideration by PEMEX. In order to enhance the role and impact of social witnesses, PEMEX may consider publishing its reports in a clear and searchable way, rather than through scanned versions in pdf format. In this context, an interesting practice is provided by Canada's Fairness Monitoring Program (Box 7.6).

Box 7.6. Canada's Fairness Monitoring Program

The Fairness Monitoring (FM) Program provides management, client departments, government suppliers, Parliament and Canadians with independent assurance that Public Works and Government Services Canada's (PWGSC) activities are conducted in a fair, open and transparent manner.

Independent third-party fairness monitors observe all or part of a departmental activity. Based on their observations, they provide an impartial opinion on the fairness of the monitored activity. The program helps PWGSC protect the interests of its clients, and Canadian taxpayers by identifying and resolving fairness issues as they arise. Dealing with any issues early makes the process fairer, and avoids possible costly after-the-fact resolutions.

When they are finished observing an activity, fairness monitors document their opinions in a Final FM Report. The report is delivered to the Director of Fairness Monitoring. PWGSC makes all Final FM Reports available to the public on PWGSC's website in a clear and user-friendly way.

Source: Government of Canada (n. d.), "Fairness Monitoring Program", Public Works and Government Services Canada, www.tpsgc-pwgsc.gc.ca/se-fm/index-eng.html (accessed 8 October 2016).

Furthermore PEMEX may consider introducing the obligation to provide written public feedback to every suggestion raised by social witnesses. As a model, it could replicate the mechanism that appears on its website to provide feedback to the Human Rights Commission, which contains reference to the recommendation, the feedback given by PEMEX, as well as the Responsibilities Unit (www.pemex.com/transparencia/Paginas/recomendaciones.aspx).

More frequent and meaningful engagement with private sector representatives would help ensure PEMEX integrity policies are well communicated and complied with.

In the OECD Recommendation on Public Procurement, the OECD (2015b) has stressed the importance of fostering the transparent and effective participation of different kinds of stakeholders, which should be subject to fairness, transparency and integrity standards. In particular, the OECD called for the establishment of mechanisms to engage potential suppliers in all the stages of the procurement process for a twofold purpose: firstly, to present public procurement objectives and to provide potential vendors with a better understanding of the country's needs; secondly, to assure government buyers a correct understanding of markets and information to develop more realistic and effective tender specifications. The importance of engaging with the private stakeholder was also identified as a priority by Mexican President Enrique Peña Nieto, who in February 2015 dedicated one of the eight Executive Orders he released on prevention of corruption and conflicts of interest to extend the mechanisms to co-operate with the private sector.

In this context, the information provided by PEMEX shows a lack of significant initiatives to involve private stakeholders in the procurement process cycle. At the same time, there were no objective criteria to assess whether they are applied constantly and consistently throughout PEMEX's procurement activity.

In order to face this challenge, two sets of initiatives could be considered by PEMEX to further involve private stakeholders and ensure their contribution to the transparency and effectiveness of the procurement process. One the one hand, PEMEX may consider the system developed by the Airport Group of Mexico City (Grupo Aeroportuario de la Ciudad de México, or GACM) allowing education institutions, schools or professional institutes to participate in the elaboration of the tender documents, independently of the participation of one or more social witnesses (Box 7.7).

Box 7.7. The participation of social observers in the construction of the new international airport of Mexico City

Besides using social witnesses, GACM has set up a further mechanism for civil society to participate in tender procedures, namely through the use of so-called "social observers". Higher education institutions, schools or professional institutes, are invited by the GACM to participate in the elaboration of the tender documents independently of the participation of one or more social witnesses.

For this purpose, GACM has created a memorandum of agreement with different higher education institutions and industrial associations, such as the Engineering Institute of the National Autonomous University of Mexico (Instituto de Ingeniería de la UNAM).

GACM also reports that in the near future they will enter into a similar agreement with the Society of Alumni of the School of Engineering of the National Autonomous University of Mexico (Sociedad de Egresados de la Facultad de Ingeniería de la UNAM).

Source: OECD (2015c), *Effective Delivery of Large Infrastructure Projects: The Case of the New International Airport of Mexico City*, OECD Publishing, Paris, http://dx.doi.org/10.1787/9789264248335-en.

On the other hand, PEMEX could consider the consultation mechanism developed by ChileCompra, the Chilean central purchasing body that manages the electronic procurement system and runs procurement procedures. The mechanism levels the playing field for suppliers as well as mitigates the risk of wrongdoing between officials and suppliers (Box 7.8).

Box 7.8. Suppliers' consultation initiatives by the Chilean central purchasing body ChileCompra: The way to transparency and effectiveness

Prior to issuing a tender, ChileCompra carries out an open consultation process with suppliers, which it announces on line at www.mercadopublico.cl. The consultation aims to obtain information about prices, the characteristics of the required goods or services, the timeline needed to prepare bids and any other information that might contribute to a successful tendering process.

Also, following the online publication of a procurement notice (request for proposals), ChileCompra conducts roundtable meetings with suppliers, which are also announced on the website. The purpose of these meetings is to inform suppliers about the main goals of the procurement and guide them on how to place a bid. For purposes of transparency, ChileCompra records the meetings and uploads them to the same website, as a folder attached to the request for proposals, so that suppliers who were not at the meetings may be informed as well.

ChileCompra has, in addition, an online forum with questions and answers for each tender in advance of deadlines for submitting bids. The forum is particularly practical for providers who are geographically distant from the capital, Santiago (where ChileCompra's offices are located), and need remote access to questions and answers. Such an arrangement ensures transparency, equitable treatment and fair competition.

With such practices, ChileCompra has achieved a high level of transparency and effectiveness in its tenders.

Source: OECD (2016), *Committing to Effective Whistleblower Protection*, OECD Publishing, Paris, http://dx.doi.org/10.1787/9789264252639-en, based on presentations at the OECD workshop on "Improving Public Procurement Practices in ISSSTE", Mexico City, 2-4 September 2014, by Marjorie Ramírez, former Head of Division of Framework Agreements at ChileCompra, the Chilean central purchasing body.

Proposals for action

PEMEX could improve the accessibility of its public procurement information, particularly through a single database.

- Simplify the existing means to publish PEMEX information and consider providing a single database containing all the information that is currently available through various channels.
- Present the information in an interactive, user-friendly, and easily accessible way on the website, giving users the possibility to select procurement information by the type of procedure used.

PEMEX could consider publishing its procurement information in open data format in order to further enhance transparency and accountability.

- Develop an open data framework and instruments taking into consideration the Open Contracting Global Principles, which would make contracting more competitive and fair, improving contract performance, and securing development outcomes through the disclosure of documents and information.
- Set up an open data portal following international best practices that monitor public infrastructures and mega-events.

PEMEX could establish and make publicly available a disclosure policy identifying what information should be publicly disclosed by law, together with the appropriate channels for disclosure, and mechanisms for ensuring access to information.

- Ensure clarity and consistency about the transparency framework in order to promote fair and equitable treatment for potential suppliers.
- Draft a set of guidelines illustrating PEMEX's policy on transparency and confidentiality, clarifying which kind of information is disclosed and publishing it on line.
- Clearly illustrate on the website the procedure to access information and provide a link to relevant mechanisms.

PEMEX could increase the transparency around the selection of social witnesses in order to increase the legitimacy of the initiative and ensure trust around its contracting activity.

- Make the section of the website on social witnesses clearly accessible from the main procurement page.
- Introduce additional integrity requirements for PEMEX's officials who select social witnesses together with the obligation to make public their asset and conflict-of-interest declarations.

PEMEX could introduce clear and non-discretionary criteria for the participation of social witnesses.

- Align the policy for social witness participation with the federal legal framework and introduce a set of thresholds above which PEMEX is legally required to include their participation in all stages of public tendering procedures.
- The participation of social witnesses in procedures below such thresholds can be considered as optional, although no criteria can be discretional.

PEMEX could improve the impact of social witness' activity through greater transparency around their observations and follow up.

- Publish reports of social witnesses in a clear and searchable way, avoiding scanned versions in pdf format.

- Introduce the obligation to provide written public feedback to every suggestion raised by social witnesses, similarly to the mechanism that appears on PEMEX's website to submit feedback to the Human Rights Commission.

PEMEX could engage more frequently and meaningfully with the private sector, thereby ensuring that its integrity policies are well communicated and complied with more effectively.

- Develop further initiatives to involve private stakeholders in the procurement process cycle.
  - One example is to allow education institutions, schools or professional institutes to participate in the elaboration of the tender documents independently of the participation of one or more social witnesses.
  - Another example is to set up an open consultation process with suppliers in order to obtain information about prices, the characteristics of the required goods or services, the timeline needed to prepare bids and any other information that might contribute to a successful tendering process.

References

Australian Government's Department of Finance (2014), "Confidentiality throughout the procurement cycle", www.finance.gov.au/procurement/procurement-policy-and-guidance/buying/contract-issues/confidentiality-procurement-cycle/principles.html.

Expo 2015 (n. d.), "OpenExpo: Data and transparency for Expo 2015", website, http://dati.openexpo2015.it/en (accessed 8 October 2016).

Government of Canada (n. d.), "Fairness Monitoring Program", Public Works and Government Services Canada, www.tpsgc-pwgsc.gc.ca/se-fm/index-eng.html (accessed 8 October 2016).

Ministry of Infrastructure and Transportation of Italy (Ministero delle infrastrutture e dei trasporti) (2016), "Opencantieri", website, http://opencantieri.mit.gov.it/.

New York City Comptroller (2014), "Checkbook NYC", official New York City website, www.checkbooknyc.com/contracts_landing/status/A/yeartype/B/year/116 (accessed 22 February 2016).

OECD (2016), *Committing to Effective Whistleblower Protection*, OECD Publishing, Paris, http://dx.doi.org/10.1787/9789264252639-en.

OECD (2015a), *Government at a Glance 2015*, OECD Publishing, Paris, http://dx.doi.org/10.1787/gov_glance-2015-en.

OECD (2015b), "Recommendation of the Council on Public Procurement", www.oecd.org/corruption/recommendation-on-public-procurement.htm.

OECD (2015c), *Effective Delivery of Large Infrastructure Projects: The Case of the New International Airport of Mexico City*, OECD Publishing, Paris, http://dx.doi.org/10.1787/9789264248335-en.

OECD (2014), *Compendium of Good Practices for Integrity in Public Procurement: Meeting of the Leading Practitioners in Procurement*, OECD, Paris. .

OECD (2007), *Integrity in Public Procurement: Good Practice from A to Z*, OECD Publishing, Paris, http://dx.doi.org/10.1787/9789264027510-en.

Open Contracting Partnership (2016), "Open Contracting Global Principles", www.open-contracting.org/get-started/global-principles/.

Ubaldi, B. (2013), "Open government data: Towards empirical analysis of open government data initiatives", *OECD Working Papers on Public Governance*, No. 22, OECD Publishing, Paris, http://dx.doi.org/10.1787/5k46bj4f03s7-en.

UK Government (2013), "G8 Open Data Charter and Technical Annex", Policy paper, www.gov.uk/government/publications/open-data-charter/g8-open-data-charter-and-technical-annex.

Chapter 8

Ensuring effective internal control and risk management in Petróleos Mexicanos' procurement activities

A robust internal control system, including risk management and independent internal audit functions, is the bedrock for improving governance and management systems, enhancing integrity, and strengthening accountability. This chapter highlights how a pre-emptive and risk-based approach is the best way for PEMEX to improve the efficiency, effectiveness and economy of operations while putting in place the proper controls and mitigating strategies to prevent, detect and respond to fraud and corruption schemes in the procurement cycle.

The Energy Reform has triggered significant changes in the existing internal control and risk-management system and processes in Petróleos Mexicanos (or PEMEX). The company is now a state-productive enterprise with a new legal framework and corporate structure.

PEMEX is implementing an ambitious action plan to align its structural organisation as well as its methodological framework, standards and tools with leading international practices. The importance of a sound and effective risk-management and control system and an independent internal audit function is highlighted in almost every corporate governance code across the globe. Equally important is having the Board of Directors actively involved in risk management, tax planning and internal audit. Attention should also be given to establishing specialised board committees in areas such as remuneration, audit, and -depending upon the company's size and risk profile - risk management.

PEMEX is adopting good corporate governance practices in risk management, control and audit requirements and arrangements. Before the Energy Reform, the internal audit function was part of the mission of the Internal Control Body (Órgano Interno de Control, or OIC), which was supervised by the Ministry of Public Administration (Secretaría de la Función Pública, or SFP). As a result there was confusion between the internal control and the internal audit functions and processes. As already explained, the current organisational structure provides for an independent internal audit unit that reports only to the Audit Committee and the Board. This approach is up to international corporate governance standards. The problem is that the internal audit function used to mainly focus on compliance audits while the issue of establishing and implementing effective internal control processes was not given proper attention. This is changing now with PEMEX's ongoing efforts to develop and mainstream sound internal control and risk-management functions. On the other hand, the external audit function is still performed by private firms, in relation to financial reporting, and the Superior Audit Office of the Federation (Auditoría Superior de la Federación, or ASF), which is Mexico's supreme audit institution (SAI), and reports to Congress (see Figure 8.1).

Figure 8.1. **PEMEX's basic control and audit structure**

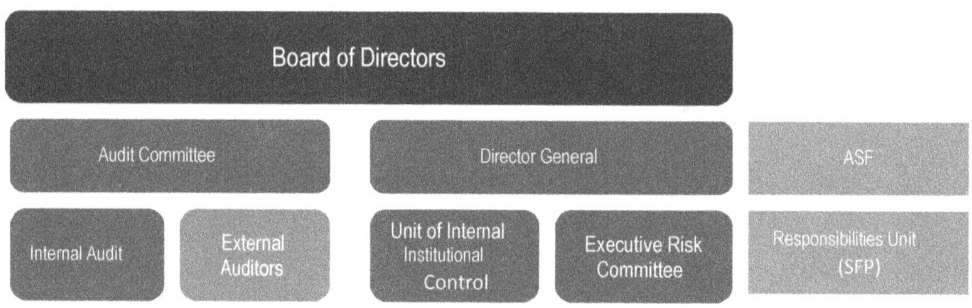

Source: Based on information provided by PEMEX.

This corporate control and risk-management model has different characteristics than the one established in line ministries and other public administration entities. One major difference is the key role of Audit Committees, which have traditionally been a key component of corporate governance regulation. This is strongly supported by the 2015 edition of the *OECD Corporate Governance Factbook* (OECD, 2015a), which tracks how countries are actually implementing the revised *G20/OECD Principles of Corporate*

Governance (OECD, 2015c), providing data on more than 40 jurisdictions, including OECD, G20 and Financial Stability Board members. More specifically, more than two-thirds of jurisdictions require listed companies to establish an independent audit committee. Key responsibilities of the audit committee, as prescribed in the relevant EU Directive (2006/43/EC) include: 1) to monitor the financial reporting process; 2) to monitor the effectiveness of the company's internal control, internal audit where applicable, and risk-management systems; 3) to monitor the statutory audit of the annual and consolidated accounts; and 4) to review and monitor the independence of the statutory auditor or audit firm. In some jurisdictions, audit committees also have a role in the oversight of regulatory compliance. In the United States, the Sarbanes-Oxley Act of 2002 required exchanges to adopt rules requiring independent audit committees to oversee a company's accounting and financial reporting processes and audits of a company's financial statements (OECD, 2015a).

Full or majority independent membership is required or recommended for the three committees mentioned in Figure 8.2, in most of jurisdictions, while provisions on chair independence in Audit Committees are more common compared to the Nomination Committee or Remuneration Committee (see also Figure 8.3).

Figure 8.2. **Requirements for establishing Board-level committees**

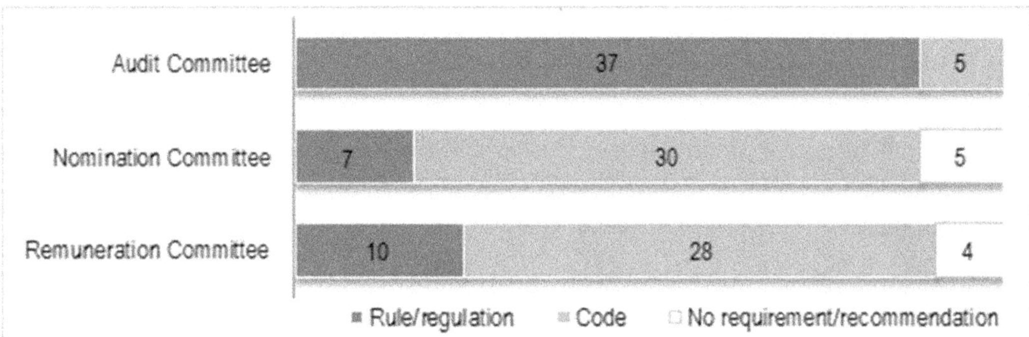

Note: This figure shows the number of jurisdictions in each category.

Source: OECD (2015a), *OECD Corporate Governance Factbook*, OECD, www.oecd.org/daf/ca/corporate-governance-factbook.htm.

Figure 8.3. **Independence of the chair and members of board-level committees**

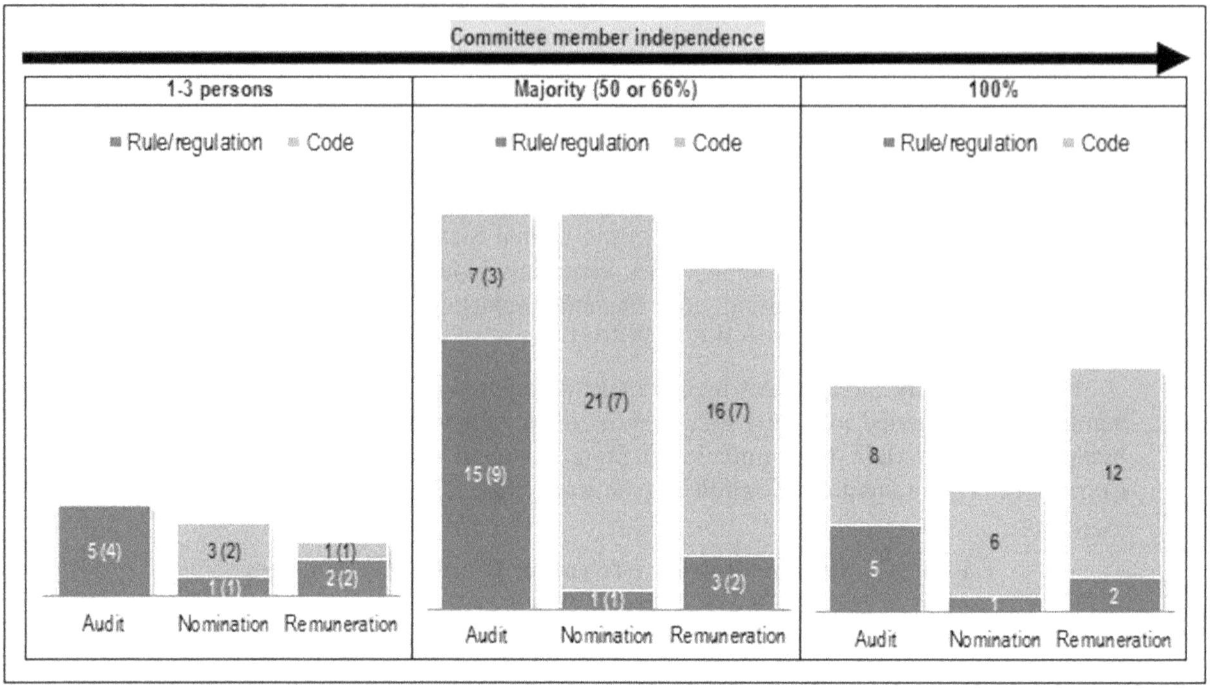

Note: This figure shows the number of jurisdictions in each category. The number in brackets shows the number of jurisdictions with an additional requirement or recommendation on the committee chair's independence.

Source: OECD (2015a), *OECD Corporate Governance Factbook*, OECD, www.oecd.org/daf/ca/corporate-governance-factbook.htm.

PEMEX has structured a lot of its reforms on promoting integrity and strengthening its internal control and risk-management system on the recommendations made by the Superior Audit Office (ASF). In 2013, the ASF conducted an evaluation exercise of the internal control system within the Mexican context, which involved 290 institutions (284 from the three branches and 6 constitutionally autonomous) and resulted in Study No. 1172. This was an initial effort that aimed to evaluate the existence and the actual implementation of the core elements of an effective internal control system. This study was supplemented by another one (No. 1173), which focused on supporting the institutions to design and implement concrete measures and activities to enhance integrity and ethical values and link them with the planning and the objectives of public institutions.

Furthermore, the ASF has followed up (Study No. 1198, Informe de PEMEX, October 2014) on the evaluation of PEMEX's actions on improving its capacity in the self-assessment of internal control and risk-management processes as well as the effectiveness of its policies to curb fraud and corruption. In the initial exercise, PEMEX scored a total of 98 points in the self-evaluation exercise of the internal control components, while the ASF's diagnosis came to 61 points. More specifically, the ASF conducted - in June 2014 - a follow-up diagnosis and concluded that PEMEX's system had improved and thus attained a score of 69 points. Main recommendations suggested that PEMEX should focus on identifying and assessing the inherent risks related with its core processes and objectives, while prioritising high-risk areas, like procurement, which pose a serious threat to the accomplishment of the company's mission and concrete objectives. Capacity building and the training of staff and management on the culture and attributes of internal control and risk management were also among the key recommendations. The most recent diagnosis undertaken in December 2015 resulted in a score of 75 points in relation to the same 37 questions structured around the five main components (control environment, risk management, control activities, information and communication, monitoring) of PEMEX's internal control framework.

It is also worth mentioning that according to the information provided by PEMEX (update 10 November 2015) deriving from the database of observations issued either by PEMEX's Office of Internal Control/OIC or the ASF in 2012-14, PEMEX and four affiliated companies (PEP [Exploración y Producción], PGPB [Pemex Gas y Petroquímica Básica], PPQ [Petroquímica] and PRF [Refinación]) had a total of 2 670 observations/findings, out of which 52% dealt with public works and procurement (Figure 8.4).

Figure 8.4. **Categorisation of observations/findings according to the applied elements of control by thematic area**

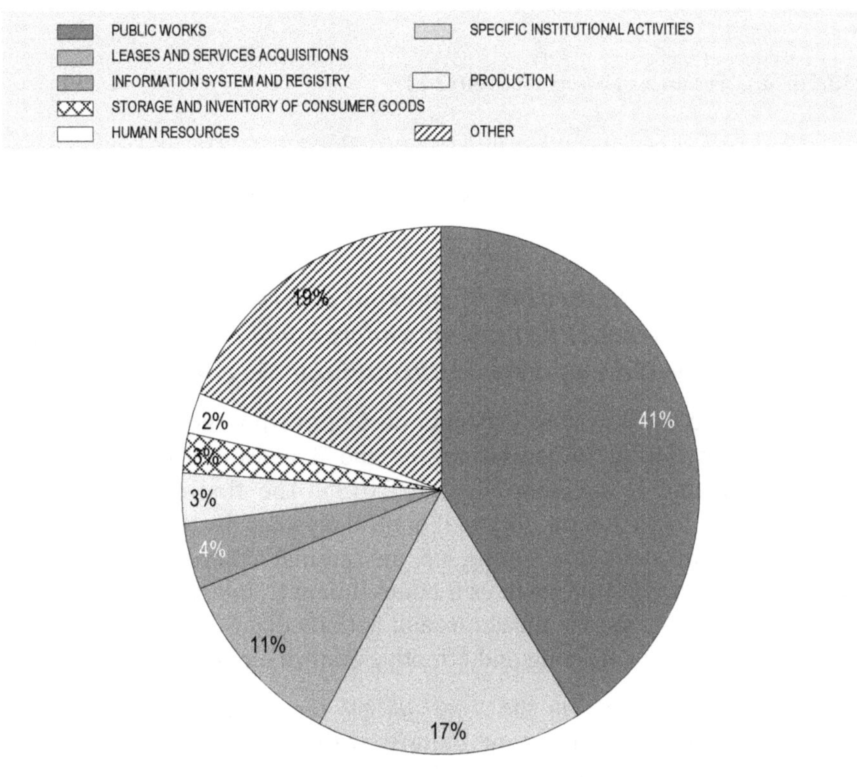

Source: PEMEX (n. d.), "Database of observations 2012-14".

Moreover, the detailed data on PEMEX indicate that 27% of the issues examined related to the acquisitions, leasing and services area with another 25% arising from the public works area (Figure 8.5).

Figure 8.5. **Categorisation of issues in PEMEX by thematic area**

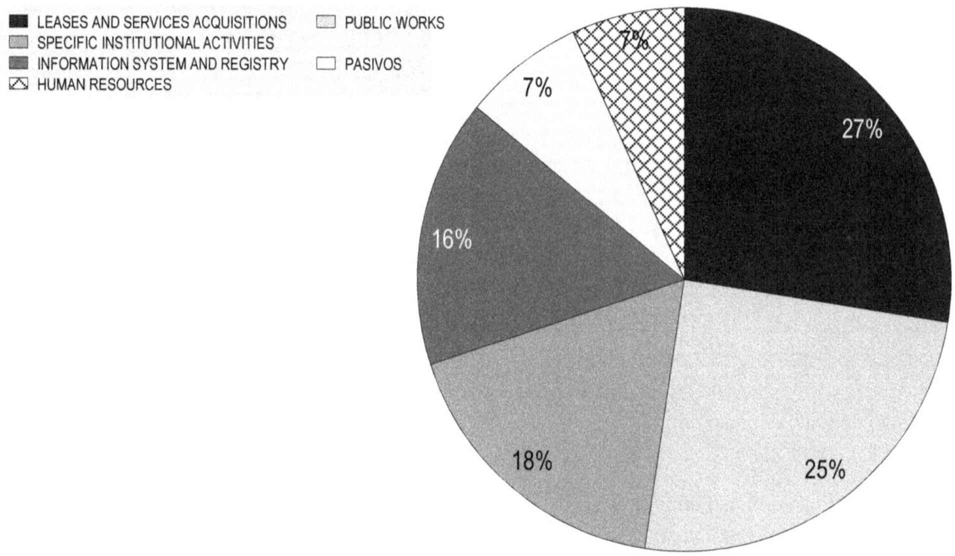

Source: PEMEX (n. d.), "Database of observations 2012-14".

Internal control mechanisms and committees

PEMEX should act on strengthening its internal control system by ensuring a sound and functional control environment underpinned by integrating ethical values and integrity into daily operations throughout the company.

PEMEX's internal control system (Sistema de Control Interno, or SCI) is based on the Committee of Sponsoring Organisations of the Treadway Commission (COSO) Internal Control-Integrated Framework (COSO, 2013). The first component and what seems to be the basis of a sound internal control system is the so-called "control environment". The cornerstone for setting up an optimal control environment is the principle that the organisation demonstrates a commitment to integrity and ethical values. The challenge lies with the concrete measures and actions that PEMEX has to implement in order to move towards a functioning and effective control environment.

One very important element is the tone set by top management, which heavily influences the corporate environment or culture within which risk-management and control activities take place. Employees usually pay close attention to the behaviour of top management and subsequently their decisions, attitudes and conduct are influenced by the tone communicated by top management. The importance of having the top executives leading by example is highlighted by a recent comment by the Institute of Internal Auditors (IIA) President, Richard F. Chambers, who stated that "a strong yet inappropriate tone at the top can easily render even viable internal control processes and policies virtually irrelevant."

Figure 8.6 illustrates the basic steps to take to create a healthy control environment as the cornerstone of establishing and maintaining an effective internal control system.

Figure 8.6. **Towards a sound and functioning control environment**

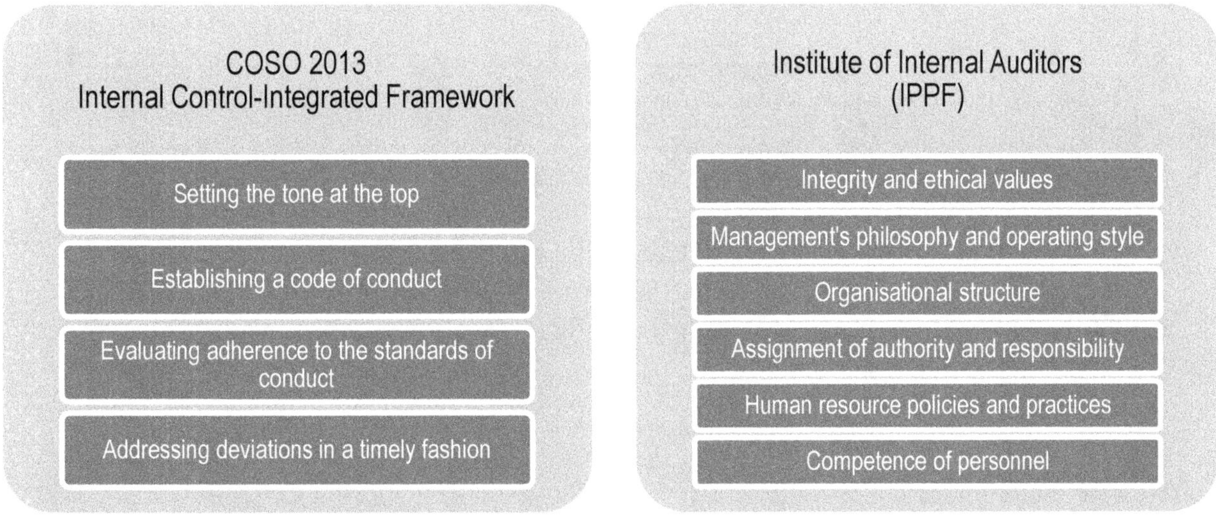

Source: Based on Internal Control-Integrated Framework (COSO, 2013) and International Professional Practices Framework-IPPF (Institute of Internal Auditors).

We can see that both COSO and IIA highlight the importance of having the board and senior management setting the example and the tone on how the organisation understands and integrates ethical values into day-to-day operations. PEMEX recently adopted a Code of Ethics (November 2014) and a Code of Conduct (February 2015). Though having manuals and written procedures is an important step forward, it is not enough. They have to be owned by the PEMEX's management and staff and followed through. This issue relates less to written instructions and more to informal, behavioural dimensions like values, beliefs and attitudes towards the character and the role of the company within the Mexican context. Although it is too soon to assess the maturity of the internal control system that PEMEX is establishing and subsequently to identify the root causes of any systemic weaknesses and gaps, it has been noted that the control environment is usually one of the main obstacles hindering the implementation of the distinct components of a control and risk-management framework. Any deficiencies in the control environment usually negatively affect the other components of internal control and, of course, this reflects on the whole organisation (Box 8.1).

Box 8.1. **Toxic corporate culture: Red flags**

The following red flags can signal a problematic control environment:

Favouritism: Managers have favourites, who receive special treatment (sometimes not held to rules that apply to everyone else) and are often the only ones given the opportunity to work on special projects.

Walking on eggshells: Employees constantly fear being rebuked or, worse, fired. Meetings consist of one-way communication because the fear of reprisal shuts down healthy debate. Employees feel disrespected and ignored. Transparency is eroded.

Bad behaviour: Cliques abound, especially those that thrive on negativity. Employees become competitors and engage in cut-throat behaviour to get ahead. Malice replaces courtesy and respect.

Box 8.1. **Toxic corporate culture: Red flags** *(continued)*

Lack of development: Management does not see the value of training and developing employees at all levels and across the organisation.

Information hoarding: Managers fail to share the information others need to do their jobs. They release information only when required to get a task done or when it is too late to be helpful to anyone else.

Lack of accountability: Transgressions may surface, but business goes on as usual and employees, managers, or executives face no consequences for rule breaking

Source: IIA (2016), "More than just setting the tone: A look at organizational culture", *Tone at the Top*, Issue 76, February, Audit Executive Centre.

PEMEX should consider taking concrete action to highlight the importance of setting a clear tone at the top to create a robust and effective control environment.

The PEMEX approach to internal control clearly links good corporate governance with a strong ethical culture, including clear expectations for acceptable conduct within the organisation and with third parties. The Board and the senior management have to set the tone at the top. The company's commitment to ethical values has to be demonstrated in the way that management makes decisions and steers corporate affairs. When individual staff face ethical dilemmas their behaviour can be influenced by their perception of management "ethics". How can we expect staff to apply the group's procedures on procurement activities if they believe that top management abides by other rules? When this approach becomes the dominant perception inside a company, it can lead to rationalised non-compliance and even fraud and corruption. A recent survey indicated that a strong majority of misconduct is committed by individuals who hold some level of managerial responsibility (Ethics Alarms, 2014). Moreover, nearly a quarter of misconduct is attributable to senior management.

PEMEX's Audit Committee should focus, among other things, on making sure that the organisation's culture aligns with its code of conduct and that behaviours are consistent top down. In order to be effective and get a true sense of the company's ethical culture, PEMEX has to do more than just rely on relevant information from senior management, who are the people who, ultimately, must be held most accountable. This is exactly why middle managers have to be actively involved, communicate these policies and lead by example. At the level of the second line of defence PEMEX's officials should pay attention when reviewing employee surveys and whistleblower reports. This way they can identify patterns and anomalies that call for closer attention with regard to whether these risks are adequately identified and at the next level, whether the proper risk responses are in place.

PEMEX's approach to internal control and integrity as a core component of a sound control environment has a lot of common characteristics with the frameworks established in other big oil companies. Box 8.2 highlights the basic components of the French oil company, Total's, control and risk-management framework. The importance of setting a strong tone at the top is a dominant attribute throughout Total's system.

Box 8.2. Total's internal control system and the role of its Audit Committee

Total's internal control system relies on the COSO 2013 framework, which is considered equivalent to the reference framework of the French Financial Markets Authority and can also cover the group's obligations under the Sarbanes-Oxley Act. The risk-management system draws on the main international standards, COSO ERM, ISO 31000:2009 as well as on the French standards.

Total's Audit Committee is responsible for monitoring the efficiency of internal control and risk-management systems, assisted by the group's Internal Control and Audit department and the internal control teams from the business segments/units.

The Risk Management, Internal Control and Audit internal charter constitutes the methodological framework on which the group relies to ensure control over its activities.

Control environment: Integrity and ethics

The basic components of Total's control environment, such as the group's values and business principles, can be found in its Code of Conduct (revised in 2014) and in its Business Integrity Guide. These documents are circulated to employees and are freely available on the group's website. They articulate the group's values and elaborate its business and behaviour principles with regard to employees, shareholders, customers, suppliers and competitors. They also set out the rules of individual behaviour expected from all employees in the countries where the group is present.

Furthermore, the Financial Code of Ethics, which also refers to the Code of Conduct, sets forth specific rules for the executive directors (Chairman of the Board of Directors and Chief Executive Officer) and Chief Financial Officer, senior Vice president Accounting, as well as for the financial and accounting officers of principal activities.

The senior management has prioritised the deployment of ethics and compliance policies and programmes since 2009. All these programmes involve awareness-raising and training initiatives and include, in particular, specific compliance audits in terms of corruption prevention, with six to eight missions per year. These missions are followed up the next year to verify that the recommendations are implemented. A compliance component has also been incorporated into the Group Audit framework. The purpose of these audits is to assess the proper implementation of the Compliance Programme and to test it, particularly by means of controls on accounting records. A network of 370 compliance officers and 110 ethics correspondents follow up the implementation of these programmes on the ground.

Source: Total (2014), "Form 20-F 2014", Annual report, www.total.com/sites/default/files/atoms/files/form_20-f_0.pdf.

As already highlighted, ethical behaviour, however, involves much more than a code of ethics. It is also very important to evaluate individual adherence to standards of conduct. The corporate values must apply at every activity and process and be enforced at all levels of an organisation. If there are exceptions and breaches then this will undermine employee morale and serve as justification for further misconduct. In PEMEX the Responsibilities Unit is the competent actor for following up on complaints, conducting investigations and sanctioning misconduct. This of course does not mean that strengthening corporate ethics and integrity involve only disciplinary and punitive actions. When employees feel valued and respected by management, ethics and compliance initiatives can be seen more as a common goal supporting the company brand and reputation standards and less as a burden and a sanctioning tool. Moreover, motivation and good behaviour are not be rewarded solely by financial policies, but encouraged by recognising individual ethical behaviour as a leading example of a company's core values. PEMEX should pay attention to the fact that adherence to policies and ethical codes heavily depend on the perception and the behaviour of humans.

At the same time, management is responsible for applying the best approach to motivate and empower people to embrace its corporate values and integrity standards. This also means that improper conduct has to be monitored and sanctioned so that management clearly demonstrates that rules apply to everyone and that unbiased consequences are applied regardless of position and performance within the organisation. One way to send a clear message on that is to publish relevant data that will make the whole process transparent while protecting the personal data of individuals. These two tasks are definitely not incompatible. Currently, PEMEX does not report and publish on a regular and structured basis any statistics on these cases. Even in the case where the data are available to third parties, upon their demand or their own initiative to actively seek them, the company must take a more proactive approach and consistently communicate both internally and externally. Potential business partners would be very interested to see that PEMEX has a rigorous system for following up on complaints, does not retaliate against whistleblowers and performs extensive and effective investigations into improper conduct. Box 8.3 illustrates an example of how an oil company can effectively communicate information and statistical data on how it creates an environment where individuals feel safe to come forward and report potential wrongdoing, fraud and corruption

Box 8.3. British Petroleum's helpline as an integrity and reporting tool

Employees, contractors or other third parties who have a question about the code of conduct or see something they feel to be unsafe, unethical or potentially harmful can get help through OpenTalk, a confidential helpline operated by an independent company.

The figures in the image above demonstrate the number of concerns or enquiries that were filed with OpenTalk. The most common concerns related to the people section of the code. This includes treating people fairly, with dignity and giving everyone equal opportunity; creating a respectful, harassment-free workplace and protecting privacy and confidentiality. British Petroleum (BP) is committed to taking steps to identify and correct areas of non-conformance and take disciplinary action where appropriate. In 2014, the Group dismissed 157 employees for non-conformance with the code of conduct or unethical behaviour (2013:113). This excludes dismissals of staff employed at retail service stations for incidents such as thefts of small amounts of money. Furthermore, BP has enhanced its human resources processes, resulting in improved identification and recording of code-related dismissals.

Box 8.3. **British Petroleum's helpline as an integrity and reporting tool** *(continued)*

BP's statement on business ethics and safety focusing on its relations with contractors and partners

Business ethics

Bribery and corruption are significant risks in the oil and gas industry. BP recognises its responsibility to shareholders and the countries and communities in which it conducts business to be ethical and lawful in all its dealings. Its code of conduct explicitly states that BP does not tolerate bribery and corruption in any of its forms. The group-wide anti-bribery and corruption policy applies to all BP-operated businesses. The policy governs areas such as appropriate clauses in contracts, risk assessments and training. BP targets training on a risk basis and to those employees for whom it is thought to be most relevant, for example, given specific incidents or the nature or location of their role.

Working with contractors and partners

BP, like its industry peers, rarely works in isolation – it needs to work with contractors, suppliers and partners to carry out our operations. In 2014, 52% of the 357 million hours worked by BP were carried out by contractors. Its ability to be a safe and responsible operator depends in part on the capability and performance of those who help BP carry out its operations. BP therefore, seeks to identify and manage risks in the supply chain relating to areas such as safety, corruption and money laundering, and aims to have suitable provisions in its contracts with contractors, suppliers and partners.

Contractors

BP expects and encourages its contractors and their employees to act in a way that is consistent with BP's code of conduct. Its operating management system (OMS) includes requirements and practices for working with contractors. The company seeks to set clear and consistent expectations of its contractors. Its standard model upstream contracts, for example, include health, safety, security and environmental requirements. Bridging documents are necessary in some cases to define how the group's safety management system and those of its contractors co-exist to manage risk on site. To help BP manage risks effectively and take advantage of economies of scale, the company focuses on developing deeper, longer term relationships with selected upstream contractors. For example, BP has established global agreements in areas such as engineered equipment and well services.

Source: BP (2014), "Annual Report and Form 20-F 2014", www.bp.com/content/dam/bp-country/de_de/PDFs/brochures/BP_Annual_Report_and_Form_20F_2014.pdf.

PEMEX should focus on establishing a robust assurance-providing function to support the Board on meeting their corporate governance obligations and the company's delivery and accountability needs.

PEMEX is currently trying to assign roles and responsibilities according to the Three Lines of Defence Model, which was first introduced by the 8th EU Company Law Directive and was further detailed in a position paper published by the Institute of Internal Auditors in 2013. During the workshops in Mexico City and Villahermosa,[1] it was evident that the attributes and the rationale of this model have not been clearly communicated and understood by operational and first-line management and staff who constitute the first line of defence. There is an ownership and implementation gap between the conceptual approach that is supported by the control and audit professionals and the personnel who are expected to own the risk, design and apply the control activities. PEMEX is trying to address this gap by launching an ambitious communication and awareness-raising campaign. Furthermore, it should be noted that maintaining a functional internal control system needs continuous monitoring and evaluation. Box 8.4 highlights the three basic steps that resulted in China Petroleum and Chemical Corporation's (Sinopec's) control and risk framework and, most importantly, the set of actions that ensure the implementation, the identification of weaknesses and gaps and subsequently the way to address arising problems and encourage continuous improvement.

Box 8.4. **Sinopec's programme on establishing, monitoring and improving its internal control system**

1. Overall scheme of internal control

Sinopec is implementing the following methodological models guidelines and standards: "Comprehensive Risk Management Guidance for Central Enterprises", "Basic Standards for Enterprise Internal Control", "Application Guidance for Enterprise Internal Control" and the "Evaluation Guidance of Enterprise Internal Control" and its related guidelines. The company revised and improved its internal control system in a comprehensive and systematic manner and established total-factor internal control:

- First, the company identified the various internal and external risk factors that it faced. After further risk recognition, recording and evaluation, the company extended the list and subdivided these risks into second-class and third-class risks categorised under five types of first-class risk: strategic risk, financial risk, market risk, operational risk and compliance risk. Moreover, after the company compiled the risk lists, it improved relevant internal controls to effectively treat all kinds of risks.
- Second, the company continued to supplement and improve its internal control at the corporate level, including the internal environment, risk assessment, information and communication and internal supervision, to satisfy the relevant requirements for corporate internal governance and social responsibility. In addition, the company established and enhanced the internal control procedure, strengthened the control measures, defined control responsibility, and enhanced controls at the operational level.
- Third, in accordance with the management principals of institutionalised management, standardised and process-oriented systems and informed processes, the company researched, developed, promoted and applied the information system for internal control management to fulfil its internal control responsibilities and improve the efficiency and effectiveness of control activities.

2. Working plans for establishment and improvement of the internal control system and their implementation

Every year, Sinopec sets goals and makes working plans for internal control, dynamically modifies its internal control system, organises trainings on internal control, enhances daily supervision and management of internal control, and conducts standard internal control evaluations. All the branches and subsidiaries of the company, under the unified direction of group headquarters, revise and improve their detailed rules for the implementation of internal control and carry out requirements of internal control. In order to form a self-supervision and

Box 8.4. **Sinopec's programme on establishing, monitoring and improving its internal control system** *(continued)*

evaluation mechanism for internal control, the company established three lines of defence: regular testing of responsible departments and units, daily supervision of the internal control department, and comprehensive monitoring and assessment for audits.

3. Set-up of the department of internal control examination and supervision

The Business Reform Administration Department, which administers the supervision of internal controls in the company, is responsible for daily supervision of internal controls, special inspections, comprehensive evaluation and assessment of internal controls and other relevant functions. The Audit Department is in charge of carrying out independent inspection and evaluation of the effectiveness of internal control design and its execution in the company.

4. Implementation of self-evaluation relating to internal supervision and internal control

In 2014, the company carried out an overall inspection and evaluation of the effectiveness of internal control design and operation. Further details can be found in "Sinopec Assessment Report on Internal Control for 2014". The Business Reform Administration Department has taken effective measures to rectify the various problems that were discovered in the internal control assessment.

5. Defects in the internal control system and their correction

There was no significant defect discovered in the internal control system in 2014. For common faults discovered during internal control inspections, the management team made the relevant correction plan and communicated with external auditors. After follow-up checks, all the internal control defects relating to financial statements were corrected by 31 December 2014.

Source: Sinopec Corp. (2014a), "Assessment Report on Internal Control for 2014", Sinopec; Sinopec Corp. (2014b), "2014 Annual Report and Accounts", http://english.sinopec.com/download_center/reports/2014/20150322/download/201503222e.pdf; Sinopec Corp. (2014c), "Internal control", webpage, http://english.sinopec.com/investor_center/corporate_governance/internal_control/.

There also seems to be confusion about which units and activities are part of the second line of defence and what their exact role is in the overall structure, since it must be clear that they should not have any direct operational responsibility and that they should be independent from delivery units (e.g. group standard setters, compliance reviews, information security assurance, ethics committee, etc.). The internal audit function is the third line of defence. The added value of a truly independent internal audit function, as described in the leading corporate governance frameworks, has different characteristics from the traditional audit function in public entities. In a company like PEMEX the internal audit unit should act as a consultant and a "key agent of change" focusing on assurance mapping. The internal audit activity must evolve from its traditional role and assist PEMEX in maintaining the proper controls by evaluating their effectiveness and efficiency and by promoting continuous improvement.

Assurance maps are a very powerful tool to provide confidence and evidence that business is conducted ethically and economically. They can be useful to managers, business partners and the public, who in the case of PEMEX, represent the shareholders. A typical assurance map usually provides a complete picture of the services being delivered, the activities undertaken and the level of associated risk. This will facilitate the identification of areas where assurance activities are either not present or insufficient as well as areas where assurance is duplicated or excessive in comparison with the value of the activity being undertaken. This will allow the competent PEMEX's actors to get a better grasp of the risk exposure, steer proportionate assurance provision and better focus their efforts and available resources.

In a fully developed and mature internal control and risk-management system, internal audit should be able to rely upon assurance mechanisms in the first and second lines of defence, enabling it to focus on areas of highest risk or where there are assurance gaps and weaknesses. However, it is always important to remember that all lines of assurance are expected to demonstrate through their directives, actions and behaviour the importance of integrity and ethical values.

The internal audit function can play a key role in assessing PEMEX's actual implementation of integrity-related objectives, programmes and activities. The annual audit plan should encompass such missions and engage in a risk-based approach to provide a robust assessment of the ethical culture of PEMEX. This is why the internal audit officials must be involved in the process of designing ethics-related activities by sharing their views on ethics, culture and values of the company coupled with their knowledge of day-to-day activities of the company. This approach includes issues like assessing the whistleblower hotline and the associated policies and procedures.

The internal audit is characterised as the only function in an organisation that is charged with monitoring and providing assurance over organisational activities without having responsibility for those activities, and this is exactly why the internal auditors can truly be objective and independent (IIA, 2016). Moreover, internal audit's direct line to the Audit Committee can be used as an "early warning" function to take corrective action on issues that could otherwise seriously damage the company's culture. This is exactly why it is important to integrate the assessment of ethical culture into virtually every audit. Internal audit is ideally situated to make a significant contribution to long-term organisational value by providing assurance that actual culture aligns with desired culture.

Moreover, PEMEX's internal audit function should consider developing a dedicated procurement audit programme. This could include audit techniques like "walkthrough tests" that allow the auditors to evaluate all the processing stages of the procurement cycle and thus fully grasp the structural and substantial core elements of the process; and identify the weaknesses and the control gaps as well as existing controls that need to be further evaluated and possibly revamped. One of the main objectives could be to assess the existence and effectiveness of procurement process controls. It may also cover existing arrangements in relation to regulatory compliance requirements that need to be tested. Information gained from sources like spend analysis exercise and previous audit reports will help identify the priority areas in the procurement audit programme. The whole evaluation and audit process should not heavily focus on compliance issues. The methodological approach should also cover performance related issues. The Board and the Audit Committee should ask for assurance that the whole procurement process is designed and implemented towards adding optimal value to PEMEX by focusing on quality outcomes rather than being cost driven.

Other important issues include the evaluation of the actual integration of risk management within the day-to-day procurement activities and the active involvement of all levels of procurement staff and managers. Performance attributes include standardised and transparent processes for keeping reliable suppliers' and contractors' performance records, based on measurable and tailor-made indicators covering issues of quality of goods and services received from vendors as well. Such indicators should address factors like: order lead times and capacity to deliver, logistics arrangements, technology innovation, environmental and conflict minerals, adherence to the corporate code of conduct and ethics standards. Moreover, when engaging in an audit mission the auditor should pay attention to attributes like the materiality of the procurement activity, the relevance, the reliability, the sufficiency and the appropriateness of evidence available. Examples of sources in relation to the procurement cycle include: contract documents; requisitions/purchase orders/invoices, etc.; interviews with third parties/vendors/contractors; physical inspection, examination and count. Furthermore, a robust procurement audit programme should identify specific high-risk components of the procurement process and design specific sets of questions that will enable the auditor to provide assurance over these activities. In the case of the purchase orders such questions could include testing that: vendor payment terms are agreed by relevant parties; purchase orders are only created from approved purchase requisitions; purchase orders are created and approved by authorised personnel; and purchase orders are recorded accurately by authorised personnel.

PEMEX's risk-management system

PEMEX must focus on addressing the implementation gap and integrating the risk-management process into day-to-day activities across all areas and organisational levels of the company.

PEMEX is currently undergoing a major reform in its risk-management system. Before the Energy Reform, the company was only focusing on financial risk and more specifically on credit and capitalisation risk. The way the company was structured and the policies regulating the procurement process did not call for a function to identify risk and assess their impact and likelihood. PEMEX's ongoing reform initiatives underpin the approach that procurement can deliver true value using an intelligent and comprehensive risk-assessment programme with suppliers and contractors.

It should be noted that out of the 120 procurement officials and practitioners that participated in the Mexico City and Villahermosa workshops, only one stated having participated in a risk-management exercise. Furthermore in Villahermosa, only one official was aware of the existence and had read the 2014 self-assessment exercise that PEMEX conducted on the maturity and the effectiveness of the internal control and risk-management system and the relevant ASF study.

A key step in addressing the implementation gap and maintaining a robust and functional risk-management system is to raise awareness and create ownership among management and staff by assigning clear roles and responsibilities across all levels of the company. In this framework, it is well established that the Audit Committees can play a critical role with respect to risk management. Furthermore, the majority of the jurisdictions surveyed for the OECD Corporate Governance 2015 Factbook stated that the board responsibilities with respect to risk management lay in either the law or in regulations (26%) or in codes (36%) (Figure 8.7). In the United States, for example, the Securities and Exchange Commission requires public companies to disclose the board's role in the oversight of risk.

Figure 8.7. **Board responsibilities with respect to risk management**

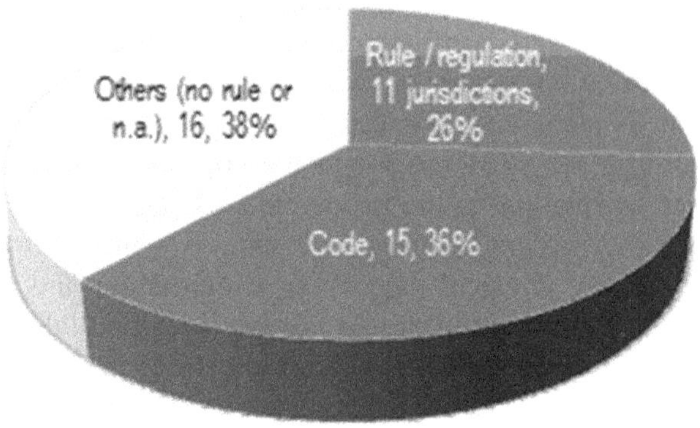

Note: This figure shows the number of jurisdictions in each category and percentage share out of all 42 surveyed jurisdictions.

Source: OECD (2015a), *OECD Corporate Governance Factbook*, OECD, www.oecd.org/daf/ca/corporate-governance-factbook.htm.

Moreover, almost two-thirds of jurisdictions require or recommend implementing an enterprise-wide internal control and risk-management system (Figure 8.8).

Figure 8.8. **Implementation of the internal control and risk-management system**

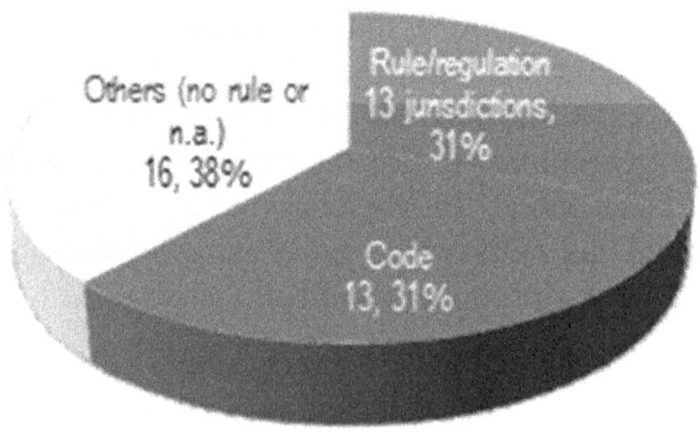

Note: This figure shows the number of jurisdictions in each category and percentage share out of all 42 surveyed jurisdictions.

Source: OECD (2015a), *OECD Corporate Governance Factbook*, OECD, www.oecd.org/daf/ca/corporate-governance-factbook.htm.

Assigning the role of risk-management oversight to a board-level committee is becoming more common in large companies, notably in the financial sector (OECD/IDB,

2014). This role is usually assigned to Audit Committees (in 26 jurisdictions) or separate risk committees (in 8 jurisdictions) (Figure 8.9).

Figure 8.9. **The role of risk-management oversight in board-level committees**

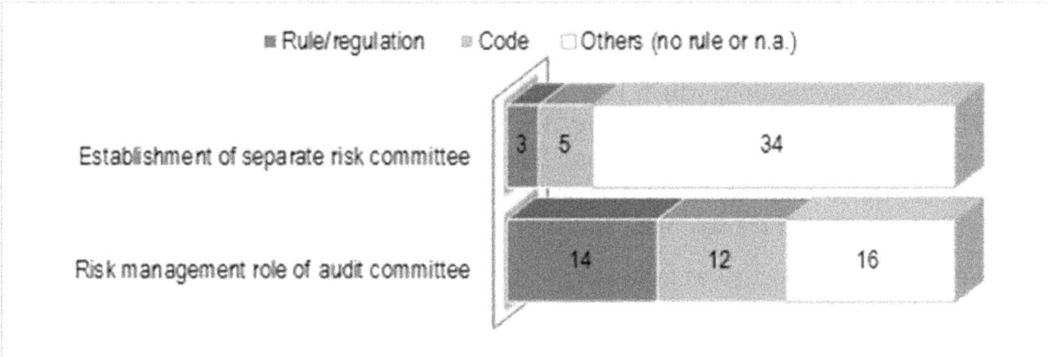

Note: This figure shows the number of jurisdictions in each category out of all 42 surveyed jurisdictions.

Source: OECD (2015a), *OECD Corporate Governance Factbook*, OECD, www.oecd.org/daf/ca/corporate-governance-factbook.htm.

PEMEX's Risk Committee (CRPEMEX) was created to ensure that risk management is integrated throughout the organisation. It should be noted that, for the first time, PEMEX is engaging in activities like due diligence with external stakeholders. PEMEX's Top Management and Audit Committee share the same three main objectives regarding risk management as their counterparts in many European countries: 1) provide reasonable assurance that major risks are identified and managed; 2) minimise operational surprises and losses; and 3) integrate a risk dimension within the decision-making process (FERMA, 2012) (Box 8.5).

Box 8.5. **PEMEX's Risk Committee**

PEMEX's Risk Committee (CRPEMEX) was created (Num DG 201505468/2015) in 10 November 2015. The president is the Corporate Director of Finance and it has nine more permanent members from senior management. It can also invite officials to attend its meetings.

CRPEMEX convened for the first time on 25 November 2015. The committee agreed on the rules for its activities and discussed the main components of the Enterprise Risk Management Framework (Marco de Administración de Riesgos Empresariales, or MARE). A special working group on commercial credit risk "GARICC" was also created. One of the main issues discussed was the project of risk management in the procurement process and the policies for exploration and production (Gestión de Riesgos en Procesos de Procura y Política para Exploración y Producción). The Committee also decided that this project would be executed with the help of an external consultant, GMS management Solutions SL (ACUERDO CRPEMEX 05/2015).

Source: Acuerdo del Director general de PEMEX, Núm. DG 201505468/2015, Creación del Comité de Riesgos de PEMEX y sus Empresas Productivas Subsidiarias PEMEX; Acta de la Sesión de Instalación CRPEMEX celebrada el 25 de Noviembre de 2015; Reglas de Operación del Comité de Riesgos de Petróleos Mexicanos y sus Empresas Productivas Subsidiarias.

In the framework of this project, PEMEX officials stated that the company has already engaged in an initial overall analysis and identified the risks related to the procurement cycle. As was mentioned, the enterprise risk-management system in PEMEX is called MARE. The risk-management exercise aims to identify, prioritise, categorise and define who is responsible for mitigating the risks focusing on the linkages between corporate objectives, risks and controls. However, there is evidence that objectives are not articulated (including the issues of risk appetite and risk tolerances) throughout the organisation, which may lead to deficiencies in the control environment. This is not uncommon for a company that is going through major changes both in structure and in how it conducts business. The Risk Committee should follow up on this problem and try to find the most appropriate solutions to integrate the procedure within its first-line operational management and staff.

The risks are categorised as follows:

- Non-discretionary risks: Required to mitigate their impact and likelihood.
- Discretionary risks: Required to determine and quantify the risk appetite and tolerance and identify the response.
- Strategic risks: Very important for planning and strategic decisions.

Discretionary and strategic risks are categorised as business (*negocio*) risks.

The methodological approach to the risk-management exercise is to address the risks issues alongside the following levels:

- entity and strategic level
- processes and business areas
- risks and controls
- Sarbanes and Oxley Act for the US affiliate company.

The Ministry of Public Administration (SFP), which until recently was the supervising authority of PEMEX's Internal Control Body, is using a different tool for risk management called Institutional Risk Management (Administración de Riesgos Institucional, orARI). This is a component of SFP's Institutional Internal Control System (SCII) that applies throughout federal public entities. On the other hand, the Supreme Federal Audit Institution (ASF) has developed a different tool called Automated System for Risk Management (Sistema Automatizado para la Administración de Riesgos, or SAAR). As previously mentioned, PEMEX has introduced its own conceptual framework called Enterprise Risk Management Framework (MARE). All of these systems are based on COSO's 2013 Internal Control-Integrated Framework. There are also elements of COSO's 2004 Enterprise Risk Management which is currently under revision and can be seen as complementary to the COSO 2013 framework.

Figure 8.10 presents a quick overview of the three different above-mentioned risk-management systems that apply in the Mexican context.

Figure 8.10. **Risk-management frameworks in Mexico**

Figure 8.11 illustrates the architecture and the basic components of PEMEX's Enterprise Risk Management Framework. This model is leveraging the three lines of defence model over the COSO 2013 Internal Control-Integrated Framework.

Figure 8.11. **PEMEX's Enterprise Risk Management Framework (MARE)**

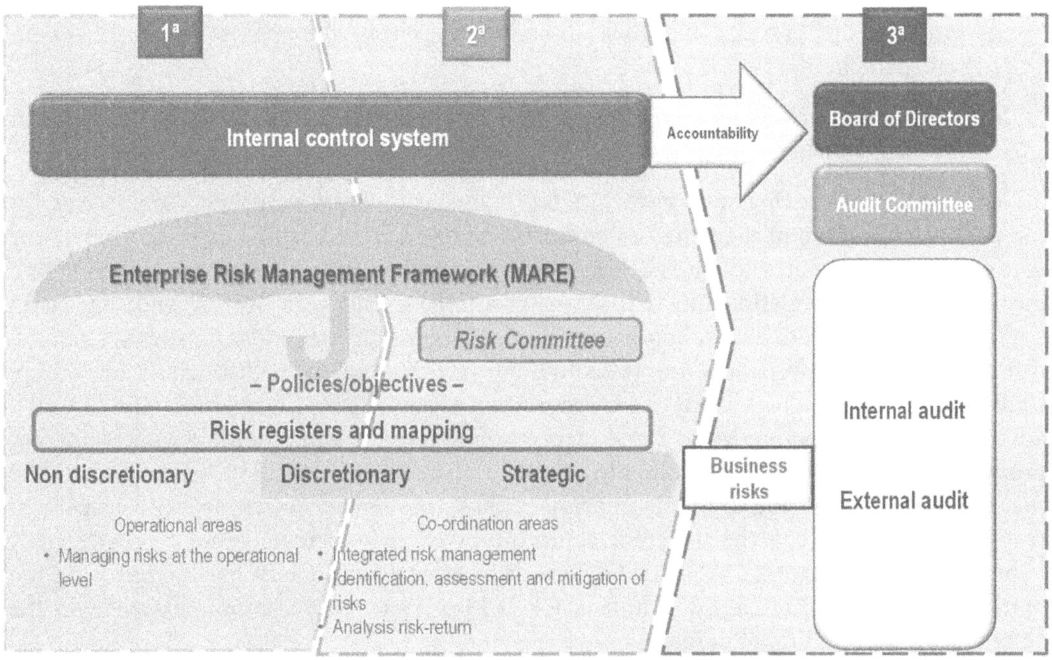

Source: Corporate Directorate of Finance, Marco de Administración de Riesgos Empresariales (MARE), presentation by the Sub-direction of Assurance and Risk Management, November 2015.

During the workshops in Mexico City and Villahermosa there was evidence that PEMEX's procurement officials working mainly in the first operational line are not very familiar with these methodological models and technical processes. The challenge seems to be quite high for those who are expected to own and respond to risk at the operational level. There is also a problem in identifying the different roles and responsibilities between the actors in the first and the second lines of defence. This is not uncommon among organisations. According to the latest IIA Common Body of Knowledge (CBOK) data, 18% of the organisations responding that they have adopted the three-lines model, say that distinctions between the lines are not clear (IIA, 2015). The basic idea behind the three lines of defence model is that when the model operates effectively, the likelihood that a risk will remain undetected by all the defence lines and harm the company's objectives diminishes. In a company like PEMEX engaging in such an ambitious transformation programme, the risk of blurring the roles and the responsibilities assigned to the different lines is very high. For example, when internal auditors perform risk-management activities that should fall under management's or second-line responsibility (e.g. due diligence), then the internal audit's independence, objectivity and reliability as an assurance provider to the Board and the Audit Committee is compromised.

On the other hand, it is also evident that PEMEX's team dealing with designing the internal control and risk-management processes has the expertise and the capacity to move the agenda forward. Integrating these functions within day-to-day activities and thus creating an enterprise-wide risk-management culture cascading throughout the organisation, providing valuable insight into decision making and contributing to the achievement of the objectives of the company, is a challenging and most rewarding task. Main challenges include issues like:

- involving the operational managers and staff
- piloting the process and then disseminating it in the affiliate and subsidiary companies
- performing rigorous monitoring and assessment of the actual degree of implementation.

CRPEMEX in its first session for 2016 (13 January) set up its primary objectives for the next months. One of them was to communicate a risk culture in PEMEX. This is one of the core prerequisites towards addressing the implementation gap and understanding the cross-functional relationships within the group. Engaging in a holistic and successful approach to risk governance requires overcoming organisational silos in order to map the full range of risks enterprise wide, reflecting the interdependencies throughout the group. CRPEMEX is working closely and reporting to the Audit Committee (CAUD) the advances in implementing MARE and incorporating risk elements in the decision-making process. The CAUD is closely following the work programme of CRPEMEX, prioritising the identification of the critical enterprise risks, the clear assignment of roles and responsibilities between the different actors involved in risk management (CAPEMEX [The Board of Directors] CAUD, DG [Director General] and CRPEMEX), ensuring the participation of the internal audit unit in CRPEMEX and good communication with the actors of the second line of defence.

PEMEX seems to be moving the right direction by focusing its efforts in strengthening its risk-management system and involving all stakeholders in this crucial business component and function, which has a central role in the strategic and operational plans of all big international oil companies (see Box 8.6).

Box 8.6. BP's risk-management system

How BP manages risk

1. BP's risk-management system is designed to be a consistent and clear framework for managing and reporting risks from the group's operations to the Board.
2. BP manages, monitors and reports on the principal risks and uncertainties that can impact its ability to deliver its strategy of meeting the world's energy needs responsibly while creating long-term shareholder value.
3. The management systems, organisational structures, processes, standards, code of conduct and behaviours together form a system of internal control that governs how it conducts its business and manages associated risks.

BP's risk-management system basic objectives

The system is designed to be a consistent and clear framework for managing and reporting risks from the group's operations to the Board. The system seeks to avoid incidents and maximise business outcomes by:

1. understanding the risk environment, and assessing the specific risks and potential exposure for BP
2. determining how best to deal with these risks to manage overall potential exposure
3. managing the identified risks in appropriate ways
4. monitoring and seeking assurance of the effectiveness of the management of these risks and intervening for improvement where necessary
5. reporting up the management chain and to the Board on a periodic basis on how significant risks are being managed, monitored, assured and the improvements that are being made.

BP's risk-management core activities

1. **Day-to-day risk management**: Staff and management are involved in identifying and managing risk, promoting safe, compliant and reliable operations. BP requirements, which take into account applicable laws and regulations, underpin the practical plans developed to help reduce risk and deliver strong, sustainable performance. For example, its operating management system (OMS) integrates BP requirements on health, safety, security, environment, social responsibility operational reliability and related issues.
2. **Business and strategic risk management**: BP's businesses and functions integrate risk into key business processes such as strategy, planning, performance management, resource and capital allocation, and project appraisal.
3. **Oversight and governance**: Functional leadership, the executive team, the Board and relevant committees provide oversight to identify, understand and endorse management of significant risks. They also put in place systems of risk management, compliance and control to mitigate these risks. Executive committees set policy and oversee the management of significant risks, while dedicated board committees review and monitor certain risks throughout the year.

The role of the Board in risk management

BP identifies certain risks as being a high priority for particular oversight by the Board. For 2015, this included risks associated with the Gulf of Mexico oil spill, geopolitical risk, security, ethical misconduct, legal and regulatory non-compliance, trading non-compliance, cybersecurity, major project delivery and incidents associated with the drilling of wells, operating facilities and the transportation of hydrocarbons.

(On 1 January 2015, the Board was composed of the chair, 2 executive directors and 11 non-executive directors).

Source: BP (2014), "Annual Report and Form 20-F 2014", www.bp.com/content/dam/bp-country/de_de/PDFs/brochures/BP_Annual_Report_and_Form_20F_2014.pdf; BP (2016), "How we manage risk", webpage, www.bp.com/en/global/corporate/sustainability/how-we-operate/how-we-manage-risk.html (accessed 22 February 2016).

The Internal Institutional Control Unit (Unidad de Control Interno Institucional, or UCII) is focusing on establishing transversal guidelines and common processes that will apply across corporate level including the seven subsidiaries. This is not an easy task since the companies that were formed after the Energy Reform are trying to adjust to the new legal and operational framework and define the roles and responsibilities among their units and personnel. The UCII is responsible for disseminating the processes and the relevant guidelines to the internal control bodies across the group and thus strengthening the co-ordination and the co-operation with the competent actors in the affiliate and subsidiary companies. They are also trying to establish Audit Committees to all the subsidiaries and ensure that enough independent members are appointed to them. For example, the Swiss subsidiary has two independent members in the Audit Committee.

PEMEX is already engaging in a process based risk-management approach. One of the areas that any big corporation should pay special attention to is the supply chain risks. According to an Accenture study (2011) involving more than 125 chief procurement officers, 70% believe procurement-related risk has increased due to financial turmoil. This is one of the reasons underlying the importance of setting up the right procedures to be more effective in supplier selection and appraisals. Furthermore, a company like PEMEX should be able to monitor changes to suppliers and screen suppliers against sanction lists for tax and financial compliance. External data sources can also be used for continuous monitoring of the supply markets and suppliers' financial health. Specific control activities rely on the analysis of existing financial and transactions data to perform "group spend analysis", which will enable PEMEX to have an overview on cases where it is purchasing from multiple companies in the same group and "supplier dependency controls" to be aware of its spending as a percentage of each supplier's turnover in order to take action to remedy the situation and thus avoid potential problems with the supply chain. The latter is being widely interpreted as being multi-tiered and being both upstream (supply) (i.e. between the organisation and the organisation's suppliers or suppliers' suppliers) and downstream (demand) (i.e. between the organisation and its market). Supply chain risks are often, and for more than 30 years, factored in strategic sourcing methodologies and project categorisation, as indicated in the categorisation matrix developed by Kraljic in 1983.

Possible answers could involve using dual sourcing, risk sharing contract clauses and regular negotiations with suppliers to anticipate supply risks related to commodity price volatility, quality and supply chain disruptions. Similar elements and responses could be strongly embedded in PEMEX procurement strategy and process. The challenge for PEMEX is to ensure that its control framework is in line with the risk assessments and develop the appropriate group-wide control activities for effectively responding to the identified risks. These controls should aim to reduce the probability of occurrence and anticipated consequences of risks. It is also important that they cover the main processes and functions outsourced to third parties through service contracts.

An effective supply chain risk mitigation process will invariably bring additional business benefits such as countering data protection or fraud risks resultant from vulnerabilities in the organisation's supply chain. A process focusing on addressing the supply chain risk should include the following elements:

- comprehensive mapping of all tiers of the upstream and downstream supply chains to the level of individual contracts
- risk scoring each contract to link in to the organisation's existing overall risk assessment

- due diligence/accreditation/assurance of suppliers (and potential suppliers) and the adoption, through contracts, of proportionate and appropriate measures to mitigate risk
- audit arrangements and compliance monitoring
- contract exit arrangements.

PEMEX has engaged in an initial risk mapping exercise focusing on the procurement cycle. The procurement process was broken down into six sub-processes, four of which were categorised as core processes and two as support processes. Furthermore, within this programme of work, another output is the identification of the universe of responsibilities concerning managing and mitigating these risks. Overall, there are 398 risks identified: 205 operational risks (52%) and 193 business risks (48%).

PEMEX is moving in the right direction, taking the exercise further than just risk identification. For example procurement risks are measured and prioritised in relation to the risk appetite and tolerance of the group.

Special attention must be given to strengthening the existing arrangements to encourage and monitor responsible practices among contractors and suppliers, thus mitigating the relevant risks. PEMEX could build on the basis that its primary interest is to ensure the interests of both parties by working with contractors and suppliers on clear, fairly negotiated contractual conditions (Box 8.7).

Box 8.7. Total's integrity policy towards contractors and suppliers

The company expects its contractors and suppliers:

- to adhere to principles equivalent to those of its own Code of Conduct, and such as those set out in the "fundamental principles of purchasing", which were set out in April 2014, specifying the commitments that the company expects from its suppliers and contractors in relation to: respect for human rights at work, health protection, assurance of safety and security, preservation of the environment, prevention of corruption, conflicts of interest and fraud, respect of competition law and promotion of economic and social development
- to agree to being audited and provide assurance over the efficiency of their internal control and risk-management processes and to ensure that their suppliers and contractors also respect equivalent principles, particularly in relation with their working standards and procedures and more specific issues like the Rule 13p-1 of the Securities Exchange Act in relation to the use of "conflict minerals" as well as other Corporate Social Responsibility (CSR) obligations and risks.

Source: Total (2014), "Form 20-F 2014", Annual report, www.total.com/sites/default/files/atoms/files/form_20-f_0.pdf.

PEMEX could further explore the added value of developing specific questionnaires to be answered by existing and candidate suppliers and contractors. Moreover, service providers can be asked to complete integrity and anti-corruption training modules similar to those developed for PEMEX's procurement staff. PEMEX could also invite people from their suppliers to participate and attend events like anti-corruption days and thematic presentations promoting the company's initiatives to foster integrity and enhance control and risk processes. Engaging in these activities is particularly important since organisations within the oil and gas community have to rely, for certain tasks, on workers, who are not company employees and subsequently grant them access to a wide range of sensitive facilities and assets. A company like PEMEX should always consider the risk that they not have been screened by their own company or agency to the same standard as the company's own employees. Practical guidelines towards secure procurement of contracting staff were developed by the Centre for the Protection of National Infrastructure (CPNI) in the United Kingdom, working closely with the Department of Energy and Climate Change, and with the co-operation of some leading oil and gas companies and trade associations (Box 8.8).

Box 8.8. Secure Procurement of Contracting Staff checklist

- A risk assessment has been conducted to determine the level of insider risk posed to the contracting authority due to the access to information/assets the contractor(s) role will afford.
- Proportionate pre-engagement screening levels(s) have been agreed that are commensurate to the risk.
- The level and standard of screening has been formally communicated to the contractor, agency or contracting company (including a mechanism to deal with any adverse information uncovered during recruitment).
- Appropriate ongoing security arrangements and policies have been drafted into the contract with clear lines of communication and defined responsibilities outlined (personnel, information technology, information and physical).
- Agreed access arrangements have been put in place.
- A system has been put in place to confirm that the contractor who arrives to work is identical to the individual who has been supplied and "screened" to work on the contract.
- A process has been put in place with the contracting company/agency to manage the substitution of a temporary member of staff when the usual contract staff member is absent.
- An effective off-boarding process has been put in place to ensure that the contractor's access to assets and information has been revoked when it is no longer necessary.
- An appropriate audit mechanism has been put in place to monitor compliance with the required security arrangements of the contract (including pre-engagement screening).
- The security controls (both pre-engagement and ongoing) demanded by the contracting authority.

Source: CPNI (2011), "The Secure Procurement of Contracting Staff - A Good Practice Guide for the Oil and Gas Industry", CPNI, April.

PEMEX should consider developing and implementing an autonomous fraud and corruption risk-management framework.

In order to develop a sound approach focusing on creating an anti-fraud environment, it would be helpful to highlight the basic concept of the fraud triangle, which was first introduced in the 1970s (Figure 8.12). It is used to illustrate the three components, i.e. pressure, opportunity and rationalisation, which create the ideal environment for fraud to occur. Opportunity is usually directly related to the existence and the effectiveness of internal controls, while pressure and rationalisation stem from inadequate integrity and ethics arrangements that can also be identified as weakness of conscience.

Figure 8.12. **The fraud triangle**

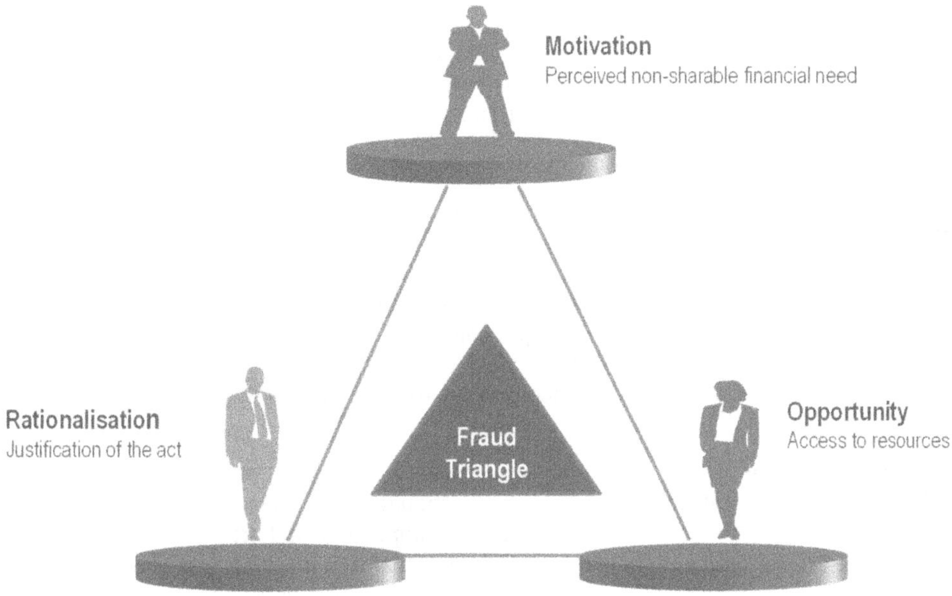

Source: Based on the fraud triangle theory developed in 1970s by criminologist Donald D. Cressesy.

Fraud prevention requires a system of rules which if correctly designed and implemented, should minimise the likelihood of fraud while setting the preconditions for detecting any fraudulent activity. The potential of being caught deters potential perpetrators from committing fraud. Dedicated fraud and corruption risk frameworks is a common characteristic among big international companies. Box 8.9 demonstrates the basic components of Total's approach in this field.

Box 8.9. Total's fraud risk assessment (integrity risks)

Focusing on fraud prevention

This is a priority for the company and the whole effort is supported by the business principles and values of individual behaviour described in the group's Code of Conduct and in the codes, charters and other standards applied by business segments'. Total has issued a directive for handling incidents of fraud which has been widely communicated and distributed, thus creating an alert system that the employees can use to report circumstances that might constitute fraud. In addition, a specific process is in place for reporting irregularities related to accounting, internal control and audit issues. This warning process was put in place at the request of, and is monitored by, the Audit Committee and may be equally used by shareholders, employees and third parties.

The system was further strengthened in 2014 by the creation of a fraud risk co-ordinator position in the Compliance and Social Responsibility department within the Group's Legal Affairs department. The deployment of the anti-fraud and fraud prevention programme relies on the network of fraud risk co-ordinators.

Preventing corruption risks

Total's senior management constantly reiterates the principle of zero tolerance with regard to corruption. This effort is supported by a set of internal standards that was published in 2011. This framework takes into account relevant applicable rules, covering various areas where high risk of corruption exposure may exist like: business partnerships, representatives, procurement and sales, etc. and is based on a due diligence process for detecting and addressing them at an early stage.

Special attention was given to raising awareness around this programme among the personnel. To this end, an e-learning module in 12 languages has been consistently deployed since 2011, and 370 Compliance Officers have been appointed and trained in the business segments and operational entities. Their role is to ensure that the programme is implemented at the local level.

On top of the above-mentioned initiatives undertaken by Total, the company had to implement further actions included in a settlement agreement, reached in 2013, on a violation case of the Foreign Corrupt Practices Act between Total, the United States Securities and Exchange Commission (SEC) and the Department of Justice (DoJ). Following this agreement, an independent monitor was appointed to conduct a three-year review of the anti-corruption compliance and related internal control procedures implemented by the Group and to recommend improvements. This assignment started on December 2013 and the monitor's first report was submitted on July 2014. Total has already started to implement the proposed improvements.

Source: Total (n. d.), www.total.com/en, official website (accessed 26 February 2016).

Investigation of potential fraud consists of several steps that require specific training and expertise in conducting interviews, collecting and analysing evidence and dealing with law enforcement and prosecution agencies. Fraud and corruption risk mapping is closely linked with effective integrity reforms. The complexity and the technical challenges arising in this field of work may require the creation of a fraud and corruption risk co-ordinator position and the hiring of certified fraud examiners (CFE) to create a dedicated team with the skills to have an actual impact in detecting, preventing and effectively responding to this kind of phenomena. Box 8.10 presents the basic components of ExxonMobil's anti-corruption initiative, including some very interesting attributes on training and capacity-building policies.

Box 8.10. ExxonMobil's anti-corruption programme

Bribery and corruption

Anti-corruption practices are an essential component of the compliance programme, given that ExxonMobil operates globally and in many challenging environments. The Anti-Corruption Legal Compliance Summary outlines ExxonMobil's commitment to comply with the US Foreign Corrupt Practices Act (FCPA), the United Kingdom Bribery Act and global anti-corruption standards in all business relationships. It also describes elements of the corporation's anti-corruption compliance programme.

ExxonMobil employees and contractors are prohibited from making payments to, or engaging in transactions with, government officials to influence the performance of their official duties improperly. Maintaining internal controls and keeping accurate and complete transaction records are required. Our standard language for procurement contracts includes a requirement to comply with all laws, keep accurate books and records, and where appropriate, contains specific anti-bribery commitments.

Training

Oil and gas exploration and production often take the company to remote parts of the world, with changing political and regulatory climates. In 2012, approximately 31 000 employees took part in anti-corruption training. This training covers the basics of the FCPA, the United Kingdom Bribery Act, global anti-corruption standards, recent developments in enforcement, and compliance with our internal anti-corruption policy, guidelines and processes. Employees in positions assessed to be higher-risk receive training every year and within three months of entering their positions. Every two years, managers and professional employees not in higher-risk positions receive training. Every four years, all ExxonMobil employees are required to attend half-day business practices reviews that include anti-corruption issues. In 2012, employees around the world attended business practices review sessions. Additionally, the company monitors legal and regulatory developments and advise employees as appropriate.

Source: ExxonMobil (2014) "2014 Annual report", www.annualreports.com/Company/exxon-mobil; ExxonMobil (n. d.), "Ethics", webpage, http://corporate.exxonmobil.com/en/investors/corporate-governance/ethics/ethics (accessed 8 October 2016).

It is essential that PEMEX deploys a robust and functioning fraud and corruption prevention programme. The company made a first significant step in this direction by launching its programme of Corporate Ethics and Integrity on 4 February 2016. The programme includes key elements and procedures aiming to support the effort to prevent, detect and respond to different types of potential fraud like bribery and conflicts of interest. Some of the most common measures and responses include:

- maintaining a strong ethics and conflict-of-interest policy
- ensuring rigorous reporting of potential conflicts of interest
- eliminating gifts from vendors and contractors

- creating an anti-fraud environment
- identifying fraud risks
- developing a robust oversight process.

PEMEX should also invest in establishing the right policies in relation to hiring and promoting staff that have the right skills and ethical values to work in high-risk areas. Policies like conducting background investigations, verifying education certificates, employment history and references can be very useful when trying to establish an anti-fraud environment. Moreover, the company should also engage in regular individual performance reviews and objective compliance review of the code of conduct and ethics policies. Addressing violations immediately and communicating a "zero tolerance" policy can also help foster such a culture inside PEMEX. The company should also clearly articulate that all employees are held accountable to act within the code of conduct and consider introducing individual code of conduct statements for certain high-risk job positions.

PEMEX has to take all the necessary steps to identify potential fraud scenarios. This requires an expert approach to conceive the potential incident and understand that this is a real possibility. Lists of typical fraud red flags must never be seen as all-inclusive. PEMEX has to focus and evaluate its major process areas based on volume of transactions/activities and budget impact. Procurement and supply chain is definitely one of these areas. Officials involved in this exercise should address the issue of assigning impact and likelihood to individual fraud and corruption scenarios identified in the risk assessment procedure. The following example in Box 8.11 illustrates a set of red flags for potential fraud and corruption schemes in the procurement cycle.

Box 8.11. Examples of red flags in procurement

Several studies have identified common indicators of potential fraud and corruption in the procurement process. Ten most common "red flags" have been cited by the World Bank, including:

- Complaints from bidders and other parties may signal that additional due diligence and investigation may be warranted in a particular procurement.
- Multiple contracts below procurement thresholds may indicate contract- splitting schemes used by corrupt officials to avoid higher level review or competitive bidding.
- Unusual bid patterns such as unexplained inflated bid prices, round or unnatural numbers, apparent rotation of winning bidders and other seemingly irregular activities may be a sign of collusive bidding by at least some of the vendors.
- Inflated agent fees, or the unnecessary involvement of middlemen or third parties may be used to disguise corrupt payments.
- Fictitious companies or consulting firms may be used by some dubious bidders to submit bids that are unreasonably high so that a real bidder can submit a higher-than-normal bid price and give the appearance it is competitive.
- Rejection of the lowest bidder on unjustifiable grounds may indicate bid rigging with project officials having a hidden interest in a contractor.

Box 8.11. Examples of red flags in procurement *(continued)*

- Sole source awards given over and over to the same bidder should be scrutinised, especially if these requests are made for reasons of urgency and with no other legitimate purpose.
- Changes in contract terms and value with regard to the price, amount or type of services between the selection and the signing of the contract, while sometimes unavoidable, may nevertheless be an indicator that warrants more review.
- Contract change orders after the contract has been signed, especially if multiple in nature, can indicate collusion between the client and contractor to increase the value of the contract without delivery of additional product or services.
- Poor performance, or deficiencies in the goods or services, or even non-delivery can indicate fraud and corruption.

Note: These red flags refer to indicators of fraud and corruption in World Bank financed projects. However, the "red flags" are a useful reference for procurement generally.

Source: World Bank (n. d.), "Most common red flags of fraud and corruption in procurement", http://siteresources.worldbank.org/INTDOII/Resources/Red_flags_reader_friendly.pdf (accessed 8 October 2016).

PEMEX is opening to competition and preparing to address the challenges of the free market. A recent case from the Colombian oil company Ecopetrol gives an example of the fraud and corruption risks that relate to procurement and the supply chain (Box 8.12).

Box 8.12. The Ecopetrol case

In 2014 the Prosecutor General's Office of Colombia announced it will be investigating the transnational bribe of an Ecopetrol official and eight others allegedly involved with the scandal. A foreign company providing production testing services to oil and gas companies is accused of having paid an official of Colombia's state-run Ecopetrol oil company a bribe in exchange for giving the company contracts from Ecopetrol.

The Head of the National Anti-Corruption Unit is investigating the involvement of eight officials from the two involved companies after an official complaint was filed by the Secretary of Transparency. The case involves charges like money laundering and wire fraud. The bribe seems to have been paid through a phony consulting contract between the involved parties. Ecopetrol, the biggest company in Colombia, stated that current executives have been suspended and the company is co-operating with Colombian prosecutors.

Source: Cassin, R. L. (2015), "Colombia arrests six linked to alleged PetroTiger bribes", *The FCPA Blog*, www.fcpablog.com/blog/2015/3/16/colombia-arrests-six-linked-to-alleged-petrotiger-bribes.html;

Proposals for action

PEMEX should act on strengthening its internal control system by ensuring a sound and functional control environment underpinned by integrating ethical values and integrity into daily operations throughout the company.

- Integrate concrete integrity objectives into the planning exercise of the company and link them with core operational objectives. Introduce measurable and simple indicators to monitor the implementation and the evolution of the integrity attributes of the control environment and culture.
- Provide dilemma training with concrete situations that focus on practical approaches regarding the organisation's values and its linkages with effective controls (special modules for management and staff).
- Introduce ethical clauses in procurement process and in contracts with external suppliers.
- Designate ethics co-ordinators with specific responsibilities to promote the linkages between integrity and effective controls.
- Work on improving the monitoring and assessment model of the internal control system and improve individual capacity by developing a set of online training modules to be completed by all heads of departments and directorates as well as employees in key positions like public procurement, financial management, core business and priority objectives.

PEMEX should consider taking concrete action to highlight the importance of setting a clear tone at the top to create a robust and effective control environment.

- Ensure a healthy tone at the top by testing ethical aspects during management selection procedures.
- Develop internal and external reporting to include statistics on ethical issues, integrity breaches, complaints treatment and sanctions.
- Draft and circulate periodic communication/reports describing detected instances of non-compliance/wrongdoing and the measures taken to redress the situation, including the sanctions applied.

PEMEX should focus on establishing a robust assurance-providing function to support the Board on meeting their corporate governance obligations and the company's delivery and accountability needs.

- Render the assurance function transparent and well-articulated with all interested parties. It must be viewed as a management tool before becoming an audit problem.
- Introduce training modules on assurance as well as on the consulting role of the internal audit function and the value of evidence-based policy choices based on existing audit reports.

PEMEX must focus on addressing the implementation gap and integrating the risk-management process into day-to-day activities across all areas and organisational levels of the company.

- Strengthen the institutional and individual capacity of PEMEX officials in internal control and risk management. This should involve concrete actions to assign clear roles and duties, empower and involve professionals across all entity levels while ensuring high quality and independent external guidance, monitoring and assessment.
- Provide concrete examples of how the early identification of risks can help avoid future problems and thus save valuable time and resources.

PEMEX should consider developing and implementing an autonomous fraud and corruption risk-management framework.

- Establish: 1) an autonomous fraud management policy focusing on specific high-risk areas; and 2) a concrete corruption risk mapping and management processes. These initiatives muse be part of, and fully aligned with, the ongoing efforts to improve the internal control and risk-management framework.
- Link human resources procedures for hiring, evaluation and dismissal with the fraud and corruption risk governance system.

Annex 8.A1

Governance of internal control and risk management

Jurisdiction	Board responsibilities for risk management[1]	Implementation of the internal control and risk-management system[2]	Board-level committee: Risk-management role of Audit Committee[3]	Board-level committee: Establishment of separate risk committee	Chief risk officers[4]
Argentina	C	C	L/R	C	C
Australia	C		-	C	
Austria	L/C	L	L**/C**	-	-
Belgium	L	L	L	-	-
Brazil			-		
Canada			-		
Chile	-	R	R	R	-
Czech Republic	C	C	-	-	-
Denmark			-		
Estonia			-		
Finland	C	C	C**	-	-
France			L		
Germany	L/C	L/C	L/C	-	-
Greece			C		
Hong Kong, China	C	C	C**	-	-
Hungary	L/C	L/C	-	-	C
Iceland			C		
India	L/R	L/R	L/R	R	-
Indonesia	L/C	-	-	C	-
Ireland	C	C	C	-	-
Israel	-	R	L**	-	L***
Italy	C	C	L	C	C***
Japan	L	L	-	-	-
Korea	C	-	-	-	-
Lithuania	-	-	C**	-	-
Luxembourg			C		
Mexico	L	-	L	-	-
Netherlands	C	C	C**	-	-
New Zealand	C	C	-	-	-
Norway	C	L/C	L**	-	-
Poland	-	L/C	L**	-	-
Portugal	-	-	-	-	-
Saudi Arabia			-		
Singapore	C	C	C	C	C
Slovak Republic			-		
Slovenia	C	C	C**	-	-
Spain	-	L/C	L**/C**	-	-
Sweden	C	C	-	-	-
Switzerland	L	C	C**	-	-
Turkey	L	L	-	L	-
United Kingdom	C	C	C**	-	-
United States	R*	L/R	L**/R**	-	-

Key: **L** = Requirement by law or regulations **R** = Requirement by the listing rule
C = Recommendation by codes or principles **"-"** = Absence of a specific requirement or recommendation

Notes:

1. This column shows the existence of specific provisions describing "Board responsibilities for risk management".
2. This column shows the existence of specific provisions describing "Implementation of the internal control and risk-management system".
3. "**"in the column of "Risk management role of Audit Committee" denotes that risk management is explicitly included in the role of the Audit Committee. In the United States, this is applicable only for NYSE-listed companies.
4. "**" in the column of "Chief risk officers" denotes that internal auditors are in charge of risk management. In Israel, internal auditors are in charge of risk management. The board of directors of a public company is required to appoint an internal auditor, in charge of examining, *inter alia*, the propriety of the company's actions, in terms of compliance with the law and proper business.

Source: OECD (2015a), OECD Corporate Governance Factbook, OECD, www.oecd.org/daf/ca/corporate-governance-factbook.htm.

Note

1. The OECD and PEMEX co-organised two workshops between 31 January and 6 February 2016 in Mexico City and Villahermosa focusing on the public procurement system of the company. The workshops were attended by more than 120 procurement officials and practitioners and the programme included dedicated sessions on internal control and risk-management systems and functions. The OECD experts and international peers (from Canada, the Netherlands and the United Kingdom) made very interesting contributions in the form of presentations and case studies, which sparked lively discussions with PEMEX officials. The workshops also benefited from the participation of the Head of the Unit of Ethics of the Ministry of Public Administration (SFP) at Mexico City and one member of his team in Villahermosa.

References

Accenture (2011), "Report on the Accenture 2011 Global Risk Management Study", www.rims.org/resources/ERM/Documents/Accenture_Global_Report%202011.pdf.

BP (British Petroleum) (2016), "How we manage risk", webpage, www.bp.com/en/global/corporate/sustainability/how-we-operate/how-we-manage-risk.html (accessed 22 February 2016).

BP (2014), "Annual Report and Form 20-F 2014", www.bp.com/content/dam/bp-country/de_de/PDFs/brochures/BP_Annual_Report_and_Form_20F_2014.pdf.

Cassin, R. L. (2015), "Colombia arrests six linked to alleged PetroTiger bribes", *The FCPA Blog*, www.fcpablog.com/blog/2015/3/16/colombia-arrests-six-linked-to-alleged-petrotiger-bribes.html.

Corporate Directorate of Finance (2015), "Marco de Administración de Riesgos Empresariales (MARE)", presentation by the Sub-direction of Assurance and Risk Management, November.

COSO (Committee of Sponsoring Organisations of the Treadway Commission) (2013), "Internal Control-Integrated Framework 2013", COSO.

COSO (2004), "Enterprise Risk Management 2004", COSO.

CPNI (2011), "The Secure Procurement of Contracting Staff - A Good Practice Guide for the Oil and Gas Industry", CPNI, April.

Ethics Alarms (2014), "Good News On Business Ethics? Maybe: The Ethics Research Center's 2014 National Business Ethics Survey", https://ethicsalarms.com/2014/02/12/good-news-on-business-ethics-maybe-the-ethics-research-centers-2014-national-business-ethics-survey/.

ExxonMobil (2014) "2014 Annual report", www.annualreports.com/Company/exxon-mobil.

ExxonMobil (n. d.), "Ethics", webpage, http://corporate.exxonmobil.com/en/investors/corporate-governance/ethics/ethics (accessed 8 October 2016).

FERMA (Federation of European Risk Management Associations) (2012), "Benchmarking Survey 2012", www.ferma.eu/about/publications/benchmarking-surveys/benchmarking-survey-2012/.

IIA (Institute of Internal Auditors) (2016), "More than just setting the tone: A look at organizational culture", *Tone at the Top*, Issue 76, February, Audit Executive Centre.

IIA (2015), "CBOK 2015 Practitioner Survey", https://global.theiia.org/iiarf/Pages/Common-Body-of-Knowledge-CBOK.aspx.

Kraljic, P. (1983), "Purchasing Must Become Management", *Harvard Business Review,* https://hbr.org/1983/09/purchasing-must-become-supply-management.

OECD (2015a), *OECD Corporate Governance Factbook*, OECD, www.oecd.org/daf/ca/corporate-governance-factbook.htm.

OECD (2015b), *G20/OECD Principles of Corporate Governance*, OECD Publishing, Paris, http://dx.doi.org/10.1787/9789264236882-en.

OECD/IDB (2014), *Government at a Glance: Latin America and the Caribbean 2014: Towards Innovative Public Financial Management*, OECD Publishing, Paris, http://dx.doi.org/10.1787/9789264209480-en.

PEMEX (n. d.), "Database of observations 2012-14".

Sinopec Corp. (2014a), "Assessment Report on Internal Control for 2014", Sinopec.

Sinopec Corp. (2014b), "2014 Annual Report and Accounts", http://english.sinopec.com/download_center/reports/2014/20150322/download/201503222e.pdf.

Sinopec Corp. (2014c), "Internal control", webpage, http://english.sinopec.com/investor_center/corporate_governance/internal_control/.

Total (2014), "Form 20-F 2014", Annual report, www.total.com/sites/default/files/atoms/files/form_20-f_0.pdf.

Total (n. d.), www.total.com/en, official website (accessed 26 February 2016).

World Bank (n. d.), "Most common red flags of fraud and corruption in procurement", http://siteresources.worldbank.org/INTDOII/Resources/Red_flags_reader_friendly.pdf (accessed 8 October 2016).

Chapter 9

Petróleos Mexicanos' review and remedy system on procurement decisions

This chapter provides an overview of the review and remedy system that applies to Petróleos Mexicanos' (PEMEX's) procurement procedures, which has evolved over time. It focuses on the current system, following amendments in 2014 to the PEMEX Law, which create a special procurement regime for the company. While it recognises that it is still early days to make an assessment on the effectiveness of the challenge mechanisms anticipated under the special procurement regime of PEMEX, this chapter provides an overview of the trends found in challenges to award decisions. Furthermore, this chapter suggests alternatives and proposes specific actions to improve the effectiveness, timeliness and accessibility of challenge mechanisms available to PEMEX bidders.

Review and remedy mechanisms contribute to increasing the overall fairness, lawfulness and transparency of procurement procedures, and support their integrity. They also build confidence among businesses and facilitate competition in public contract markets. Review and remedy systems serve a procurement oversight function by providing means to scrutinise the activities of government procurement officials, enforce their compliance with procurement laws and regulations, and correct their improper actions. These systems provide an opportunity for bidders to contest the process and verify the integrity of the award.

To guarantee an impartial review, a body with enforcement capacity independent of the procuring entity needs to rule the review decisions. Complaints must be resolved in a fair manner while ensuring administrative efficiency through timely resolutions and adequate remedies (Box 9.1). In order to be effective, a review and remedy system needs to:

- provide timely redress
- be effective in correcting (and thus preventing) instances of unlawfulness on the part of economic operators and/or contracting authorities
- be transparent and clear (i.e. understandable and easy to use by economic operators)
- be non-discriminatory and available to all the bidders wishing to participate in a specific contract award procedure.

Box 9.1. Recommendation of the Council on Public Procurement

The 2015 OECD Recommendation of the Council on Public Procurement recommends that adherents apply oversight and control mechanisms to support accountability throughout the public procurement cycle, including appropriate complaint and sanctions processes. To this end, adherents should handle complaints in a fair, timely, and transparent way through the establishment of effective courses of action for challenging procurement decisions to correct defects, prevent wrongdoing, and build confidence of bidders, including foreign competitors, in the integrity and fairness of the public procurement system. Additional key aspects of an effective complaints system are dedicated and independent review and adequate redress.

Source: OECD (2015), "Recommendation of the Council on Public Procurement", www.oecd.org/corruption/recommendation-on-public-procurement.htm.

This chapter provides an overview of the review and remedy system that applies to Petróleos Mexicanos' (PEMEX's) procurement procedures, which has evolved over time (see Table 9.1). It focuses on the current system, following amendments in 2014 to the PEMEX Law, which create a special procurement regime for the company. In fact, PEMEX had been excluded from the application of the Law of Acquisitions, Leasing, and Services of the Public Sector (Ley de Adquisiciones, Arrendamientos y Servicios del Sector Público, or LAASSP) and the Law of Public Works and Related Services (Ley de Obras Públicas y Servicios Relacionados con las Mismas, or LOPSR), which apply to the entire federal public administration since the publication of the PEMEX Law in 2008. The 2014 amendments modified the conditions for filing formal complaints against procurement procedures.

Table 9.1. **Evolution of the review and remedy system applicable to PEMEX procurement**

Period	Challenge mechanisms	Authority reviewing the challenge	Applicable regulation	Details
5 January 1966-6 May 1972	*Amparo Indirecto*	District Judge	Contract Inspection and Public Works Law (Ley de Inspección de Contratos y Obra Pública)	Challenge to be filed against awards of public works contracts held through tender.
7 May 1972-31 December 1979	*Amparo Indirecto*	District Judge	Procurement Inspection Law (Ley de Inspección de Adquisiciones)	Challenge to be filed against procedures for the acquisition of real estate through tender.
1 January 1980-8 February 1985	Administrative challenge against awards	Hierarchical superior of the public official in charge of the award decision	Law on Acquisitions, Leasing, and Warehouses of the Federal Public Administration (Ley sobre Adquisiciones, Arrendamientos y Almacenes de la Administración Pública Federal)	Possibility to request the suspension of the award by the complaining bidder.
	Amparo Indirecto against the resolution of the administrative challenge	District Judge		
1 January 1981-8 January 1988	*Amparo indirecto*	District Judge	Public Works Law (Ley de Obras Públicas)	Challenge to be filed against awards of public works contracts through tender.
9 February 1985-8 January 1988	Administrative challenge (*inconformidad*)	Tendering institution or the Comptroller's Office	Law for Acquisitions, Leasing, and Services related to Movable Property (Ley de Adquisiciones, Arrendamientos y Prestación de Servicios relacionados con Bienes Muebles)	Challenge to be filed against awards in procurement processes for acquisitions, leasing, and services, through public tender.
	Amparo Indirecto against the resolution of *inconformidad* or directly against the award decision	District Judge		
8 January 1988-4 January 2000	*Inconformidad*	General Comptroller of the Federation (Secretaría de la Contraloría General de la Federación, SECOGEF)	Public Works Law (Ley de Obras Públicas) Law for Acquisitions, Leasing, and Services related to Movable Property (Ley de Adquisiciones, Arrendamientos y Prestación de Servicios relacionados con Bienes Muebles)	Amendments harmonise the mechanism of *inconformidades* in both laws and introduce intervention by default (*intervención de oficio*) to assess the legality of procurement procedures dealing with public works, acquisitions, leasing, and services related to movable property.
	Amparo Indirecto against the resolution of *inconformidad* or directly against the award decision	District Judge		
1 December 1994-4 January 2000	*Inconformidad*	SECOGEF	Acquisitions and Public Works Law (Ley de Adquisiciones y Obras Públicas)	Challenge to be filed against award decisions of procurement dealing with acquisitions and leasing, services of any kind, public works and services related. *Recurso de Revocación* challenges the resolution to a *inconformidad* Since 1 January 1995, the *recurso de revocación* was substituted by a challenge review (*Recurso de Revisión*).
	Challenge recourse (*Recurso de Revocación*)	SECOGEF		
	Annulation trial (*Juicio de Nulidad*)	Federal Tribunal for Fiscal and Administrative Justice		
	Amparo Directo against the trial resolution	Collegiate Circuit Tribunal for Administrative Matters (Tribunal Colegiado de Circuito en Materia Administrativa)		
4 January 2000-Entry into force of PEMEX Law	*Inconformidad*	Ministry for Control and Administrative Development (Secretaría de Contraloría y Desarrollo Administrativo, SECODAM)	LAASSP and LOPSR	Amendments provide more details regarding the process of *inconformidad* and the corresponding suspension of the award, as well as intervention by default.
	Resolution of *inconformidad* can be challenged through *recurso de revisión* or a contentious administrative trial	SECODAM or Federal Tribunal for Fiscal and Administrative Justice		
	Amparo Directo against the trial resolution	Collegiate Circuit Tribunal for Administrative Matters (Tribunal Colegiado de Circuito en Materia Administrativa)		

Source: Based on legal compendiums that can be found at www.dof.gob.mx and www.diputados.gob.mx/LeyesBiblio/index.htm.

Current review and remedy mechanisms on procurement procedures

The PEMEX Law states in its introduction that, in order to advance the principles of justice and timeliness, there will be mechanisms to challenge award decisions. Article 81 of the PEMEX Law dictates that challenges against award decisions in public tenders or restricted invitations can be filed through a reconsideration request (*recurso de reconsideración*, or RR) or a jurisdictional action called the administrative-contentious trial (*juicio contencioso administrativo*, or JCA). The RR is filed before the collegiate body established in Articles 27 and 28 of the Bylaws (Reglamento de la Ley de PEMEX), while the JCA is filed before the Federal Tribunal for Administrative Justice (Tribunal Federal de Justicia Administrativa, or TFJA). All this is explained to potential suppliers in the calls for tender.

The collegiate body that reviews RR is regulated in Articles 236-240 of the Organic Statute of PEMEX (Estatuto Orgánico de PEMEX). According to this regulation, the collegiate body is integrated by three members with vote and opinion capacities, with the hierarchical level of managers, at least. The three members are a public official appointed by the Head of the Institutional Internal Control Unit (Unidad de Control Interno Institucional, or UCII), who presides over the collegiate body; a public official appointed by the Corporate Director for Planning, Co-ordination and Performance; and a public official appointed by the Legal Director. The collegiate body:

- decides on the RR and their incidents
- provides instructions to the Technical Secretariat to take the necessary actions to substantiate the RR
- approves its internal operations rules.

The Manager for Legal Affairs and Administrative-Contentious (Gerencia Jurídica Contenciosa Administrativa, or GJCA) or someone appointed by it plays the role of Technical Secretariat of the collegiate body. The GJCA provides legal advice to the collegiate body and is responsible for putting together the file for the body to reach a decision. It prepares the draft resolutions, notifies the resolutions, and executes the administrative acts required by the collegiate body (i.e. inspections). Resolutions are taken by simple majority and the members of the collegiate body cannot abstain from voting, except when there is a legal obstacle. In case of a tie, the vote of the president of the collegiate body prevails.

The RR can lead to overturning, modifying, or confirming, totally or partially, and definitively, an award decision. It can only be filed by bidders who actually participated with a proposition in a tender. It should be filed in written form within five days of the public meeting in which the award decision was taken or the notification to the awarded entity, in case such public meeting did not take place.[1] In the case of joint proposals, the RR should be filed with the signature of all the co-bidders. If this condition is not met, the RR is disregarded. Among other items, the RR should explain the facts or omissions that provide background to the award decision, the estimated damages, and the evidence related to the above-mentioned acts or omissions. Resolutions on RR take on average between 30 and 35 days.

The filing of a RR suspends the award of a contract until resolution when: 1) the bidder filing the RR requests it; 2) there are no damages implied to the public interest or contradictions to public order regulations; and 3) the bidder filing the RR meets the requisites established by Article 30 of the Bylaws. Furthermore, when the collegiate body in charge of reviewing a RR identifies the possibility or the actual occurrence of acts violating applicable regulations, it may suspend the award decision, only when the resolution has not been dictated.

When the suspension of the award decision is feasible, but implies damages to PEMEX or the awarded bidder, the participant filing the RR should provide a guarantee to repair damages, in case the RR is not decided in his favour. Such a guarantee consists of an amount between 10% and 30% of the economic proposal of the bidder filing the RR. When such an amount could not be calculated, the guarantee will be equivalent to the budget for the corresponding tender procedure. This requirement can make the obtaining of a suspension of the award onerous. In addition, the suspension is overturned if the winning bidder provides a counter guarantee (*contragarantía*) of the same amount as the one paid by the bidder filing the RR.

Once the RR is received by the collegiate body, it calls on the PEMEX unit in charge of the bidding process in question to provide a report within five working days to justify the award of the contract. The awarded bidder is also called to provide evidence and arguments. Once all evidence is provided, the instruction process is complete and the parties have three more working days to provide arguments. Once this term is finished, the collegiate body concentrates on preparing a resolution, which cannot be appealed through administrative means. If the PEMEX unit in charge of the bidding process does not comply with the resolution, the awarded bidder or the one who filed the RR can inform the collegiate body so that it requires compliance and, if necessary, informs the Responsibilities Unit so that it applies the Federal Law for Administrative Responsibilities of Public Officials (Ley Federal de Responsabilidades Administrativas de los Servidores Públicos).

The JCA, filed before the TFJA, is regulated by the Federal Law of Contentious-Administrative Procedures (Ley Federal de Procedimiento Contencioso Administrativo). The parties to the JCA are the filing bidder, the sued entities (i.e. the authority that awarded the contract or the entity benefited by the award), or a third party with an incompatible right with the pretention of the filing bidder. The bidders have 45 working days to file for the JCA. The length of time taken by the JCA is variable and depends basically on the TFJA's workload, but it certainly takes several months or even years.

Contrary to what happens with the RR, in the case of the JCA there is not a minimum amount for the guarantee that should be provided by the filing bidder who requests to suspend the award decision, with corresponding damages to third parties. This difference may create incentives for bidders to prefer the JCA over the RR. Another factor which may cause bidders to prefer the JCA is that the entity reviewing the RR is, at the end, a PEMEX body and its autonomy may be questioned. On the other hand, the JCA takes much longer than the RR, which is a strong disincentive.

The bidder who wants to challenge an award decision can choose to file for a RR or a JCA, so there is no precedence of one over the other. Notably, the information on the number of RRs or JCAs filed against PEMEX and their corresponding resolutions are not publicly available on the PEMEX website.

Keeping public information on the challenges filed against PEMEX award decisions increases transparency and encourages compliance with the legal framework. However, such information will only allow interested parties and the general public to be better informed if it is presented in a user-friendly and effective manner. As such, PEMEX should explore ways to increase transparency by committing to making the RR and JCA resolutions public on its website in a regular, user-friendly manner, and by putting in place an effective search engine.

As said, the resolution of the collegiate body after the review of the RR cannot be challenged by administrative means, but only through an annulation request (*demanda de nulidad),* filed before the TFJA, or the *Juicio de Amparo Indirecto,*[2] before a District Judge for Administrative Matters (*Juez de Distrito en Materia Administrativa*). Likewise, the resolution dictated by the TFJA on a JCA can be challenged through a *Juicio de Amparo Directo* by the bidder or through a fiscal review challenge (*recurso de revisión fiscal*) by PEMEX, both filed before a Collegiate Circuit Tribunal for Administrative Matters (*Tribunal Colegiado de Circuito en Materia Administrativa*). The challenging bidder can even skip the RR and the JCA and go directly to the *Amparo Directo* alternative (see Figure 9.1).

Figure 9.1. **Challenge mechanisms for PEMEX award decisions**

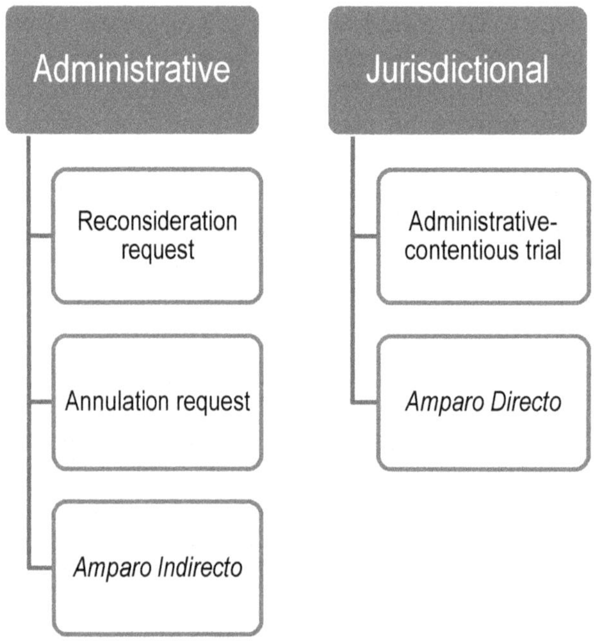

Source: Based on the analysis of PEMEX Law and other regulations described in Table 9.1.

One more alternative for bidders to contest the fairness of procurement procedures, particularly with regard to the actions of public officials involved in such procedures is that of a complaint (*quejas y denuncias*). Since the first secondary law on administrative responsibilities was published on 31 December 1982, specific units were established in each public agency for citizens to file complaints against public officials for lack of compliance with their duties and hence launch the corresponding disciplinary processes. Until the entry into force of the PEMEX Law, complaints against PEMEX public officials' actions or omissions were filed before the Internal Control Body (*Órgano Interno de Control*, or OIC) of the company. Since the publication of the PEMEX Law, such complaints are filed before the Responsibilities Unit (*Unidad de Responsabilidades,* or UR), which is now in charge of investigating, substantiating procedures for administrative responsibilities, and imposing the corresponding sanctions.[3] The UR is hierarchically subordinate to the Ministry of Public Administration (*Secretaría de la Función Pública*, or SFP); its head is appointed by the SFP minister, and its organisation and operations are regulated by the rules applicable to responsibilities units of OICs. Hence, regarding the management of complaints against PEMEX public servants, not much has changed, aside from the formal name of the unit receiving the complaints and the fact that severe violations of an administrative nature are now sanctioned by the TFJA, not by OICs, as established in the General Law of Administrative Responsibilities, published in the Official Gazette on 18 July 2016.

Despite the observations above, complaints are of limited usefulness for bidders, who tend to prefer the challenge mechanisms to contest the award of contracts. The legal effect of complaints is limited to investigating the possible administrative responsibilities of public servants and, if applicable, launching the corresponding disciplinary process. However, complaints cannot lead to the suspension of an award of a contract.

An important change deriving from the new regulatory framework applicable to PEMEX procurement is the elimination of the intervention by default (*intervención de oficio*). According to Article 76 of the Law of Acquisitions, Leasing, and Services of the Public Sector and Article 94 of the Law of Public Works and Related Services, the intervention by default is the power of the authority to get to know the complaint (*inconformidad*) against an award decision to verify the legality of the award and suspend the procurement process and its corresponding actions, when breaches to the legal framework are evident, considering no damages are caused to social interests and there are no contradictions to public order regulations. In such a case, the authority can declare the whole procurement process, or a part of it, null.

Intervention by default allows the authority to review the legality of the procurement process even if the complaint is flawed. This provides for some additional protection for complaining bidders, even when their complaints are not well substantiated or even when a complaint is not filed, but the illegality of the process is evident. As said before, the laws mentioned in the previous paragraph do not apply to PEMEX any longer and neither the PEMEX Law nor its Bylaws consider the intervention by default. The only intervention that exists is carried out by the collegiate body when it realises the actual or possible occurrence of illegal acts, but there has to be a RR filed by a bidder and the suspension of the award decision can only take place before the RR is settled.

The difference described above is important since the procedures inherent to the RR and the JCA are considered of "strict legal application" (*estricto derecho*), which means that the entity reviewing the challenge can only consider the arguments of the complaining bidder and cannot comment beforehand to address deficiencies or fill the voids left in the RR or the JCA.

Another important difference from the special procurement regime applicable to PEMEX is that, previous to its entry into force, the authority reviewing challenges to award decisions filed through the administrative channel (*inconformidades*) was the SFP of the federal government, while under the new regime the entity that reviews RR is the collegiate body within PEMEX.

According to PEMEX Law, all contracts in which the company takes part are of an administrative nature until the moment they are awarded. Once the contract is signed, it becomes a matter of commercial and civil law. Controversies dealing with contract execution between PEMEX (or one of its subsidiaries) and a supplier will be settled through the competent tribunals of the Federal Judicial Power (*Poder Judicial de la Federación*), except in cases when there is an agreement to settle controversies through alternative mechanisms, which include the following:

- A claim (*reclamo*) which settles technical or administrative controversies. The supplier files the claim before the responsible department of PEMEX in charge of managing and supervising contract execution.
- A conciliation is filed as a result of disagreements dealing with compliance with contractual requirements. This procedure is filed before SFP.
- Contracts may also include articles or arbitration commitments, aligned with the applicable commercial regulations and the international treaties to which Mexico is a party.

Formal challenges against PEMEX procurement procedures

It is early days to assess the effectiveness of the challenge mechanisms anticipated under the special procurement regime of PEMEX. Since PEMEX is still in transition from the previous regime to the new one, the use of the challenge mechanisms anticipated in the latter is incipient. The learning curve of suppliers might also have to do with the low number of RRs filed (see Table 9.2).

Table 9.2. **Reconsideration requests filed before the PEMEX collegiate body, as of June 2016**

	Revoked	Inadmissible (*improcedente*)	In process of substantiation
2015			
Total: 1	1	0	0
2016			
Total: 6	3	2	1

1. A RR is considered inadmissible when: 1) it is filed against acts considered in another challenge process pending resolution; 2) it is filed against acts that do not affect the legal interest of the filing bidder; 3) it is filed against acts explicitly accepted; 4) the challenged award cannot legally or effectively take place because the matter of the tender process becomes inexistent; 5) the complaining bidder files the JCA; and 6) it is filed against procedures settled previously.

Source: Based on information provided by PEMEX.

According to PEMEX, the low number of RRs is a result of three additional factors: 1) budget restrictions have led to fewer total tender procedures; 2) the concentration of procurement procedures by categories; and 3) the work by PEMEX to standardise procurement activities. Indeed, these numbers contrast sharply with the number of administrative challenges (*inconformidades*) filed under the previous regime (see Table 9.3).

Table 9.3. ***Inconformidades* filed under the previous administration, 2010-15**

Year	Procurement procedures	*Inconformidades* filed	*Inconformidades* admitted into process
2010	11 981	211	44
2011	12 602	222	48
2012	10 800	228	47
2013	9 609	157	31
2014	8 057	98	14
2015	1 883	34	3
Total	54 932	950	187

Source: Based on information provided by PEMEX.

While the more recent number of RRs contrasts with the challenges filed during 2015-16, it is also true that the number of *inconformidades* followed a decreasing trend from 2012. In fact, from 2012 to 2015, *inconformidades* decreased by 85%. Again, PEMEX explains this trend by the decreasing number of tender procedures, as a consequence of lower procurement budgets, and the implementation of strategic supply and category management. Furthermore, PEMEX recognises that the increasing number of direct awards also had an impact on the number of administrative challenges.

The Corporate Directorate for Procurement and Supply (Dirección Corporativa de Procura y Abastecimiento, or DCPA) would benefit from regularly performing analyses of past challenges so as to identify areas of opportunity to improve procurement procedures. For example, the analyses could identify which purchases are challenged the most and in what stage of the procurement process (see Figures 9.2 and 9.3 for such an analysis of *inconformidades*). With regard to the RRs, from 2015 up to 21 September 2016, eight RRs had been filed: five of them on processes applied to services and leasing and three for works and related services, while none had been filed against purchases of goods. Five of those RRs had been filed against the award stage.[4]

Figure 9.2. ***Inconformidades* as a percentage of total calls for tender, 2010-2015, by type of purchase**

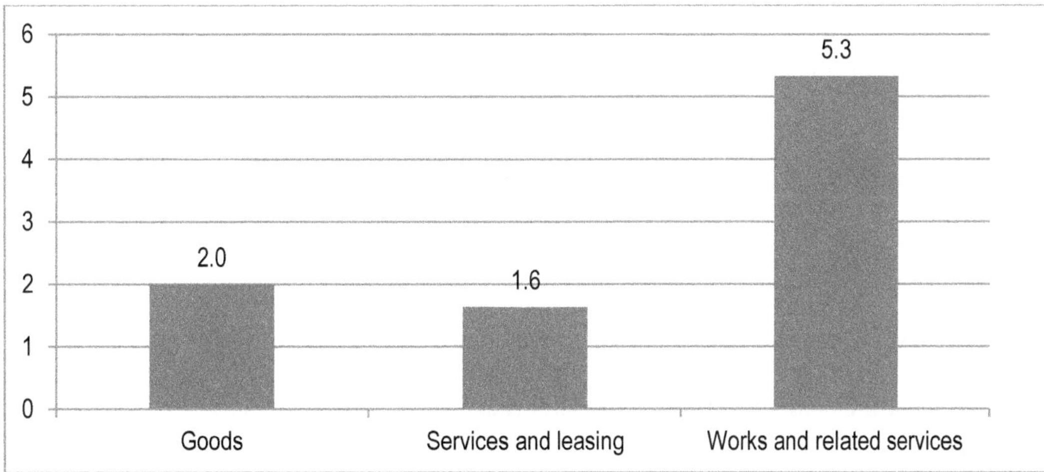

Source: Information provided by PEMEX.

Figure 9.3. **Percentage of *inconformidades* filed, by stage of the procurement process 2010-15**

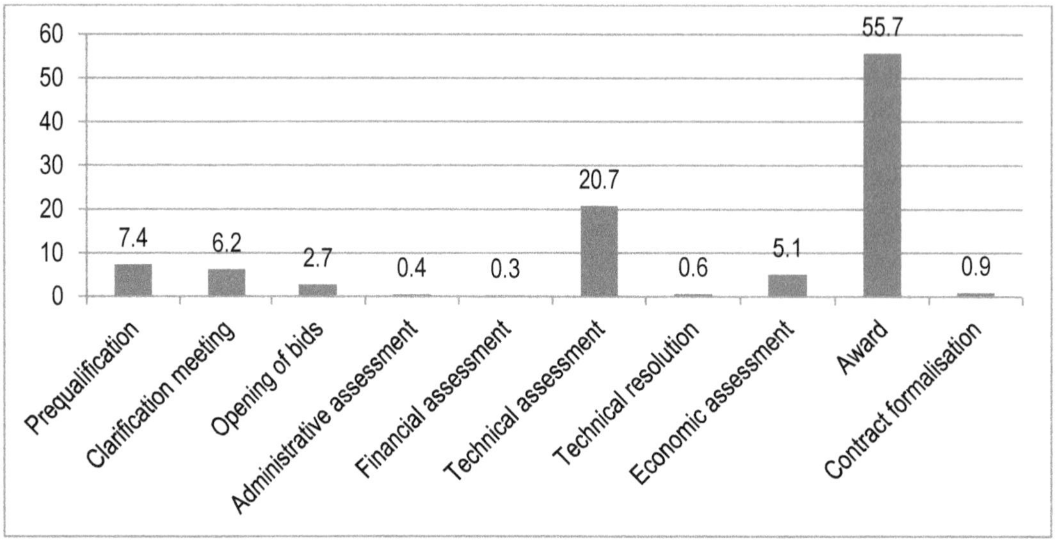

Source: Information provided by PEMEX.

Opportunities to reduce the number of challenges

PEMEX would benefit from a low number of challenges on its procurement procedures in the long term. Various actions can be taken by the company to keep this number low, irrespective of the current transition period. First, PEMEX could implement the proposals regarding integrity, transparency, and accountability, as suggested in Part II, to increase the integrity of the evaluation process by ensuring compliance with the requirements and rules established in the solicitation documentation. In support of that activity, PEMEX could perform a detailed analysis of the resolutions of the challenges in the last years, even under the previous regime. This would make it possible to identify areas of opportunity to improve the relevant procedures and mechanisms.

Furthermore, PEMEX could strengthen its engagement with suppliers through the verbal debriefing procedure suggested in Chapter 12. This would assist suppliers in understanding the results of the evaluation of their proposals and show them that the process has been carried out in accordance with the rules of procurement and probity.

Finally, PEMEX could maximise the participation of civil society in public tendering, and particularly social witnesses, to identify and correct potential deficiencies in the process and ensure that all stages of the procurement procedure are managed in accordance with the legal framework and the applicable solicitation documentation. Social witnesses may also strengthen trust in procurement procedures from the side of suppliers.

Proposals for action

A review of the recent evolution of the challenge and remedy systems available for bidders participating in PEMEX procurement processes leads to several conclusions. First, in essence, administrative and jurisdictional mechanisms persist, which might hurt the timeliness of remedies and the determination of definitive resolutions to challenges of procurement processes. Hence, it is not clear that any simplification, in terms of time or number of procedures involved, has been achieved. Second, the autonomy of the authority reviewing administrative challenges, the collegiate body, is questionable. In the recent past, the authority reviewing administrative challenges was SFP (previously SECODAM and SECOGEF), which is an entity outside of PEMEX. As mentioned in the introduction, in order to guarantee an impartial review, a body with enforcement capacity independent of the procuring entity needs to rule the review decisions. This is not the case for RR and might lead bidders to distrust the collegiate body and prefer challenges through the JCA, even when this mechanism takes much more time.

In essence, there has been no change on the restrictions applicable to the suspension of an award when challenging through administrative mechanisms, which basically require a guarantee of between 10% and 30% of the economic proposal of the complaining bidder or, when this amount cannot be determined, of the authorised budget for the particular procurement process under contest. This can also create a bias towards the JCA, in which case there is no minimum amount for the guarantee to be provided by the complaining bidder when requesting the suspension of an award. Furthermore, intervention by default is not considered any longer in the regulations applicable to PEMEX, which in fact eliminates any additional protection in place for the fairness and legality of procurement processes.

In light of the previous conclusions, PEMEX review and remedy mechanisms could be strengthened to favour the principles of justice and timeliness by taking the following actions:

- Given that PEMEX's GJCA is in charge of substantiating the RR and proposing the collegiate body a draft resolution, it is advisable to implement a rigorous training and certification process for the public officials of this unit. This should help the GJCA to issue robust resolutions to RR.
- The process of implementation of the mechanism of RR should be constantly monitored, assessed and improved in accordance with the principles of justice and timeliness. PEMEX should implement a performance audit programme to assess the timeliness, efficiency and effectiveness of RR and the training process for the GJCA. Likewise, audits on the legality of the resolutions to RR should be useful to assess how robust such resolutions are and where the opportunities for improvement are.
- PEMEX and its UR should ensure the effective application of sanctions when integrity breaches are identified in the preparation of draft resolutions to RR. Likewise, a Code of Ethics specifically designed for the collegiate body should be prepared to raise awareness about the importance of the objectivity of its decisions. These measures should favour the perceived degree of autonomy of the collegiate body.
- PEMEX should analyse and, if constitutionally feasible, propose amendments to the PEMEX Law in order to incorporate the possibility of the intervention by default. Such a mechanism would decrease the risks of awards violating the principles of legality and fairness.
- In addition to seeking to re-establish intervention by default, PEMEX could implement self-correcting actions to identify and provide timely and effective

solutions to potential infringements to the procurement legal framework. This could be done, for instance, by increasing civil society participation in public tenders, notably social witnesses.

- PEMEX should facilitate the filing of complaints by those who have witnessed integrity breaches (i.e. public officials and bidders) during procurement procedures. For example, Chapter 6 recommends protecting whistleblowers from retaliatory actions, so that they may feel confident about coming forward and reporting wrongdoing.
- PEMEX and particularly, DCPA, should regularly perform analysis of past challenges so as to identify areas of opportunity to improve procurement procedures. For example, the analysis should identify which stages of procurement procedures are challenged the most[5] and which types of processes are contested more frequently (i.e. national or international public tender, restricted invitation).
- PEMEX should explore ways to increase transparency by publicising on its website (and perhaps others, such as the Transparency Duties Portal or POT) the resolutions on RR, JCA, and *Amparos,* as well as relevant statistics, in a timely and user-friendly manner. A search engine could be available to facilitate finding specific procedures.[6]
- DCPA should provide guidelines for procurement officials to know when, where, and how to engage with potential suppliers, as well as the information that can be shared with them (see Box 9.2). Timely and transparent engagement should mostly be perceived as a preventive measure, but it is also useful to inform the business community about the alternatives available to challenge an award decision.

Box 9.2. Constructive market engagement in New Zealand

The New Zealand Government Procurement Branch of the Ministry of Business, Innovation and Employment developed a manual providing guidance for public officials on market engagement. The manual includes recommendations on why, how, and when to engage with the market, the types of market engagement, the information that can be required from suppliers, the risks implied in market engagement, and engaging with integrity.

The manual states that, used properly, market engagement can:

- change and improve the way procurement is planned and managed
- improve the understanding of the market
- increase trust and credibility with suppliers
- create the market conditions needed to deliver the best solutions
- help agencies identify opportunities for innovation.

Source: New Zealand Government (2015), "Constructive market engagement: A guide to engaging effectively with suppliers", Wellington, August, www.business.govt.nz/procurement/pdf-library/agencies/guides-and-tools/Constructive-Market-Engagement.pdf (accessed 22 August 2016).

Notes

1. This is a notable difference from the previous regime since administrative challenges (*inconformidades*) could be filed in any stage of the tender process, while RR can only be filed after the award decision.
2. The *Amparo* is a mechanism through which citizens can challenge any infringement by the government of individual rights granted by the Constitution This specific *habeas corpus* enables citizens and businesses to successfully oppose and even repeal flawed rules or improper actions by the administration.
3. Chapter 1 describes the latest adjustments to PEMEX corporate governance, including the disappearance of PEMEX's OIC and the establishment of new audit and control functions and institutions.
4. Even though RR can only be filed after the award of a contract, the challenge can refer to any stage of the procurement process.
5. Even though RR can only be filed after the award of a contract, the challenge can refer to any stage of the procurement process.
6. Article 70, Bullet XXXVI, of the General Law for Transparency and Freedom of Information establishes that public institutions should proactively disclose resolutions and rulings issued as part of processes carried out in the form of a trial.

References

New Zealand Government (2015), "Constructive market engagement: A guide to engaging effectively with suppliers", Wellington, August, www.business.govt.nz/procurement/pdf-library/agencies/guides-and-tools/Constructive-Market-Engagement.pdf (accessed 22 August 2016).

OECD (2015), "Recommendation of the Council on Public Procurement", www.oecd.org/gov/ethics/OECD-Recommendation-on-Public-Procurement.pdf.

Part III

Connecting Petróleos Mexicanos' competencies with suppliers' capabilities for a new procurement

Chapter 10

E-procurement: Implementing a strong information technology environment to support Petróleos Mexicanos' procurement activities

This chapter describes Petróleos Mexicanos' (PEMEX's) current information technology (IT) environment and assesses the recent development of the e-procurement system. The importance of a point-to-point platform that PEMEX is trying to achieve cannot be understated in terms of the potential benefits, i.e. more efficiency and standardisation of processes. While the company is going through a transitional period, so is the procurement system. PEMEX realises the potential of the system, but needs to fully commit to transforming it in order to reap the benefits, which include more efficient use of time and resources in a competitive environment.

Use of information and communication technologies (ICT) in procurement processes is widely considered as a tool with strong potential to deliver major benefits to public and private entities. Electronic public procurement has an established track record of streamlining and accelerating public purchasing, benefiting both public purchasers and suppliers along the way. It is a way to improve automation and standardisation, by reducing time to complete tasks and the probability of human error. In the public sector, the use of digital technology has been a strategic driver for improving efficiency and supporting effectiveness of policies by creating more open, transparent, innovative, participatory, and trustworthy government. In light of this, the use of e-procurement not only increases efficiency by facilitating access to tenders by increasing competition and decreasing administrative burdens, but can also improve transparency by holding public authorities more accountable. The challenge for Petróleos Mexicanos (PEMEX) is to lay the foundations for such a system and make it work in practice so that suppliers and PEMEX can both enjoy the benefits.

The 2015 Recommendation of the Council on Public Procurement stresses the importance of harnessing the use of digital technologies to support appropriate e-procurement innovation throughout the procurement cycle for the purpose of improving the public procurement system (Box 10.1). The OECD recognises that employing integrated e-procurement solutions can ensure transparency, increase competition, and simplify processes for contract award and management. The integration of two or more electronic platforms is crucial to ensure greater efficiency of the process. Realising the potential of e-procurement systems is just the first step. Designing, creating, and implementing an e-procurement system is a challenge for most countries or companies. While pursuing a state-of-the-art e-procurement system, the OECD recommends that the system be simple to use and fit for purpose. Excessively complicated systems can create implementation risks and challenges for new entrants or small and medium enterprises.

Box 10.1. Recommendation of the Council on Public Procurement

VII. RECOMMENDS that Adherents improve the public procurement system by harnessing the use of digital technologies to support appropriate **e-procurement** innovation throughout the procurement cycle.

To this end, Adherents should:

i) **Employ recent digital technology developments that allow integrated e-procurement solutions covering the procurement cycle.** Information and communication technologies should be used in public procurement to ensure transparency and access to public tenders, increasing competition, simplifying processes for contract award and management, driving cost savings and integrating public procurement and public finance information.

ii) **Pursue state-of-the-art e-procurement tools that are modular, flexible, scalable and secure** in order to assure business continuity, privacy and integrity, provide fair treatment and protect sensitive data, while supplying the core capabilities and functions that allow business innovation. E-procurement tools should be simple to use and appropriate to their purpose, and consistent across procurement agencies, to the extent possible; excessively complicated systems could create implementation risks and challenges for new entrants or small and medium enterprises.

Source: OECD (2015a), "Recommendation of the Council on Public Procurement", www.oecd.org/corruption/recommendation-on-public-procurement.htm.

This chapter describes the development of e-procurement for the last couple of years while PEMEX has been going through a transitional period of becoming a state productive company. The chapter gives an account of the different digital platforms PEMEX is using to manage data and information. Furthermore, the integration of different platforms is assessed and whether the system in place is efficient and supplier friendly. PEMEX's main objective throughout this process has been to design a point-to-point platform (end to end) that covers all functions, linked to vendors, procurement and planning. However, PEMEX is not moving from using five systems (Enterprise Resource Planning Systems [ERPs]) to a one-system platform (SAP – Ariba) supporting all procurement processes. The SAP – Ariba is providing support for three transactional systems, PEP (Exploracion y Produccion), TRI (Transformación Industrial) and CORP (Corporativo) for the processes of spend analysis, negotiation, contracts and information requirements with suppliers. The unification of the ERPs is only to have the same templates in three SAPs. The long-term view is to create a system that is integrated and managed in the right manner, with a suppliers market actively using the system to support procurement processes, and thus being more cost-efficient in the long run.

Laying the foundations for an interoperable procurement system

PEMEX is making an effort to standardise the automation of procurement by using technology to create common procurement processes so as to ensure greater transparency and access to information vital to the tendering process. There are different platforms (tools) being developed to meet the needs for different stages of the procurement process, such as for category management, electronic catalogues, and the registration of suppliers. The current situation at PEMEX is that the different platforms that together create a framework for the e-procurement system are currently not integrated, though there is a commitment to move in that direction. Some steps have been taken and there is partial integration already in place between ERP and Bóveda Electrónica, SAP – Ariba and HIIP (Herramienta Integral de Información de Proveedores).

Overall, PEMEX shows a high level of digitisation of processes and information management with a centralised data master system (SAP-Ariba) to keep track of the overall volume of purchases and the list of suppliers. Before the reforms, each subsidiary had developed its own information technology (IT) system, which hindered the full harvesting of the benefits of the IT investments made. This has had a negative impact on the overall process efficiencies, economies of scale, rationalisation and standardisation of procedures across PEMEX. The use of different IT platforms, paired with different business processes, different catalogues of products, different encodings for each organisation, have most likely limited the positive impact of digitisation on the efficiency of decisional processes in the past.

More than five years ago, PEMEX decided to streamline procedures across the entire oil industry and develop an integral business solution for the supply process at the organisational level, including the Integral Electronic Platform (PTI). This was to increase process efficiencies, but also shift from a compliance-based to a more performance-based system. The PTI was never fully implemented, but produced some definitions of business processes, some of which were used as a starting point for implementing the ERP for transactional operations and for the functionality of the platform for institutional procurement. It is estimated that the PTI platform contributed to more streamlined procurement procedures, enhanced transparency and prevented collusion.

There was a strategic need to modernise, reorganise, and streamline the management of internal business processes with the support of a harmonised platform for the entire company (e.g. harmonisation of the catalogues managed by the various organisations to have a single catalogue for PEMEX). The procurement process for the harmonised basic platform is SAP – ECC (Enterprise Central Component), which is a modular system that combines many areas of the organisation together, thus forming an integrated whole that allows for the communication and interaction of data. Furthermore, the SAP – ECC processes large amounts of data and obtains useful information for decision making. It includes functionality and links between internal processes like finance, maintenance, commercial and human resources. The procurement process is linked with finance for budget checking, and specific functionality to other processes in relation to the procurement process (e.g. maintenance). SAP-ECC is complemented by other systems to ascertain the whole functionality (e.g. SAP-Ariba for electronic procurement). PEMEX efforts are now focused on keeping three SAP-ECC operated by EPS, by standardising formats and the procedures. The three SAP ECC are complemented by a unique solution for the planning phase of the SPyA System (Sistema de Seguimiento de Procura y Abastecimiento), as well as a unique solution for electronic procurement, SISCeP (based on SAP-Ariba).

The SAP-ECC system is being improved and supplemented to harmonise for all PEMEX, including the SPyA system for the planning stage, SAP-Ariba cloud solution for e-procurement, RFx and reverse auctions, supplier information and performance management, reverse management contracts and visibility and Documentum for content management. For the procurement process, there are two phases of the platform: the transitional phase in which PEMEX and companies use three SAP-ECC solutions with the same master data, formats and process execution, complemented with the SPyA solution for the planning phase and the SAP-Ariba solution for the electronic procurement, and a final phase in which the platform will be integrated to approved systems that meet the process from end to end. PEMEX is currently working on the implementation of this platform final institutional purchases.

End-to-end platform for e-procurement and the challenges ahead

With the incorporation of the new system, PEMEX is no longer actively using Compranet. In 2015 PEMEX launched the e-procurement tool SAP – Ariba. No data is yet available on the proportion of contracts carried out electronically for 2015. However, from 1st November 2016 all contracts should be negotiated and made with the electronic platform of SAP-Ariba. Up until that date some PEMEX contractors were still sending and receiving documents by paper. The new structure of PEMEX has resulted in three subsidiaries (EPS) using SAP-ECC for basic operation as well as the SPyA platform for planning purposes. SAP-ECC is meant to provide an integrated environment (e.g. information on purchases, human resources, accounting, project management, detailed information on procurement volumes from each supplier, prices). The system provides an integrated business environment (procurement, human resources, finance, etc.); however it is still working on some definitions of transversal processes to achieve the necessary integration. Furthermore, there are some other minor systems that are part of the procurement platform transition.

PEMEX is currently moving towards a single e-procurement platform across all subsidiaries (SAP-Ariba). The company is working to create a single institutional platform to support the electronic procurement processes and electronic exchange of information with suppliers. The three ERP platforms, based on SAP-ECC for all subsidiaries have areas of opportunity within descriptions, standardised data, processes, documents and templates, and even the functionality of ERP systems. The three existing ERPs allow for the integration of management of internal and external information across the entire organisation; each person involved in the decision-making process could be making decisions on line, but at the moment that function is not operable. This could, however, help increase the level of accountability, transparency and effectiveness of the decision-making process.

OECD countries and the challenges they face in this area are common and need to be understood in order to be addressed successfully. The PEMEX implementation process has been running for over two years now and the company has faced many challenges during this period, which are also found in some other countries. When responding to the OECD Survey on Public Procurement, the main challenge faced by both procuring entities and potential bidders and suppliers to use e-procurement systems are low knowledge and skills of ICT (48%). Low innovative organisational culture (41%) and low knowledge of the economic opportunities raised by e-procurement systems (32%) were identified as additional challenges for procuring entities. These issues have also been identified as challenges for PEMEX personnel. Related to potential bidders and suppliers, 12 OECD countries (41%) identified difficulties in understanding or applying the procedures and challenges in the use of the functionalities (see Table 10.1).

The challenges facing PEMEX during this transitional period since becoming a state productive company have prolonged the implementation process excessively. Some of the main hurdles which the DCPA has had to overcome while implementing an end-to-end platform are lack of project support when it comes to executing the necessary changes. The project has been progressing slowly but the vision is clear: a platform with complete functionality, use of homologated processes providing recording and visibility of the complete process. Other challenges await PEMEX that will need to be addressed if the company is to succeed in setting up the SAP-Ariba system. Challenges have already been identified for the use of e-procurement systems, such as employees with limited ICT skills, low knowledge of the economic opportunities raised by the tool and, in general, low innovative organisational culture. The effectiveness of the system depends on suppliers actively using the system. However, among PEMEX suppliers, low ICT knowledge is also an issue along with low propensity to innovation and lack of confidence.

Table 10.1. **Main challenges to the use of e-procurement systems in OECD countries**

	Procuring entities				Potential bidders/suppliers					
	Low knowledge/ ICT skills	Low knowledge of the economic opportunities raised by this tool	Low innovative organisational culture	Do not know	Low knowledge/ ICT skills	Low knowledge of the economic opportunities raised by this tool	Difficulties to understand or apply the procedure	Difficulties in the use of functionalities (e.g. catalogue management)	Low propensity to innovation	Do not know
Australia	No major challenges faced by procuring entities				No major challenges faced by potential bidders/suppliers					
Austria				●						●
Belgium			●						●	
Canada	●				●	●	●	●	●	
Chile				●		●	●	●		
Denmark				●			●	●		
Estonia		●				●				
Finland				●						●
France				●						●
Germany	●	●	●			●		●		
Greece		●	●		●	●			●	
Hungary	●		●		●		●	●		
Ireland				●			●			
Italy	●		●		●		●	●	●	
Japan	●	●			●	●	●	●		
Korea	●		●		●				●	
Luxembourg				●						●
Mexico	●	●	●							●
New Zealand	●	●			●	●				
Norway		●				●	●		●	
Poland	●		●		●		●	●		
Portugal	●				●		●			
Slovak Republic		●			●			●		
Slovenia	●	●	●		●	●	●	●	●	
Spain		●	●		●	●			●	
Sweden				●						●
Switzerland				●						●
United Kingdom	●		●			●		●		
United States	●		●		●		●	●	●	
Brazil	●	●	●		●	●	●	●		
Colombia	●	●	●		●	●			●	
OECD 29	13	10	12	9	13	11	12	12	9	7

Source: OECD (2015b), *Government at a Glance 2015*, OECD Publishing, Paris, http://dx.doi.org/10.1787/gov_glance-2015-en.

Improving information management through supplier's registration and performance assessment

There are databases in place to capture information that can be useful for future tenders, particularly in the case of registration and evaluation of suppliers. The purpose is to make available information about suppliers that can reduce risks to the procurement process. Additionally, for the procurement strategy (SISCeP), information of expenditure is collected relating to contracts, invoices, category analysis, performance information, market analysis with comparative prices, terms of contract, business scenarios, library of standard clauses, preparatory repository, open contracts and framework agreements. All the information is likely to be used for future procurement procedures.

Before 2014, the Directory of Suppliers and Contractors (national suppliers) and HITEC (international suppliers) had 10 500 registered suppliers. The suppliers have now been migrated to the new solution and are in the process of being validated by the suppliers themselves. PEMEX recently introduced a new supplier registry managed by Achilles that is servicing the registration and validation of information that the suppliers register on two levels: basic and extended. Achilles is considered to be the registration module of HIIP. The basic level is for minor contracts (under USD 200 000) and the extended level for contracts greater than the threshold or those that PEMEX deem strategic. For the extended registration, Achilles also contemplates an assessment of commercial risk.

At the end of 2015, there were 975 basic registrations and 76 extended registrations in the database. Over 3 000 contractors were completing their registration, approximately 250 were under review, but information concerning over 5 000 suppliers had been migrated with suppliers updating or registering. About 5 000 suppliers are active on average over a whole year and approximately 60% are suppliers to PEMEX refineries. The e-procurement system provides tools for officials for the search, collection, consolidation, extraction and visualisation of the information required by them in decision making, through dashboards and standard reports. PEMEX also has the opportunities to approach additional suppliers through a global network of suppliers from other companies in the oil and gas business (a list of suppliers of other oil companies). This will extend the list of suppliers beyond the local list. PEMEX could invite those on the global list to participate but they will need to register in Achilles first.

There are several internal systems that interface with PEMEX procurement officials, but only Achilles, SAP-Ariba and HIIP interface with users (see Figure 10.1). The functional interoperability of these three platforms starts with the registration process. The registration takes place on the PEMEX website when the contractor is automatically transferred to the Achilles website. All suppliers and contractors must complete the basic registration, where they will be required to provide generic information about their company, including financial records. Depending on the strategic or risk profile of the company, and the amount of contracts it holds with PEMEX, suppliers and contractors may be invited to register at the next level (extended registration). Suppliers should provide their administrative information for each event when participating in the tendering. With the implementation of the new registration system, the supplier keeps his registration updated and the PEMEX employee responsible for the tendering process obtains the vendor information through the management information system.

As part of a comprehensive procurement process, there are stages of registration and evaluation for future suppliers. PEMEX can generate a report on commercial risks where it has ratings and comparisons based on the information provided through the registration process. The purpose of the report is to show the financial health of the company and establish whether the suppliers are black-listed. PEMEX has been operating this system since 2015 and it is progressively being adopted. Information from the audits is still not part of the decision-making process.

Figure 10.1. **PEMEX's interconnected system for the registration process**

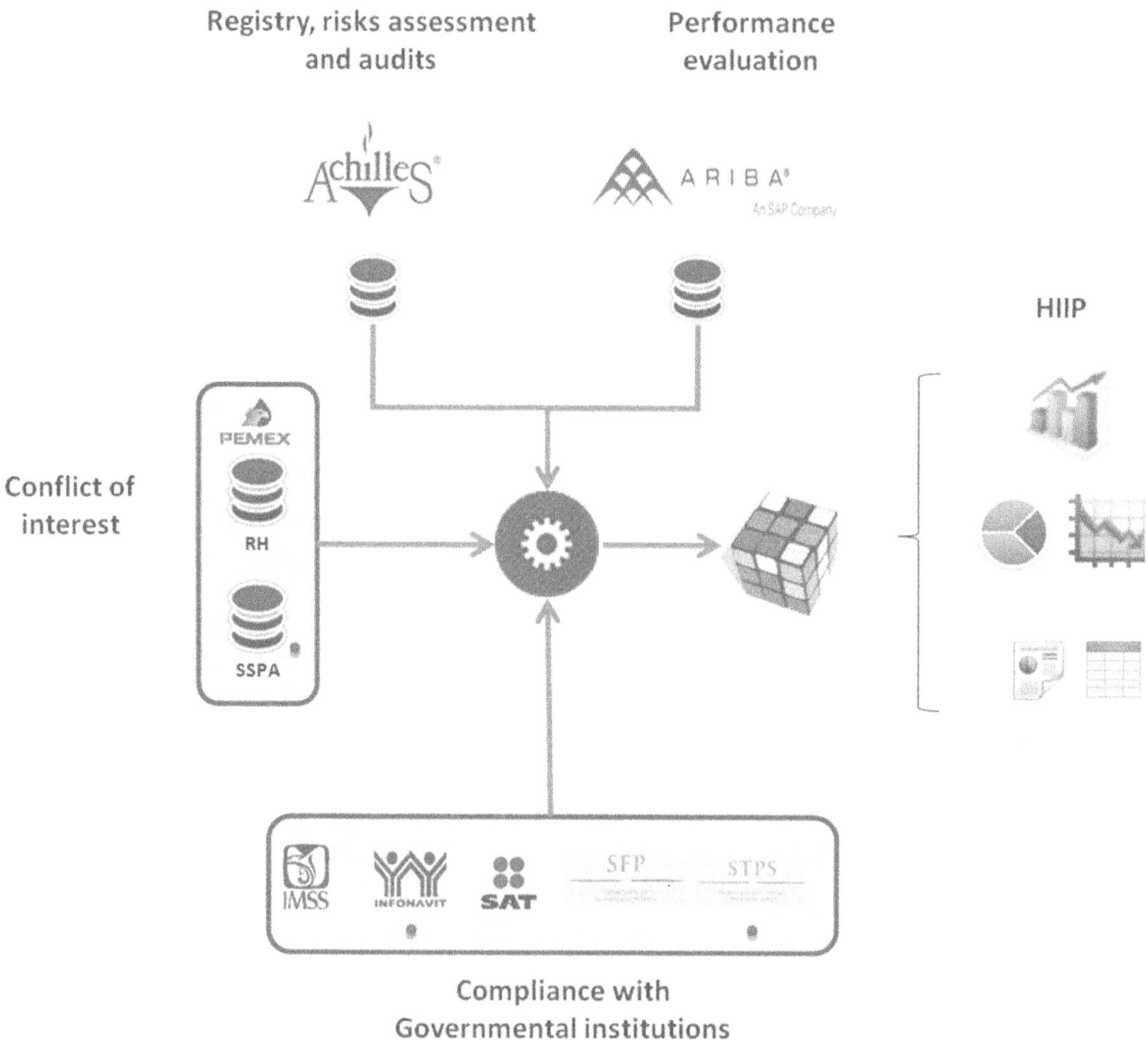

Source: Figure provided by PEMEX

Part of the registry process includes the assessment of previous performance. That information on performance is stored on the SAP-Ariba platform and obtained through ERPs for the purpose of evaluating contract performance and to find key business users that fulfil certain criteria. Assessment of work is based on the complexity of the project. Companies do not see this internal assessment.

The HIIP is a comprehensive query platform that provides data visualisation. The system is interconnected to Achilles (which functions as it registry) and SAP-Ariba. Information can be consolidated from suppliers from different internal and external sources, performance evaluation can be recorded and risk can be reported, improving the knowledge about suppliers. Statistical information is not the main focus of this platform, however; rather it accumulates data on specific companies for the purpose of identifying trends to assist PEMEX in deciding which suppliers to select.

An interactive communication tool

The Relationship with Suppliers and Contractors (RPC) is a new route for PEMEX to interact with suppliers. The RPC performs actions beyond the established limits in seeking continual improvement in the interests of elements such as quality, innovation, delivery time and logistics, among others. RPC consistently exceeds the established conditions of the contract and even in the applicable regulations to distinguish itself in a competitive market.

Another communication tool is the PEMEX PASS (Point of Access to Supply System) system, which refers to the point of contact and assistance to suppliers, contractors, and users of PEMEX. It is the means by which assistance is provided to the companies who approach PEMEX, channelling offers to user areas, and obtaining an understanding of the market. It also offers information on how to register on line and upload necessary documents (supplier registration). It is also a guide (supplier development) so that potential suppliers know the company's needs concerning goods, equipment, services, supplies, etc. The aim of PEMEX PASS is to create value through collaboration with suppliers and contractors, becoming a specialised channel linking supply with demand. It works to link the needs of users with opportunities identified in the market, starting from elements such as assistance to suppliers and contractors, categories, market research and other initiatives of the Corporate Directorate for Procurement and Supply (Dirección Corporativa de Procura y Abastecimiento, or DCPA).

The institutional context and governance of SAP-Ariba

PEMEX Law and its regulations establish the preferential use of electronic communication media, i.e. the SAP-Ariba. The administration of SAP-Ariba is run by the "Gerencia de Mejora del Proceso, Integración y Catálogación", belonging to the DCPA, it includes users and templates for business scenarios. The objective of the SAP-Ariba is not only to contribute to the systematisation of strategic tendering and category management, with a comprehensive supplier management, expenditure analysis, strategic negotiation, and model contracts, but also to be used for the operational procurement by developing all public biddings, restricted invitations and direct award procedures. The system and services is maintained on a cloud-based solution, both for internal PEMEX users and for suppliers. Information on spending visibility is loaded periodically by PEMEX administrators on the Spend Visibility Module. The information is enriched and deployed by SAP–Ariba personnel. Information on particular contracting processes is uploaded by PEMEX suppliers. There is a reporting module with around 200 established reports based on the information that suppliers have registered onto the platform. The SAP-Ariba platform offers certain services designed to meet the following stages of strategic and operational tendering:

- creation of projects and supplier evaluation
- search and identification of suppliers in Ariba's global platform related to goods and/or services of particular requirements
- visualisation and analysis of spending in different dimensions

- creation and project management for:
  - development, updating, and implementation of categories
  - implementation of strategic tendering defined by commodities
  - negotiation and formalisation of preliminary contracts, referential agreements and agreements of terms and conditions
  - implementation of operational procurement: public bidding, restricted invitations and direct award procedures
  - particular requirements on the inclusion of social witnesses.
- creation of major contracts resulting from strategic negotiation.

Access to the system is controlled by creating individual user names and passwords, depending on the role of the procurement officials. However, for each individual tendering project, the access is controlled by the owner of each specific project. Only the owner of the tender can make changes, other participants can only execute the assigned tasks. The completeness and quality of data entered by potential contractors can be ensured by a specific functionality of SAP–Ariba. This is done by configuring fields, formats and the capture of information that allow potential contractors to continue capturing further information.

For now SAP– Ariba is not linked to other systems. PEMEX plans to link it up to the planning system (SPyA), to the three ERPs for the creation of the purchase requisition and to create contracts for the execution. The future plan envisages the inclusion of complementary systems and the corresponding links, to complete the whole landscape. The flow of information is always the same; it is defined by the process independently of the systems. On the other hand, depending on the systems implemented and the links developed, the flow of information is partially automated. As discussed previously, the SAP-ECC system will combine many areas of the organisation together forming an integrated whole that allows for the communication and interaction of data.

The efficiency of the procurement process has significantly increased with the incorporation of the SAP-Ariba solution using standard templates, documents and approved procedures and reference times for each activity. SAP-Ariba is based on international best practices and provides full traceability of each transaction, documents created or modified, and the current status of tasks in a project supply, including workflow authorisation and collaboration rooms. It also allows for the participation of a "social witness" in supply projects, in accordance with federal regulation. Moreover, each activity in the system automatically creates audit trails for full traceability, increasing transparency. In the current platform there is still some duplication in capturing the same information more than once. The final institutional provisioning platform is being designed and constructed to prevent duplication and redundant procedures.

To ensure the ability of PEMEX staff to use SAP-Ariba in electronic trading and to support procurement processes, a programme called "training of trainers" has been developed, based on identifying, selecting and training a group of people who will be trainers for the entire company. Additionally, PEMEX has initiated the deployment of an "On Boarding Program Provider". There is also a help desk service and documentation available on line for PEMEX personnel.

The scope of functions and usage of the e-procurement system

As previously discussed in this chapter, PEMEX is going through a transitional period while at the same time developing and implementing a single end-to-end platform for e-procurement. The procurement system was fairly complex and inefficient in the past when the subsidiaries had the freedom to set up their own procurement systems without any consideration for what another subsidiary was doing. PEMEX realised that that the lack of interconnectivity and standards for processes between the systems were not ideal and PEMEX is now implementing a centralised support system to three ERPs with SAP-Ariba for specific processes of the procurement cycle, leading to more cost efficiency in the long run. A list of procurement phases and IT systems supporting them are found in Table 2.1, "Information technology systems where PEMEX and DCPA procurement-related information is stored" (see Chapter 2). This list is very extensive and portrays a picture of a system that could be streamlined and made more efficient. PEMEX's objective is to create a framework to incorporate several platforms that are all integrated with a high level of interoperability. Any transition of this sort involves risks, some substantial, to the continuity of the operations of the system. Ensuring appropriate management and skills is crucial, both in terms of ensuring continued and effective service and in achieving the right balance between contractor support and internal capabilities to manage the system. As the system is being developed, PEMEX should recognise the importance of developing key performance indicators that can be derived from information available from within SAP-Ariba and other related systems. See Box 10.2 for indicators across four key target areas defined in Colombia by way of example.

Box 10.2. Indicators to measure the national procurement system in Colombia

Indicator	What does it measure?	Description
	Value for money	
Opportunity of the contracting process	The level of budgetary commitments in a fiscal year	Ratio between the commitments and the appropriation during the fiscal year, which does not include staff costs, budgetary transferences, and debt expenses
Changes in value according to specifications	The variation in the value of the contracts between the initial value established in the tender documents and the final value awarded	Average difference between the estimated value for the selection and the final value of the contract
Average time of the selection process according to the award mechanism	Difference in time of the selection process by award mechanism	Period of time between the signature date of a contract and the starting date of the process
	Integrity and transparency in competition	
Average of new contractors	Percentage of new contractors in a public entity regarding the former year	Ratio of new contractors of a public entity regarding the number of contractors working in the public entity in the previous year
Concentration of the contracts' value by contractor	The concentration of resources by contractor that perform for a public entity through public procurement	Concentration of a public entity's budget by contractor measured by the GINI coefficient
Percentage of contracts awarded to plural bidders	Frequency of awarded contracts to plural bidders by a public entity	Ratio of the contracts and the value of the contracts awarded by a public entity to plural bidders
Percentage of contracts awarded in non-competitive processes	Percentage of public contracting that is done under non-competitive processes	Percentage of awarded contracts without a competitive process, not including inter-administrative contracts, reserve spending of the defense sector and professional services

Box 10.2. Indicators to measure the national procurement system in Colombia *(continued)*

Indicator	What does it measure?	Description
	Accountability	
Percentage of public entity users of SECOP	SECOP use by the public entities that are obligated to use it	Percentage of public entities using SECOP
Percentage of public entities that publish their annual acquisition plans on SECOP	The progress in the compliance of the publication of the Annual Acquisition Plan on SECOP	Percentage of public entities that publish every year their annual acquisition plan on SECOP
Percentage of publicity of the contracting processes in SECOP	The level of publication on SECOP of the contracts signed in a fiscal year	Percentage of the value of the procurement processes that a public entity publishes on SECOP
	Risk management	
Percentage of contracts with modifications in time and/or value	Proportion of contracts modified after their signature regarding the total of contracts done by a public entity	Proportion of contracts modified in the value or in the duration of their performance after their signature

In 2015, Colombia Compra Eficiente made the first indicators estimation of the public procurement system using the procurement information of the state entities in 2014. The baseline results are presented in the following table.

Dimension	Indicator	Results baseline (2014)
Value for money	Opportunity of the contracting processes	7.4%
	Changes in value according to specifications	0.1%
	Average time of the selection process according to the award mechanism	Open tender: 37 days
		Merit contest: 38 days
		Abbreviated selection: 37 days
		Reverse auction: 38 days
		Abbreviated selection in instruments to aggregate demand: 9 days
		Direct contracting: 26 days
		Special regime: 38 days
		Selection with small budget: 12 days
		Lower value: 38 days
Integrity and transparency in competition	Average of new contractors	24.1%
	Concentration of the contracts' value by contractor	0.638
	Percentage of contracts awarded to plural bidders	10%
	Percentage of contracts awarded in non-competitive processes	38.5%
Accountability	Percentage of public entities users of SECOP	99%
	Percentage of public entities that publish their annual acquisition plan on SECOP	58%
	Percentage of publicity of the contracting processes in SECOP	49%
Risk management	Percentage of contracts with modifications in time or value	23%

Source: OECD (2016), *Towards Efficient Public Procurement in Colombia: Making the Difference*, OECD Publishing, Paris, http://dx.doi.org/10.1787/9789264252103-en.

In Table 10.2, the key functionalities of the PEMEX e-procurement system are benchmarked against four topics in an attempt to assess the effectiveness and service orientation of the system. The topics are:

- Is the function part of the e-procurement system?
- Is the function transactional with the e-procurement system?
- Are the functionalities provided for free?
- Are the functionalities mandatory?

The answers are very clear: more or less every e-procurement function, according to answers provided by PEMEX during the fact-finding mission, state that all key functions are part of the system, they are transactional, free for suppliers to use and mandatory by law. The only exception being framework agreements, but they are uploaded to the system to give visibility of the contracts, negotiated prices, and commercial conditions to satisfy requirements. This visibility is used to avoid purchasing out of such framework agreements. However, it is not possible to order on line and the system seems to lack catalogues of products offered in the framework agreements.

The main e-procurement system is the new SAP–Ariba, which incorporates all the main stages of the procurement process. Furthermore, there is the Portal of PEMEX and Achilles for supplier registration, performance assessment, and audit findings. In addition to these platforms, there is a planning and budgeting system that plays a crucial part within ICT procurement. As mentioned above, PEMEX uses a platform called SPyA for the planning and budgeting of procurement projects. A more direct translation of SPyA would be the "Procurement and Supply Tracking System". The SPyA system is designed to store information about future needs. The system is used to develop an annual programme of acquisitions, leasing, works and services. The objective of the system is to integrate information on planning, processes, and contract management into a corporate database. The planning requirements are based on business rules that the project is aligned to the business plan of PEMEX and the budget. SPyA is a living platform in the sense that resources can move between projects and tasks can be reprioritised. The functionalities of the system are that from April to June, procurement officials can register data and information about projects in the database for the forthcoming year. Several key issues need to be taken into consideration when registering the projects, for example, who made the contracting request, location of work, results from market studies, planning and invitation of tenders.

There is flexibility within the system with regard to the projects going through the planning stages. The planning phase establishes an overview of all future projects, from cleaning to building oil rigs, but every tender has to be aligned with the PEMEX strategy. The platform can include a contracting plan for a project lasting several years but it must always be in line with the PEMEX strategy. SPyA is not only a planning tool; up-to-date information on the progress of a project is supposed to be uploaded onto the platform. Hence, SPyA is capable of issuing progress reports quarterly. The planning platform requires additional information on the progress of the projects to be registered since there is no current integrated solution that collates information from Achilles, SAP-Ariba or HIIP to be transferred to SPyA. Those systems are currently not interconnected. There is a need for an integrated solution. The double entering of data is likely to lead to error, resulting in decisions being made based on wrong data and information.

Table 10.2. **Functionalities of PEMEX's e-procurement system**

	The function is part of the e-procurement system	The function is transactional within the e-procurement system	The functionalities provided by the e-procurement system are free of charges for suppliers	The functionalities provided by the e-procurement system are mandatory[1]	IT system responsible this function
Informational platform	●	◘	◘	◘	Portal de PEMEX Web page (SRPC)
Publishing procurement plans (about forecasted government needs)	●	●	●	●	Portal de PEMEX SAP–Ariba
Supplier registry and risk assessment.	●	●	●	●	Achilles / HIIP
Publication of opportunities	●	●	●	●	Portal de PEMEX SAP–Ariba
Announcing tenders	●	●	●	●	SAP–Ariba
Provision of tender documents	●	●	●	●	SAP–Ariba
E-submission of bids (excluding by e-mails)	●	●	●	●	SAP–Ariba
Notification of award	●	●	●	●	SAP–Ariba
E-submission of invoices (excluding by e-mails)	●	●	●	●	Boveda electronica
Ex post contract management	●	●	●	●	SAP–Ariba
E-reverse auctions	●	●	●	●	SAP–Ariba
Online catalogue	○	○	○	○	
Ordering on line	○	○	○	○	
Framework agreements module	●	●	●	●	SAP–Ariba
Business intelligence module	●	●	●	●	SAP–Ariba
● Yes	13	12	12	12	
○ NO	2	2	2	2	
◘ to a certain extent	0	1	1	1	

1. The procurement law or other institutional decrees state when and how PEMEX must use the e-procurement system.

Source: Based on information provided by PEMEX.

Moving towards an integrated e-procurement system

Despite a wide range of functions, PEMEX needs to further enhance the integration of the e-procurement system to become a leader in terms of scope and coverage, even when compared to other OECD country systems. In fact, while the use of e-procurement systems in the form of portals or websites among OECD countries is omnipresent, when moving along the procurement cycle the role actually played by e-procurement in public procurement processes is reduced. As of 2014, all OECD countries report having procurement opportunities and provide tender documents through their e-procurement systems; most of these countries are mandated by law to provide these functionalities. Functionalities at the beginning of the procurement cycle - in particular publishing of procurement plans (86%), electronic submission of bids (90%), and e-tendering (86%) - are provided in most OECD countries. In contrast, those towards the end of procurement cycle (except for notification of award [97%]) are provided by a lower number of OECD countries. Fewer countries provide e-auctions, ordering, electronic submission of invoices, and *ex post* contract management through their e-procurement systems. It is worthwhile to mention that the majority of countries provide these functionalities in their e-procurement systems even though they are not obliged by law (see Table 10.3).

Table 10.3. **Functionalities provided in e-procurement systems in OECD countries**

	Mandatory and provided	Not mandatory, but provided	Not provided
Publishing procurement plans (about forecasted government needs)	AUS, BEL, CHL, DMK, GRC, HUN, IRL, KOR, MEX, NZL, NOR, PRT, GBR, USA	AUT, CAN, FIN, DEU, ITA, JPN, POL, SVN, ESP, SWE, CHE	EST, FRA, LUX, SVK
Announcing tenders	AUS, AUT, BEL, CAN, CHL, DNK, EST, FIN, FRA, DEU, GRC, HUN, IRL, ITA, KOR, LUX, MEX, NZL, NOR, POL, PRT, SVK, SVN, ESP, SWE, CHE, GBR, USA	JPN	
Provision of tender documents	AUS, AUT, BEL, CHL, EST, FIN, FRA, DEU, GRC, HUN, IRL, KOR, MEX, NZL, NOR, POL, PRT, SVK, SVN, SWE, CHE, GBR, USA	CAN, DNK, ITA, JPN, LUX, ESP	
Electronic submission of bids (excluding by e-mails)	BEL, CHL, EST, FRA, GRC, ITA, MEX, PRT, USA	AUS, AUT, CAN, DNK, FIN, DEU, IRL, JPN, KOR, LUX, NZL, NOR, SVK, SVN, ESP, SWE, GBR	HUN, POL, CHE
E-tendering	BEL, CAN, CHL, EST, GRC, IRL, ITA, MEX, CHE, USA	AUT, DNK, FIN, FRA, DEU, JPN, KOR, NZL, NOR, PRT, SVK, SVN, ESP, SWE, GBR	AUS, HUN, LUX, POL
E-auctions (in e-tendering)	GRC, MEX, SVK, SVN, USA	DNK, EST, FIN, FRA, DEU, IRL, ITA, NZL, NOR, PRT, SWE, CHE, GBR	AUS, AUT, BEL, CAN, CHL, HUN, JPN, KOR, LUX, POL, ESP
Notification of award	AUT, BEL, CAN, CHL, DNK, EST, FIN, DEU, GRC, HUN, IRL, KOR, MEX, NZL, NOR, POL, PRT, SVK, SVN, ESP, SWE, CHE, USA	AUS, FRA, ITA, JPN, GBR	LUX
Ordering	CHL, FIN, ITA, CHE, USA	AUT, BEL, CAN, DNK, FRA, DEU, JPN, KOR, NZL, NOR, SVN, ESP, SWE, GBR	AUS, EST, GRC, HUN, IRL, LUX, MEX, POL, PRT, SVK
Electronic submission of invoices (excluding by e-mails)	AUT, DNK, FIN, ITA, ESP, SVN, SWE, CHE, USA	FRA, DEU, JPN, KOR, NZL, NOR, GBR	AUS, BEL, CAN, CHL, EST, GRC, HUN, IRL, LUX, MEX, POL, PRT, SVK
Ex post contract management	CHE, USA	AUT, DNK, FIN, DEU, ITA, JPN, KOR, NZL, NOR, SWE	AUS, BEL, CAN, CHL, EST, FRA, GRC, HUN, IRL, LUX, MEX, POL, PRT, SVK, SVN, ESP, GBR

Source: OECD (2015b), *Government at a Glance 2015*, OECD Publishing, Paris, http://dx.doi.org/10.1787/gov_glance-2015-en.

PEMEX's new procurement system should leapfrog the current Mexican public procurement system, Compranet. The SAP–Ariba has already some advantages in terms of added functions and interoperability that should be in place when the system goes fully functional in 2016. The PEMEX system will be missing the ordering option linked to the incorporation of framework agreements. However, with Bóveda Electrónica and SAP–Ariba functions, such as electronic submission of invoices and *ex post* contract management, there will be additional tools available within the e-procurement framework.

Proposals for action

One of the most significant steps taken since the reform of PEMEX is the acceptance of how e-communications can help reduce the process costs for suppliers, improve timescales, facilitate compliance with the rules, and promote traceability, transparency and auditability in the procurement process. One of the more significant changes compared with the old regulatory framework is that electronic means of communication are now mandatory means of communication and information exchange in regulated procurement procedures. The review does indicate that many positive steps have been taken towards moving the management of procurement in that direction.

The e-procurement system, incorporating several different platforms, is relatively new. Hence, the experience of suppliers with the newly established SAP-Ariba is fairly limited and more time is needed to assess whether the system will meet employee and supplier expectations. Certain modules of the system have not been fully tested, i.e. reverse auctions, and there are still opportunities to improve parts of the system, for example with the incorporation of e-catalogues. To fully capture the returns on investment of large IT platforms and solutions, ensuring the interoperability and integration of systems is a must in order to avoid duplication and redundancies of procedures, which leads to inefficient use of time and resources. Therefore, PEMEX could consider the following proposals for action:

- Have a clear vision for change from the senior management of PEMEX and ensure that the development of the e-procurement system receives full support by the senior management team.
- Adopt a firm change management approach given the complex network of connections between e-procurement platforms. Consulting key stakeholders should be at the forefront of any change management strategy.
- Increase the integration and interoperability of the different systems used by PEMEX. Increased integration between SAP–Ariba, SPyA and HIIP could help secure the benefits of the new investment, taking into account the identified limitations.
- Develop a strategic approach to ensure the presence of the right level of capacities across the whole of PEMEX where the levels of sophistication in the use of ICT to support public procurement processes vary greatly.
- Consider integration of audit findings for the development of training activities, to better incorporate lessons learned, which could potentially lead to better targeting of training resources.
- Consider leveraging the deployment of SAP–Ariba as an opportunity to level the strategic capacity and skills across the various subsidiaries.
- Empower employees to grasp the potential of the different e-platforms and how to take advantage of economic opportunities raised by these tools.

- Improve the management of data and information with HIIP across the whole of PEMEX to support the pooling of homogenous needs.
- Ensure that DCPA continues playing a leading role in developing and using tools to improve procedures, reducing duplication and achieve greater value for money, including centralised purchasing, framework agreements, e-catalogues.
- Regularly evaluate the performance of the system by gathering qualitative data through satisfaction surveys from users. This will provide PEMEX with a wide variety of suggestions for improvements and provide information concerning customer satisfaction with the overall system.
- Set up a call centre and ensure the ability of the call centre to address technical questions from end-user buyers and suppliers. Make sure that the call centre is capable of addressing questions that are directed to matters beyond the function of the e-procurement system.
- Set up an Online Shopping Mall with specific search functionalities, including, e.g. social objectives, to further achieve the full potential of the procurement system.
- Ensure that transparency is provided through the collection and publication of procurement information. Make sure that access for vendors and other stakeholders is assured not only through standardised and simplified processes, but also through regular trainings and the availability of a help desk that is readily available to answer questions about the use of the system.
- Deliver clear and integrated tender documentation, standardised where possible and proportionate to the need.
- Consider implementing tools that help ensure that the extent and complexity of information required in tender documentation and the time allotted for suppliers to respond is proportionate to the size and complexity of the procurement.
- Track complaints from suppliers from within the SAP-Ariba, and make the outcomes publicly available.
- Improve the tenders search functionality for suppliers. A progressive filtering option to narrow down open tenders by type, requirements for social category, etc. would be helpful for suppliers looking to identify relevant tender opportunities.
- Ensure that procurement data is collected in a centralised manner, eliminating the need for manual transmission and entry of statistics to satisfy reporting requirements. Building on this improved centralised data, PEMEX should consider developing procurement metrics and indicators to monitor the health and efficiency of the procurement system.

References

OECD (2016), *Towards Efficient Public Procurement in Colombia: Making the Difference*, OECD Publishing, Paris, http://dx.doi.org/10.1787/9789264252103-en.

OECD (2015a), "Recommendation of the Council on Public Procurement", www.oecd.org/corruption/recommendation-on-public-procurement.htm.

OECD (2015b), *Government at a Glance 2015*, OECD Publishing, Paris,

http://dx.doi.org/10.1787/gov_glance-2015-en.

Chapter 11

Revising Petróleos Mexicanos' pre-solicitation activities for a stronger procurement function

This chapter assesses the alignment of Petróleos Mexicanos (PEMEX) pre-solicitation activities with the mandate of its procurement directorate, which is maximising value creation. Pre-tendering activities support and often shape how procurement operations are carried out and have the potential to transform the positioning of the PEMEX procurement unit, from an intermediary to a strategic enabler. This chapter suggests actions in the collection and analysis of users' procurement needs and strategic interactions with suppliers to further reinforce the competitiveness of PEMEX procurement processes and their overall attractiveness.

Improving the efficiency of PEMEX's operations, and thus increasing its productivity, is of vital importance, particularly in view of PEMEX's financial performance compared with that of its main competitors. While producing a number of barrels somehow comparable to other international oil companies, PEMEX's capital is negative (Figure 11.1). Industrial reasons are well known: costs in exploration and production are high; taxes and rights are greater than the returns; and in industrial transformation sales, costs are higher than revenues (PEMEX, 2016a).

Figure 11.1. **Production vs. assets in major oil companies in 2014**

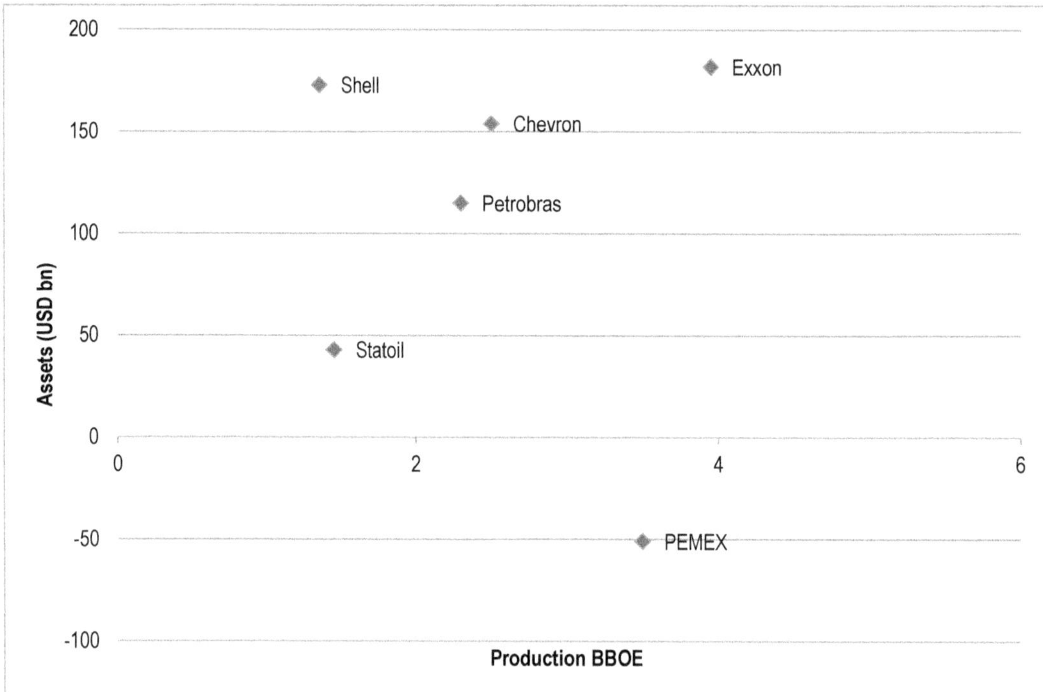

Source: PEMEX (2016a), "Business Strategy 2016-2020", www.pemex.com/acerca/plan-de-negocios/Paginas/default.aspx.

In a low oil-price environment, few means have been identified to address the structural challenges. Like other oil companies PEMEX has been looking first at cutting costs, both internally and externally. Between 2014 and 2015, PEMEX saw its number of employees reduced by approximately 10% (SEC, 2016).

According to the economic significance of outsourced services in PEMEX's overall balance sheet, suppliers have been rapidly targeted as natural candidates for cost reductions. Yet, requiring hard discounts from awarded suppliers will only generate immediate, marginal savings and cannot prove sustainable in the long term. Therefore, PEMEX should identify alternative ways to improve the efficiency of its procurement operations and maximise value creation, while being sustainable over time.

Revisiting pre-solicitation strategies could help PEMEX maximise value creation

Well before the preparation and issuance of specific procurement processes, pre-solicitation activities, both internal and external, could pave the way to develop a stronger procurement function, strategically interacting with business units and suppliers. In doing so, the Corporate Directorate for Procurement and Supply (Dirección Corporativa de

Procura y Abastecimiento, or DCPA) would therefore move away from playing a middle-man or interface role to an enabling role.

Because of PEMEX's structural organisation, strategies presiding over pre-solicitation activities impact on the DCPA's robustness and positioning in the company. In line with trends observed in the oil industry, PEMEX transformed its procurement activities into a centre-led function. This hybrid structure is often identified as having the potential to merge the most beneficial elements of centralised and decentralised procurement functions (Hartman, Trautmann and Jahns, 2008). Yet, it also comes with inherent challenges linked to the level of control the central entity has on the decentralised purchasing units.

By devoting additional attention to pre-solicitation activities, mirroring efforts on the post-award phase, the DCPA could implement a strategic shift, unlocking further efficiencies in procurement operations (Figure 11.2).

Figure 11.2. **Different approaches to procurement**

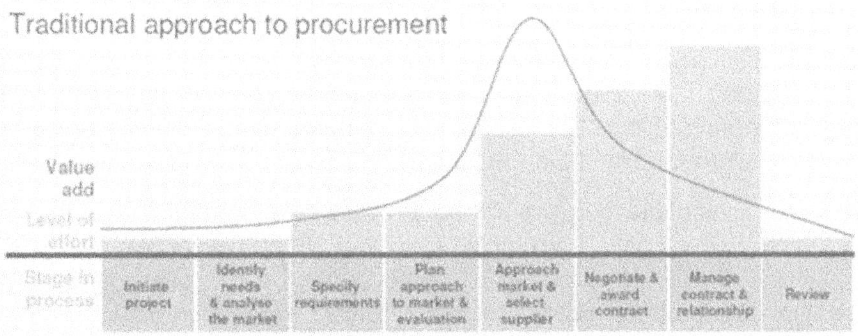

vs.

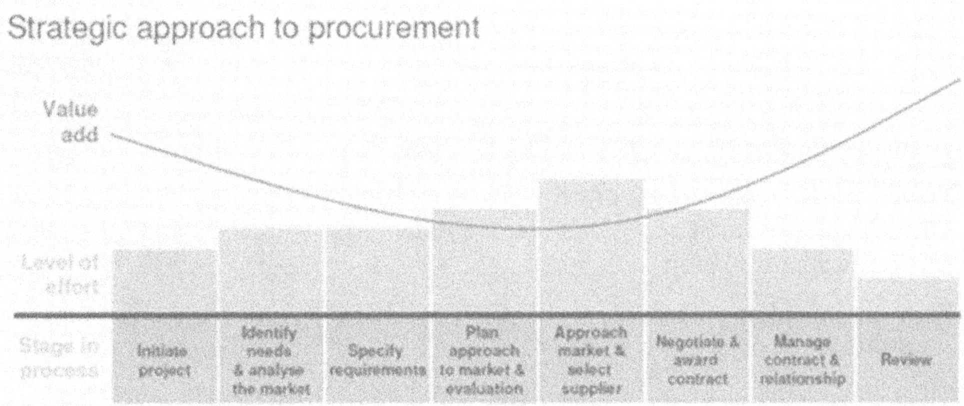

Source: Ministry of Business, Innovation and Employment of New Zealand (2011), *Mastering procurement a structured approach to strategic procurement*, www.procurement.govt.nz/procurement/for-agencies/strategic-procurement/mastering-procurement-the-guide.

Those preliminary activities are mainly twofold: developing a co-ordinated and strategic approach to plan future procurement processes, and designing tender documentation that would create a competitive environment conducive to value maximisation. These activities imply both internal and external efforts.

To support strategic procurement decisions PEMEX should implement a comprehensive collection of procurement needs reflected in a holistic procurement plan

Considering the operational structure of PEMEX and its subsidiary productive companies, coupled with a centre-led procurement function, a strong and strategic procurement function starts with a robust procurement planning exercise. Beyond gathering and structuring procurement needs, state-of-the-art planning activities could also provide additional opportunities to create and maximise value of procurement operations.

Indeed, centralised processes and strategies need to be grounded in exhaustive, structured, and as-accurate-as-possible needs assessment. According to procurement forecasts,[1] PEMEX is expected to spend more than USD 18 billion in 2016 for outsourced services, resulting from not less than 9 000 distinct procurement processes. Trying to increase PEMEX productivity, thus creating additional value, necessitates a thorough and strategic planning of those operations, both to maximise internal efficiencies and to identify potential external synergies.

Procurement planning is the primary function that sets the stage for subsequent procurement activities. It is the process of determining the procurement needs of an entity, their funding and timing of their acquisition such that operations are met as required in an efficient manner (Arrowsmith and Hartley, 2002).

The OECD Recommendation on Public Procurement highlights the importance of identifying functional overlap, inefficient silos and other causes of waste in driving efficiency throughout the procurement cycle. Because of the number of stakeholders involved in the definition of needs (technical units, budgeting officials, procurement workforce), comprehensive procurement planning can be a strategic tool to identify and overcome overlap and silos.

Article 3 of PEMEX Procurement Guidelines (Disposiciones Generales de Contratación para Petróleos Mexicanos y sus Empresas Productivas Subsidiarias), published on 10 June 2015, stipulates that procurement needs shall be planned, programmed and budgeted in accordance with the following:

I. They must be aligned with the PEMEX Business Plan.

II. They integrate requirements of acquisitions, leasing, services and works necessary for the implementation of projects and their alignment with goals and objectives of an already approved project.

III. They are aimed at generating economic value and allowing for the evaluation of results based on objective indicators.

IV. Their complexity, nature and magnitude shall be identified by the project manager, considering deadlines or delivery, so that, together with the DCPA, procurement timelines are established.

V. The project manager, with the support of the Finance Directorate, determines and obtains budget approval for the said procurement, as well as financing mechanisms in accordance with the guidelines established by the latter.

VI. The DCPA considers the Risk Policy and market conditions that could have an impact on procurement and its results, providing options to address them, supported as the case may be by the risk area, together with the project manager.

Those needs are therefore integrated into a consolidated Annual Programme of Acquisitions, Leases, Public Works and Services (Programa Anual de Adquisiciones, Arrendamientos, Obras y Servicios, or PAAAOS) prepared jointly by the business units and the DCPA. It contains the general description of acquisitions, leases, public works and services intended to be procured during the fiscal year in question, but also multi-annual needs, their estimated amounts for each year and the projects they are associated with.

The procurement process formally starts in April of the preceding year, when all business units are required to input information into the procurement-planning tool, SPyA (Sistema de Seguimiento de Procura y Abastecimiento), by 30 June of the preceding year. The procurement needs are subject to budget availability and are assessed against the company's strategic objectives.

Once needs are collected from business units, the DCPA analyses them and identifies those which can be subject to consolidation. The approved procurement needs are then integrated into the PEMEX budget, which is submitted in the Draft Budget of the Federation prepared by the Ministry of Finance and Public Credit (Secretaría de Hacienda y Crédito Público, or SHCP) and proposed to the Congress in September.

Providing strategic oversight on procurement strategies and operations, the procurement plan is then submitted to the Committee of Acquisitions, Leases, Works and Services (Comité de Adquisiciones, Arrendamientos, Obras y Servicios, or CAAOS) for recommendations. This committee is also responsible for approving quarterly updates and integrating modifications in line with the company's evolving strategic directions or external causalities.

At the end of the process, it is authorised by the Director General of the subsidiary productive company and the Director of the DCPA, and in the case of PEMEX by its directors in conjunction with the Director of the DCPA. The PAAAOS is issued and published on the PEMEX website no later than 15 November of the preceding year to which they intend to carry out procurement (Figure 11.3).

Figure 11.3. **The procurement planning process in PEMEX**

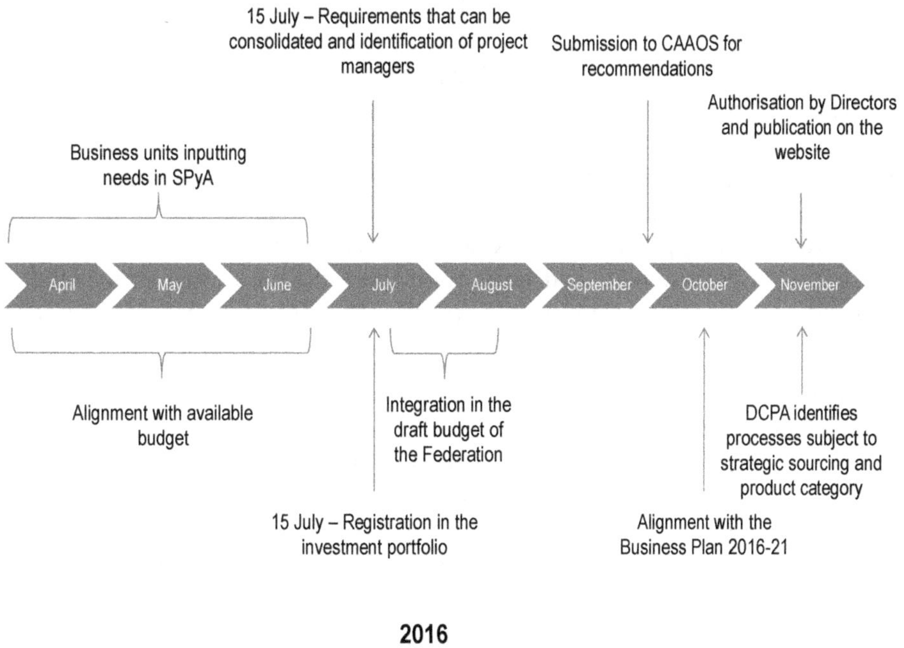

Source: Adapted from PEMEX (2016b), "Presentation of SPyA (Sistema de Procura y Abastecimiento)".

Yet, the PAAAOS only contains information relative to procurement operations carried out by PEMEX and its subsidiary productive companies. It does not include information relating to procurement opportunities with PEMEX Procurement International (PPI) or PEMEX International Trade (PMI), representing a significant share of the group's procurement activities. In fact, information about future procurement opportunities with PPI is absent from its website. While not being subject to the same mandatory requirements, information on procurement plans disclosed by PEMEX subsidiaries would help the DCPA ensure a co-ordinated approach when defining procurement strategies and would allow interested suppliers to gain a better understanding of the overall group procurement strategies.

The procurement-plan process follows prescriptions of the PEMEX Law and is somehow similar to the formalisation of procurement plans for other Mexican public entities. However, some institutions are going further in adhering to these legislative requirements and provide longer term information about future procurement needs. For example, the Mexican Federal Commission of Electricity (Comisión Federal de Electricidad, or CFE) established in 2014 a nine-year procurement forecast for goods and equipment in order to provide the market with longer term visibility about the company's recurring needs. Developing accurate estimates of procurement needs over an extended period, however, necessitates drawing on extensive spend analysis so as to be able to understand product lifecycle and procurement patterns.

The OECD fact-finding mission revealed that PEMEX is analysing past procurement information only for goods and services managed under specific product categories. Yet, as shown in Figure 11.3, the link between future procurement needs and strategic sourcing or product category management is carried out once the procurement plan is finalised and approved by directors. This prevents PEMEX from integrating spend analysis into the budget planning exercise.

Identifying which business units are spending budgets according to the previously approved procurement plan could be an important input for the allocation of the budget for the year to come. Also, understanding the most significant purchasing units for a specific product category could foster strategic exchanges with business units when the DCPA seeks to rationalise the supply base.

This collection exercise aims to consolidate procurement needs so that the DCPA is able to define the most suitable procurement strategies from needs aggregation to recourse to specific contracting instruments, such as preparatory contracts or referential agreements. Procurement planning is not only important to ensure co-ordinated and efficient procurement operations, it also helps to reduce undue recourse to emergency procurement and direct award. Defining purchasing synergies in a decentralised business environment is a challenge to which governments and large companies alike are often confronted with. In the public sector, Central Purchasing Bodies (CPBs) face the same issues when designing procurement plans that are aligned with contracting authorities' decentralised needs.

In addition to comprehensively describing future needs, regularly assessing the effectiveness of procurement plans could further streamline procurement operations and maximise value creation. Once defined and corresponding budgets are agreed, the PAAOS serves as a route map for procurement operations carried out throughout the year. Yet in practice, this route map, while being quarterly updated, is not capturing all procurement forecasts information. Indeed, unplanned procurement operations are still occurring in such proportion that the exhaustiveness and the efficiency of the agreed plan are questioned.

In the literature, the performance of procurement planning is long admitted to be a major component allowing for the assessment of strategic procurement maturity within an organisation (Barry et al., 1996; Schiele, 2007). In PEMEX, no such assessment is carried out. But the number of requests submitted to CAAOS for exceptions could provide insights on the extent of procurement-planning performance. Based on information provided by PEMEX, of the 148 requests submitted to CAAOS, only 47 were foreseen in the procurement plan.

Targeted implementation efforts would maximise the impact of the procurement plan

The annual procurement-plan process ends with the publication of the corresponding document on the PEMEX website. This strategic tool will only help increase procurement operations' efficiency, however, if it goes beyond reflecting procurement needs analysis and allows for needs management on a regular basis. It could first serve the purpose of raising awareness among suppliers on future business opportunities. It also needs to be continuously assessed to ensure that procurement operations are carried out to the fullest extent possible according to the plan.

The static format used does not allow for dynamic searches of future business opportunities, preventing suppliers from easily accessing the information they might be interested in. External and dynamic disclosure of procurement plans could provide suppliers with enhanced visibility and knowledge of business opportunities with PEMEX. By way of comparison, the procurement plan disclosed by CFE on its website provides search filters that allow interested users to identify specific business opportunities. In other OECD countries, websites publishing aggregated procurement plans sometimes provide enhanced functionalities (Box 11.1).

Box 11.1. Procurement information in Australia

The Australian e-procurement system, AusTender, provides centralised publication of Australian government business opportunities, annual procurement plans, multi-use lists and contracts awarded. Agencies are required by the Commonwealth Procurement Rules to publish on AusTender standing offer arrangements and contracts with a value of AUD 10 000 or more. Since 2005, Commonwealth Authorities and Companies Act bodies are also required to publish details of certain contracts and standing offers.

Agencies are required to publish an Annual Procurement Plan (APP) on AusTender. An APP is a statement of an agency's significant planned procurements. It consists of a short strategic procurement outlook for the agency, supported by details on planned strategic and major procurements.

For planned procurements converted to an open approach to market (ATM), information on obtaining request documents is specified on individual ATM notices on AusTender. Planned procurements can be viewed for twelve months (four quarters) from their estimated date of approach to market before they are archived and removed from public view. Withdrawn planned procurements are archived 30 days after their withdrawal.

AusTender allows for users to browse procurement plans by agency or to search for a specific planned procurement. The search engine contains the following features:

- search by keywords
- filter of annual procurement plans by agency

Box 11.1. **Procurement information in Australia** *(continued)*

- filter by product category
- filter by estimated date of approach to market
- download procurement plans in an exploitable format
- following progress of planned procurement by adding them to a watch list

Source: Australian Government (n.d.), "Annual Procurement Plan List", Department of Finance, Canberra, www.tenders.gov.au/?event=public.APP.list (accessed 25 July 2016); OECD (2016) *Improving ISSSTE's Public Procurement for Better Results,* OECD Public Governance Reviews, OECD Publishing, Paris. http://dx.doi.org/10.1787/9789264249899-en.

Besides annual forecasts synthesising procurement needs, PEMEX provides more detailed information about upcoming open tenders in the month to come. For example, and along with a short description of the subject matter, the estimated timing for the completion of the works or the delivery of the goods or services is indicated. This could help potential suppliers in assessing their capacity to respond to the advertised needs. However, the website contains partial, uneven information and sometimes obsolete information. Indeed at the time of drafting, among PEMEX and its productive subsidiary companies, only PEMEX Production and Exploration disclosed information on upcoming tenders for the month to come. Information published for some entities of the PEMEX group dates back to January 2015. The absence of regularly updated information hinders the impact of the procurement plan on raising awareness among suppliers about future processes.

In addition to the electronic disclosure of future procurement information, another means to increase suppliers' understanding of PEMEX business objectives requires physical interactions either in specialised fairs or in dedicated events organised directly by PEMEX.

Early engagement with suppliers can prove crucial to raise awareness of the private sector about future procurement opportunities. It can also foster strategic exchanges on specific projects before designing the procurement processes. These initiatives, if planned sufficiently in advance and widely communicated to allow the supplier community to mobilise, should help reduce asymmetry of information often evidenced in complex procurement projects (Saussier and Tirole, 2015).

The OECD Recommendation on Public Procurement calls upon countries to engage in regular and transparent dialogues with suppliers and business associations so that public procurement objectives are clearly exposed and markets correctly understand future requirements (Box 11.2). Not only could these activities could prove useful in providing markets with greater visibility on future procurement opportunities, they could also foster closer interactions between the supply and demand sides so that collaborative synergies could be found to generate operational efficiencies and foster participation in procurement processes.

Box 11.2. Principles of the OECD Recommendation on Public Procurement relating to suppliers' engagement

While the 2015 OECD Recommendation on Public Procurement spells out principles aiming at driving efficiencies throughout the procurement cycle, some principles convey concepts that aim to encourage suppliers' engagement in procurement processes. The OECD Council notably:

II. RECOMMENDS that Adherents ensure an adequate degree of **transparency** of the public procurement system in all stages of the procurement cycle.

To this end, Adherents should:

i) **Promote fair and equitable treatment for potential suppliers by providing an adequate and timely degree of transparency in each phase of the public procurement cycle,** while taking into account the legitimate needs for protection of trade secrets and proprietary information and other privacy concerns, as well as the need to avoid information that can be used by interested suppliers to distort competition in the procurement process. Additionally, suppliers should be required to provide appropriate transparency in subcontracting relationships.

ii) **Allow free access, through an online portal, for all stakeholders, including potential domestic and foreign suppliers, civil society and the general public; to public procurement information** notably related to the public procurement system (e.g. institutional frameworks, laws and regulations), the specific procurements (e.g. procurement forecasts, calls for tenders, award announcements), and the performance of the public procurement system (e.g. benchmarks, monitoring results). Published data should be meaningful for stakeholder uses.

iii) **Ensure visibility of the flow of public funds, from the beginning of the budgeting process throughout the public procurement cycle** to allow: (i) stakeholders to understand government priorities and spending; and (ii) policy makers to organise procurement strategically.

VI. RECOMMENDS that Adherents foster **transparent and effective stakeholder participation.**

To this end, Adherents should:

i) **Develop and follow a standard process when formulating changes to the public procurement system**. Such standard process should promote public consultations, invite the comments of the private sector and civil society, ensure the publication of the results of the consultation phase and explain the options chosen, all in a transparent manner.

ii) **Engage in transparent and regular dialogues with suppliers and business associations to present public procurement objectives and to assure a correct understanding of markets.** Effective communication should be conducted to provide potential vendors with a better understanding of the country's needs, and government buyers with information to develop more realistic and effective tender specifications by better understanding market capabilities. Such interactions should be subject to due fairness, transparency and integrity safeguards, which vary depending on whether an active procurement process is ongoing. Such interactions should also be adapted to ensure that foreign companies participating in tenders receive transparent and effective information.

Box 11.2. Principles of the OECD Recommendation on Public Procurement relating to suppliers' engagement *(continued)*

iii) **Provide opportunities for direct involvement of relevant external stakeholders** in the procurement system with a view to increase transparency and integrity while assuring an adequate level of scrutiny, provided that confidentiality, equal treatment and other legal obligations in the procurement process are maintained.

Source: OECD (2015a, "Recommendation of the Council on Public Procurement", www.oecd.org/corruption/recommendation-on-public-procurement.htm.

In Canada, the province of Alberta directly supports the organisation of specialised recurring events aiming at connecting oil and gas companies with suppliers in the industry. The Canadian Energy Supply Chain Forum became Canada's largest energy sector event, exclusively dedicated to improving the performance and effectiveness of all stages of the supply chain.

PEMEX participates in specialised international fairs such as the Offshore Technology Conference, which in May 2016 attracted more than 2 600 companies, providing opportunities to develop business partnerships (OTC, 2016). Yet, according to interviews carried out during the fact-finding mission, PEMEX does not seize this kind of opportunity to share and communicate on its procurement plan.

Some of PEMEX's competitors in the oil industry, like Shell or Statoil, organise supplier days that aim to reinforce strategic links between the supply and demand sides. First and foremost, such events allow oil companies to share their objectives and strategic orientations, thereby communicating their upcoming projects to the supplier community (Box 11.3).

Box 11.3. Statoil Supplier Day

Supplier Day held on 8 March 2012 was hosted by Statoil's chief procurement officer. The annual value of Statoil's procurements is around USD 14.5 billion and the total number of suppliers globally is approximately 12 000.

Between 60% and 95% of Statoil's operations are handled by suppliers that significantly contribute to the company performance and that of its partners and customers. Supplier Day is an important arena to interact with suppliers, ensure dialogue and discuss challenges, and to give the industry an update on Statoil's strategic objectives and ambitions.

Presentations insisted on Statoil's procurement improvement agenda:

- standardising and simplifying procurement procedures and documentation
- improving planning and predictability
- developing innovative sourcing strategies
- strengthening suppliers relations

Box 11.3. **Statoil Supplier Day** *(continued)*

- developing compliance and leadership.

Underpinning all these efforts, collaboration between Statoil and its suppliers has been identified as key. Supplier Day highlighted the need for technology and innovation in Statoil's portfolio, and the important role the supplier industry plays in this. Discussions focused on Statoil's new technology strategy and how to take improved oil recovery and subsea technology to the next level. Key speaker stated how important it is for Statoil and its suppliers to have a common understanding of the challenges ahead and to work closely together.

Source: Statoil (2012), "Supplier Day 2012 – Highlights", webpage, www.statoil.com/en/NewsAndMedia/Events/Pages/SupplierDay2012.aspx (accessed 27 July 2016).

These types of events prove useful not only to communicate on oil companies' future needs and business opportunities for suppliers but also help to create a community in the industry favouring a greater understanding of the market structure and dynamics. Experiencing transformational reforms and strategic shifts, PEMEX would therefore reap tangible benefits in reinforcing its ties with suppliers. Suppliers interviewed during the OECD fact-finding mission stressed the importance of these activities in building strategic relationships between PEMEX and its suppliers.

Ensuring that PEMEX technological and operational needs meet or develop market capabilities

Beyond gathering, structuring and communicating on aggregated procurement information, PEMEX could further reinforce pre-solicitation activities on specific procurement projects. In order to satisfy its business needs and maximise value creation PEMEX has to develop clear and effective requirements before formally soliciting suppliers with the issuance of tenders. By defining the scope of competition, tender documentation plays a strategic role in shaping the outcomes of procurement processes. In fact, technical specifications have an effect on the procurement that lasts its entire lifetime — from planning, through bid evaluation, award and contract performance up to completion and post-contract evaluations (UN, 2012).

Technical specifications and requirements are being drafted by business units that have the expert knowledge to ensure that responses from the market to procurement processes indeed meet PEMEX operational needs. Although they have an undisputed technical knowledge of outsourced goods and services that will encourage PEMEX industrial development, however, they might lack a procurement understanding in drafting technical specifications.

The issue of too narrow or unclear technical specifications is a long-lasting problem that eventually diminishes competition in the procurement process. The definition of such specifications is also a source for direct award. The DCPA includes a unit responsible for standards that supports business units in developing technical specifications according to commonly accepted standards. Specialised business associations, such as the International Association of Oil and Gas Producers also developed a set of technical standards that are relevant to the oil and gas industry and benchmarked practices (IOGP, 2015).

Support or templates designed by procurement experts in the DCPA could help business units when drafting technical specifications to ensure they are logically structured and clear enough to ensure a good understanding of the needs. They could also help to reduce the number of clarification meetings where suppliers seek additional or clearer information.

To ensure the clarity of technical specifications, but more importantly their matching with market capabilities, PEMEX could also reach out to suppliers in the preparation phase of the tender documentation. Indeed, Article 13 of the Procurement Guidelines foresees the possibility to disseminate draft tender documentation in advance so that it could benefit from suppliers' input on the definition of the needs and requirements.

However, unlike public entities in Mexico subject to the public procurement laws, publication of the draft tender documentation to collect potential feedback from suppliers is not mandatory beyond a certain threshold and does not contain any minimum period for which this draft documentation should be publicised. This loose formulation could question its effective use.

Indeed, although a section on the PEMEX website is dedicated to draft tender documentation for PEMEX and its subsidiary productive companies, this section is empty and has not been updated for more than a year (since June 2015). This signals that such a possibility is not used by PEMEX to benefit from potential suppliers' input on the definition of the needs and the structure of the procurement process.

Although procurement or technical expertise supporting business units when defining the needs is provided, the mere structure of tenders and assessment mechanisms of offers are hindering competition and the identification of proposals offering the best value for money. Indeed Section V.1 of the General Guidelines for Procurement (Lineamientos Generales de Procura y Abastecimiento) of 11 June 2015 stipulates that the tender documentation shall indicate that compliance with requirements asked of participants will be verified using a binary mechanism.

This implies that technical specifications included in the tender documentation shall list requirements that will allow for the identification of technically suitable proposals on a pass or fail basis. The consequence of this assessment mechanism is twofold. First it further emphasises the role of the technical specifications in the outcomes of procurement processes. It forces business units responsible for the drafting of the technical elements of the tenders to cautiously formulate each of the requirements in order to precisely assess whether they are mandatory from a technical viewpoint or just nice-to-have technical features.

A second consequence is that, de facto, suppliers are only aiming at meeting minimum requirements and do not genuinely compete on technical terms. Because of the assessment mechanism, suppliers will rather focus on pricing elements. Yet, the complexity of oil and gas procurement projects implies that technical or organisational elements significantly play a role in projects' outcomes. As evidenced by discussions with suppliers during the OECD fact-finding mission, PEMEX is locked into contracts with old technologies and do not benefit from innovative solutions.

Open, performance-based technical specifications would provide substantial benefits to PEMEX since it could incentivise suppliers to propose alternative solutions in often extremely complex areas. However, this remains largely unexploited in PEMEX procurement processes because of the assessment mechanisms of bidders' responses.

PEMEX competitors in the oil industry, notably because of remote operating locations, however benefit from innovations in their production processes (Erdal, 2013) (Box 11.4). The current climate has been a catalyst for looking more closely at the oil and gas industry's supply chains and there has been much discussion on collaboration and adopting the latest supply chain innovation to remain profitable against the low oil price.

Box 11.4. BP's assessment of 3D printing in the oil industry

In the seemingly short time it has been with us, 3D printing has raised a number of new possibilities, from paleontologists making replicas of dinosaur bones to would-be designers creating their own plastic shoes. For industry, the prospect of low-cost printing of customised parts – in a range of materials – gives the technique plenty of potential.

Until now, the technology has mainly been used for prototyping. However, production of complex, tailored parts at a low volume is on the rise in fields such as aerospace, for example.

The oil and gas industry – and many others – see opportunities to use this technology, especially to produce parts on demand in a specific material. For example, 3D printers on an offshore facility may mean complex components can be manufactured in remote locations, saving time and improving efficiency. Uses of 3D printing is set to grow over the next ten years as applications are identified and opportunities arise with new materials and equipment.

Source: British Petroleum (2015), "8 technology breakthrough that may change the energy landscape", www.bp.com/en/global/corporate/bp-magazine/innovations/8-technology-breakthroughs-that-may-change-the-energy-landscape.html (accessed 27 July 2016).

The impact of innovative products on procurement efficiency and on an entity's productivity is a recent focus, yet initial findings suggests that procurement processes that foster innovation have a strong potential in generating economic value, thus enhancing productivity. This is why a growing number of countries implement strategies and plans aiming to increase the use of public procurement to encourage innovation.

The concept of encouraging innovation through procurement is not new and some countries have pursued policies to that end for decades. The United Kingdom, for instance, has actively sought to integrate procurement for innovation across government since 2003. Germany, too, has introduced the Agreement on Public Procurement of Innovation. Under the terms of the agreement, six federal ministries (the interior, economics, defence, transport, environment, and research) publish long-term demand forecasts, engage in continuous market analysis to identify potential new solutions, offer professional training on legal options for promoting innovation, and encourage a strategic dialogue and the sharing of experience between procuring agencies, end users, and industry (OECD, 2016). The Netherlands and Spain operate programmes for innovation through procurement and Finland's programme provides for a target of 5% to be spent on procurement for innovation (OECD, forthcoming). In Mexico, in 2013, the president instructed the Ministry of Economy to create a programme to drive innovation through public procurement.

Innovation is often a collaborative process and a recent survey showed that among the partners contributing to the success of procurement projects involving innovative solutions, the private sector is the most important (Figure 11.4).

Figure 11.4. **Partners in innovation procurement**

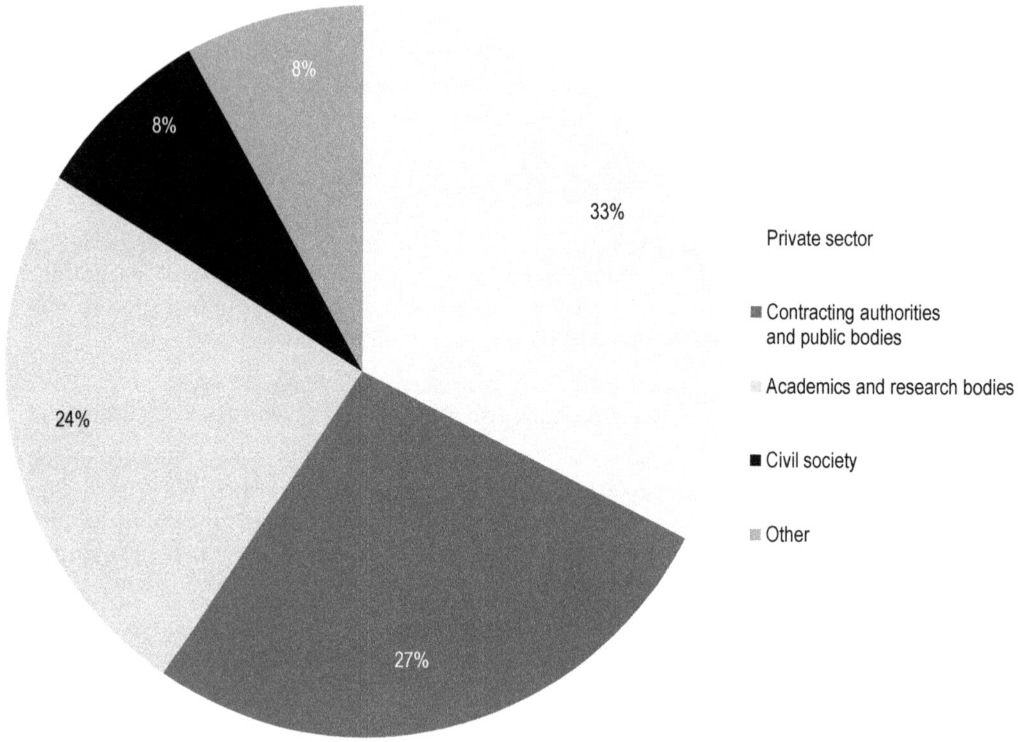

Source: OECD (2017), *Public Procurement for Innovation: Good Practices and Strategies*, OECD Publishing, Paris. http://dx.doi.org/10.1787/9789264265820-en

While the quantifiable contribution of public procurement on innovation is confronted with challenges, notably relating to missing information allowing for its assessment (Appelt and Galindo-Rueda, 2016), the literature insists on the importance of the demand-driven policies to foster innovation. Indeed demand affects the development of new products, as firms modify and differentiate products to increase sales and market share, or create new markets. Demand factors can force firms to improve their production and supply processes in order to reduce costs and lower prices. In many cases, they are also the main driver of innovation.

However, to do so procurement processes need to be framed so as to favour innovation among suppliers. This can be achieved by designing performance-based technical specifications that would set only expected performance rather than imposing technical requirements to reach those objectives or by involving suppliers at an early stage in the tender process.

A 2012 survey by the OECD indeed suggests that most OECD countries had at some point used performance-based tender specifications to encourage innovation, given guidance to procurement officers, or involved suppliers at an early stage in the tender process to encourage innovation (Figure 11.5).

Figure 11.5. **Use of procurement to promote innovation in selected OECD countries**

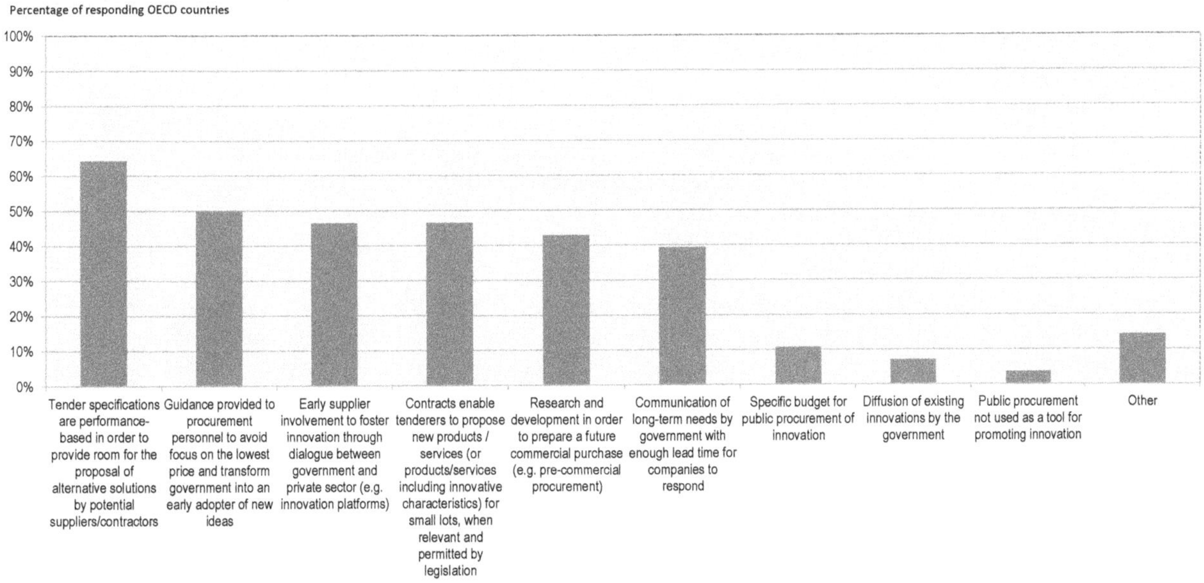

Source: OECD (2014), "Intelligent demand: Policy rationale, design and potential benefits", *OECD Science, Technology and Industry Policy Papers*, No. 13, OECD Publishing, Paris, http://dx.doi.org/10.1787/5jz8p4rk3944-en.

As suggested by Figure 11.5, another factor conducive to innovation is the early engagement of suppliers in procurement process so that they can participate in the definition of project requirements according to market capabilities. Collaborative sourcing has been implemented by many large organisations in an attempt to maximise value creation through mutual shareholder benefits. This approach to procurement has often been found to be conducive to enhanced procurement performance. Yet, these initiatives need to build on shared values and common understanding (Box 11.5).

Box 11.5. **Strategic alliances in the oil industry**

With few new oil fields discovered around the world, oil and gas companies need to maximise value creation in the existing fields, including marginal fields.

The oil and gas markets' structure has been steadily deteriorating. Easy to exploit oil fields are becoming scarce and companies are now forced to undertake increasingly complex projects, such as deepwater and remote developments, to generate profits. From 2004 to 2013 operators' upstream returns on average capital employed decreased by about 40% although oil prices increased by almost 60%. Entering now into an era of low oil prices, companies are looking more and more at the best possible solutions to maximise capital expenditure. Strategic alliances have been found to provide several benefits, from increased overall projects efficiencies to revisited working relationships between clients and suppliers. Several oil and gas companies, along with governmental programmes, implemented such alliances.

Box 11.5. Strategic alliances in the oil industry *(continued)*

BP's Andrew Alliance

BP formed a strategic alliance with seven contractors for the development of its Andrew Project in the North Sea in 1996. The Andrew Alliance included construction of a fixed platform with topside facilities supported on a four-legged steel frame. The contracting team comprised Brown and Root, Santa Fe, Saipem, Highlands Fabricators, Allseas, Emtunga, and Trafalgar House. BP structured the alliance to link the cost of the project to the financial rewards, which were shared among the alliance members. Functioning as a single team, alliance members shared common objectives and incentives and reduced the need for contract interactions. Despite challenging targets, the project came in 20% under budget and six months ahead of schedule.

CRINE

The Cost Reduction Initiative for the New Era, or CRINE, was an industry-wide programme adopted in the 1990s with the objective of reducing operating and capital costs for projects on the UK continental shelf without compromising either safety or production volumes. A number of North Sea operators and contractors participated in the programme, which aimed to eliminate waste and inefficiency in the platform-construction supply chain. The companies defined functional specifications, developed standard contracts, and simplified the contracting process by creating a single industry pre-qualification body, which eliminated duplicative effort. The alliance succeeded in reducing the industry's overall costs by 40% while improving safety at North Sea facilities, although some of the benefits were later eroded by rising oil prices and the ensuing inflation. Many of the strategies and business processes developed then are still in use today.

Shell's FLNG Alliance

Shell is constructing the world's first floating liquefied natural gas (FLNG) facility. The massive ship will chill natural gas produced in the field — generating at least 5.3 million tonnes of liquids per year, according to company press releases. A framework agreement formed in 2009 with Technip and Samsung Heavy Industries was strengthened in 2012 to enhance collaboration on the design, engineering, procurement, construction, and installation of future FLNG facilities.

BG Group and KBR

In January 2015, BG Group entered into a single-partner alliance with KBR, under which KBR will provide front-end-loading engineering services, project management expertise, and technical support across BG's global upstream portfolio. According to press releases from both companies, the alliance, which could last as long as ten years, involves a new method of work between operators and contractors and includes a level of integration and collaboration that is deeper than such parties have shared in the past. The alliance will enable BG to minimise its fixed costs while retaining access to high-value technical expertise and support. It will enhance BG's productivity and agility while also providing a steady pipeline of work for KBR.

Source: Adapted from Groves and Melville (2015), "Strategic alliances in upstream oil and gas", www.bcgperspectives.com/content/articles/energy_environment_strategic_alliances_upstream_oil_gas/ (accessed 28 July 2016).

While having the potential to create additional value with the identification of alternative technical solutions, leveraging on public procurement to foster innovation is a complex process and could prove suboptimal if not cautiously carried out. Indeed it could generate adverse consequences such as organisational disruption minimising the expected outcomes of procurement processes. Case studies highlight the importance of intermediation in those complex processes to mitigate adversarial effects. Intermediation in innovation is a concept relating to establishing or enabling the link between different actors with complementary skill sets or interests in order to support the generation and diffusion of innovation (Box 11.6).

Box 11.6. Connecting supply and demand in procurement, triggering innovation

The UK National Health Service Blood and Transplant (NHSBT) is a special health authority set up to provide a limited set of clearly defined services nationally. For many years, NHS Blood and Transplant searched to procure a new blood donation chair to replace their current beds, one that would fit a modern environment, satisfy all the health and safety issues and concerns, and improve their service delivery efficiency.

The inability to formulate the concrete need and to articulate it to the market resulted in several failed procurement attempts that wasted time, money and resources. The organisation also tried to work with their incumbent supplier to design a new chair, but to no success. There was a concern expressed by the Assistant Director of Nursing that a failure to procure a new chair to meet their changing needs could impact on their service delivery efficiency. In 2009, the Assistant Director of Nursing became aware of the National Innovation Centre (NIC) and its role in the NHS innovation process and realised they could assist NHSBT in getting a bespoke chair designed, built and procured. From a clinical and operational perspective, the Assistant Director of Nursing had a clear idea about what functionalities the chair would have to deliver, but was unable to translate that into clear technical specifications. She lacked the necessary skills for this, and could not assess how the various functions would be best delivered. NIC presented the possible options available to procure a new chair to NHSBT, making sure they had already considered "conventional" procurement routes and framework agreements.

NIC introduced a formal process in which relevant stakeholders are invited to participate in a workshop to identify, validate and rank the clinical needs of the innovation in question, ranging from those that are essential to those that are "nice to have". NHSBT subsequently carried out a staged project with a design contest as an initial, separate step of the procurement process to reduce risk. This entire process was new to NHSBT, where previously products were chosen in traditional procurement procedures and rolled out through the organisation without a proper trial and improvement phase. Through separating the design phase and the procurement phase of the new donation chair, this approach allowed multiple specific service contracts to compete for the best designs, established a close interaction between the public agency and those working on a solution, and led to sharing the risks and benefits.

As a result of working in this new way with NIC, NHSBT saw an opportunity to use the NIC process to procure other pieces of kit to support blood donation. The result was the development of a Session Environment Design Authority (SEDA) within NHSBT, which subsequently took on some of the intermediary functions through testing of innovations and trust-building exercises. An external intermediation not only succeeded in delivering a new technology, but also led to institutional learning for future processes.

Source: Adapted from Edler and Yeoh (2016), "Connecting demand and supply: The role of intermediation in public procurement for innovation", www.sciencedirect.com/science/article/pii/S0048733315001638 (accessed 28 July 2016).

Proposals for action

While the DCPA defines and develops centralised processes and strategies, procurement operations are carried out by decentralised business units. To ensure that this centre-led model indeed reaps the benefits of this procurement structure, greater attention and strategic efforts could be placed in pre-solicitation activities. They indeed support and often shape how procurement operations are carried out and have the potential to transform the positioning of the DCPA within PEMEX, from an intermediary to a strategic enabler.

To do so, in view of the OECD Recommendation on Public Procurement along with practices from countries and sectorial competitors, PEMEX could consider the following proposals for action:

- The DCPA could benefit from integrating in a comprehensive procurement plan the procurement needs of the entire PEMEX group, including its affiliates.
- In addition to those carried out for defined product categories, systematically analysing past procurement expenditures provides strategic insights to inform future procurement decisions. It helps define and prioritise future procurement needs and would help PEMEX in developing more accurate estimates and assess the needs against the available budget.
- Like other similar Mexican entities, PEMEX could expand its procurement plans beyond needs for the next calendar year so as to provide suppliers with longer term visibility and develop internal strategic spend management.
- Being a central element of streamlined procurement processes, PEMEX could implement regular assessments of its procurement plan efficiency, notably by defining indicators relating to its effective coverage against actual procurement expenditures.
- Developing dynamic procurement plans, allowing for the identification of specific future procurement opportunities according to suppliers' areas of interest, would help raise awareness among the private sector on procurement processes in which they estimate being in a position to bring value add to PEMEX.
- PEMEX should ensure that its website provides structured and harmonised information on the various steps of its procurement processes and notably on the pre-solicitation phase. This would provide interested suppliers with a greater understanding of the group structure and business opportunities.
- In order to reduce asymmetry of information and to create an environment conducive to strategic relationships between PEMEX and its suppliers, the former could further develop communication activities on its procurement plan.
- To ensure that expression of needs correspond to market capabilities and encourage competition, the DCPA could develop guidance and templates to support business units developing technical specifications.
- PEMEX could more systematically disseminate draft tender documentation before the issuance of the procurement process so as to benefit from the industry perspective when defining technical requirements.
- To unlock the technical innovation potential of the industry, PEMEX could consider revising its Procurement Guidelines and Manuals to allow for a

comparative assessment of technical merits of the proposals submitted by bidders, rather that evaluating them on a pass or fail basis.

- PEMEX could define policies and guidance on the development of performance-based specifications, allowing suppliers to propose technically competing solutions.
- To leverage on public procurement to encourage innovation, PEMEX should reinforce early exchanges with suppliers in large procurement projects while ensuring fairness and transparency in the selection process.
- PEMEX could define specific risk management strategies to mitigate potential disruptive effects of innovation so that projects adequately deliver their expected outcomes.

Note

1. For more information, see the 2016 Annual Procurement Plan available at www.pemex.com/procura/procedimientos-de-contratacion/Paginas/programas.aspx (accessed 16 June 2016).

References

Appelt, S. and F. Galindo-Rueda (2016), "Measuring the link between public procurement and innovation", *OECD Science, Technology and Industry Working Papers*, No. 2016/03, OECD Publishing, Paris, http://dx.doi.org/10.1787/5jlvc7sl1w7h-en.

Arrowsmith, Sue and Keith Hartley (2002), *Public Procurement*, Volume 1.

Australian Government (n.d.), "Annual Procurement Plan List", Department of Finance, Canberra, www.tenders.gov.au/?event=public.APP.list (accessed 25 July 2016).

Barry, J. et al. (1996), "A development model for effective MRO procurement", *International Journal of Purchasing and Materials Management*, 32 (3), pp. 35–44.

British Petroleum (2015), "8 technology breakthrough that may change the energy landscape", www.bp.com/en/global/corporate/bp-magazine/innovations/8-technology-breakthroughs-that-may-change-the-energy-landscape.html (accessed 27 July 2016).

Edler and Yeoh (2016), "Connecting demand and supply: The role of intermediation in public procurement for innovation", www.sciencedirect.com/science/article/pii/S0048733315001638 (accessed 28 July 2016).

Erdal, O. (2013), *The Impact of Technological Innovation on the Oil and Gas Industry*, Cambridge University Press.

Groves and Melville (2015), "Strategic alliances in upstream oil and gas", www.bcgperspectives.com/content/articles/energy_environment_strategic_alliances_upstream_oil_gas/ (accessed 28 July 2016).

Hartmann, E., G. Trautmann and C. Jahns (2008), "Organisational design implications of global sourcing: A multiple case study analysis on the application of control mechanisms", *Journal of Purchasing and Supply Management*, *14*(1), 28-42.

IOGP (International Association of Oil and Gas Producers) (2015), "Benchmarking on Standards and Technical Specifications", Report 500.

Ministry of Business, Innovation and Employment of New Zealand (2011), *Mastering procurement, a structured approach to strategic procurement*, www.procurement.govt.nz/procurement/for-agencies/strategic-procurement/mastering-procurement-the-guide.

OECD (2017), *Public Procurement for Innovation: Good Practices and Strategies*, OECD Publishing, Paris. http://dx.doi.org/10.1787/9789264265820-en

OECD (2016) *Improving ISSSTE's Public Procurement for Better Results*, OECD Public Governance Reviews, OECD Publishing, Paris.

http://dx.doi.org/10.1787/9789264249899-en.

OECD (2015), "Recommendation of the Council on Public Procurement", www.oecd.org/corruption/recommendation-on-public-procurement.htm.

OECD (2014), "Intelligent demand: Policy rationale, design and potential benefits", *OECD Science, Technology and Industry Policy Papers*, No. 13, OECD Publishing, Paris, http://dx.doi.org/10.1787/5jz8p4rk3944-en.

OTC (Offshore Technology Conference) (2016), "2016 Offshore Technology Conference Attendance Ranks in Top 15", webpage, http://www.otcnet.org/page.cfm/Action=Press/libID=1/listID=8/libEntryID=48?_ga=1.24209459.882315.1482226990 (accessed 27 July 2016).

PEMEX (2016a), "Business Plan 2016-2021", PEMEX.

PEMEX (2016b), "Presentation of SPyA (Sistema de Procura y Abastecimiento)", PEMEX.

Saussier, S. and J. Tirole (2015), "Renforcer l'efficacité de la commande publique", *Conseil d'analyse économique* 2015/3, No. 22, http://dx.doi.org/10.3917/ncae.022.0001.

SEC (Security Exchange Commission) (2016), "Form 20-F, Petroleos Mexicanos Annual Report", www.sec.gov/Archives/edgar/data/932782/000119312516591959/d179072d20f.htm.

Schiele (2007), "Supply-management maturity, cost savings and purchasing absorptive capacity: Testing the procurement–performance link", *Journal of Purchasing and Supply Management*, 13(4), pp. 274-293.

Statoil (2012), "Supplier Day 2012 – Highlights", webpage, www.statoil.com/en/NewsAndMedia/Events/Pages/SupplierDay2012.aspx (accessed 27 July 2016).

UN (United Nations) (2012), "Public Procurement Handbook", www.ungm.org/Areas/Public/pph/channels/PPH.pdf.

Chapter 12

Increasing efficiency and fairness in Petróleos Mexicanos' solicitation and contract award process

This chapter discusses the path Petróleos Mexicanos (PEMEX) has paved for making the procurement system, processes, and procedures more efficient. Furthermore it discusses how PEMEX is engaging with stakeholders and the processes in place for supplier engagement. While PEMEX has improved the process for evaluations of bids, the company has been slower in adopting new techniques such as the debriefing of suppliers or applying standstill periods.

This chapter looks at the results of reforms and strategies implemented in recent years to make Petróleos Mexicanos' (PEMEX's) procurement system, processes, and procedures more efficient. With PEMEX becoming a state productive enterprise (empresa productiva del Estado) in 2014, the market environment in which it works has been transformed and the company is now forced to takes steps as it enters a much more competitive market. Part of that process is to identify good practices of supplier engagement, since in Mexico excessive controls and a legalistic culture make it difficult to engage with suppliers for consultation and development purposes.

Throughout this chapter two key recommendations from the 2015 OECD Recommendation of the Council on Public Procurement will be highly visible. First, the relevance of stakeholder participation, and how PEMEX can engage better in a transparent and regular dialogue with suppliers and business associations. For this part, an assessment is carried out for two stages of the procurement cycle, clarification meetings and debriefings. Both methods can contribute to a more efficient and fair solicitation and contracting process. The second recommendation encourages organisations to drive efficiency throughout the public procurement cycle with the aim of satisfying the needs of the government and its citizens (OECD, 2015). Furthermore, the OECD emphasises the importance of evaluating existing processes and institutions to identify functional overlap, inefficient silos and other causes of waste (see Box 12.1).

Box 12.1. OECD Recommendation on Public Procurement

VI. RECOMMENDS that Adherents foster transparent and effective stakeholder **participation**.

To this end, Adherents should:

i) **Develop and follow a standard process when formulating changes to the public procurement system**. Such standard process should promote public consultations, invite the comments of the private sector and civil society, ensure the publication of the results of the consultation phase and explain the options chosen, all in a transparent manner.

ii) **Engage in transparent and regular dialogues with suppliers and business associations to present public procurement objectives and to assure a correct understanding of markets.** Effective communication should be conducted to provide potential vendors with a better understanding of the country's needs, and government buyers with information to develop more realistic and effective tender specifications by better understanding market capabilities. Such interactions should be subject to due fairness, transparency and integrity safeguards, which vary depending on whether an active procurement process is ongoing. Such interactions should also be adapted to ensure that foreign companies participating in tenders receive transparent and effective information.

iii) **Provide opportunities for direct involvement of relevant external stakeholders** in the procurement system with a view to increase transparency and integrity while assuring an adequate level of scrutiny, provided that confidentiality, equal treatment and other legal obligations in the procurement process are maintained.

Box 12.1. **OECD Recommendation on Public Procurement** *(continued)*

VII. RECOMMENDS that Adherents develop processes to drive **efficiency** throughout the public procurement cycle in satisfying the needs of the government and its citizens.

To this end, Adherents should:

i) **Streamline the public procurement system and its institutional frameworks.** Adherents should evaluate existing processes and institutions to identify functional overlap, inefficient silos and other causes of waste. Where possible, a more service-oriented public procurement system should then be built around efficient and effective procurement processes and workflows to reduce administrative red tape and costs, for example through shared services.

ii) **Implement sound technical processes to satisfy customer needs efficiently.** Adherents should take steps to ensure that procurement outcomes meet the needs of customers, for instance by developing appropriate technical specifications, identifying appropriate award criteria, ensuring adequate technical expertise among proposal evaluators, and ensuring adequate resources and expertise are available for contract management following the award of a contract.

iii) **Develop and use tools to improve procurement procedures, reduce duplication and achieve greater value for money**, including centralised purchasing, framework agreements, e-catalogues, dynamic purchasing, e-auctions, joint procurements and contracts with options. Application of such tools across sub-national levels of government, where appropriate and feasible, could further drive efficiency.

Source: OECD (2015), "Recommendation of the Council on Public Procurement", www.oecd.org/corruption/recommendation-on-public-procurement.htm.

With a new methodology for defining its strategies for the acquisition of goods and services, the "Strategic Supply and Management by Categories" (Abastecimiento estratégico y gestión por categorías), PEMEX has identified an appropriate procurement strategy to develop solicitation documents, terms of the contract models, and how offers will be evaluated to select the winning bidder(s). However, during the solicitation process, PEMEX must: 1) provide clarifications to potential bidders, including any resulting changes to the solicitation documents; 2) receive and evaluate the offers in strict adherence with the process and criteria established in the solicitation; 3) award any resulting contract(s); and 4) debrief unsuccessful bidders.

This section will assess the context of clarifications to bidders, the evaluation process, the timing of issuance of the contract and the debriefing provided. According to international experience, these phases are particularly prone to errors or lack of integrity, high scrutiny and potential challenges. The principles of objectivity, equal treatment and transparency are therefore paramount throughout this process.

Embrace more systematic tools and platforms to achieve value for money

PEMEX contracting strategies aim to satisfy the supply needs while getting the best deal in terms of value for money. PEMEX seeks to optimise, streamline, and better manage available resources, by business orientation, process improvement and integration. Furthermore, PEMEX aims to plan and execute in less time with an approved centralised process, and implement contracting strategies supported by the methodology of strategic supply and category management of products.

Strategic supply is key to streamlining the procurement process and to achieving savings through tendering strategies. The Corporate Directorate for Procurement and Supply (Dirección Corporativa de Procura y Abastecimiento, or DCPA) strategies include preparatory contracts and framework agreements, while also categorising products centrally. The preparatory contract is a voluntary agreement by which a supplier or contractor establishes a unilateral promise or exclusive rights of sale to supply PEMEX goods, services, leases or works. PEMEX has been quite active in making preparatory contracts, which now total over 200. Preparatory contracts are made by direct awarding and can save both time and money, but a decision that involves exception from the open tendering procedures needs to be justified with proper data and evidence. The objective of these contracts is to ensure the best conditions of purchase for PEMEX relating to substantive productive activities through competitive, open, and transparent processes. These contracts create a unilateral obligation of the suppliers to sell goods or services to PEMEX, if requested. PEMEX does not have any obligation in terms of the volume or value of goods or services that it will acquire from these suppliers.

The objective of PEMEX is to move more towards product management as a process for maximising the economic value of contracts and reduce costs through new and better conditions. Furthermore, PEMEX has established a model based on centralisation that should maximise the use of purchasing power of PEMEX to generate value. It seeks to optimise the resources of DCPA to increase productivity and efficiency of the procurement process, by creating multidisciplinary teams in regional representations, called Centres for Procurement and Supply (Centros de Atención de Procura y Abastecimiento, or CAPAS), which have the function of being an executor of the process. Categorising products allows the company to simplify its procurement processes and make them more efficient by defining a contracting strategy for the whole category of products, instead of analysing the market and defining a contracting strategy for each individual product.

Standardisation of the templates and review processes could increase the quality of the solicitation documents and contracts

Contractual terms must be clear and specific to avoid establishing unnecessary requirements, and they should favour free competition and equality of opportunity to increase the number of participants in the tendering process. As a result of an effort to standardise and simplify, PEMEX has developed prototypes of solicitation documents in various forms for open competition, restricted invitation, and direct award. There are guidelines and policies relating to the creation of model contracts that have been developed in various forms for public events and formats and which are essential for operation under the existing regulatory framework.

According to the General Guidelines for Procurement and Supply, the model contracts are included in the information with the solicitation documents for open competition or restricted invitation, as well as the submission of an offer for direct awards. The model contract is prepared considering the provisions of the contracts and should include at least: the type of contract, the identification of risks linked to the project, processes and the execution of the contract, prevention and mitigation, the concentration of contracts in a single supplier and scale and complexity of the object of the contract.

The type of model contracts and the clauses for contracts are prepared beforehand. The legal department provides DCPA with an ad hoc tendering model in line with the strategic sourcing on the request of the DCPA within a reasonable time prior to the start of the procurement process. Once the contract is awarded, the DCPA customises the draft contract with the data, which the contractor or supplier sends to the DCPA accompanied by supporting documentation for it to conduct a legal review and proceed with the processing. The legal review of contracts is performed according to the tasks entrusted to the legal department in terms of the PEMEX Law.

The average opening period of public tenders (from the issuance of the tender notice until the deadline for responses) varies depending on whether the tender is national, international or restricted. The relationship between open and restricted for this period is estimated to average 2.5 times higher in the open competition with respect to the restricted invitation (see Table 12.1).

Table 12.1. **DCPA's average number of tendering days per type of tender for the year 2014 and first half of 2015**

Type	Average tendering period (days)
National public tendering	49
International public tendering	66
International public tendering according to treaties	65
Restricted tendering with less than three suppliers	25

Source: Based on information provided by PEMEX.

In the case of North American Free Trade Agreement (NAFTA) processes, there is an estimated average of 1.5 times longer period for international open tendering, compared to national ones. The period is determined according to the characteristics, complexity, and nature of the procurement in question; as well as the type of procedure that will be used, considering the strategy, attributes such as pre-qualification of companies, level of competition (participants), and volume clarifications received, among others.

Communicating with and assessing strategic vendors

Overall the impact has been positive regarding the comprehensive technology platform on vendor registration with 3 794 registered suppliers, of which 3 167 are in the form of basic registration and 627 in extended registration. This information has been used to identify potential suppliers for market analysis and sending requests for information (RFIs) to specifically selected suppliers. The PEMEX PASS (Point of Access to Supply System) solution is another portal that allows suppliers, contractors and users of PEMEX areas to find and identify business opportunities swiftly; it is also targeted at small, medium and large suppliers or contractors that have a business relationship with PEMEX, or are interested in starting a relationship. Furthermore, PEMEX PASS can be used by those that are looking for new business opportunities, or who wish to strengthen their business relationship with a strategic approach or proposal that creates value solutions.

Audit strategically important vendors

In December 2015, PEMEX set up an audit programme with third-party auditors carrying out independent audits of strategically important vendors. Currently, the first 14 audits have taken place but it is foreseen that a total of 120 audits will be carried out in 2016. Through this programme, suppliers know the issues important to PEMEX for compliance. Suppliers are chosen based on a risk management scheme that is very closely linked to the value chain. There is a selection process where PEMEX invites suppliers to a face-to-face meeting to explain the mechanics and scope of the audit. The audit protocol reviews five main topics: corporate sustainability, environment, human resources management, process and business quality, health and safety. The outcome of the audit is shared with supplier as a tool for continuous improvement and with internal areas as part of a due diligence assessment.

Provision of clarifications through established meetings and e-tools helps accelerate the process

Advancing symmetry of information for all suppliers is a key requirement to ensure equal opportunity and fairness to all potential suppliers. Failure to achieve that objective is recognised as a particular risk during the solicitation period (OECD, 2009). Despite improvements, technical specifications and requirements for participation remain the main areas where PEMEX can improve, according to a recent survey of PEMEX's suppliers. Furthermore, one-third of suppliers believe that procurement procedures are an area for improvement and close to one-quarter of suppliers consider that requirements for tenders need to improve. Technical specifications and calls for tender require more attention in terms of equity. According to survey results, a significant majority of suppliers perceive PEMEX to be a fair company in the tendering process; however, that has decreased slightly compared to the 2012 survey (PEMEX, 2014). Before reaching the clarification stage, suppliers interested in becoming contractors of PEMEX have to go through a recruit ment process that can be considered a pre-qualification stage. The stage is used to explain to all suppliers the rules of the game but also to assess the ability of potential suppliers to deliver a certain product. The process of asking suppliers questions is something that PEMEX applies. It can get potential contractors disqualified from the process if the answers don't meet requirements or if PEMEX does not receive any responses.

Clarification meetings

Potential contractors have to submit an interest in participating in the procurement procedure for tender through a *manifiesto de interés.* PEMEX publishes the invitation and a schedule including dates for clarification meetings and the rules of bidding. Then there is an expression of interest to bid and potential contractors have to supply PEMEX with questions no later than 24 hours before the clarification meeting takes place. They have a chance to have their questions answered at the meeting. PEMEX can have one or a series of meetings for clarification in a tender. Before the regulatory reforms PEMEX used to only publish answers that led to changes to the rules of the bidding. Now all answers are published, including all the questions, and names of the suppliers.

Technical clarification meetings are performed in accordance with the current regulations; they are carried out during the clarification meetings, which appear in the records at the end of the meetings. PEMEX is beginning to use a SAP-ARIBA solution for electronic exchange of information through RFx, including technical clarifications and pre-qualification of suppliers. Clarification meetings are held at specific points in time, with the possibility of having more clarification meetings, based on the need for clarification of the participants, and according to the period of clarification set in the schedule of the relevant procurement procedure. PEMEX can collect all the issues addressed in clarification, formulate answers, and share with the rest of the participants. The clarification meetings currently represent an efficient form of communication, allowing for direct interaction with interested suppliers and clarifying their doubts. They are held at PEMEX offices and normally all those interested are invited to participate in the clarification meeting at the same time (see the PEMEX clarification process in Box 12.2).

Box. 12.2. How PEMEX organises clarification meetings

The clarification meetings are held in accordance with Article 21 of the General Provisions of the Contract. There is a mechanism for participants to request clarification of doubts and there are predefined processes on how to respond to them. Requests for clarification may be submitted, inter alia, in writing or through electronic means. Unlike the general public procurement regime which obliges contracting authorities to hold clarification meetings, PEMEX has a margin of discretion in relation to this matter. PEMEX may decide whether to carry out clarification meetings. Bidders may ask the contracting officials for technical explanations and propose amendments to the call for tender through clarification meetings when this has been specified by the tender terms.

PEMEX holds clarification meetings in accordance with the policies and guidelines for procurement. The clarification meetings are organised as follows:

1. The stage for formulation and clarification of doubts should be initiated after a reasonable period before the submission of proposals.
2. It is recommended that at the beginning of this stage the DCPA, in conjunction with the project manager, will reveal to the participants, the terms and conditions subject to a specific tendering procedure.
3. At a pre-qualification phase, clarification of doubts should be segmented to focus in the first instance on the terms and conditions of pre-qualification and not on the solicitation documents. Once this stage is finished, requests from qualified participants concerning the terms and conditions of the contract can be shared.
4. DCPA should secure throughout the contracting process and prior to the submission of proposals that changes to contractual terms are consistent and appropriate.
5. The clarifications from participants should be objective, concrete and clear, preferable indicating the motivation for amending the content. Furthermore, the answer from PEMEX should not refer to an individual participant.
6. DCPA verifies that any clarifications made by the project manager will not impact the contracting strategy and maintain the integrity and consistency of the contractual terms. It will also make sure that conditions do not favour any one particular brand or supplier.
7. If the result of the clarifications lead to the need to alter the contractual terms or the model contract, the DCPA with the support of the project manager, will document the reasons motivating the alterations.
8. Minutes should be taken for each of the clarification meetings and published on PEMEX's website (www.pemex.com/Paginas/default.aspx). The minutes of the clarification meetings include the date, time and venue of the meeting; the names of the participants; their questions and the explanations; and any modification to the call for tender made by PEMEX.

All clarifications that lead to modification of the Terms of Contract shall be reflected in the final version of the Terms of Contract.

There is no legal obligation for PEMEX to hold a minimum of one clarification meeting for public tendering. While the PEMEX Law and the associated procurement framework do not explicitly state a similar requirement, various provisions also make reference to clarification meetings being held. PEMEX assessment is based on the complexity and scope of the procurement when complying with that requirement. It is the procurement procedures that set the stage for the clarification of a tender (Open Competition and Restricted Invitation).

Issues are resolved in face-to-face meetings or by e-mail option, where the representative of the company sends its queries to the server Procura, which presides over the tendering procedures. PEMEX answer the queries in the same way they were received and publishes the answers on line.[1] Apart from the above, there are channels established by the SDRPC (Subdirección de Desarrollo y Relación con Proveedores y Contratistas), like the PEMEX PASS for suppliers to seek advice or request for general information about tenders. PEMEX has relied to a limited extent on electronic channels to correspond on contracts clarification. It was not until recently that PEMEX started using the Procura solution with SAP-Ariba procurement, where suppliers can submit their clarifications and receive answers.

The possibility that a potential provider is dissatisfied with clarification is reduced since several meetings of clarification can be held. Hence, they can rethink their questions and have a second chance to discuss matters with PEMEX officials. Apart from the above, if a contractor is not satisfied with the answer given by the convenor, the contractor can send a complaint to the Internal Audit of PEMEX. An internal control body is invited to all clarification meetings where it is allowed to interact and even communicate to the PEMEX officials.

Through the provision of faster and clearer clarifications, PEMEX could obtain various benefits, such as a higher level of competition, more innovative solutions being offered by suppliers, reduced efforts and time required in the solicitation process, as well as improved communication and relationship with its supply base.

Evaluating proposals in accordance with the rules established in the solicitation documents significantly impacts the integrity of procurement processes

Bid evaluation has been identified as a particularly vulnerable step of the procurement process.[2] The procurement laws and regulations to which PEMEX is subject require that solicitation documents contain specific criteria that will be used for the evaluation of the proposals and selection of the winning bidder. It is essential that these criteria be directly linked to the requirement, be as objective as possible and not favour a particular supplier. Furthermore, these criteria as well as other requirements for compliance must be clearly identified in the solicitation document, and the evaluation must entirely adhere to them (no other elements being considered). Doing so is critical to ensure clarity, preserve the integrity of the process, and maintain certainty and trust of the suppliers.

Concerns have been raised regarding breaches of that crucial principle within PEMEX, as the evaluations are not always held in accordance with the criteria and requirements specified in the solicitations. According to reports by CORP (Corporativo), PEP (Exploracion y Produccion), PPQ (Petroquímica), REF (Refinación) and PGPB, this issue appears to be significant in PEMEX. The rate of claims (*inconformidades)* against the organisation and its subsidiaries over the period 2007 to 2010 was 7%, which was considered quite high at that time compared to other federal entities (5%), and rising to 14% of the number of procedures in PEP.[3] Recent numbers indicate a slight decrease has occurred with rate claims at 6% for the period 2014-15, which could be because of the reduction in tendering processes. However, PEP continues to have the largest number of claims against them, with approximately 16% of those considered to be founded. Most of these claims (more than 80%) are linked to the technical evaluation and the selection of the winning bid (see Figure 12.1).

Figure 12.1. **Proportion of claims *(inconformidades)* for breaches during the evaluation phase against PEMEX and its subsidiaries, 2014-15**

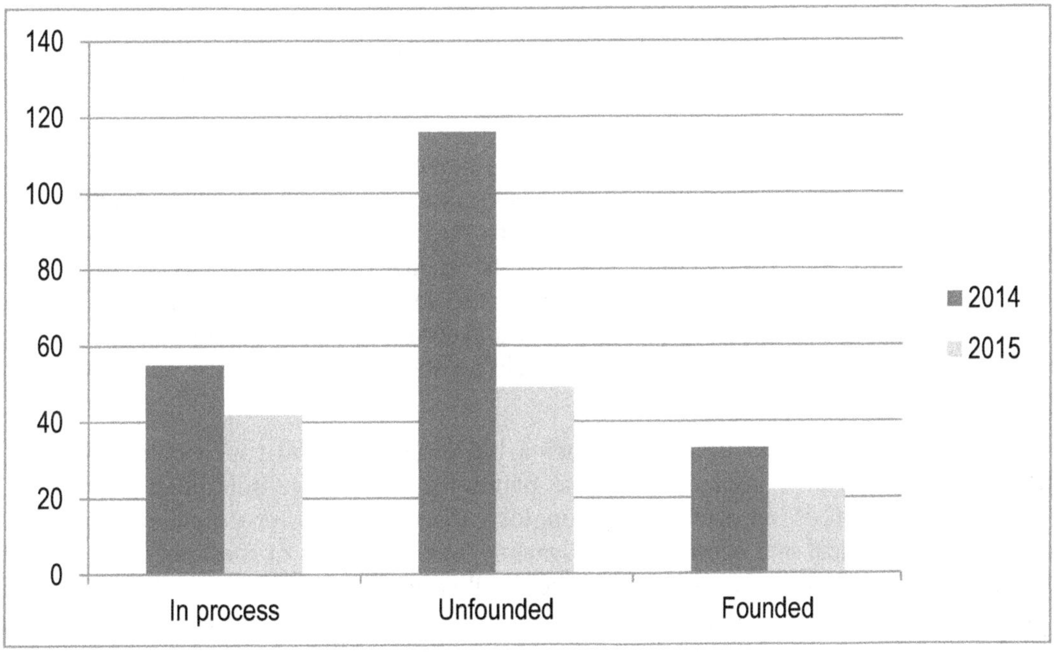

Source: Based on information provided by PEMEX.

Such occurrences significantly compromise the integrity of the procurement system and prevent the organisation from meeting its needs under the best conditions. They also create legal risks for the organisation and the possibility of a reduction of its supply base, suppliers refraining to submit a proposal under a system they perceive as "fixed" or "tainted".

For some contracts (such as high-value contracts), this process could also take the form of an *ex ante* audit prior to issuance of the decision. Furthermore, all evaluators sign their evaluation reports (technical, economic and commercial), so the final bid evaluations are collected in a final document that recounts the chronology of the procurement procedure, including assessments from start to finish. Prior to the awarding of a contract, a process of verification of the report is carried out jointly by those involved in the evaluation process: Procurement Management, Cost Engineering Management and Market Analysis and the project manager. This indicates that there is a review mechanism in place where technical evaluation is carried out prior to the issuance of the decision (*fallo*) to determine any divergence from the established process and criteria.

Automated systems, such as the Integral Technology Platform, could provide opportunities to increase compliance with the established solicitation rules. The use of automated systems facilitates the exchange of information, improves process efficiency and increases transparency, but compliance with the rules established in the tendering process depends entirely on the participants and the evaluators.

Evaluation mechanisms can stimulate innovation among suppliers

The binary method is linked to other awarding criteria such as points and percentages, net present value, cost benefit, etc. set out in contractual terms. It is for the convener to evaluate the tender proposals in detail under the criteria and requirements established in the tendering documents by analysts participating in the preparation, review and approval of the evaluation results of the legal, technical, and economic proposals of the participant's evaluations. Ensuring compliance with those requirements and specifications is the work of the legal representative of PEMEX for the outcome of an evaluation.

The DCPA has developed several documents that constitute a guide for the use of the method of binary evaluation itself as the award criteria, among which is the virtual course entitled, "Methods of Evaluation of Proposals" (by the designation receiving in the previous legal system, with the consideration that they be updated to the more recent regulatory framework), in which different criteria and cases are described, procedures for application, and how it is possible to develop precise criteria according to each situation. Furthermore, the DCPA has instructed that courses will be held for staff regarding the use and application of such criteria.

The DCPA declares in writing whether a bid is unsuccessful (open competition) or successful (in restricted invitation), to the participants that have submitted a proposal. Failure or allocation of bid contains a chronological review of the procurement procedure, the result of technical and economic assessments, and the result of the application of the award criteria, the name of awardees, and the deadline for the formalisation of the contract. The result of the tender will be announced through the Internet portal area, Procurement and Supply, and include only the name or names of bidders and the contract amount.

PEMEX provides information about what will be assessed, what needs to be presented and how they are going to determine the winner. It is a customised requirement and in the hands of each specific procurement area to determine. The first part of the evaluation process is the technical assessment, which is the responsibility of the project manager. The evaluation can be carried out by a group of technicians; sometimes up to ten people are working on the assessment. However, the project manager is responsible for the technical evaluation. The purpose of this process is, among others, to reduce the number of contractors in the process before the economic or legal assessment takes place. The technical evaluation is based on the binary approach; there is no comparative assessment of the bidders carried out. There are additional challenges to the technical specifications because of the binary approach. There is a need for high-level capacity among employees when using the binary approach as this does not incentivise companies to come up with new solutions during the bidding approach. By using the binary system, PEMEX might be deterring more innovative companies (this is further discussed in Chapter 11). The economic evaluation is based on prices of the bids and in some cases the total cost of ownership. The analysis has to be signed by the procurement division.

PEMEX has mainly used the lowest price criteria for public works and points and percentages for service contracts. The lowest price method is mainly used during the second stage, leading to the rejection of some contractors scoring higher for the overall assessment if their offer is not the lowest. The approach to this method needs to be re-evaluated; if PEMEX does not adhere to the results of their own evaluations, this can undermine the integrity of whole process. However, with the change in regulation there is an intention to use other methods in the future. In the current system, the evaluation criteria used is the method of binary evaluation; this on the basis of Article 25 of the General Provisions of Contract for Petróleos Mexicanos and Subsidiary Companies. The regulatory framework requires PEMEX to use the binary approach in the awarding process. The approach is operationalised in two phases, the first using solely mandatory requirements to narrow the field of bidders. The second stage can include several awarding criteria. Article 57 indicates that procurement and supply activities, during the procurement process and execution of contracts, is subject to the following:

> "D) Procurement procedures and supervision of the execution of the contracts will be performed by trained and qualified personnel in order to promote the right decision making. Technical evaluations are the responsibility of the project manager and may be assisted by trained and qualified personnel.
>
> n) Technical and economic evaluations will be conducted in adherence to the provisions of the contractual terms and considering the provisions of the Operational Guidelines for Procurement and Supply, to ensure fairness between suppliers or contractors and the best conditions for PEMEX. The economic evaluations must verify that the price stated in the proposals is commensurate with the quality, delivery conditions and deadlines. ..."

The number of employees participating in the evaluation phase depends on the type of procurement (goods, services, works, etc.) as well as its complexity. For public works it can be various specialists, such as civil, structural, process, piping, etc., that require a larger team to conduct evaluations. The documentation of evaluations is carried out in accordance with the General Provisions for Contracting of PEMEX. Article 26 states that the technical evaluation of the proposals made by the project manager and the economic assessment carried out by the management of Procurement and Supply shall be made in writing:

- The result of the evaluation of financial and commercial legal aspects, shall be entered in a document entitled, "Outcome of the Commercial Evaluation", which will be signed by an employee of the DCPA.
- The result of the technical evaluation shall be recorded in a document called "Technical Evaluation Results", which will be signed by the project manager.
- The result of the economic evaluation shall be recorded in a document entitled, "Economic Assessment Results", which will be signed by the employee appointed by the DCPA.

A standstill period can diminish the impact of potential ineffectiveness claims

A standstill period should provide PEMEX with a short pause between the point when the contract award decision is notified to bidders, and the final contract conclusion, during which time suppliers can challenge the decision. Before the PEMEX reforms, the company was limited under the procurement legislation due to the fact that the obligations of both parties became effective at the moment of the award (*fallo*) rather than at the time of signature of the contract. With the new legislation, there are no legal obligations that limit the possibility of having a standstill period in place, between the date bidders are notified of the contract award decision and the date it can enter into the contract. The terms for any standstill period is required to be stated in the documentation for the formalisation of the contract, which is part of the contractual terms, the date on which the supplier or contractor is awarded the contract is established. Despite being allowed the flexibility of a standstill period, PEMEX tends not to take advantage of that possibility.

PEMEX could consider implementing a minimum standstill period between the date bidders are notified of the contract award decision and the date it can enter into the contract. This practice promotes fairness and integrity of the procedure by providing dedicated and sufficient time for bidders to use existing remedies and permitting the suspension and annulment of the decision at a stage where the infringement can still be rectified or its impacts minimised.

Standstill periods are currently implemented in many countries. PEMEX should consider implementing it for a minimum of 6 working days, i.e. the period available to bidders to raise claims against the award (*fallo*), and a maximum of 15 calendar days, the maximum time allowed by law to sign and issue the contract when not otherwise specified in the solicitation document. The implementation of the standstill period in the United Kingdom is presented in Box 12.3.

Box 12.3. The use of a standstill period in the United Kingdom

Main steps to take

1. Send Award Decision Notice to all tenderers and candidates right away by the fastest means possible.
2. Award Decision Notice should include:
   - award criteria
   - reasons for the decision, including:
     - characteristics and relative advantages of the successful tender
     - the scores of: the winner; and the recipient of the notice
     - any reasons why the recipient did not meet the technical specification.
   - the name of the party to be awarded the contract
   - a precise statement of when the standstill period is expected to end, including any reasons that it may not end when envisaged.
3. Duration of standstill:
   - Minimum 10 calendar days, when notice sent electronically.
   - When sent by other means:
     - 15 days from day of sending; or
     - 10 days from day of receipt.
   - Standstill must end on a working day.

Source: Crown Commercial Service (2015), "The Public Contracts Regulations 2015", www.gov.uk/government/uploads/system/uploads/attachment_data/file/417945/Guidance_on_Standstill.pdf.

Setting up a formal mechanism for debriefing

PEMEX has no regulatory framework for debriefing bidders. There are also no procedures for debriefing meetings with suppliers as such. In general, the answers provided by PEMEX to contractors are in writing, but may in some cases be oral at the request of participants. However, clarifications will be written for general knowledge of the participants and published on the PEMEX website. At this time, PEMEX's procurement units are usually strictly adhering to the minimum requirement of the law and solely provide in writing the elements of non-compliance. PEMEX tends to hold a public event when a decision is made to disclose information about the procurement process and provide feedback. There is nothing in the regulatory framework that states that PEMEX is obliged to provide information on non-compliance. But companies can approach PEMEX officials and ask about issues or request feedback. There are no one-on-one meetings with suppliers for debriefing.

Unsuccessful tenderers may want to know why their tender failed. The amount of information that can be conveyed will vary according to the circumstances of the particular contract, but PEMEX could give a broad indication of the reasons and, on cost and where they ranked in the tender list. This culture of limiting the feedback to the bidders is evidenced by the current practice of the unit in PEMEX Exploration and Production to provide verbal debriefing, which has raised concerns in other PEMEX entities.

The OECD Secretariat recognises verbal debriefing as a good practice commonly used in many OECD countries to engage with the market and expand the supply base. Implementation of adequate debriefing with the suppliers provides a valuable opportunity for both parties to benefit from the process. Verbal debriefings can improve the relationship with suppliers and the quality of their offers while providing valuable insight to the organisation. However, verbal debriefings must be used judiciously and under a clear framework in order to reduce any associated risks and costs. A debriefing can also be made available to the successful bidder as a first step in establishing a sound working relationship and setting a precedent for a constructive feedback. In order to increase the benefits of such debriefings while mitigating any potential risks, PEMEX should develop guidelines creating a clear framework for that activity. It is recommended that certain generic content be considered in its development (see Box 12.4).

Box 12.4. The benefits of debriefing

Debriefing is beneficial to bidders by:

a. helping them to rethink their approach in order to make future bids more successful

b. offering targeted guidance to new or smaller companies to improve their chances of doing business in the public sector

c. providing reassurance about the process and their contribution or role (if not the actual result)

d. providing a better understanding of what differentiates public sector procurement from private procurement.

That dialogue can also assist PEMEX by:

a. identifying ways to improve subsequent solicitation processes, including the associated communications

b. making sure best practice and guidance is updated to reflect any relevant issues that have been highlighted

Box 12.4. The benefits of debriefing *(continued)*

c. encouraging better bids from those suppliers in the future

d. getting a better understanding of how that segment of the market thinks, enhancing the organisation's market intelligence

e. helping establish a reputation as a fair, open and ethical buyer with whom suppliers will want to do business in the future

f. potentially reducing the number of challenges.

Source: United Kingdom Office of Government Commerce (2003), "Supplier Debriefing".

Proposals for action

PEMEX is constantly working towards improving the process for evaluations of bids. Part of that work has been improvements to the process of clarifying bids and the incorporation of an Audit Module House. Despite improvements, issues can be raised about how PEMEX continuously uses the binary approach for the technical assessments of bids. Furthermore, PEMEX has been relatively slow in incorporating new techniques such as debriefing of suppliers or applying standstill periods. In order to improve the transparency and integrity of its solicitation and contract award process, as well as the efficiency and value of its procurement function, PEMEX could consider the following proposals for action:

- Enhance the adequacy, clarity and quality of the solicitation documents and requirement specifications by implementing supporting tools and documents (such as checklists, best practices, templates and a regularly updated catalogue of authorised goods) as well as necessary training.
- Further improve project planning and tenders. Despite having taken steps to improve the clarification process, the number of suppliers requesting such meetings and the number of questions put to PEMEX concerning tender are significant cause for concern about the clarity of projects and the need for better planning and writing of tenders.
- Put in place measures to assess the quality of all technical specifications developed, given a high risk of corruption in the development of technical specifications.
- Consider revising the requirements at the pre-qualification level. The requirements at the pre-qualification level can be too strict, leading to certain companies being prematurely excluded from the procurement process. Certain requirements for certification from other countries are likely to exclude Mexican contractors participating in tenders.
- Look more at the lifecycle cost in the economic assessment and do not only apply the lowest cost-win model.
- Respect the time needed for preparing proposals; asking for quotes with fixed prices with no adjustment in prices can lead to higher offers. It is important to include adjustment clauses in the contracts.

- Ensure that clear and complete answers are provided to all valid questions raised by potential bidders.
- Provide answers electronically via the PEMEX website, to the extent permitted by the legislation, and hold clarification meetings only to the extent necessary or required by law.
- Improve the efficiency and adequacy of the evaluation and selection process by implementing a mandatory review process for all solicitations, taking into account the value and risk of the requirements. For that purpose, a dedicated quality assurance unit could be created and used for larger or more sensitive requirements.
- Mandate that solicitation documents are modified immediately after each clarification meeting to reflect changes agreed upon. These should be issued with the meeting minutes.
- Require all technical evaluators to sign an "Evaluation Code of Conduct", clearly spelling out their obligations, the evaluation process to be followed, and the criteria to be considered.
- Create a clear framework, as well as checks and balances for the evaluation of proposals and determination of the winning bidder through the automatisation of various associated activities.
- Implement a mandatory standstill period of a minimum of 6 working days and a maximum of 15 calendar days between the date bidders are notified of the contract award decision and the date of entry into the contract, so as to allow sufficient time for bidders to exercise available remedies and challenge the decision.
- Hold verbal debriefings (either by telephone or face to face), making them part of the company's formal communication policy. PEMEX should support this activity with clear guidelines that provide a structured framework, and clarify elements such as when and where debriefings take place, what information can and cannot be provided, and the standard discussion structure to be followed.

Notes

1. The answers are published at http://www.pemex.com/procura/procedimientos-de-contratacion/concursosabiertos/Paginas/default.aspx
2. This was highlighted, among others, in the discussions at the OECD Symposium: Mapping out Good Practices for Integrity and Corruption Resistance in Public Procurement and the back-to-back Global Forum, November 2006.
3. Excessive or frivolous claims would not explain the higher rate observed for PEMEX, the same percentage of its claims having been ruled valid (28%) than the average for all federal Mexican entities.

References

Crown Commercial Service (2015), "The Public Contracts Regulations 2015", www.gov.uk/government/uploads/system/uploads/attachment_data/file/417945/Guidance_on_Standstill.pdf.

OECD (2015), "Recommendation of the Council on Public Procurement", www.oecd.org/corruption/recommendation-on-public-procurement.htm.

OECD (2009), *OECD Principles for Integrity in Public Procurement*, OECD Publishing, Paris, http://dx.doi.org/10.1787/9789264056527-en.

PEMEX (2014), "Encuesta Externa de Percepción de Transparencia de Procura y Abastecimiento de Bienes y Servicios" (External Survey on Perceptions of Transparency in Procurement and Supply of Goods and Services).

United Kingdom Office of Government Commerce (2003), "Supplier debriefing".

Chapter 13

Procurement data and performance management systems: Towards evidence-based decision making in Petróleos Mexicanos' public procurement

This chapter provides an overview of the evaluation process of the procurement function and the indicators being considered in the evaluation methodology, although its design is still incomplete. An adequate monitoring of supplier performance is also critical to facilitate the effectiveness of procurement strategies, allowing for the anticipation, identification, and correction of failures before relationships with suppliers suffer and before the optimal use of resources is jeopardised. This chapter analyses the strategies and methodologies used by Petróleos Mexicanos (PEMEX) to monitor the performance of its suppliers and suggests specific actions to use previous performance as an award criterion. Finally, this chapter puts forward proposals for action in order to upgrade the evaluation of PEMEX's procurement function and make the assessment and monitoring of suppliers' performance more systematic.

Procurement data

The evaluation process of the procurement function, which measures efficiency and costs, was in the definition and design stages at the moment of the OECD fact-finding mission. The definition of the Evaluation Model of Procurement 2.0 (Modelo de Evaluación de Procura 2.0) anticipated mechanisms to generate and consolidate data for the different components needed for the operative, tactic, and strategic dimensions (see Figure 13.1). The Unit for the Management and Evaluation of the Business Model (Gerencia de Gestión y Evaluación del Modelo de Negocio) is the one responsible for developing and implementing the evaluation model.

Figure 13.1. **Data flow for the operative, tactic, and strategic dimensions of PEMEX**

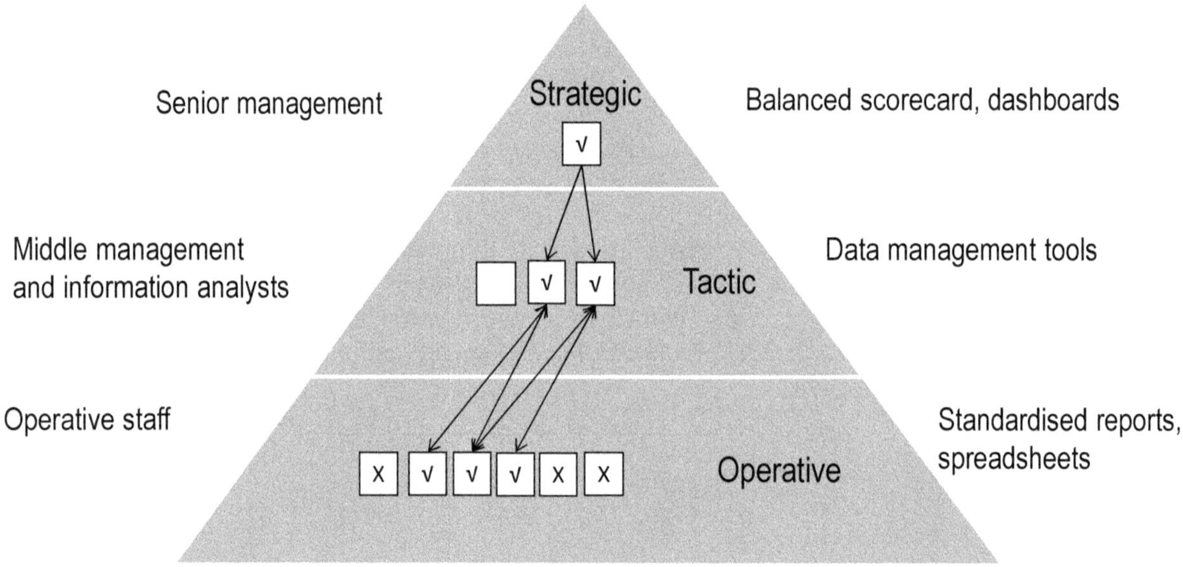

Source: Information provided by PEMEX.

Petróleos Mexicanos (PEMEX) aims to develop a robust evaluation model allowing for a comprehensive assessment of the Business Model for Procurement and Supply, with timely and reliable information to support decision making and continuous improvement. The development of the evaluation model requires the following:

- reviewing the set of reports, management and evaluation indicators considering the new regulatory and organisational frameworks
- strengthening the processes to verify the consistency, integrity, and quality of information
- analysing the sources of reports and the processes to generate indicators to be incorporated to the corporative evaluation scheme
- updating criteria for data extraction and management, as well as to produce reports and indicators
- systematising processes for data analysis and benchmarking
- reviewing current indicators.

Currently, the Corporate Directorate for Procurement and Supply (Dirección Corporativa de Procura y Abastecimiento, or DCPA) is in a process of review of corporative indicators, as well as good practices, to determine which ones will be incorporated into the evaluation model. The model will include the following:

- Metrics: Generic reports to measure an activity, process, or outcome
- Key performance indicators (KPIs): Indicators to measure progress in critical objectives for the company, which should be specific, measurable, realistic, relevant, and time-based
- Baseline: Inputs for KPIs, which support the calculation of metrics.

DCPA has also developed some dashboards to monitor procurement performance, which allow senior management to have a wide perspective. These dashboards are under review, but the indicators they provide are illustrative of the elements that will constitute the evaluation model, among others:

- Acquisitions annual programme: It provides the amount of the annual programme divided into investment and operations.
- Progress of the annual programme: It illustrates progress in compliance with the acquisitions programme in relation to the estimated amount.
- Status of order requests: It shows information on order requests by stage of the procurement process.
- Reconsideration requests (*recursos de reconsideración,* or RR): It provides the number of RRs received per month.[1]
- Uncontested procedures (*procedimientos desiertos*): It illustrates the number of uncontested tender procedures in relation to the total number of procedures organised per month.
- Contracts and suppliers (business volume): It shows the volume of acquisitions according to the Catalogue to Classify Acquisitions and Works (Catálogo de Clasificación de Adquisiciones y Obra) and by supplier.
- Compliance with procurement times: It compares the real-time length of procurement procedures in relation to a standard and identifies deviations to address opportunity areas. It illustrates the procedures carried out on time by type (i.e. direct award, restricted invitation and public tender). This indicator is measured by month. Currently, DCPA is developing the standard time against which each area will be measured.
- Saving strategies: It calculates the amounts saved by each strategy implemented.
- Best practices: It indicates the use and leverage of best practices for procurement and supply, such as reverse auctions, pre-qualification of suppliers, negotiation, maximum reference prices, cost-benefit, net present value, points and percentages, and annual equivalent cost.
- SME participation: It provides the total amount of purchases to small and medium-sized enterprises (SMEs).
- Order requests status (SolPeds): It illustrates the status of order requests, whether they are with the user area, DCPA, or under a contract already.

In terms of engagement with suppliers, the following indicators are used:

- Service time: It measures the time taken to address requests and identify gaps to be taken care of to improve the procedures.
- Addressed requests: It illustrates progress in addressing suppliers' requests and allows for taking corrective action.
- Meetings organised: It focuses on high relevance suppliers and measures meetings organised in relation to meetings requested.
- Partner satisfaction: It evaluates the service provided by PEMEX staff through a customer service survey.

Box 13.1 sets out the benefits expected from the development of this evaluation model.

Box 13.1. **Benefits expected from the Evaluation Model of Procurement 2.0**

- Strategic vision: Harmonised vision of PEMEX's results, allowing the company to make better decisions.
- Company alignment: Having common objectives and goals in the different departments participating in the supply processes to ensure fulfilling the procurement strategy.
- Consolidation of efforts: Consolidating and sharing actions and necessary resources to achieve PEMEX's objectives.
- Results orientation: Providing support for effective and objective decision making.

Source: Information provided by PEMEX.

All indicators are to measure performance through time and consider the possibility of comparisons to analyse differences leading to decision making. However, the frequency in which they will be measured may vary and is still to be determined.

DCPA launched a pilot to measure efficiency in the procurement process and customer satisfaction by calculating the time taken in each stage of procurement procedures, based on a timeline designed for category implementation. A generic template in the SAPRE (Solución de arranque para la procura estratégica) system includes information on stages, tasks, responsible unit, and time for each activity. For example, for the stage "executing the procurement procedure", in the case of open tender, the activities measured are: publication of the tender, pre-qualification, technical/economic/legal clarification meetings, technical/economic/legal evaluations, negotiation, award decision, contract award, and evaluation of the process. The estimated time length for each activity is then measured against a standard to be defined by DCPA, considering the applicable regulations, and as established in the calls for tender.

The SAPRE system also displays information on expenditure by contract, invoice, and supplier, category analysis, supplier performance, market research comparing prices and commercial terms, business scenarios, model articles for contracts, and referential agreements.

As concluded in Chapter 10, it will be important to ensure that procurement data is collected in a centralised manner that eliminates the need for manual transmission and entry of statistics to fulfil reporting requirements. An important constraint in PEMEX data management is that currently it is carried out through different electronic platforms that do not always communicate with each other. Building on the upgraded centralised procurement data system under development, PEMEX will be able to develop procurement metrics and improve the ones it is envisioning for the evaluation model.

In addition to the previous indicators, DCPA also carries out surveys to get to know the opinions of participants on the transparency of the procurement processes and identify areas of opportunity. These surveys are applied during the opening of biddings. PEMEX is currently working to develop the alternative to apply the survey through electronic means. Perception surveys are applied both internally and externally, and results are reported to PEMEX's Commission for Sectorial Co-ordination of the Procurement Macro-function for Transparency and Anti-Corruption (Comisión de Coordinación Sectorial de la Macrofunción de Adquisiciones para la Transparencia y el Combate a la Corrupción), whose members include representatives from business chambers and associations and PEMEX staff linked to procurement activities (Box 13.2).

Box 13.2. Results from surveys applied to suppliers by PEMEX

During 2014, PEMEX issued the External Survey on Perceptions of Transparency in Procurement and Supply of Goods and Services (Encuesta Externa de Percepción de Transparencia de Procura y Abastecimiento de Bienes y Servicios 2014) to measure the satisfaction of suppliers and contractors regarding integrity and equity in PEMEX's procurement processes. Some 2 800 surveys were collected from companies of all sizes (see the table below), identifying opportunities for improvement mainly in technical specifications, participation requirements, the reasons to terminate contracts and payment procedures.

Size of the company	Number of surveys collected
Micro	180
Small	2 350
Medium	187
Large	83

Source: Information provided by PEMEX.

Performance monitoring mechanisms for PEMEX suppliers

Poor performance by suppliers can have strong negative impacts in the efficiency of operations and the ability of the company to meet its objectives. No matter how well a contract was planned or drafted, it will only add value to the extent that suppliers actually comply with what they are required to do. An adequate monitoring of supplier performance is therefore critical to facilitate the effectiveness of procurement strategies, allowing for the anticipation, identification, and correction of failures before relationships with suppliers suffer and before the optimal use of resources is jeopardised. Indeed, supplier performance management strategies can lead to several benefits, such as the following:

- Ensuring adequate supply: Proactive management of supplier performance diminishes the risks of lack of inventories, ensuring the right quantity and quality of supply of products and services at the right moment and the right time.

- Process efficiency: Workloads are streamlined and internal operation costs are reduced by managing supplier performance and avoiding lack of inventories.
- Customer service: Good performance by suppliers is a prerequisite for high-quality customer service and increases satisfaction and trust by internal and external clients.
- Risk control: Monitoring supplier performance offers information on trends and emerging issues, which means measures can be taken to avoid or mitigate unplanned, unexpected, and potentially dangerous supply problems (see the case of targeted interventions by BP in Box 13.3).
- Supplier relationships: An effective and systematic supplier performance management process strengthens the working relationship and communications with suppliers, increases mutual trust and understanding, minimises the risk of conflicts, and potentially increases the supply capacity.

Box 13.3. BP's approach to supplier performance management

In 2015, 52% of the 353 million hours worked by BP were carried out by contractors (52% in 2014 and 54% in 2013). BP focuses on developing deeper, longer-term relationships with selected contractors. This helps to take advantage of economies of scale and manage risks. BP seeks to set clear and consistent expectations of its contractors. Its standard model contracts include health, safety, security, and environmental requirements. Bridging documents are necessary in some cases to define how safety management systems and those of contractors will co-exist effectively.

Contracts involving work that could result in the most serious risks, according to their potential impact and probability, demand the highest scrutiny. The selection process for these contractors includes pre-contract quality, technical and health, safety, security, and environmental audits that are carried out on a risk-prioritised basis. Current work includes plans that address health, safety and environmental management, contractor self-verification, BP oversight, key performance measures, and joint performance review meetings.

BP also holds workshops with senior executives from the company and its suppliers to provide opportunities for engagement. For example, in 2015 BP hosted a forum for upstream strategic suppliers, where discussions focused on how to effectively collaborate in areas such as operational safety, increased efficiency in a lower oil price environment, and safe and reliable operations.

BP's approach is to work collaboratively with contractors in a way that seeks to avoid the need for intervention. Where contractors do not meet requirements, they may be put on a performance improvement plan. For example, following poor performance in key areas, BP placed an engineering contractor on a performance improvement plan until clear improvement was observed. During this time, BP awarded no additional contract work and met regularly with the contractor in order to measure progress. In some instances, BP will dismiss contractors that do not meet requirements or are unable to demonstrate improved performance.

Source: BP (n.d.), "Working with contractors, suppliers and partners" webpage, www.bp.com/en/global/corporate/sustainability/how-we-operate/working-with-contractors-suppliers-and-partners.html (accessed 10 August 2016).

According to Article 85 of the PEMEX Law, the company and its subsidiaries should develop a system with public information about their suppliers and contractors, which should be periodically updated and contain information for the last five years on contracts and compliance with them, including, if any, extensions of time and adjustments in amounts.[2] This platform is called the System of Public Information on Suppliers and

Contractors (Sistema de Información Pública de Proveedores y Contratistas, or SIPPC), which among other things, should include the following items:

- Information on suppliers and contractors: Nationality, address, activities, and legal status.
- Information on contracts with suppliers and their performance: Compliance with timeline, quality of the goods or works, and sanctions imposed on the supplier, if any.
- Compliance with environmental, industrial security, and labour regulations.
- Certifications of compliance with technical and quality management norms.
- Results from evaluations applied on suppliers and contractors by specialised companies.

The information collected from suppliers and contractors is communicated externally via the SIPPC itself and internally via the comprehensive tool for supplier information (Herramienta Integral de Información de Proveedores, or HIIP).[3] Registration in the SIPPC cannot be a requirement for participation in tenders. The system is managed by DCPA, but it is PEMEX's Board that regulates its operation and the information to be collected. However, information collected through the SIPPC is not used for pre-qualification purposes. The HIIP, on the contrary, provides some elements for the purchasing units to determine supplier participation, although not for a comprehensive pre-qualification. Pre-qualification is indeed common in the energy industry (see Box 13.4 on the case of Shell).

Box 13.4. The Shell Supplier Qualification System (SQS)

The Shell Supplier Qualification System (SQS) was introduced in January 2012 to support a common approach to supplier pre-qualification across the Shell Group. SQS streamlines the pre-qualification process by gathering standard supplier data and carrying out detailed pre-qualification assessments in line with Shell's requirements. SQS is managed by Achilles on Shell's behalf. Registration in SQS enables suppliers to:

- Complete the required pre-qualification process: If the supplier is being considered for a potential contract or is renewing a current contract with Shell, it will be asked to register in SQS. Once the supplier provides the required details in SQS, Achilles will complete the necessary pre-qualification assessments and will publish the outcome in SQS. The results of completed assessments will then become available to the Contracting and Procurement specialist who invited the supplier to register. However, registration in SQS does not guarantee any business with Shell.
- Keep pre-qualification results valid for three years: Once registration in SQS is complete, details and the outcome of assessments will remain valid and visible to Shell Contracting and Procurement specialists for three years.
- Demonstrate compliance with the Shell Supplier Principles: The results of the completed pre-qualification assessments will enable Contracting and Procurement specialists to ensure the supplier adheres to the core requirements set out in the Shell Supplier Principles.
- Identify gaps and improve business performance: If the supplier is required to complete a more detailed assessment in the area of health and safety and/or labour rights, Achilles, as an independent party, will perform the assessments and provide detailed feedback on the supplier's policies in these areas. This feedback enables it to identify gaps and drive further business improvements.

SQS provides critical intelligence and important insights into Shell's supply base and delivers a common approach to supplier pre-qualification.

Source: Shell (n.d.), "Supplier Qualification System", www.shell.com/business-customers/shell-for-suppliers/qualify-as-a-supplier-to-shell/_jcr_content/par/textimage_1243601949.stream/1447247715709/57dc82b8dd6ca544a447fccfc5015086a988f1df1bd6446d90194d30cc990587/supplier-qualification-system.pdf (accessed 10 August 2016).

There are several opportunities for improvement regarding the SIPPC. First, as of August 2016, the SIPPC was not really a system but rather an Excel spreadsheet. Second, as illustrated in Tables 13.1 and 13.2, the data on suppliers and contracts is notably incomplete. One-third of suppliers had no recorded information on certificates, while 98% of contracts had no information on sanctions and performance. There are mainly two reasons why information is incomplete: 1) given that the registration in SIPPC is not mandatory, it is difficult to collect the relevant information, and 2) during 2015 most contracts were subscribed before the new regulations entered into force illustrating purchasing units about the importance of registering suppliers in the SIPPC. For SIPPC to be a useful tool, on the one hand, it should provide complete and accurate information, and on the other hand, facilitate interoperability with other electronic platforms used by PEMEX, something which cannot be achieved through an Excel spreadsheet.

Table 13.1. **Percentage of suppliers with no data available in SIPPC**

	Information on suppliers		
	Total companies	Companies with no information recorded	%
Environmental certificate	199	64	32
Labour responsibility certificate		58	29
Industrial security certificate		65	33
Technical norms certificate		76	38
Quality assurance certificate		66	33
Average		66	33

Source: PEMEX (2015), "Sistema de información pública de proveedores y contratistas", www.pemex.com/procura/relacion-con-proveedores/Paginas/info-proveedores-contratistas.aspx (accessed 3 August 2016).

Table 13.2. **Percentage of contracts with no data available in SIPPC, 2016**

	Information on contracts		
	Total contracts	Contracts with no information recorded	%
Sanctions	1 606	1 606	100
Delivery performance		1 606	100
Qualitative performance		1 491	93
Average		1 568	98

Source: PEMEX (2015), "Sistema de información pública de proveedores y contratistas", www.pemex.com/procura/relacion-con-proveedores/Paginas/info-proveedores-contratistas.aspx (accessed 3 August 2016).

Information on delivery performance could be useful, for example, to assess whether contracts with foreign companies have a notably different performance record from the ones with national companies. If this were the case, PEMEX could find out the underlying reasons and take measures to correct the problem by, for instance, adjusting the procurement strategy or managing supplier performance with different tools. Such information would also be useful for PEMEX to analyse the enforcement of sanctions.

A robust system of supplier performance evaluation would allow for managing risks according to the historic performance of suppliers and even provide incentives for good performance. Indeed, the General Guidelines for Procurement and Supply (Lineamientos Generales de Procura y Abastecimiento), Section VIII.6.3., establish that suppliers could be exempted from the requirement of providing guarantees to ensure compliance with contractual duties, considering the risk policies dictated by the Risk Committee of PEMEX Board. The same idea is ratified by the Policies and Guidelines for Procurement and Supply

(Políticas y Lineamientos para Procura y Abastecimiento) in Section II.13. Likewise, PEMEX could introduce the possibility of paying incentives when the company realises savings due to reduced time in the completion of works or when it benefits from innovations or new technologies provided by suppliers. On the contrary, PEMEX could use information on poor historic performance to avoid those suppliers getting more contracts and, particularly, to avoid inviting them to restricted tenders or consider them for direct awards.

According to PEMEX, supplier performance is measured on a permanent basis, not only through the indicators in SIPPC, but also through performance surveys applied to project managers in the different business units of PEMEX. Depending on the contract characteristics, the evaluation can take place at its completion, in the case of short-term contracts, or periodically in the cases of medium or long-term contracts. In some cases, meetings could be organised to define and implement corrective and preventive actions, such as audits.

In addition, PEMEX Procurement International, Inc. (PPI), which is the international branch of PEMEX procurement that provides comprehensive management solutions for the supply chain of imported goods and services, carries out an evaluation every four months for each supplier who has participated in any procurement activities with PEMEX. The evaluation follows specific criteria, such as best price, on-time delivery (i.e. compliance with delivery time), quality (i.e. successful inspections against rejections, including claims submitted by customers), and customer service (i.e. responsiveness and correctness of information). Each of these criteria is assigned a weight, which combined can produce a maximum possible score of 100%. Suppliers with a score of 80% or above qualify for consideration in bids and other purchasing processes that PEMEX and its subsidiaries carry out through the services provided by PPI. However, the results of these evaluations carried out by PPI could not be found in its website (http://pemexprocurement.com, consulted on 3 August 2016).

PEMEX (and PPI) could consider a Pareto strategy to manage supplier performance. For example, an analysis of contracts and spending would identify critical suppliers (i.e. those with the highest amounts of sales to PEMEX or those who supply important materials or equipment), whose performance is decisive for the efficiency of PEMEX operations. A survey of 23 companies in the oil industry in 2010 indicated that they usually have a high level of concentration of suppliers; on average 4.6% of suppliers represent 80% of total procurement costs. Likewise, the survey indicated a trend towards greater concentration: More than half of those surveyed reported a higher concentration of suppliers, while 39% reported a decrease relative to a previous report. More importantly, 68% of the surveyed companies had established programmes to manage relationships with suppliers (Table 13.3).

Table 13.3. **Supplier concentration and performance management in selected companies of the oil industry, 2010**

	Average	Minimum	Maximum	Median	Average of previous report
Percentage of active suppliers that concentrate 80% of total procurement expenditure	4.64	1.01	13.14	3.79	3.74
Percentage of companies in which the supplier base decreased	54.55		-		38.89
Percentage of companies with an established programme to manage supplier relationships	68.18		-		68.75

Surveyed companies include Aera Energy LLC, Alyeska Pipeline Service Company, BHP Billiton Petroleum (Americas) Inc., BP plc, Chevron Corporation, Ecopetrol, El Paso Corporation, EnCana Corporation, Eni S.p.A., Exxonmobil Global Services Company, Hess Corporation, Nabors Industries Ltd., National Cooperative Refinery Association (NCRA), Nexen Inc., Plains All American Pipeline L.P., Pride International Inc., Repsol YPF, Sasol Limited, Shell International, Statoil ASA, Tesoro Companies Inc., and TransCanada Pipelines Ltd.

Source: Adapted from CAPS Research (2010), *2010 Supply Management Performance Benchmarking Report – Petroleum Industry*, jointly sponsored by the Institute for Supply Management and J.P. Cary School of Business, Arizona State University.

The cycle of performance management and its corresponding strategy

Suppliers' performance management is usually considered an *ex post* activity, meaning that it is carried out after a contract is awarded. However, special attention should be paid at the initial development stage since it is in this phase that the basis for performance assessment and communication are set and, therefore, it is at this moment when efficiency and benefits are determined, as well as costs and inherent risks.

Adequate planning, the framework for implementation, and the successive activities are indispensable for a supplier performance management programme to maximise its benefits for PEMEX. Likewise, the programme should be communicated and understood by the relevant stakeholders (i.e. internal clients, procurement officials, senior management, and suppliers) well before it is actually used in a call for tender or a contract. Indeed, supplier performance management is a cycle of activities that starts from strategic design and runs through to evaluation (see Figure 13.2).

Figure 13.2. **The cycle of supplier performance management**

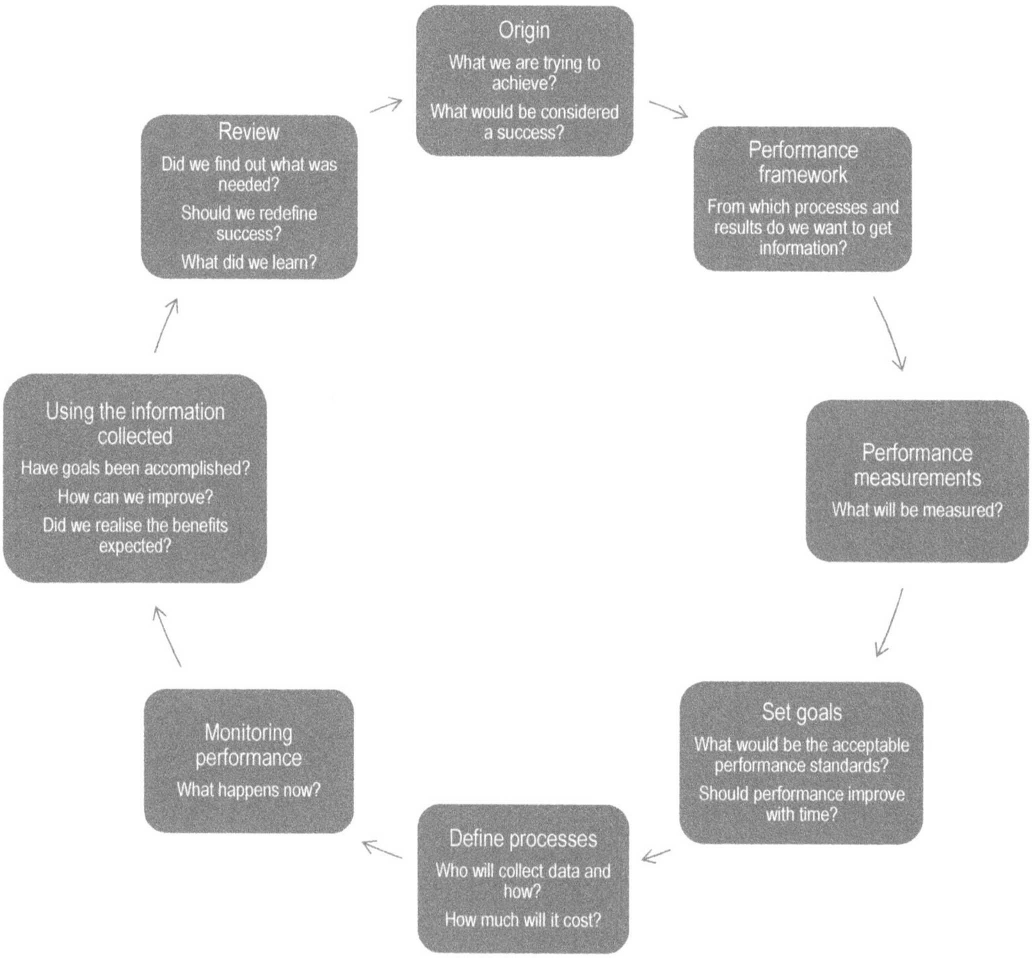

Source: UK Office of Government Commerce (2007), "Improving performance project evaluation and benchmarking", London, www.ccinw.com/images/publications/OGC%20Procurement%20Guide%208%20Improving%20Performance.pdf (accessed 8 August 2016).

The strategy should include, at least, the following elements:

- Identifying critical performance areas, including the results expected and risks to be mitigated. This requires looking at contracts and performance by suppliers in the past, as well as conducting an analysis of the main sources of obstacles to ensure supply. Likewise, it involves identifying KPIs to support priorities and defining the minimum performance standards to be achieved.
- The methodology used to collect data and the calculation of performance results for each KPI.
- Resources by which performance results will be measured between PEMEX and its suppliers, as well as potential disagreements to be addressed.
- Consequences of performance results, such as penalties, fees, termination of contracts, and use of data for future bid assessments, as well as the degree of communication of such results.

Procurement KPIs can be used to measure all important elements concerning supplier performance. For example, the UK Office of Government Commerce (2008) identified different categories: 1) quality (performance as set in the contract); 2) cost (paid price); 3) time (delivery as set forth in the contract); 4) communication (delivering reports, information exchange); and 5) management (risk control, contract management).

In order to minimise subjectivity in performance measurement and avoid disagreements, the strategy should favour objective KPIs, limiting the use of subjective indicators to those cases that do not allow for any other alternative. PEMEX may want to consider indicators used by other oil companies to review the ones used by the SIPPC (see Table 13.4).

Table 13.4. **Percentage of surveyed oil companies that periodically include the following elements in their systems for supplier performance assessment**

Element	Average	Average of previous report	Trend
Cost reduction	68.75	62.50	+
Environmental indicators	75	68.75	+
Health indicators	50	50	=
Experience with innovation	43.75	31.25	+
Management experience	25	31.25	-
Timely delivery	75	81.25	-
Operative performance	87.50	81.25	+
Meeting expectations of management levels	31.25	6.25	+
Quality	93.75	87.50	+
Response ability/flexibility	43.75	50	-
Risk reduction	37.50	37.50	=
Safety	87.50	100	-
Reliability in the supply chain	37.50	37.50	=
Social responsibility	31.25	37.50	-
Supplier reliability	37.50	18.75	+
Sustainability	50	50	=
Total cost of property	43.75	43.75	=
Others (continuous improvement, emergency response ability, financial stability, national content, supplier evaluation)	12.50	12.50	=

Surveyed companies include Aera Energy LLC, Alyeska Pipeline Service Company, BHP Billiton Petroleum (Americas) Inc., BP plc, Chevron Corporation, Ecopetrol, El Paso Corporation, EnCana Corporation, Eni S.p.A., Exxonmobil Global Services Company, Hess Corporation, Nabors Industries Ltd., National Cooperative Refinery Association (NCRA), Nexen Inc., Plains All American Pipeline L.P., Pride International Inc., Repsol YPF, Sasol Limited, Shell International, Statoil ASA, Tesoro Companies Inc., and TransCanada Pipelines Ltd.

Source: Adapted from CAPS Research (2010), *2010 Supply Management Performance Benchmarking Report – Petroleum Industry*, jointly sponsored by the Institute for Supply Management and J.P. Cary School of Business, Arizona State University.

While experts on market research, category products, and procurement should develop the indicators, it is particularly important to ensure market participation (i.e. business chambers) through a structured, fair, and transparent dialogue with suppliers to advance pertinence and buy-in.

Methods for monitoring supplier performance

The right combination of performance measurement methods is critical to maximise benefits and effectiveness in communicating the practice, while minimising the related costs. An important element to define the strategy is determining who is in the best position to get the necessary information to monitor supplier performance. There are several methods, each one with advantages and disadvantages, so the right mix should be selected based on needs, risks, and their specific features (Government of Queensland, 2010).

- Direct supervision by the procurement unit: It allows direct control of the assessment process, as well as the timely identification and solution of problems, but costs and the scope of efforts by the procurement unit can be significant.
- Supervision by the supplier itself: This method increases the participation of suppliers and decreases costs for the public agency. However, it requires periodic audits of the information provided by the supplier to ensure its reliability.
- Supervision through follow-up with users: It allows for a more precise perception of supplier performance quality relative to delivery conditions, but users may not report all cases of lack of compliance and this method may be costly and slow.
- Supervision by a third party: It consists of directly entrusting the supervision responsibility to a third party or indirectly through a certification. Although this method may imply important costs and delays, it brings expertise into the assessment, which would be hard to incorporate through other methods. In addition, the independence of the third party may prevent conflicts between the parties.
- Combining supervision methods: The right combination should ensure fulfilment of the contract's objectives while minimising costs and risks. For example, third-party tests can verify compliance with technical specifications, follow-up with users would be useful to collect information on the quality and timeliness of services, and suppliers can provide information on compliance with delivery conditions.

Performance reports should be carried out jointly by PEMEX and its suppliers periodically, as established in contracts. These reports are useful not only for record purposes, but also to assess performance against objectives and duties as established in contracts, as well as to proactively identify emerging issues and as the basis for subsequent interactions with suppliers. Discrepancies in performance reports should be settled as soon as possible, preferably within a set period established in contracts.

In order to avoid missing opportunities in performance management, PEMEX should put into practice the results of performance reports in a timely fashion. Constant communication with suppliers, for example, through periodic meetings to analyse performance, can help identify emerging problems and increase supplier participation. Although procurement officials should have flexibility to call for such meetings based on the actual performance of suppliers, a minimum should be pursued to maintain open dialogue.

An effective supplier performance monitoring system would alert PEMEX that suppliers are having trouble meeting contractual conditions or agreed performance standards. Any deficiency should be informed to the suppliers as soon as possible so that they can take timely corrective measures and avoid major problems. However, supplier performance management can only be effective if PEMEX applies contractual provisions comprehensively and systematically. Tolerating lack of compliance can lead to increasing cases of poor performance by suppliers and undermine the legal standing of the company in case of a dispute. Likewise, missing the opportunity to reward an outstanding performance decreases the incentive for suppliers to make an extra effort.

The implementation of a modern and comprehensive system for supplier performance management would allow PEMEX to establish specific objectives and standards of acceptable performance in order to maximise the benefits of a specific contract and minimise the main risks (Box 13.5). As mentioned before, mechanisms should not only be punitive (i.e. sanctions), but also positive incentives. PEMEX should take the initiative to review its regulatory framework to allow it to use such positive motivations.

Box 13.5. **Elements for a structured model for management and monitoring of supplier performance**

- Daily management: Any problem emerging from daily operations should be documented and analysed for reference in future performance assessments. Major problems may call for immediate attention.
- Management and performance information: Data should be continuously or periodically collected to measure performance against agreed KPIs. This decision should balance the efforts required to collect information in relation to the inherent risks to the relevance of the goods or services provided by a supplier.
- Expected performance and progress reviews: Periodic progress and performance reviews should be established before the contract is awarded. The frequency would depend on the moment and nature of the contract. Review protocols such as who should participate, who will collect information, and which documents will be required should also be agreed before the contract is awarded.
- Anticipated reviews by the leading unit: Senior management meetings could be adequate for complex or fundamental contracts. These reviews, although less frequent, provide a strategic perspective on achievements, issues and future plans.

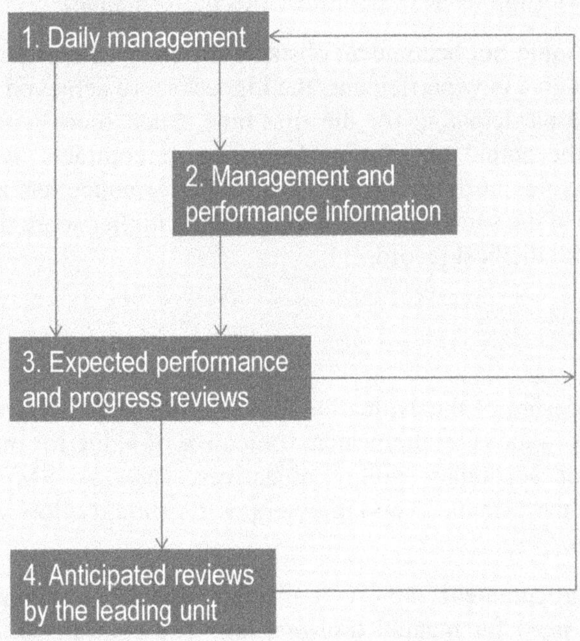

Source: Government of Ontario (2009), "Performance Measurement: Phase II – A Framework for Action", BIS Supply Chain Secretariat, Ontario.

Using previous performance as an award criteria

The information to be uploaded in the SIPPC to make it a comprehensive performance management data repository and its use in the selection of suppliers invited to participate in direct awards or restricted invitation procedures would be strong incentives for suppliers to improve their performance. Public tenders also provide an important opportunity to motivate improved performance when past experience is used as criteria in the award process. PEMEX could implement this innovation for the main products and services, or for categories, subject to competitive tenders. In this way, PEMEX would benefit from improved risk management, for example, the possibility of a supplier with a poor past performance winning a tender by offering the lowest price, while increasing the responsibility and incentives of suppliers to achieve an outstanding performance and, in consequence, allowing PEMEX to improve quality and value added.

This strategy calls for a gradual implementation. First, it is important to complete the information in the SIPPC and define the KPIs to be used for evaluation as part of the calls for tender. Second, once enough suppliers have a complete record in the SIPPC, more and more calls for tender could consider past performance as part of the official award criteria. When designing the strategy, special attention should be paid to the following:

- All suppliers should be evaluated on the same basis, according to their respective contracts and through time. Hence, KPIs, the assessment methodology, and the scores punctuation (i.e. formulas, weighting) should be identical and clearly expressed in contracts.
- Only the previous performance assessments that are relevant should be applied (i.e. those related to the same products or services, or categories).
- Once previous performance is used as award criteria, it should be applied in all subsequent calls for tender. Failing to do so would defeat the purpose of the strategy, hurt incentives, and lead to discretion, creating opportunities for integrity breaches (i.e. a procurement official excluding past experience as award criteria in order to favour a supplier with poor previous performance).
- The strategy should not become an obstacle for entry of new suppliers. One way to avoid this is to give new participants the highest score achieved during the tender in which they are participating for the first time. Such score would subsequently be replaced for the actual one for performance in contracts awarded to any new entrant. This avoids hurting suppliers whose performance has not been assessed in the past, while at the same time not giving them a higher score than that obtained by the supplier with the best record.

Proposals for action

- Complete the design of the evaluation model of the PEMEX procurement function, including KPIs to measure the primary objective of value for money, as well as the achievement of secondary policy objectives, such as SME participation and environmental performance, among others. KPIs should allow time comparisons to assess progress.
- Ensure that procurement data is collected through a centralised system that eliminates the need for manual transmission. The centralised system should have access privileges so that procurement officials and senior managers can access information according to the scope of their responsibilities. The system would be

even more useful if it displayed dashboards with a user-friendly visualisation scheme, which in some cases could even be open to the public.

- Continue applying internal and external perception surveys of the procurement processes. Allowing participants to answer the surveys on line and confidentially will likely increase the rate of response.
- Upgrade and complete the supplier information to be recorded in SIPPC, as well as its functionalities (i.e. make it an electronic system, not a spreadsheet). The usefulness of the system will depend on the comprehensiveness and accuracy of the information recorded, which could be used for pre-qualification purposes, as Shell does with its SQS system.
- Consider the KPIs used by other oil and gas companies (see Table 13.4) to review the comprehensiveness of the SIPPC. Consult suppliers and business chambers when carrying out such a review.
- Leverage the experience of PPI assessing the performance of suppliers and pool expertise with its officials to develop a "whole-of-PEMEX" model.
- Communicate widely the supplier performance assessment programme to suppliers, making sure they understand what is expected from them. To the extent possible, consult suppliers when addressing the gaps that the system still has. Likewise, involve the Institutional Internal Control Unit (Unidad de Control Interno Institucional, or UCII) in the discussions.
- Following the practice of BP, implement performance improvement plans for suppliers who have repetitively failed to meet PEMEX standards and specifications. Regulations should be amended to incorporate this figure and establish that suppliers unable to demonstrate improved performance may be at a disadvantage in future tenders (i.e. by assigning a low score for poor past performance).
- Ensure the implementation of positive incentives for suppliers with an outstanding performance by first reviewing the regulatory framework to incorporate this possibility, and then establish clear criteria for which such incentives will be considered (i.e. savings, innovation, timely delivery). Under no circumstance should this decision be left to discretion, and it should be taken by a group of officials, not a single one. Positive incentives could include exemptions from the requirement of providing a guarantee, reward payments, or using previous performance as part of the award criteria (without limiting entry to new suppliers).
- On the contrary, poor past performance should be considered in tenders to score technical capabilities of bidders or to avoid inviting those companies to restricted tenders or consider them for direct awards. Again, it should be clear what "poor past performance" means to avoid discretional decisions.
- Ensure poor performance has consequences for suppliers (i.e. penalties, fees, termination of contracts, etc.). Sanction enforcement should be reviewed periodically to assess its effectiveness.
- Given that supply in the oil industry is highly concentrated, consider the implementation of a Pareto strategy to assess first those suppliers with the highest amounts of sales to PEMEX and those who provide critical inputs, equipment, or services.

- Consider the use of different methods for monitoring supplier performance, according to needs, risks, and the specific advantages and disadvantages of each method. The right mix should minimise costs and risks, and at the same time ensure compliance with contract objectives.

Notes

1. Chapter 9 on challenges and remedies describes RR in more detail.
2. Article 24 of the General Rules for Contracting (Disposiciones Generales de Contratación) also establishes the mandate to evaluate supplier performance, as well as the General Guidelines for Procurement and Supply (Lineamientos Generales de Procura y Abastecimiento).
3. See Chapter 10 on e-procurement for a detailed description of the HIIP.

References

BP (British Petroleum) (n.d.), "Working with contractors, suppliers and partners" webpage, www.bp.com/en/global/corporate/sustainability/how-we-operate/working-with-contractors-suppliers-and-partners.html (accessed 10 August 2016).

CAPS Research (2010), *2010 Supply Management Performance Benchmarking Report – Petroleum Industry*, jointly sponsored by the Institute for Supply Management and J.P. Cary School of Business, Arizona State University.

Government of Ontario (2009), "Performance measurement: Phase II – A framework for action", BIS Supply Chain Secretariat, Ontario.

Government of Queensland, (2010), "Managing and monitoring suppliers' performance", Department of Public Works, Brisbane.

PEMEX (2015), "Sistema de información pública de proveedores y contratistas", www.pemex.com/procura/relacion-con-proveedores/Paginas/info-proveedores-contratistas.aspx (accessed 3 August 2016).

Shell (n.d.), "Supplier Qualification System", www.shell.com/business-customers/shell-for-suppliers/qualify-as-a-supplier-to-shell/_jcr_content/par/textimage_1243601949.stream/1447247715709/57dc82b8dd6ca544a447fccfc5015086a988f1df1bd6446d90194d30cc990587/supplier-qualification-system.pdf (accessed 10 August 2016).

UK Office of Government Commerce (2008), "Performance indicators", *Category Management Toolkit*, London.

UK Office of Government Commerce (2007), "Improving performance project evaluation and benchmarking", London, www.ccinw.com/images/publications/OGC%20Procurement%20Guide%208%20Improving%20Performance.pdf.

Chapter 14

Ensuring results for Petróleos Mexicanos: Implementing robust post-award contract management

This chapter evaluates the current contract management system developed in PEMEX and suggests actions to shift from ensuring contract compliance to promoting contract performance. Strategic contract management provides additional assurances towards the effective delivery of suppliers' contractual commitments. It also contributes to strengthen PEMEX relationships with its suppliers, being a stepping stone for the development of more strategic alliances creating additional value.

Considering the share of procurement expenditure against oil and gas industry revenue (44%), suppliers provide central contributions to deliver on Petróleos Mexicanos' (PEMEX's) business objectives. While procurement strategies developed by PEMEX aim to identify and select suppliers that offer the best value for money, the Corporate Directorate for Procurement and Supply (Dirección Corporativa de Procura y Abastecimiento, or DCPA) should ensure that such suppliers indeed deliver on their initial commitments.

Besides strategic sourcing and complex assessment mechanisms to evaluate bids submitted in response to tenders, effective contract management is a decisive factor to ensure that suppliers participate in the maximisation of value creation in PEMEX operations. The OECD Recommendation of the Council on Public Procurement highlights the importance of adequate resources and expertise in contract management to foster efficiency throughout the public procurement cycle. It also insists on the benefits of a comprehensive evaluation of procurement operations to inform future procurement decisions (Box 14.1).

Box 14.1. Principles of the OECD Recommendation on Public Procurement relating to performance management

The OECD Council notably:

VII. RECOMMENDS that Adherents develop processes to drive **efficiency** throughout the public procurement cycle in satisfying the needs of the government and its citizens.

To this end, Adherents should:

i) **Streamline the public procurement system and its institutional frameworks.** Adherents should evaluate existing processes and institutions to identify functional overlap, inefficient silos and other causes of waste. Where possible, a more service-oriented public procurement system should then be built around efficient and effective procurement processes and workflows to reduce administrative red tape and costs, for example through shared services.

ii) **Implement sound technical processes to satisfy customer needs efficiently.** Adherents should take steps to ensure that procurement outcomes meet the needs of customers, for instance by developing appropriate technical specifications, identifying appropriate award criteria, ensuring adequate technical expertise among proposal evaluators, and ensuring adequate resources and expertise are available for contract management following the award of a contract.

iii) **Develop and use tools to improve procurement procedures, reduce duplication and achieve greater value for money**, including centralised purchasing, framework agreements, e-catalogues, dynamic purchasing, e-auctions, joint procurements and contracts with options. Application of such tools across sub-national levels of government, where appropriate and feasible, could further drive efficiency.

X. RECOMMENDS that Adherents drive performance improvements through **evaluation** of the effectiveness of the public procurement system from individual procurements to the system as a whole, at all levels of government where feasible and appropriate.

To this end, Adherents should:

i) **Assess periodically and consistently the results of the procurement process**. Public procurement systems should collect consistent, up-to-date and reliable information and use data on prior procurements, particularly regarding price and overall costs, in structuring new needs assessments, as they provide a valuable source of insight and could guide future procurement decisions.

ii) **Develop indicators to measure performance, effectiveness and savings of the public procurement system** for benchmarking and to support strategic policy making on public procurement.

Source: OECD (2015), "Recommendation of the Council on Public Procurement", www.oecd.org/corruption/recommendation-on-public-procurement.htm.

By monitoring and documenting suppliers' performance, public officials are in a position to require corrective actions when performance fails to meet the contract requirements. Performance monitoring can also inform the selection of suppliers when their past performance is assessed for award of contracts (OECD, 2016).

A comprehensive and effective contract management framework typically includes the following:

- planning, information collection and analysis providing a clear understanding of the contract surrounding the environment (regulatory, commercial, etc.), allowing for the identification of project risks, mitigation measures and potential effects
- contract administration as it refers to the definition of roles and responsibilities in managing the contract, allowing for responsiveness in mitigating risks and ensuring objectives are delivered
- effective performance reporting and monitoring, providing access to relevant standardised information on which controls could be based and supports informed decision
- efficient relationship management, creating a long-term relationship of mutual benefit between the parties, enabling them to more effectively anticipate risk before they occur
- governance and integrity mechanisms, providing an appropriate setting for interactions with suppliers
- effective knowledge sharing and information management, ensuring that information relating to the project can be easily retrieved and accessed, enabling the parties to comply with obligations relating to information retention, disclosure and protection
- change management, which ensures that change events are managed smoothly without creating unnecessary risk or the unintended acceptance of risk
- contingency plans, allowing for prompt and appropriate reactions to unplanned events
- ongoing review of the contract management framework, adapting the framework to changes in the strategic business orientations.

Effective contract management is found to be conducive to contractual performance in many different industries: the oil and gas industry is no different. As detailed above, it goes significantly beyond strict contractual compliance, which is a reactive exercise focused on sanctions. A contract management framework follows a more proactive approach targeted at improving buyer-seller relationships and preventing problems (Figure 14.1).

Suppliers' performance monitoring and reporting plays a central role in the implementation of an effective contract management system. Such an exercise, however, relies on a clear definition of roles and responsibilities and on the availability of the necessary data integrated into dedicated information technology (IT) tools to allow for a qualitative assessment of the suppliers' performance.

Figure 14.1. **Contract management's contribution to performance**

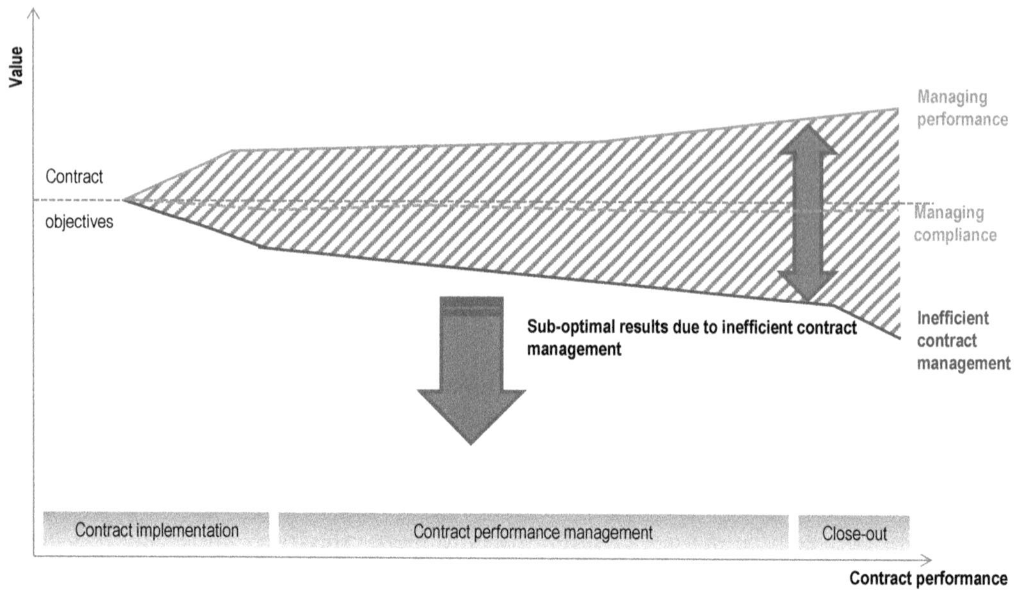

Source: Based on National Audit Office (2008), "Good practice contract management framework", www.nao.org.uk/wp-content/uploads/2013/03/Good_practice_contract_management_framework.pdf; Chartered Institute of Procurement and Supply (2007), "Contract management guide", www.cips.org/documents/CIPS_KI_Contract%20Management%20Guidev2.pdf.

By aggregating various sources of information, PEMEX can monitor the performance of its suppliers

According to Section VII.7 of the Procurement Guidelines, the DCPA is responsible for carrying out, possibly with the assistance of specialised companies, the commercial and financial risk assessments and performance assessments of suppliers. While the former evaluation is carried out when suppliers register, the latter is meant to verify the proper execution of the contracts signed between suppliers and PEMEX, its subsidiaries and affiliates, as the case may be.

The DCPA oversees the Sub-Directorate Responsible for the Development and Relations with Suppliers and Contractors (Subdirección de Desarrollo y Relación con Proveedores y Contratistas, or SDRPC). In accordance with Article 151 of the Organic Status of PEMEX, SDRPC is responsible for the following:

- promote, co-ordinate and manage relations with suppliers and contractors engaged by PEMEX, its subsidiary productive companies and, as the case may be, its affiliates
- establish strategies for the management of the entire supplier base
- co-ordinate the implementation and management of the suppliers' and contractors' information system integrating their evaluation
- co-ordinate the implementation of mutually beneficial contractual arrangements with suppliers and contractors

- link market capacity with the needs of PEMEX, its subsidiary productive companies and, where appropriate, affiliates
- define mechanisms for segmenting suppliers and contractors with the purpose of building strategic alliances
- oversee the implementation of relationship and development strategies with suppliers and contractors and promote new related mechanisms
- administer and conduct specialised forums with suppliers and contractors for PEMEX, its subsidiary productive companies and, where appropriate, affiliates
- co-ordinate with chambers and associations of suppliers and contractors for developing mutually beneficial business strategies
- co-ordinate the implementation of procurement strategies regarding the conclusion of preparatory contracts, referential agreements or other special contracting schemes defined by the strategic sourcing strategy
- co-ordinate actions for the assessment and reporting of national content in contracts
- define and implement best practices for the development and relations with suppliers and contractors for PEMEX, its subsidiary productive companies and, where appropriate, affiliates.

The centre-led procurement function poses some challenges, however, in objectively assessing suppliers' performance. Being responsible for the overall suppliers' oversight, the SDRPC liaises with business units to collect necessary information regarding contractors' performance. Indeed the effective assessment of the performance of suppliers in delivering on their contractual commitments requires information and feedback that can only be provided by the end users working closely with those suppliers. To do so several IT systems are used to gather information from different sources.

PEMEX contracted out the provision of commercial and financial risks assessments of bidders to a third party, a US-based company named Achilles. Although performance assessment of existing contracts with suppliers is absent from this evaluation, all current contractors are required to register on the Supplier Registration and Evaluation System and to provide updates as they pertain to their financial or legal situation. The Supplier Registration and Evaluation System is an important step for improving supply chain visibility for both suppliers and for the different business areas of PEMEX, providing updated information about the products and services offered by suppliers and delivering insights into their capacity to meet the operational needs of PEMEX.

This tool is meant to act both as a qualification system but also as a living repository of technical or environmental standards and certifications. It comprises a two-step registration process with different requirements. All suppliers and contractors must complete the basic registration, where they will be required to provide generic information about their company, including financial records.

Depending on the strategic or risk profile of the company, and the amount of contracts they hold with PEMEX, suppliers and contractors may be invited to register at the next level (extended registration). As part of the extended registration, suppliers and contractors will be asked to provide additional information and documentation related to a wide range of business aspects, including financial, product and service-quality certifications, health and safety and corporate social responsibilities policies (see Figure 14.2).

Figure 14.2. **Suppliers Registration and Evaluation System**

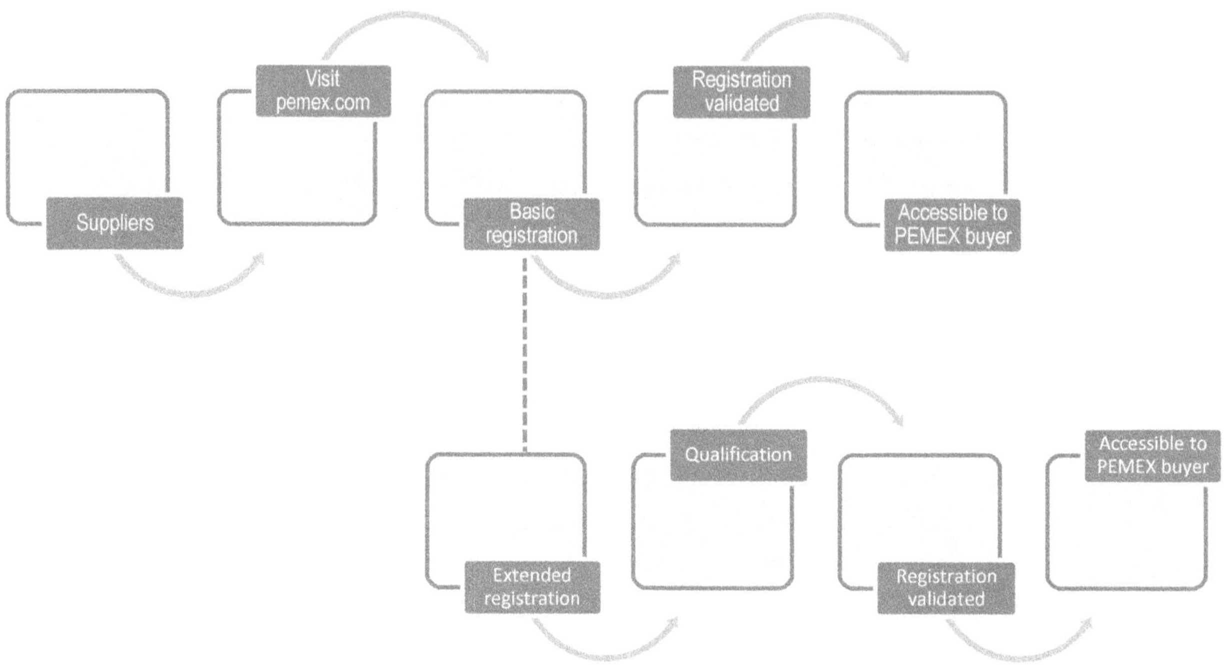

Source: Information provided by PEMEX.

With this system, PEMEX is provided with up-to-date information on suppliers and contractors allowing it to mitigate potential risks in the supply chain. In this sense, a regular monitoring of contractor's financial health participates to a comprehensive contract management system.

The SDRPC also manage the interactive platform called PEMEX PASS (Point of Access to Supply System), providing technological support to information exchanges between the DCPA, business units and suppliers. This platform however does not provide information on suppliers' performance. It is more of a forum for general discussions between the different stakeholders involved in procurement processes.

To carry on performance assessment of existing contracts with suppliers, the DCPA is retrieving transactional information in the SAP-Ariba system. This tool, coupled with the system for electronic invoicing is central to the contract administration and includes information that can provide insights on suppliers' performance. Indeed, an approval workflow makes possible the tracking of the submission of invoices, their validation by business units and corresponding payments processed by the Finance Corporate Directorate.

Yet, such transactional information only partially and indirectly depicts suppliers' performance in executing contracts signed with PEMEX. To address this information gap and considering the centre-led procurement function in place in PEMEX, additional information is gathered from projects managers by the means of periodic surveys asking them for feedback on suppliers on the following aspects:

- understanding of the business and client service

- innovation and technology
- quality
- contract management and compliance
- human resources
- security and social responsibility.

Results of these surveys are then integrated into the Integral Platform (Herramienta Integral de Información de Proveedores, or HIIP) and analysed by the DCPA to inform future procurement decisions. With all these various sources of information, the DCPA is able to retrospectively assess suppliers' compliance in executing the contracts they hold. Yet, this consolidated assessment does not provide for ongoing and regular performance evaluation of contractors, which contributes to performance improvement. It is also a non-inclusive process gathering information solely from the buyer perspective and does not integrate inputs from the supply side. PEMEX should therefore address these information gaps.

A comprehensive contract management framework is necessary to ensure the maximisation of suppliers' value added

In accordance with its mandate, the SDRPC is responsible for defining assessment frameworks applicable to suppliers in all phases of the procurement cycle, from capacities evaluation to contract execution. As such, the SDRPC can stimulate a strategic shift for the management of suppliers, from contract compliance to contract management.

Managing suppliers' performance is often perceived as a "downstream" activity undertaken after the contract is awarded. However, particular attention and resources must be channelled into its upstream development phase as it creates the foundation for subsequent performance assessment and communications, and therefore determines not only its effectiveness and benefits, but also its costs and risks (OECD, 2013).

Defining a robust contract management framework with specific milestones and review points would allow the SDRPC to guide contractual relationships between PEMEX business units and suppliers (Figure 14.3). It would also provide structured and reliable information, further supporting future procurement decisions.

Figure 14.3. **Development of a contract management framework**

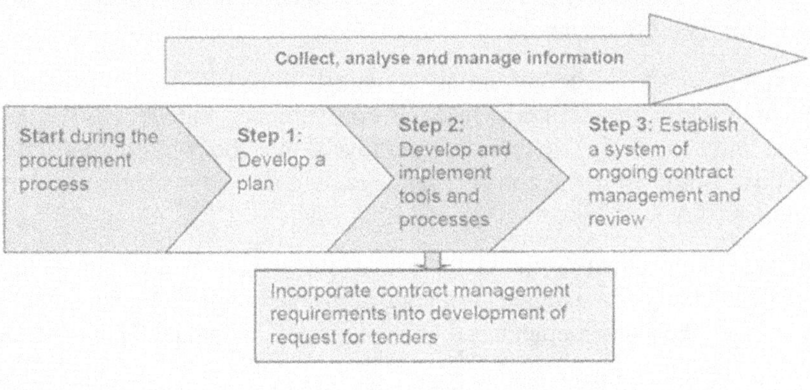

Source: Partnerships Victoria (2003), "Contract Management Guide", Department of Treasury and Finance.

Considering the organisation of the procurement function in PEMEX, a contract management framework has to be defined and understood by all stakeholders, including business units and suppliers. Being at the forefront of performance assessments and reviews, a structured framework would ensure that evaluation is carried out consistently across the different product categories and business units.

A contract management framework (or supplier management framework) consists in a structured engagement with suppliers to adequately and meaningfully track and manage their performance in various contractual dimensions, which should be aligned with PEMEX strategic orientations. This alignment could provide PEMEX with tools to leverage suppliers' capabilities, maximise value creation and foster innovation.

Indeed a thorough understanding of the specific buyer-supplier relationship is necessary to the development of a framework supporting the regular review and monitoring of suppliers' performance. The underlying question to which an answer should be given is how better supplier performance can contribute to the attainment of PEMEX's overall business goals and strategies.

Supporting PEMEX strategic orientations can be achieved by unveiling hidden cost drivers and risks, finding business and performance improvement opportunities, reducing risks and supplier costs, or discovering additional value from suppliers. Those elements need to be understood so that assessment frameworks are aligned with business strategic orientations and operations.

Frameworks for contract management can reinforce strategic relationships between PEMEX and its suppliers

As shown in Figure 14.3, a performance assessment framework and its related tools and processes should be an inherent component of the tender documentation to ensure its effectiveness. This would allow suppliers to clearly understand performance requirements and regular measurements from the outset, thereby contributing to aligning suppliers and PEMEX business operations. It would not only support an effective framework but would also define the associated resources on both sides.

With the integration of such a framework into the tender documentation, performance assessment becomes a mandatory requirement for the future contractual relationship between the awarded supplier and PEMEX. It will therefore require specific attention on the development of assessment mechanisms. If not adequately designed or understood, these additional requirements could indeed harm competition by imposing restrictive conditions or question their effectiveness.

Indicators and targets should be commonly agreed between PEMEX and the supplier and should provide opportunities for performance improvements. Indeed, while compliance management seeks only to verify whether suppliers have met their contractual obligations and impose sanctions if not, strategic contract management develops rooms for continuous supplier development (NAO, 2008).

All these elements are to then be translated into a Service Level Agreement that spells out the details of the contract management framework. Signed by both parties at the time of award, it allows for the development of an integrated approach into performance assessment.

With the view to promote suppliers' improved performance over time, PEMEX could also introduce formal debriefings towards the end of the contracts. They could prove useful for PEMEX to better understand challenges and issues faced by suppliers during contract execution and adapt future procurement process accordingly. Debriefings could respond to the benchmarking appetite signalled by different suppliers interviewed during the OECD fact-finding mission. Sharing information on contract execution also reinforces trustworthiness, which in turn might lower transaction costs and result in competitive advantage (Dyer and Chu, 2003).

Performance assessment frameworks should be proportionate to the complexity and criticality of goods and services delivered by suppliers

Although proving beneficial to increase the efficiency of the contractual relationship between PEMEX and its suppliers, a contract management system involves complex and time-consuming tasks requiring extended communication, both internally and externally. Therefore a balance should be found to develop a sustainable model.

To do so, PEMEX could build upon its methodology for strategic sourcing and notably the supplier segmentation against the criticality and value of the services and products provided by them. It will provide PEMEX with opportunities to strategically allocate internal contract management resources according to the impact it might generate.

To address complexity and sustainability issues, PEMEX could also define a flexible governance structure of its contract management framework. Indeed, experience in other oil and gas companies suggest that framing tailored interactions with business units and suppliers and clearly defining roles and responsibilities in this exercise are crucial to the effectiveness of the framework (see Box 14.2).

Box 14.2. Implementing supply management in Chevron Canada

A key component of supply management (SM) is performance review meeting (PRM). PRMs are organised at periodic intervals whose frequency depends on suppliers' segmentation. The purpose of the PRM is to analyse the supplier service and product lines' performances based on pre-agreed key performance indicators (KPIs) for a specific timeframe; understand operational highlights and lows and discuss short- and long-term value-added initiatives and strategic plans. PRMs enable the senior leadership teams from both sides to see the whole picture and gain awareness and information on suppliers' performance on a regular basis.

Challenges

While implementing SM, the specific challenges Chevron Canada's team faced at the initial stage were the inefficiency and the lack of standardisation in the performance measurement and management process demonstrated by:

- too many PRMs, without relevant prioritisation based on value and criticality
- unclear roles and responsibilities
- issues being "fixed" at PRMs reactively, not proactively
- wrong attendees and wrong conversations within the PRMs
- too retrospective with minimum look-ahead initiatives
- PRMs that took a full day fixing operational issues rather than focusing on value-added initiatives and strategic plans for future

- poor or no data reflecting the performance
- lack of resources to catch up with this time-consuming process
- poor PRM scheduling.

To overcome these challenges, numerous SM engagement and enrolment sessions have been held with internal teams and suppliers to ensure the SM details are communicated and awareness increased. A member of business units has been assigned per product and service line with clear SM roles and responsibilities. This role is to develop and agree KPIs with suppliers and focus on suppliers' performance. The Supply Chain Management Category Manager in the meantime supports regular operational meetings, PRM co-ordination and all other contractual support.

Benefits

Since its implementation, the benefits of SM have been acknowledged both by the company and the supplier. They include:

- continuous performance tracking per pre-agreed KPIs
- drop in non-productive time (NPT) rate
- quick problem resolutions due to leadership involvement
- focusing on operational highlights and on how to improve performance, rather than finger pointing at each other by discussing operational lows
- focusing more on future rather than past by discussing possible value-adding initiatives and plans
- open discussions involving people from all categories including field engineers who are involved in daily operations and senior leadership from both sides
- providing high-level regular updates on operational performance to senior leadership
- achieving deeper relationships with fewer suppliers, based on mutual trust and benefit.

Source: Adapted from Contracting Excellence (2013), *Supplier Management – Key Components, Challenges and Benefits*.

Setting the overarching parameters for assessing suppliers' performance also necessitates defining targets and evaluation methods against which they will be measured. PEMEX indicated having developed performance indicators, yet they are only meant to assess internal efficiencies. Implementing indicators aiming at evaluating suppliers' performance would therefore be a decisive step towards the introduction of an effective contract management framework.

When developing performance indicators and evaluation methods, PEMEX could draw on experience of other entities or countries, like Italy (see Box 14.3).

Box 14.3. Consip's monitoring of suppliers

Consip, the Italian central purchasing body, has a monitoring method based on the analysis of five so-called "macro-categories".

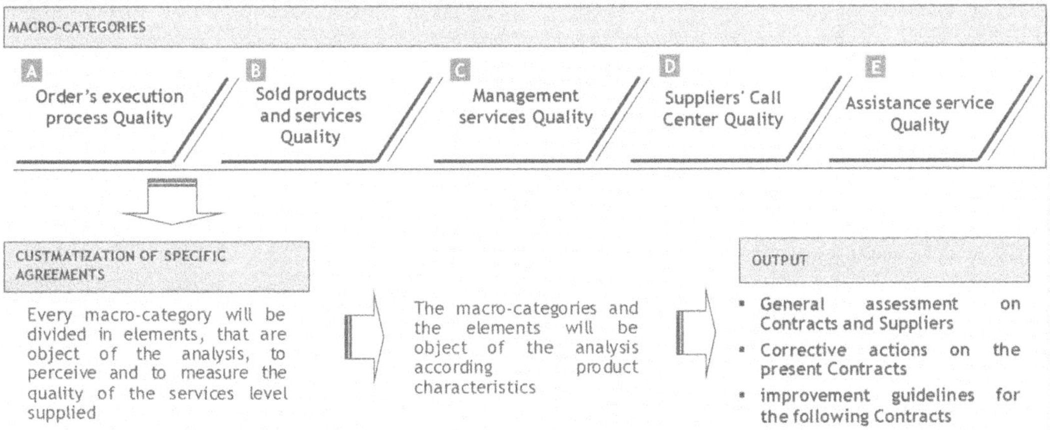

The monitoring team employs the following three tools:

- **Inspections**: Inspections verify suppliers' compliance with technical requirements. An external inspection body carries them out with the costs paid by suppliers being inspected.
- **Surveys**: Surveys measure the buyers' perceptions of suppliers' service levels. An external call centre conducts the surveys.
- **Claims**: Consip collects and analyses public administration complaints to judge whether supplier performance failed to meet the agreed quality standard.

All procurement contracts factor in a specific budget for financing inspections, which is included in the supplier's payment. It is proportionate of the amount of money spent as a result of the contract, the maximum amount being 0.5% of the sum spent. The supplier pays the external inspection body.

The findings of surveys and inspections are weighted to show levels of performance.

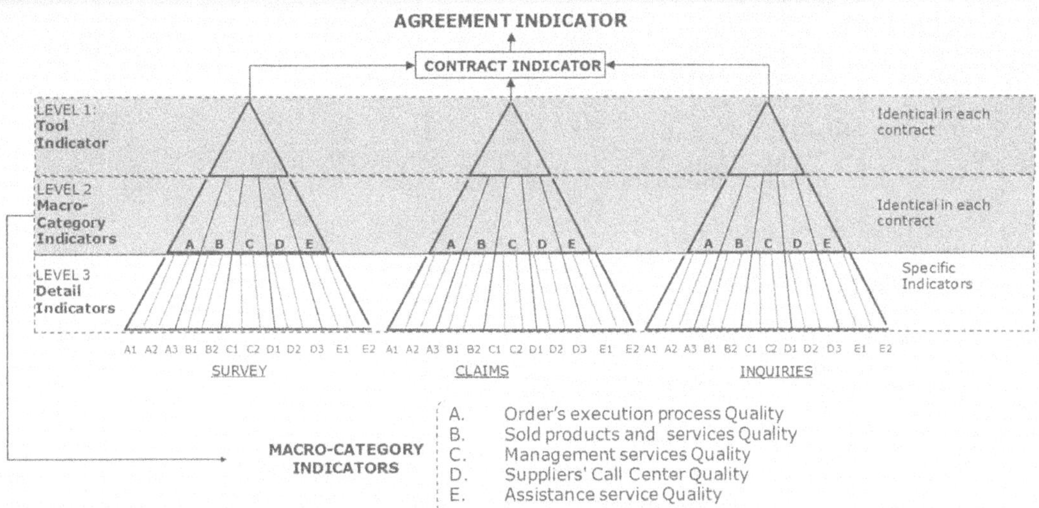

Box 14.3. Consip's monitoring of suppliers *(continued)*

The monitoring team draws on survey and inspection findings to score each component in the indicator. The final assessment is as follows:

Score	1	2	3	4	5
Level of service % indicator	0%	25%	50%	75%	100%
Range	Alert		Warning		On target

- "Alert" when the score is equal to or lower than 50%
- "Warning" when the score is between 51% and 74%
- "On target" when the score is equal to or greater than 75%.

Source: OECD (2016), *Improving ISSSTE's Public Procurement for Better Results*, OECD Publishing, Paris, http://dx.doi.org/10.1787/9789264249899-en

A shown by the experience of Consip, the Italian central purchasing body, the definition of indicators against which suppliers' performance will be assessed follows a structured approach. While all contracts are subject to the same general objectives, translating into common indicators, they also include specific targets according to the nature of the goods or services contracted. This hybrid approach provides a general alignment of performance assessments as well as tailored evaluation in accordance with the specific value the contract has for the buyer.

Based on the objectives pursued, the attributes against which suppliers' performance will be assessed can vary. For some product categories or services, qualitative aspects might outweigh considerations relating to the timeliness of deliveries or the exchange of information. Examples of attributes that could form the basis of performance assessments are:

- quality level
- service level
- correct quantity (especially when stocks incur a high cost)
- on-time delivery
- willingness to share information (notably for projects implying knowledge transfer)
- certifications or standards
- ability to respond to unexpected changes
- communication abilities
- responsiveness in case of emergency

After identifying factors that shall be subject to regular assessment and review, methods for performance evaluation should be defined. The three most common methods are the categorical system, the weighted-point average system and the cost-based system. The categorical system is the most subjective technique since it does not differentiate between the weights of the attributes considered. The weighted-point average system overcomes this drawback by assigning weights to each attribute. The cost-based system is the most objective of the three methods because it also considers non-performance costs (Arsan and Shank, 2011).

Proposals for action

In order to maximise the outcomes of its procurement processes, PEMEX could consider the following proposals for action:

- Develop a comprehensive contract management framework defining roles and responsibilities between the DCPA and the business units. This framework should not only allow PEMEX to carry out *ex post* evaluations, but also to implement regular reviews of suppliers' performance.
- Reinforce regular and structured exchanges with suppliers during contract execution to understand potential shortcomings.
- Adapt this framework to complexity and criticality of the goods or services procured so as to ensure the sustainability of the system for both PEMEX and its suppliers.

References

Arsan, A. and Shank, A. (2011), "Performance measurements and metrics: An analysis of supplier evaluation", https://scm.ncsu.edu/scm-articles/article/performance-measurements-and-metrics-an-analysis-of-supplier-evaluation.

Chartered Institute of Procurement and Supply (2007), "Contract management guide", www.cips.org/documents/CIPS_KI_Contract%20Management%20Guidev2.pdf.

Contracting Excellence (2013), *Supplier Management – Key Components, Challenges and Benefits.*

Dyer, J. and W. Chu (2003), "The role of trustworthiness in reducing transaction costs and improving performance: Empirical evidence from the United States, Japan, and Korea", *Organization Science*, 200314:1 , 57-68.

NAO (National Audit Office) (2008), "Good practice contract management framework", www.nao.org.uk/wp-content/uploads/2013/03/Good_practice_contract_management_framework.pdf.

OECD (2016), *Improving ISSSTE's Public Procurement for Better Results*, OECD Publishing, Paris, http://dx.doi.org/10.1787/9789264249899-en.

OECD (2015), "Recommendation of the Council on Public Procurement", www.oecd.org/corruption/recommendation-on-public-procurement.htm.

OECD (2013), *Public Procurement Review of the Mexican Institute of Social Security: Enhancing Efficiency and Integrity for Better Health Care*, OECD Publishing, Paris, http://dx.doi.org/10.1787/9789264197480-en.

Partnerships Victoria (2003), "Contract Management Guide", Department of Treasury and Finance.

ORGANISATION FOR ECONOMIC CO-OPERATION AND DEVELOPMENT

The OECD is a unique forum where governments work together to address the economic, social and environmental challenges of globalisation. The OECD is also at the forefront of efforts to understand and to help governments respond to new developments and concerns, such as corporate governance, the information economy and the challenges of an ageing population. The Organisation provides a setting where governments can compare policy experiences, seek answers to common problems, identify good practice and work to co-ordinate domestic and international policies.

The OECD member countries are: Australia, Austria, Belgium, Canada, Chile, the Czech Republic, Denmark, Estonia, Finland, France, Germany, Greece, Hungary, Iceland, Ireland, Israel, Italy, Japan, Korea, Latvia, Luxembourg, Mexico, the Netherlands, New Zealand, Norway, Poland, Portugal, the Slovak Republic, Slovenia, Spain, Sweden, Switzerland, Turkey, the United Kingdom and the United States. The European Union takes part in the work of the OECD.

OECD Publishing disseminates widely the results of the Organisation's statistics gathering and research on economic, social and environmental issues, as well as the conventions, guidelines and standards agreed by its members.

OECD PUBLISHING, 2, rue André-Pascal, 75775 PARIS CEDEX 16
(42 2017 01 1 P) ISBN 978-92-64-26854-8 – 2017

www.ingramcontent.com/pod-product-compliance
Lightning Source LLC
Chambersburg PA
CBHW061200240926
51846CB00006B/1071